Not Hollywood

Sherry B. Ortner

Not Hollywood

Independent Film
at the Twilight of the
American Dream

Duke University Press   Durham and London   2013

© 2013 Duke University Press

All rights reserved

Printed in the United States of America on acid-free paper ∞

Typeset in Arno Pro by Keystone Typesetting, Inc.

Library of Congress Cataloging-in-Publication Data appear
on the last printed page of this book.

For Tim and Gwen

With love as always

Contents

Acknowledgments

I want to say in advance how inadequately the following bare lists of names convey the depth of my gratitude to each and every person named for his or her contribution, large or small. An anthropologist really does depend in the most profound way on the kindness of strangers, and every name noted below carries a history of some act(s) that, at a given moment, or throughout the project, made all the difference in the world.

First thanks go to (chronologically) documentary filmmaker Murray Nossel, producer and studio executive James Schamus, and screenwriter John Romano, all of whom patiently gave me their time in the very earliest stages of the project, and helped me begin to define what this project could and could not be.

Also in the early stages of the project, when I knew virtually no one in the industry, I relied on friends and relatives who in turn had friends and relatives in the industry, and I thank them all for the contacts and connections they gave me: Leo and Dorothy Braudy, Alice Kessler Harris and Bert Silverman, Fran Markowitz, Chuck Ortner, Karen Seeley, Elaine Showalter, and Amy Swerdlow.

And again in the early stages, I plucked up my courage and cold-contacted professors in the UCLA School of Theater, Film, and Television (TFT). I expected condescension at best. Instead, I received a warm welcome and the beginnings of a process of ongoing support that lasted throughout the project. I want to thank Barbara Boyle, Kathleen McHugh, Bob Rosen, and Vivian Sobchack for their wonderful collegiality, and especially John Caldwell, who was extraordinarily supportive and helpful in more ways than I can count.

Once I broke in and began interviewing key people in the world of independent film, I was blessed to encounter people of great openness and generosity. I want to single out here for thanks those who gave me multiple interviews, further contacts and access to their networks, and, last but not least, a sense of friendly and warm inclusion in their world: independent producer Albert Berger, filmmaker Rodrigo García, independent producer Ted Hope, screenwriter and independent producer Vanessa (Wanger) Hope, independent producer Lydia Dean Pilcher, and independent producer Ron Yerxa. All of these folks not only gave me rich and thoughtful interviews but became friends I felt I could return to for more kind assistance—more interviews, more contacts, more access.

Next, I thank the people who specifically facilitated my access to sets. My neighbor, TV composer Jan Stevens, got me a gig as an extra on the set of *Scrubs*, where I performed brilliantly in the role of a patient lying in a bed. Albert Berger put me in touch with Jonathan Dayton and Valerie Faris, directors of *Little Miss Sunshine*; Jonathan and Valerie in turn got me admitted to the set of *Sunshine Cleaning*. Rodrigo García, one of the kindest human beings on earth, and not just for this, agreed to let me observe for a week on the set of *Passengers* and also invited me back for a day of observation when he was shooting *Mother and Child*. Producer Lydia Dean Pilcher put out a call on her e-mail networks for someone to get me on a set in New York; line producer Matt Myers agreed to bring me on the set of Franc. Reyes's *The Ministers*, and Franc. in turn was welcoming and good-natured about my presence.

Special thanks to anthropologist Kate Hohman and film editor Chad Beck. Chad was one of the editors of (among other things) the prizewinning film *No End in Sight*, and Chad and Kate were at the Sundance Film Festival in 2007 with the film. They warmly included me in their group, and I was able to observe the festival as a quasi-insider, which made for both richer ethnography and much more fun.

And so finally the research was declared done and the writing began. This of course set in motion a whole new army of people for whose help I am also deeply grateful.

For student assistance with transcriptions of interview tapes, reference checking, bibliography compiling, transportation, and many other details of project performance and management, I thank Sasha David, Sarah Evershed, Rebecca Feinberg, Hanna Garth, Kayla Noonen, Michael Strickland, and Eric Vanstrom. Here I need to especially single out Adam

Fish, who worked for this project for five (!) years, performing every kind of task with excellence, and also lending his incredible energy and enthusiasm and friendship to me and the project at every step of the way.

Next, for reading and very helpful comments on various chapter drafts of the manuscript I thank Sam Anderson, Leo Braudy, Rebecca Feinberg, Andrew Grant, Timur Hammond, Purnima Mankekar, Kathleen McHugh, Luis Felipe Murillo, Dan Segal, and Vivian Sobchack.

Major thanks to heroic friends, students, daughter, and colleagues who read and commented on the entire manuscript: Jessica Cattelino, Adam Fish, Ted Hope, Vanessa Hope, Douglas Kellner, Gwendolyn Kelly, and Elinor Ochs. Major-plus thanks to an even more heroic partner, and to several colleagues, who read the whole thing twice: Timothy D. Taylor, Elizabeth Traube, and one anonymous reader for Duke University Press. Individually and collectively, the comments from all these extremely smart, thoughtful, and knowledgeable people improved the manuscript literally beyond measure.

Ken Wissoker has been an outstanding editor throughout the process, offering, as always, just the right balance of criticism and support for the project. I thank him for all that, and for his friendship above and beyond.

And finally, for his sharp critical perspective, as well as his diffuse, enduring support, solidarity, and love, I thank my partner, Timothy D. Taylor.

Notes for the Reader

Names and Pseudonyms

Most names in the book are real names. Where individuals have requested that their real names not be used, pseudonyms have been created and are marked with an asterisk.

Sources and Citations

Recorded and transcribed interviews are cited as "(Interview, [month] [day], [year])." Quotes from transcripts of recorded interviews are verbatim, except for stylistic cleanup. The interviewee of course speaks and is quoted in the first person.

Quotes from field notes are cited as "(Field notes, [month] [day], [year])." Field notes include notes on many individual and group interviews that were not recorded. They are thus written in the third person ("he told me x," "she said y") and are not verbatim, though they are as close as possible as I could get.

Published interviews and all other published materials are cited in the usual *American Anthropologist* format as "([author] [year]: [page])."

Quotes from films are verbatim.

What is happening to the world lies, at the moment, just outside the realm of common understanding. The only revenge is to work, to make cinema that illuminates this common understanding, that destabilizes the dull competence of most of what is produced, that infuses life with idiosyncrasy, whimsy, brutality, and like life, that captures that rare but fabulous energy that sometimes emerges from the juxtaposition of tragic and comic.

FILMMAKER MIRA NAIR (CINEMA MILITANS LECTURE, 2002)

Go to your favorite movie theater and buy a ticket to one of the little pictures. . . . Do this because you want something uncommon. Because you want a story where the actors look like people you know. Where there's not some symphonic score lacquering over every scene, telling you what to feel. . . . Do this because you want to go where an interesting story can take you.

INDEPENDENT PRODUCER CHRISTINE VACHON (VACHON 2006: 269–70)

Studios are now looking for what they call "edge." When I was young, they weren't even looking.

FILMMAKER JOHN WATERS (IN TIMBERG 2004: 5)

Introduction

In January 2007 I attended the Sundance Film Festival, the premier American festival for independent film, as part of the research for this project. Park City, Utah, where the festival is held, is a ski resort, cold, snowy, and beautiful in January. The main street of the town is located at 7,000 feet above sea level, with snow-covered slopes all around rising to 10,000 feet, all of it bringing back memories of my earlier high-altitude fieldwork in Nepal.

I had registered for the festival and sought housing relatively late in the game, so I stayed in a condo on the far edge of town, at the outer limits of the shuttle service. This turned out to have its ethnographic benefits, as people on the shuttle were very friendly and chatty and I could have conversations with all sorts of people with various connections to the world of independent film. Indeed, the friendliness among festival-goers was noteworthy throughout, and as one stood in line after line in the cold and snow, with everyone bundled up in coats and hats and boots, one could always turn to one's neighbor and say, "So! What have you seen so far?" and everyone was happy to engage in these conversations.

By luck I had a personal connection to a specific film in the competition, Charles Ferguson's documentary about the 2003 American invasion of Iraq, *No End in Sight*.[1] Ferguson and key members of the production group, together with friends and relatives, were at the festival in a kind of dispersed network, occupying hotel rooms and sharing sublet houses around town. I viewed the film with some members of the group, was introduced to

Ferguson, and became an informal member of the party, which also included editor Chad Beck, cinematographer Antonio Rossi, and others. The awards are always announced on the final night of the festival, and there is an enormous gala party for everyone who either is part of the festival or (like me) had bought the right level of pass. We learned just before the party that *No End in Sight* had won the Special Jury Prize. Simply being accepted into the competition at Sundance is itself enormously prestigious; actually, winning a prize there is a mark of the utmost distinction in the world of independent film. Needless to say, there was a lot of happy celebrating in the group; even the anthropologist got to share in the collective effervescence.

I begin with this vignette because it captures and forecasts several of the main themes of this book. First and foremost, this project combines both ethnographic research on the world of independent film (including things like film festivals) and a study of many of the films themselves (including an extended examination of *No End in Sight*). Most anthropologists who work on the ethnography/film nexus emphasize the ethnographic side; a few emphasize the film side; I had decided—possibly impossibly—to try to do both. Second, although it was sheerest luck that I had a connection to the group that made that particular film, it was no accident that I was watching, out of the hundreds of offerings at Sundance, a political documentary. I had begun to view independent film as a culturally and politically critical art form, and I had made a decision even before going to the festival to focus on documentaries in general and political documentaries in particular. And finally, Sundance itself is a phenomenon that encapsulates, for better and for worse, the tension between art and commerce that animates all creative work in capitalist society. But this tension is perhaps felt in unique and exquisitely self-conscious ways in an artistic world that thinks of itself as "independent." All of these themes will of course be explored at much greater length in the course of this book.

My original intention for this project was not to study independent film, but rather to do a re-study of "Hollywood," sixty-plus years after Hortense Powdermaker's pioneering work (Powdermaker 1950). My interest was in Hollywood as still one of the most powerful sites for the production of hegemonic (what the folk would call "mainstream") American culture, and for the seduction of American and global audiences into the values of that culture. As it turned out, I found it almost impossible to get access to the Hollywood studios, but in the course of trying, I more or less stumbled into the world of independent film. At first I was intrigued; soon I was hooked. This scene, which had begun emerging strongly in the 1980s, was producing films like I had never seen before, and seemed urgently to be trying to say something, and be something, new. I came to feel that, for all the many and large changes in Hollywood in the past decades, it was after all still in the same business of making "entertainment" (and money). The only genuinely new thing on the scene seemed to be this quirky little world of film people, styling itself as the anti-Hollywood, making films that violated one's Hollywood-adapted expectations and that forced one to think. Or rather, what was new was that these people and these films had emerged from the art houses and had begun to achieve both critical and commercial success, playing at a theater near you.

This is thus a book about the relationship between independent film, "Hollywood," and contemporary American society. One part of the book is ethnographic, an account of the social world in which independent films are made and circulate. Within that world we encounter a value system in which "Hollywood" is seen as presenting false pictures of reality, as "telling lies," while independent film sees itself as trying to tell the truth, to represent reality "as it really is." The other part of the book consists of interpretations of selected groups of films. One of the striking features of these films is that many of them are very dark—depressed, angry, violent, "edgy." Here then I ask about the "reality" that these films are representing, and how they go about representing it. I argue that they are best understood as grappling with a range of profound changes wrought in American society under the regime of neoliberal capitalism, that is, the more brutal form of capitalism that has become dominant in the United States since about the 1970s. Although some of the films are directly critical of contemporary society, most of them use a more implicit form of "cultural critique" (Fischer 1995; Marcus and Fischer 1986), exposing the harsh realities of many people's lives in this culture as a way of making audiences think about their own values and assumptions.

What is an independent film? Social theorist Pierre Bourdieu has argued that one should not even try to give a provisional definition of an artistic genre, but rather should attend to the way in which the genre is constructed, defended, and transformed within a "field of cultural production" (1993). I take this point seriously and will devote much of the next chapter to examining the social field within which "independent cinema" has taken shape and is continuously evolving under various social and cultural pressures. Nonetheless, it seems to me that I have to begin by providing the reader with some sense—some images, some reference points—of the object under discussion. Here then I will spend the next few pages simply establishing a few general—and hopefully not too contentious—rules of thumb for picturing what it is I am writing about in this book.

The simplest place to start is to say that an independent film is defined to varying degrees and in varying ways as the antithesis of a Hollywood studio film.[2] The contrast can be seen in a variety of relatively objective indicators. Where studio films are very expensive, independent films are made on relatively low budgets; where studio films are in the business of "entertainment," independent films often set out to challenge their viewers with relatively "difficult" subject matter and/or techniques; where Hollywood films generally eschew taking sides on political issues, independent films are often explicitly political and critical; where Hollywood films are in the business of fantasy and illusion, independent films include virtually all documentary films, and even features are usually highly realist; and finally, where Hollywood films classically have happy endings, independent films rarely do.[3]

Before going on, I have to say that this whole notion of a clear contrast between independent films (indies) and Hollywood movies has been contested almost from the moment independent films emerged from the art houses in the late 1980s. In a nutshell the argument holds that indies are best seen as one kind of Hollywood product, serving a particular consumer niche. I both agree and disagree, and I will take on this issue at some length in the next chapter. For the moment I will simply say that there is a spectrum of what counts as independent films, with a more Hollywood-y end of the spectrum and a more radically avant-garde and experimental end. For present purposes, in order to give the reader some initial fix on the objects (independent films and filmmakers) to be discussed in the pages that follow, the above list of typical indie characteristics—low budget, challenging subject matter, few happy endings, etc.—can provide some simple rules of thumb for distinguishing an independent film from a "Hollywood" or "studio" film.

As a further aid to picturing the "indie" object, let me provide some examples. Selecting such examples is by no means a cut-and-dried exercise. At first I thought to provide some of the more well-known examples, films that crossed over and received wide circulation, such as *Little Miss Sunshine* (Dayton and Faris 2008). But then for various reasons, including precisely its wide success (and its happy ending), it might not seem very "indie" to readers. Actually it was an independent film in the sense discussed here, although toward the Hollywood end of the spectrum. On the other hand, I could provide the names of many indies the reader probably has never heard of, but that would defeat the purpose of providing some visualizable examples.

After some thought, I devised the strategy of providing lists of winners of the two leading American independent film competitions, the Sundance Film Festival and the Independent Spirit Awards. The strategy has the benefit of objectivity, rather than being a compilation of my subjective choices. It also underlines the role of festivals/competitions in defining what counts not only as an independent film but as a good independent film. Finally, the two festivals/competitions give some idea of the range of variation within the independent film world. The Independent Spirit Awards, based in Los Angeles, are much closer to the Hollywood end of the spectrum. At the other extreme are some of the smaller and more artistically radical festivals like Slamdance. Occupying the broad middle and in a sense the high ground of the independent film festival world is Sundance, which remains the gold standard—at least in the United States —of independent film.

Table 1 lists the winners of the Grand Jury Prize (Dramatic) of Sundance and the "Best Feature Film" award of the Independent Spirit Awards for the past ten years. I'm guessing that most readers will have seen more of the Independent Spirit Award winners than the Sundance winners; most of them, being closer to the Hollywood end of the spectrum, received wider circulation, while many of the Sundance winners may never have made it to a theater. In addition to these feature (i.e., fiction) films, virtually all documentaries are independent films. With rare exceptions, Hollywood studios do not make documentaries as they are not considered commercially viable, and in any event are not seen as fulfilling the fundamental mandate to entertain. Even some of the more well-known documentaries of recent years—most of Michael Moore's films, as well as *An Inconvenient Truth* starring Al Gore—were originally made as independent films, although they have now crossed over to a much wider audience.

TABLE 1

Best Picture Winners of the Top Two American Independent Film Competitions

YEAR	SUNDANCE	INDEPENDENT SPIRIT AWARDS
2003	American Splendor	Far from Heaven
2004	Primer	Lost in Translation
2005	Forty Shades of Blue	Sideways
2006	Quinceañera	Brokeback Mountain
2007	Padre Nuestro	Little Miss Sunshine
2008	Frozen River	Juno
2009	Precious	The Wrestler
2010	Winter's Bone	Precious
2011	Like Crazy	Black Swan
2012	Beasts of the Southern Wild	The Artist

A few words first about my film-viewing practices for this project. When Hortense Powdermaker conducted her study of the Hollywood studios in the mid-twentieth century, she did not discuss the movies produced in those studios except largely to dismiss them. For me, and for this project, it was unthinkable to study the independent film scene without immersing myself in the films. Thus, from the beginning of the research—roughly the end of 2005—I began intensively watching films across a spectrum ranging from super-low budget indies made entirely outside the studio system to somewhat higher budget "semi-indies" (Merritt 2000) made with some kind of studio involvement. Within the indie spectrum I include both features and documentaries, mostly American-made but also some foreign-made. I also occasionally checked out a Hollywood movie, either because it won an award, or because I wanted to see what Hollywood was up to within a particular genre. By the end (although there is no real end) I had watched about six hundred fifty films, the vast majority of which were somewhere on the independent spectrum.

There was no systematic principle of selection. I tried to watch everything I could. I tried to watch all the films of the people I interviewed. I tried to watch everything that won or was nominated for a major award, everything that people I talked to recommended, everything that got good reviews in my various regular newspapers and magazines.[4] I also signed up for the UCLA extension course called "Sneak Preview" for two years, attended several festivals (to be discussed below), and attended many preview screenings hosted by various film organizations in Los Angeles.

I intentionally tried to be as open-ended and, one might say, as "ethnographic" as possible in my film viewing, attempting to get a sense of what these films in some collective sense were trying to do and be. In the beginning especially I was often stunned or shocked by the heaviness or darkness of the films and found many of them hard to watch. Over the course of the project I became more accustomed to the filmic themes, moods, and strategies that were distinctive of independent film. I began to recognize patterns and styles, what one might think of as mini-genres. These thematic groupings of films, rather than individual films, will be the focus of most of the film interpretations in the pages that follow.

In a later section I will discuss my approach to reading the films, an approach that, I warn the reader in advance, draws mostly from interpretive anthropology and cultural studies rather than "film studies" per se. Most basically, the films are seen throughout as part of the place/time in which they were made, emerging from it, reworking it, and in the process critiquing it. Without dismissing important questions of aesthetics, style, and cinematic techniques, my primary issues for this book concern the films' relationships to the social, cultural, and historical world. Specifically, I will treat independent films as part of a story of profound changes in American society and culture that began in the last quarter of the twentieth century and have been intensifying ever since.

Public Culture and Cultural Critique

In the late 1980s, about the same time that independent film was emerging as a significant force in the cinema world, anthropologist Arjun Appadurai and historian Carol Breckenridge launched a new journal called *Public Culture*. Subtitled "Bulletin of the Project for Transnational Cultural Studies,"[5] the journal addressed itself to the workings of culture in an unevenly globalizing world. Included within the category of "public culture" is everything we would think of as "media," but also academic works, literary and artistic works, film, nowadays everything on the Internet, and more. Appadurai and Breckenridge explain their choice of the phrase "public culture" in terms of the ways in which it "allow[s] us to hypothesize not a type of cultural phenomenon but a *zone* of cultural debate, . . . an arena where other types of cultural phenomena are encountering, interrogating, and contesting each other in new and unexpected ways" (1988: 6). With the case of India particularly in mind, they expand on the idea as follows: "The actors in the contest are a variety of producers of culture and their audiences; the materials in the contest are . . . many [different] cultural modalities . . . ; and the methods . . . involve the mass media, as well as mechanical modes of reproduction. What is at stake in the contest is . . . no less than the consciousness of the emergent Indian [or any] public" (Appadurai and Breckenridge 1988: 7). There are clear echoes of the work of Jürgen Habermas here, particularly his theorization of the emergence of the "public sphere" of political debate, in turn part of the emergence of the new bourgeois class in European history ([1962] 1994). The relationship between public culture and a changing class configuration will be central to the present work as well, and I will return to that in the next section.

Equally important in Appadurai and Breckenridge's formulation, however, is the idea of public culture as a partially organized space or zone in which a variety of cultural forms operate in various relationships with one another. As Appadurai and Breckenridge say, this is a zone of constant contestation, but that does not mean that a particular historical ordering of forms is easily rearranged. Rather, there are powerful hegemonies in place, in which certain cultural formations dominate and which are aligned with the dominant culture/ideology of the society. But as Raymond Williams (1977) has classically argued, no hegemony remains uncontested, and there are both old ("residual") and new ("emergent") cultural forces that challenge the existing ("dominant") arrangement.

This then is precisely the story of "Hollywood movies" and independent film. "Hollywood movies" are indeed hegemonic within American public culture, having borne the messages of dominant American culture, and having powerfully shaped American consciousness in line with dominant ideologies, over the course of the past hundred or so years. Of course, this is something of a caricature, since Hollywood movies themselves could be read as a zone of contestation, both across time (see especially Biskind 1998; Sklar 1975) and at any given moment (see, e.g., Caton 1999; Kellner 2010; Pfeil [1985] 1990). Nonetheless, there is little question that Hollywood dominates the huge space of "entertainment" within the public culture, and all other kinds of films and filmmaking must position themselves in relation to it.

There are different kinds of positioning vis-à-vis a hegemonic formation. There is a long tradition of "experimental" and very un-Hollywood
filmmaking in America, but those films were shown in extremely small and
marginal locations, the so-called art houses to be found in only a few major
American cities. One could say that the earlier experimental film move-
ments were not so much challenging the hegemony as virtually withdrawing from the public sphere. What is different about the independent film
story since the 1980s is that these films were successfully moved out of the
art houses and into more mainstream theaters, playing for more mainstream audiences. The story of how this happened, which involved a kind
of cross-fertilization of Sundance Film Festival aesthetics and Harvey
Weinstein/Miramax marketing genius, is very well told in Peter Biskind's
*Down and Dirty Pictures: Miramax, Sundance, and the Rise of Independent
Film* (2004).

It would be too much to say that independent film poses a serious
challenge to Hollywood movies, in the sense of suggesting that independent films might, for example, become greater money-makers than the
blockbusters and rom-coms (romantic comedies) that fill up the box office
charts in *Variety* magazine. But I would argue—and independent film
people would argue—that, unlike the old "experimental" films, independent films today have clearly made themselves felt as viable alternatives to
the standard Hollywood movie. Indies are attracting both talented filmmakers and sizable, committed audiences, and a case could be made that,
collectively, they are at least destabilizing, if not overturning, the Hollywood hegemony. Of course, this does not take place in some magic space
cut off from the rest of society; it takes place within the space of "public
culture," in turn deeply tied to the real practices of producers and filmmakers, and deeply tied to the kinds of class, gender, and generational
changes that will be the stuff of this book.

But if Hollywood is hegemonic and independent films are (self-defined
as) counter-hegemonic, then they call for different kinds of interpretive
perspectives. For Hollywood movies the job is to, using the term loosely,
deconstruct them, to take them apart in terms of their coded ideological
messages, their forms of subjectivation of viewers, their false pictures of
the real world. There is a strong tradition of this kind of work across
anthropology (e.g., Abu-Lughod 2005; Mankekar 1999; Traube 1992a),
feminist studies (e.g., de Lauretis 1984; Modleski 1988; Mulvey [1975]

2004), and cultural studies (e.g., Biskind 1983; Kellner 2010; Pfeil [1985] 1990, 1995; Ryan and Kellner 1988; Shohat and Stam 1994).

Independent films, on the other hand, form a kind of "counter-cinema" (Steven 1985). They are in the business of "cultural critique," going up against the dominant culture by way of being "not Hollywood." At one level, of course, they are themselves full of unexamined elements of the dominant ideology, and of various political and cultural contradictions, just like Hollywood movies. How could they not be? They are part of American culture too. But insofar as one is sympathetic with what they are trying to do, it does not make sense to deconstruct and demystify them as if they were Hollywood movies. Rather, the effort must be to figure out how and in what ways they are constructing themselves as critiques of, and alternatives to, Hollywood and the dominant cultural order.

As I will discuss at length in the next chapter, the independent film world thinks of itself as "telling the truth," as against the "lies" and falseness of Hollywood movies. It also thinks of itself as showing "reality," as opposed to the fakeness and unreality of Hollywood movies. In the pages that follow, then, I look at the films in terms of how they go about this work of telling truths and showing realities that Hollywood movies do not tell and show. Much of this has to do with the kinds of stories independent filmmakers choose to tell, stories that for the most part Hollywood simply would not touch. The stories are often too violent, too sexually perverse, too depressing, too morally ambiguous, or perhaps simply too weird for Hollywood screens. While looking at stories constitutes a small and marginal part of certain kinds of film studies, it is absolutely central to this kind of work. It is not irrelevant that independent filmmakers themselves often talk about their films in terms of stories they felt they urgently wanted to tell.

How then to make sense of the relative success of this movement, and of the kinds of relatively uncommercial films they make? There are several levels on which this question can be answered. The first derives from the so-called culture- (or cultural-, or creative-) industries perspective. This important line of thinking begins with the work of Horkheimer and Adorno in 1944 and is developed further in the 1980s and 1990s by Raymond Williams (1981), Bernard Miège (1989), Pierre Bourdieu (1993), and Richard Ohmann (1996). The 2000s saw a veritable explosion of work in this area, including work by Richard Caves (2000), Toby Miller et al.

(2001), John Hartley 2005, Edward Jay Epstein (2006), David Hesmond-halgh (2007), and Scott Lash and Celia Lury (2007). Within a cultural industries perspective, new developments within any sector of the culture industries—like the flourishing of the independent film scene in the 1990s —need to be understood in the first instance in relation to changes in the political economy and strategic culture of the larger industry. In particular, cultural industry scholars have argued that big media corporations have increasingly pursued a strategy of diversification of offerings, including offerings for both "mass" and "niche" audiences, under a single corporate umbrella (see especially Curtin 1996). Although I have not seen any discussion specifically of independent film from this point of view, it is clear that indies would be one kind of niche-oriented product, directed toward an upscale, highly educated audience. The cultural industries perspective is thus very important for our story, as it will go a long way toward accounting for the opening or expansion of studio "specialty divisions" in the 1980s and 1990s, designed to finance and market low-budget "edgy" films that were in many ways the antithesis of movies being produced elsewhere in the same studio.

But this book is primarily concerned with understanding the emergence and flourishing of the indie scene at a different level of discussion, namely, at the level of changes in American society and American culture. If, from the point of view of the studios, indies served a particular niche, this book argues that the niche itself needs to be explored and understood as an emergent product of its times. The landscape of American society and culture has changed dramatically over the past several decades, opening up (or closing down) significant social spaces and cultural imaginaries. In particular, there have been massive shifts in the class structure at every level, and these will be central to our story. Without in any way losing sight of the inescapable influence of the culture industries, the arguments of this book situate the independent film scene, as a distinctive social world and a distinctive body of work, in the context of these broader social changes.

Neoliberalism and Class Transformation in the United States

This book is informed throughout by an eclectic blend of different Marxist perspectives—political economy, Frankfurt school, Birmingham/British cultural studies, and a kind of Marxist-inflected feminism. These perspectives will be discussed in the context of their uses in various chapters. Here

I begin from the basic Marxist insight that important cultural shifts are generally tied in some ways to class transformations in capitalist societies, usually to the emergence of new classes. As Raymond Williams has noted,

> It is true that in the structure of any actual society, and especially in its class structure, there is always a social basis for elements of the cultural process that are alternative or oppositional to the dominant elements. One kind of basis has been valuably described in the central body of Marxist theory: the formation of a new class, the coming to consciousness of a new class, and within this, in actual process, the (often uneven) emergence of elements of a new cultural formation. . . . A new class is always a source of emergent cultural practice (1977: 124).

Thus, working within this Marxist framework, Jürgen Habermas explored the cultural transformations surrounding the emergence of the modern bourgeoisie in England, France, and Germany in the eighteenth and nineteenth centuries ([1962] 1994), while E. P. Thompson did the same for the emergence of the modern working class in England in the same period (1966).

With respect to Hollywood, the case for the connection between the early development of the movie industry and the changing American class structure—specifically the massive growth of the American working class at the turn of the twentieth century—has been powerfully made by Steven J. Ross in his *Working Class Hollywood: Silent Films and the Shaping of Class in America* (1998). I have not seen similar, class-related arguments made for later periods of Hollywood history; in my view they are very much worth pursuing, but beyond the scope of this book. I will, however, pursue this kind of argument with respect to the emergence of the independent film movement in the late 1980s. Specifically, I will argue that the takeoff of independent film at that time is best understood in relation to major changes in the American class structure that had been developing since the 1970s.[6] Of course, independent film is only one piece of a larger set of changes in the public culture, including changes in popular music (1990s "grunge" is key), architecture (as Fredric Jameson 1984b has particularly emphasized), and so forth. Any of them could be looked at in terms of the issues at stake in this book.

The changing class configuration of American society has been well documented and widely recognized. Quite simply, since the 1970s, the rich have gotten richer, the poor have gotten poorer, and the middle class is coming apart (Krugman 2002; Shapiro and Greenstein 1999; G. Thompson 2008; Perucci and Wysong 2008). Behind this is a particular theory of the capitalist economy called "neoliberalism," which appears on the surface to be economically rational and socially neutral, but which is actually highly skewed toward the upward accumulation of wealth. Although I assume that most people reading this book will know what neoliberalism is, I need to provide a quick overview of it here (the following discussion draws especially on Harvey 2005; Klein 2007).

According to neoliberal economic theory, capitalism works best if there are no constraints on the free play of the market. Government regulations on corporate and financial activity simply impede the possibilities for greater profit. In the ideal capitalist economy, there would be no checks on profit seeking, including not only no government regulations but also no labor "privileges" like seniority, tenure, or collective bargaining.

In pursuit of the realization of this theory, major changes in the American economic system were initiated, starting in the 1970s. There was a decisive break with past economic policy and practices, involving two somewhat interrelated shifts. The first was a shift from a so-called Fordist to a post-Fordist framework defining the relationship between capital and labor: under Fordism there was a kind of working relationship between capital and labor, and (organized) labor did fairly well in terms of pay and job security; under post-Fordism, the working relationship is over, and labor has become dispensable, disposable, and replaceable. The second is a shift from a Keynesian theory of the relationship between the government and the economy to a post-Keynesian ("neoliberal") theory: under Keynesianism, the government was expected to play a role in regulating the economy and in sustaining social programs for the general well-being; under post-Keynesianism/neoliberalism, the government is supposed to get out of the way.

Another piece of the picture has to do with "globalization." Various technological advances have allowed for the increasingly rapid circulation of people, ideas, media, money, and so forth, around the globe. Some of this has had quite positive effects (see, e.g., Appadurai 1990; Hannerz 1996; Inda and Rosaldo 2002). But with respect to the American working class, among other things, the effects have been nothing short of disastrous. American companies began outsourcing production to countries where labor was cheaper, and the American working class more or less collapsed, both economically and politically. Factories all over America shut down; industrial workers were thrown out of work in huge numbers; America "deindustrialized" (see, e.g., Dudley 1994).

The weakening of labor and the deregulation of the economy together had the effect of unleashing the worst possibilities of a capitalist system: the pure pursuit of profit with virtually no concern for its negative social effects. And although the working class was hit first by these policies and practices, the effects worked their way up the ladder fairly quickly. Corporations began "downsizing" to both increase profits and remain competitive in the global marketplace, and white-collar jobs became almost as insecure as blue-collar ones (Ehrenreich 2005; Sennett 1998).

Finally, all of this has reshaped the American class structure. The inhabitants of the uppermost layers have become vastly richer, while the inhabitants of the poorest layers have become poorer or, at least, poverty has become more devastating due to the removal of many social services under neoliberal (in this case, smaller government) policies. Most dramatic has been the impact on the once prosperous and growing middle class. As white-collar unemployment has risen, and as white-collar pay has been held down even for those fortunate enough to still have jobs, downward social mobility has been prevented (when it has) almost entirely through both spouses working full-time and/or multiple jobs.

Actually neoliberalism alone has not created these effects. As David Harvey has emphasized, under conservative political regimes it is aided by active transfers of wealth to the rich, in the form of tax cuts, special deals, lucrative contracts, and bailouts. American society today—mitigated only slightly by the election of Barack Obama—is a picture of the cumulative effects of neoliberal economic policies and conservative political agendas that favor the wealthy, producing polarization of wealth, growing poverty, and widespread economic insecurity.

Here let me zoom in more closely on the "polarization of wealth," which will be central to the arguments in this book. Although the gap between rich and poor began to expand in the late 1970s (again see G. Thompson 2008), the issue of increasing inequality only began to become news starting in the late 1980s, when it began to be tracked in both academic studies and the media. Moreover, the polarization of wealth has, with minor ups and downs, been accelerating since that time. "You might think that 1987, the year Tom Wolfe published his novel, 'Bonfire of the Vanities,' and Oliver Stone released his movie 'Wall Street,' marked the high tide of America's new money culture. . . . The America of [that time] was positively egalitarian compared with the country we live in today" (Krugman 2002: 65; see also Phillips 2002).

The polarization of wealth represents a profound transformation of the class structure, including both the social organization and the culture of wealth, of the United States. After the Second World War, the New Deal and the GI Bill had the effect of creating a large and economically comfortable middle class. That class, moreover, was arguably culturally hegemonic, in the sense that its values came to be the dominant values of the nation (see Ortner 2003, drawing on a large literature about postwar America). Now, as author Douglas Coupland has recently written, "The middle class is over. It's not coming back" (Coupland 2010). The rapid erosion of that formerly comfortable and in many ways powerful middle class has produced a new American class configuration, an increasingly bottom-heavy two-tier structure of haves and have-nots. *Washington Post* columnist Harold Meyerson has written, "These are epochal shifts of epochal significance" (quoted in Gusterson and Besteman 2010: 5).

The End of the American Dream

The cultural shift that accompanies these economic and social changes has been captured in the phrase "the end of the American Dream," that is, the end of the widely accepted belief that hard work was virtually guaranteed to bring economic success and security in America. Observers began commenting on "the end of the American Dream" in the early 1990s when, as noted earlier, the effects of the neoliberalization of the economy began to be felt. To take a few random examples, in 1991 an article in the *Ann Arbor News* proclaimed, "American Dream Fades, Changes for Middle Class" (Nesbitt 1991).[7] In 1992 Bill Clinton said in a campaign speech, "Millions of young people growing up in this country today can't count on [the American] dream. They look around and see that their hard work may not be rewarded. Most people are working harder for less these days, as they have been for well over a decade. The American Dream is slipping away" ("The Economy," quoted in L. King 2000: 11). And in 1993, anthropologist Katherine Newman subtitled her ethnography of a suburban community in New Jersey "The Withering of the American Dream."

In the early part of the twentieth century, the "American Dream" was closely connected with immigrant visions of America as a "land of opportunity." In contrast with other nations in which, as the story went, people were trapped in low social positions by birth (or worse, were persecuted for their lowness), in America there were no social barriers, and anyone willing to work hard enough could rise up from lowly origins. The early Hollywood moguls were themselves living embodiments of this story, and the idea became part of American public culture in part through early Hollywood movies (Gabler 1988). After the Second World War, the American Dream became more closely associated with upward class mobility within the American nation itself, as a previously quite radical working class was offered access to a middle-class lifestyle by way of better wages, affordable houses, consumer goods, and higher educations.

The American Dream was always a complicated thing, both myth and—until recently, for many—reality. As myth, it was in part a highly ideological construct, a picture of upward mobility that could not in fact be realized by many, above all by African Americans. But for large parts of the white working and middle classes, as well as many immigrant minorities, it was embraced as an ideal, a "dream," of upward mobility, or at least material comfort, to which people could aspire for themselves and their families. Moreover, for large numbers of people this dream corresponded to real material possibilities generated by the post–World War II boom economy of the 1950s and 1960s. Middle-class Americans began to take a relatively high level of prosperity and security for granted.

With the downturn of the economy starting in the 1970s, and registering strongly by the late 1980s, people could no longer take the American Dream for granted. This sense of the dream slipping away took shape affectively as a bundle of fears, anxieties, insecurities, and, suffusing all that, anger. This is what we hear in the ethnographic literature (Newman 1993; Gusterson and Besteman 2010) and what we see and hear throughout the public culture. The central fears and insecurities are economic. People are worried about finding jobs, losing jobs, and (not) finding jobs again. People worry about jobs with respect to themselves, their parents, their partners/spouses, and their children. Surrounding the fears about jobs are the fears about larger forms of social loss—loss of home, loss of social identity, "downward mobility." And alongside these economic and social fears are more amorphous anxieties: a rise in fear of class and racial

Others, a rise in fear of crime and violence (despite the fact that the crime rate has been declining), and a rise of obsessions with "security" in relation to all that. While 9/11 was in no way the beginning of this massive shift in the cultural mood, it certainly provided an additional charge to it.

For the (unionized) working class, the American Dream was crushed slightly earlier, with all the industrial plant closings in the 1980s. Anthropologists and other observers have provided a number of close-up accounts of the aftermaths of these closings. For example, anthropologist Christine Walley provides a very personal account of her father's and her family's experience in the wake of the closing of the Wisconsin Steel Works in southeast Chicago in 1980 (Walley 2010). In a more ethnographic vein, anthropologist Katherine Newman documented the experiences of workers following the closing of the Singer Sewing Machine plant in Elizabeth, New Jersey, in 1982 (Newman 1988). Anthropologist Kathryn Dudley studied the experiences of individual workers, as well as of the town collectively, in the wake of the Chrysler plant closing in Kenosha, Wisconsin, in 1988 (Dudley 1994). And in 1989 filmmaker Michael Moore made *Roger and Me*, in which he revisited his hometown of Flint, Michigan, and documented the damage wrought by the closing of the General Motors plant there. From all these accounts we get powerful portraits of the devastation of individuals, families, and whole towns by the loss of jobs.

Many middle-class observers at the time did not foresee the degree to which the plant closings in the 1980s and related events such as Reagan's breaking of the air traffic controller strike in 1981 (Newman 1988) were a forecast of things to come for the middle class itself. However, I will suggest later that the (representation of the) fate of the American working class will become, within the context of some independent films, both a thing in itself and a parable for the fears of the middle class.[8]

Some would argue that the working class never entirely bought into the American Dream, at least not the dream of full-blown upward mobility. For many, there was a desire for material comfort and economic security without necessarily leaving a familiar class/ethnic social world. But if the working class was ambivalent about the American Dream, this was much less true, if at all, for the middle class, for whom it was deeply part of their culture. Middle-class life was proof that the Dream had worked and was working; the nightmare was downward mobility, "fear of falling." As part of her multi-group study of downward mobility in America, Katherine Newman (1988) studied the difficult experience of downward mobility suffered by the fired air traffic controllers in the 1980s, but at the time their experience seemed to be unusual, within what middle-class people still thought of as a stable and productive economy. Subsequently Newman studied experiences of social class in a middle-class suburb in New Jersey. Her book *Declining Fortunes: The Withering of the American Dream* (1993) was one of the first anthropological works to pick up on middle-class people's experiences within the new, neoliberalized economic environment, and we begin to hear the voices of the new culture: the anxiety, fear, frustration, and anger about working hard and yet losing ground, economically and socially. Newman never uses the term "neoliberalism," which did not in fact come into common usage until about 2000 (Ortner 2011), but there is little doubt that that is what she is talking about.

A note about journalist Barbara Ehrenreich, a great fellow traveler of anthropology, is in order here. Ehrenreich has been tracking social class in America since the 1980s, and her early book *Fear of Falling: The Inner Life of the Middle Class* (1989) looks at the ways in which fears of downward mobility have played themselves out in the American middle class since the 1950s. In subsequent books, she began to focus on the fact that the entire economic environment was changing. In *Nickel and Dimed: On (Not) Getting By in America* (2001), which was a New York Times bestseller, Ehrenreich looks at the deteriorating condition of the working class as wages go down and social services are cut. In 2005 she published *Bait and Switch*, which comes back to the middle class, this time confronting the impossibilities of the new job market for white-collar workers. For *Bait and Switch*, Ehrenreich spent several months undercover as an out-of-work middle manager trying to get a new job. She learned much about a rather desperate new infrastructure of seminars on resumé preparation, wardrobe selection, interview comportment, and so forth, designed to help such people get (new) jobs, but she never even got close to actually getting one. The subtitle again makes the point: "The (Futile) Pursuit of the American Dream."

There is one more piece to this picture of what we might call "post–American Dream" culture. In addition to this large cluster of fears and anxieties about economic security, there is simultaneously a large cluster of fears about physical security. Middle-class people were experiencing elaborate fears of violent crime at a time when the crime rate in America was dramatically declining, even before the events of 9/11. In 1990, cultural journalist Mike Davis published *City of Quartz*, about class and race issues throughout the history of Los Angeles. In one chapter, called "Fortress LA," Davis documents the degree to which Los Angeles has become a fortified and virtually militarized city, organized around the race/class fears of middle-class homeowners. In 2002, Michael Moore made *Bowling for Columbine*, about middle-class Americans' rising fears of violence and the extraordinary growth of gun ownership at a time when, as he pointed out in the film, the crime rate was going down. (The film won Best Documentary Oscar of that year.) And in 2010, anthropologists Hugh Gusterson and Catherine Besteman published an edited collection titled *The Insecure American*, with articles on the exponential growth of physical security arrangements and institutions: more gated communities, more jails and prisons, more schemes for walling out immigrants. Middle-class people's deep anxieties for their own economic futures are simultaneously transmuted into exaggerated fears of physical violence by aggressive Others.

"The First Generation since the Great Depression That Will Not Do Better Than Their Parents"

In a completely different zone of the public culture, there was a seemingly different but in fact closely related attempt to grasp the big cultural shift that appeared to be taking place. This was the zone of popular rather than academic culture, and the cultural shift was seen as a generational shift. The idea of "generations" as important indicators of cultural change is not for the most part taken seriously by academic analysts (but see Traube 1992a), and usually for good reason: it originates largely in marketing culture, where it represents an attempt to capture trends for marketing purposes, or to construct consumer entities (e.g., "the Pepsi generation") as targets for marketing campaigns. As the Pepsi example indicates, many of the attempts to articulate generational differences can be quite trivial. But at certain points in time, generational breaks take place along historically significant fault lines, and when this is the case, a focus on that break can be very productive.

In the mid-1980s, media statements began to appear announcing the arrival of a significant new generation.[9] The new generation was initially defined demographically, as the "baby busters" who followed the "baby boomers." The baby boom, that is, the upward trend of the American birthrate, started right after World War II, in the mid-1940s, and ran until the mid-1960s, producing the huge baby boom generation. The birthrate first decreased in 1965 and continued to move downward until the mid-1970s, producing the smaller baby buster cohort. The boomers had ridden two decades of a strong growing economy and collectively did very well financially. The busters were born into that same good economy, and many were born into well-off or at least comfortable middle-class families, but starting in the 1970s the economy under neoliberalism began the "long downturn" (Brenner 2003). By the time the first wave of the new generation reached their twenties, the economy had begun to take the form we see today: the relentless shrinking of the job market, and especially the shrinkage of the market in good jobs—jobs with decent wages, benefits, and some kind of security, and also jobs involving some kind of meaningful work.

The main growth sector of this economy has been in what author Douglas Coupland called "McJobs," "low-pay, low-prestige, low-dignity, low-benefit, no-future job[s] in the service sector" (1991: 5). Coupland published a very influential novel in 1991 about three educated young people stuck in McJobs, titled *Generation X: Tales for an Accelerated Culture*, and the label "Generation X" was quickly taken up as the label for the new generation. And where the baby busters were defined strictly demographically (1965–76), the idea of Generation X was expanded to include people born between 1961 and 1981; this has become the standard time frame in the literature.[10]

Readers may have negative associations with the idea of "Generation X." For many it is one of those empty, trumped-up marketing concepts mentioned earlier. For others it may have been a useful idea at some earlier moment, but its value has long passed. I will address these and other objections in the course of the following discussion. For the moment I ask the reader to bear with me as I attempt to set out my case.

The relevance of "Generation X" for the present study is this: the overwhelming majority of independent filmmakers were born within that 1961–81 generational time frame, give or take a few years at the transitional front end. This connection between Generation X and the independent film movement has in fact been recognized before: in both *The Cinema of Generation X* (Hanson 2002) and a special issue of the film journal *Post Script* (2000), authors explore various connections between this emerging new generation and (mostly) independent film.[11] As we will see in chapter 2, some Gen X filmmakers self-consciously set out to make films about the experiences of their (emerging) generation. But for the most part the connection between generational experience and what we see in films is much more complicated; part of the point of this book will be to disentangle the various strands of that connection.

The importance of Generation X is this: they are the first generation to begin to feel the full impact of the neoliberal economy. They have been repeatedly characterized in the media as the first generation since the Great Depression that will not do better than their parents (see, e.g., *Business Week* 1991, quoted in Ortner [1998] 2006c; Newman 1993: 3). It is much harder for them to get decent jobs, to keep those jobs, and to save money for the future. On the contrary, many of them are deeply in debt before they even start out in life. In addition, they are viewed, and view themselves, as having encountered extremely problematic social conditions, including a soaring divorce rate, high rates of working mothers and latchkey children, ecological disaster, the AIDS epidemic, and so forth (this is much condensed from a longer discussion in Ortner [1998] 2006a). As a result, they express themselves—in their writings, their music, and their films—as angry and frustrated, damaged and depressed, or, as a defense against all that, ironically removed from, and with a dark sense of humor about, the world.

Generation X will be a central category in the present work. But as noted earlier, the phrase carries a certain amount of baggage, and I need to do some deck clearing here.

First, there has been some question as to whether Generation X is a real social phenomenon or some kind of marketing construct. In fact, the answer is both. This can be seen in the two kinds of literature available on the subject. On the one hand, there is a literature written by outside observers who try to define Generation X in contrast to the preceding boomer generation (e.g., Howe and Strauss 1993; for overviews see Ortner [1998] 2006c; L. King 2000); on the other hand, there is a kind of "subculture" literature, in which Gen Xers themselves appropriate the term and try to define who they are (e.g., Rushkoff 1994; Holtz 1995; Ulrich and Harris 2003). Self-styled Gen X films of the early 1990s, including *Slacker*, *Reality Bites*, and others, were also part of that process of self-definition and will be discussed in chapter 2. In other words, while Gen X was initially a construct imposed from above, it also developed into an "authentic" (i.e., self-conscious, self-aware, self-productive) social and cultural entity in a complex feedback loop with the public culture that sought to define it.

This is not at all to say that everyone born within the Gen X parameters identifies with the category. On the contrary, although it is clearly "emic" for some people, that is, part of their conscious identity, for probably the vast majority of chronological Gen Xers it is not. Thus, I am using it primarily as an "etic" category, that is, a category that describes some social reality, whether people identify with it or not.

Second, I propose that we need to think differently about the temporal parameters of Generation X. Just as the bad effects of the neoliberal economy have not ended, neither, I would argue, has Generation X. Thus, rather than treat Generation X as a finite cohort, I treat it as an open-ended and ongoing generational entity, born after the end of the baby boom and continuing into the present. There have been various attempts to label new generations after the "official" end of Generation X, but none of them have really stuck. There was an attempt to label and characterize a "Generation Y," mainly related to the emergence and spread of the Internet in the 1990s; the Internet has indeed been massively important, but I would argue that it has not overridden the continuity between the "generations" in economic terms. There was also an attempt to demarcate something called "the Millenials" (possibly a variant of Generation Y), but they turn out to be the same thing, or in fact worse. Thus, in 2010 we see a story in the *New York Times* about the Millennials titled "American Dream Is Elusive for New Generation." The writer tells us that "for young adults, the prospects in the workplace, even for the college-educated, have rarely been so bleak" (Uchitelle 2010).

Third, I need to connect the Gen X concept with the earlier discussions of class. Although a "generation" would seem to include everyone born within a certain time frame, a constructed category like "Generation X" actually contains specific inclusions and exclusions. In fact, it refers primarily to the children of the (mostly white) middle class who had been brought up in reasonable (or more) material comfort and with solid (or better) educations, but who enter a world reordered by the neoliberal agenda. Working-class people and people of color have been hit at least as hard economically by neoliberalism as the children of the white middle class, but for the most part they had lower expectations to begin with. The Gen X concept, by contrast, includes the idea of a kind of generational shock for children of the middle class, who face the prospects of a loss of comfort and security that the middle class had come to take for granted.

In sum, the idea of Generation X is meant to capture what we might think of as "neoliberalism on the ground," specifically in its middle-class manifestations. But as I alluded to above, there is more to the idea—and the reality—of Generation X than its economic situation, as central as that may be. In fact, one of the useful things about the generational framing is that it does go beyond the narrowly economic "neoliberalism" story. There are actually two other large areas of life in which Generation X is seen as having, and sees itself as having, a more difficult time than the preceding boomer generation. One is the whole area of intimate life, where Gen X is the first (middle-class) generation to feel the full impact of the new configurations of the family, of a rising divorce rate and all its economic and emotional consequences, or of both parents working (more than) full-time even when the family is intact. As part of that, but distinct, are the upheavals surrounding the new sortings of sexual identities and gender roles. The second large area in which life is more difficult for Gen Xers than the preceding generation is the area of political life, including the new generation's complex and fraught relationship to feminism and other forms of political activism that had been central to the political life of the boomers. I will take up all of these issues in the chapters that follow.

The Roles of Ethnography

This is a work of anthropology. At the heart of it is an ethnographic study of the world of independent film, including both the production and the circulation of those films. But as is increasingly common in anthropological work today, the ethnographic elements of the book are both contextualized within and enlarged by accounts of the wider political, economic, historical, and cultural contexts (see Marcus 1998; for a recent example, see Ortner 2003). In addition, because this is a book about films, the ethnographic discussions are linked, in various ways, to cultural interpretations of significant films or groups of films. All of this is to say that ethnography today rarely stands alone and is usually part of a larger tool kit (see also Marcus 1998). At the same time, it is, for anthropology, the sine qua non of all the rest, and I want to conclude this introduction with a discussion of the specifically ethnographic dimensions of this book.

Ethnographic studies of media production have recently emerged as a very dynamic field in anthropology, sociology, and media studies. All such work involves extended ethnographic immersion in one or more sites of media production with an aim of understanding how the forms of the public culture—film, television, music, advertising, etc.—are produced. These studies may include information on the mechanics of production, but they are primarily oriented toward understanding the culture and the politics that shape what the public is offered (or not offered) by way of news and information, advertising and marketing, and art and entertainment.

Early work in ethnographically based production studies was sparse. There were, first, the two early ethnographies of Hollywood, Leo Rosten's 1941 *Hollywood: The Movie Colony, The Movie Makers*[12] and Hortense Powdermaker's 1950 *Hollywood the Dream Factory*. Fast forward, then, to the 1980s, with sociologist Todd Gitlin's *Inside Prime Time* (1983), a detailed ethnography of the politics of prime-time programming inside several television networks. Then there is another significant gap of time.

Finally, in the late 1990s we start to see a marked acceleration of this kind of work. In sociology, continuing in the tradition of Gitlin, Laura Grindstaff published a remarkable ethnography of two TV talk shows (2002). In anthropology, Faye D. Ginsburg, Lila Abu-Lughod, and Brian Larkin published the influential reader *Media Worlds: Anthropology on New Terrain* (2002), providing a rich range of articles on ethnographic studies of media production from all over the world (see also Askew and Wilk 2002). In those and other collections, Faye Ginsburg launched a series of very influential articles on indigenous media production (e.g., 1999, 2002). Recent anthropological monographs on cultural production would include Barry Dornfeld's study of the politics of producing a PBS series (1998), Lila Abu-Lughod's ethnographic work on Egyptian television production (2005), Georgina Born's studies of the Institut de Recherche et de Coordination Acoustique/Musique (IRCAM) in Paris (1995) and of the BBC in London (2005), William Mazzarella's study of advertising production in India (2003), and Brian Larkin's study of film production and circulation in Nigeria (2008).[13] In media studies, John Thornton Caldwell has launched an ethnographic movement with his multi-sited work on production practices in film and television. His pathbreaking monograph *Production Culture: Industrial Reflexivity and Critical Practice in Film and Television* (2008) was followed in 2009 by a collection of articles coedited by Vicki Mayer, Miranda J. Banks, and himself titled *Production Studies: Cultural Studies of Media Industries*.

Moving to the present work, I want to unpack the various uses of ethnographic methods in this book. As a minimal definition I will say that ethnography entails an attempt to understand a particular social world from the point of view of the participants in that world. This minimal definition, emphasizing an effort to hear voices that would otherwise not be heard, was particularly relevant to the study of societies or groups with relatively less social power than the anthropologist's own, which was the case with most anthropological work until recently. In recent years anthropologists have begun to "study up" (Nader 1969) or "sideways" (Hannerz 2010b; Ortner 2010), that is, to study people/groups who are in positions of equal or greater power than the anthropologist. Even with more powerful people, however, the effort to understand their thinking, to see the world from their point of view, is fundamental to the ethnographic enterprise and must precede any critique one might also wish to make of their power and privilege.

I emphasize this at the outset as many readers of this book may not be familiar with the ethnographic perspective. Ethnography is not just a bunch of "methods," though I will discuss some methods in a moment. It is an open-ended set of strategies for getting at how people differently positioned than oneself, socially, culturally, and historically, see the world in their own terms.

Ethnography is most commonly equated with participant observation, with the ethnographer entering physically, and in every other way possible, into the cultural spaces or life-worlds in question, and ideally spending a relatively long time there. I had initially hoped to do long-term ethnography in this sense in a movie studio or a film production company but, despite many attempts, was unable to obtain permission (see Ortner 2010 on access issues). The participant-observation parts of this project were thus relatively limited (though intense), confined mainly to several observation opportunities at film festivals and on movie sets.

At the same time, I continued to feel the need for live and relatively "natural" encounters, in addition to formal interviews. I thus improvised a method that I called "interface ethnography." The idea of interface ethnography is that, apart from truly "secret societies" like (say) the Freemasons, most relatively closed communities have events where they interface with the public. In the case of the independent film world, one could join a variety of film organizations and subscribe to a variety of screening series, whereupon one would be invited to large numbers of preview screenings of films, with Q&A afterward with the director or other people importantly connected with the film.[14] Some of these organizations and groups also hold special programs for which one can buy tickets and hear panels of directors, screenwriters, and others talk about their work. One could also buy passes to film festivals, in my case to Sundance once and the Los Angeles Film Festival twice, and attend more screenings with Q&A, as well as panel discussions, poolside chats among groups of filmmakers, public interviews of individual filmmakers, and so on and so forth. The notes from more than one hundred live, close-up, often hour-long discussions between independent filmmakers, interviewers and/or other onstage participants, and audience members constitute the largest body of my data, other than the formal interviews.

And then there are the interviews. Altogether I interviewed, in varying degrees of depth, and in several cases more than once, about seventy-five people in various positions within the media industry in general and independent film in particular. But again I felt I had to improvise, partly for reasons of quantity, but also because of a problem particular to this project: that I could see all the films of the people I interviewed, but I could not interview all the filmmakers whose films I saw. The solution in this case came from the fact that film people are interviewed all the time, and that one can both attend live public interviews (as at the film festivals) and find published interviews more or less ad infinitum. This strategy more than doubled the pool of interviews on which I could draw in writing this book.

The interviews (of whatever provenance) are used in two rather different ways in the discussions that follow. On the one hand, people tell stories about their own experiences, and in many cases I retain their stories intact. The stories are particularly important in chapter 3, in which I piece together many accounts to provide a kind of insiders' oral history of the way in which the independent film scene came together in the late 1980s and early 1990s.

But the interviews, as well as all the field notes from the Q&A sessions, public interviews, and panels, are also used in a different way. Specifically, I treat them as texts to be taken apart in order to understand the language, the discourse, and the modes of self-expression of the world of independent film. This represents another way to get "inside" a cultural world, through the interpretation of social and cultural texts broadly conceived, in this case texts of ordinary talk and conversation. The study of culture as the interpretation of texts is associated especially with the work of Clifford Geertz (1973a) and was later adapted and expanded for the distinctive kind of literary/cultural analysis developed by Stephen Greenblatt under the rubric of "the new historicism" (e.g., 1999).[15] Recently John Caldwell has put it to powerful use in his own version of "production studies" (2008). Within this Geertzian framework a text can be anything—formal textualized objects such as Shakespeare's plays or independent films, but also games such as Balinese cockfights, rituals such as Sherpa offerings to their gods, three filmmakers talking to one another on a panel, and so on. Throughout this book I will treat the interviews and field notes as texts in this sense and mine them for the distinctive expressions and tropes that seem to open up independent film people's distinctive ways of thinking about their work and their world.

Looking at the book as a whole, there are film chapters and ethnographic chapters, alternating with one another. But there are films in some of the ethnographic chapters, namely, films about independent filmmaking, which I treat as another kind of ethnographic text. And there is ethnography in all of the film chapters, including both what I earlier called "stories" (people's accounts of events and experiences taken substantively) and "texts" (people speaking in the language of independent filmmaking, where the important thing is the language). The point of it all will be to understand independent films as stories meant to shake up and disturb audiences about the condition of American society today.

We turn then to the first chapter, where I will look closely at various discourses prevalent in the indie world, to try to understand and convey what independent film people mean by "independence." As part of that discussion, I will tackle the debate over what happens to filmmaking "independence" in the context of new conditions and strategies in the wider cultural industries.

Making Independence

I will argue throughout this book that the independent film movement that emerged in the late 1980s represented a critical cultural movement, an attempt to critique the dominant culture (represented by "Hollywood") through their films. Cultural critique (Marcus and Fischer 1986, Fischer 1995) in the films takes several forms. Some films, mostly but not entirely to be found among documentaries, are explicitly critical of the existing cultural and political order. These films are very important, in my view, and probably constitute my favorite genre of independent films. But they are in the minority among independent films, as well as the least favorite with most audiences. They will be discussed in chapter 8. More often, independent films perform cultural critique by way of embracing a kind of harsh realism, by making films that display the dark realities in contemporary life, and that make demands on the viewer to viscerally experience and come to grips with those realities.

Most independent filmmakers would not see themselves as engaged in "cultural critique," at least not in those specific terms. But they do have very strong ideas about the importance of "independence," which is to say, independence from Hollywood and all that it stands for. I will approach this central issue through an examination of the discourse, the self-representations, circulating within the world of independent filmmaking. The notion of discourse has had a long and complex life in the field of linguistics, and also plays a distinctive role in the philosophy of Michel Foucault (see especially Foucault 1986). But I use it here in the non-technical sense of the vocabulary of terms, tropes, and styles distinctive to a particular social universe, in this case, the universe of independent film-making and all its associated institutions and support structures.

The discourse of independent filmmaking is always a reactive discourse, always set strongly against certain stereotypic notions of "Hollywood." Producer Larry Drubner* called Hollywood blockbusters "disgusting" (interview, March 23, 2007), and said, "I don't love the industry, I hate it." Independent filmmaker Ramin Bahrani (e.g., *Man Push Cart, Chop Shop*) said that Hollywood movies "just don't make any sense. They create massive confusion" (in Scott 2009: 43). Producer Ted Hope, one of the pioneers of the indie movement, talked about his early move toward independent film production: "[I was 19, 20, but] was already [thinking], what is this junk that Hollywood is producing? . . . It was all supposed to be hip and cool, and I was just, this is such saccharine crap, and I remember just being angry at what was supposed to be groundbreaking and wasn't" (interview, March 15, 2006). Not all indie film people are literally angry about "Hollywood," but all by definition are in some sense against what "Hollywood" is and stands for; that is the basis of the decision to work independently and to go against the grain of the standard Hollywood movie.

But this negative stance toward Hollywood is set at two relatively distinct levels. The first level might be called the level of cultures and practices: independent filmmaking sees itself as different from, and better than, Hollywood in its ethos and practices of making films, specifically in terms of the commercial intention of "the studios" and the relatively noncommercial intention of independent filmmaking. The critique of Hollywood, and of commercialism in general, constitutes independent filmmaking as a form of cultural critique at the most general level, even before one looks at specific films.

The other level concerns the nature of the films themselves in the two worlds. Here there is a critique of the stereotypic Hollywood movie as not only informed primarily by the commercial intent but also by a relatively unquestioning relationship to the dominant culture. Here then we can find in the discourse of independent filmmaking a more articulated set of ideas about critical filmmaking: making films that challenge the dominant culture, making films that challenge the audience, making, in the words of independent producer Christine Vachon, "films that matter" (Vachon and Edelstein 1998: cover).

Before getting to that discussion, I need to say a few words about the interpretation of discourse in the context of this book. I will not be doing what is called "discourse analysis" in linguistic anthropology, a method that entails a close examination of conversational texts, exploring the ways in which conversational styles and gambits enact and co-construct various kinds of intentions, positions, and social outcomes. Instead, I will be doing something we might call cultural ethnography through discourse, listening to the ways in which people spontaneously seem to say or write the same things in many different contexts. For example, many people in the independent film world will say things like "I hate Hollywood," or "Hollywood is crap," or "You have to stay out of the studios or they will destroy your film." After the fourth or fifth repetition of these sorts of statements by different people in different contexts, it seems reasonable to conclude that there is something like a relatively established discourse of contempt for Hollywood prevalent in the indie world.

But—and this is very important—this does not mean that everyone who says something like this has the same intention or relationship to the discourse. For some people it expresses a genuine and deep-seated personal feeling. For others it's a kind of posturing: to say something like this is to declare one's status as an *auteur*, an artist of great individuality. For yet others (and we will see examples), they might say something like this today and sign up for a studio contract tomorrow.

For the most part I am not interested in this kind of individual variation or the quest for getting behind informants' backs that this would imply. At the level of discourse, informants are always right, that is, regardless of their intentions or their subjective relationship to what they are saying, they nonetheless say what they say, and what they say is, from this perspective, an instance of a particular discourse. I am, on the other hand, interested in contestations over the discourse itself, as when people question the reality of the indie/Hollywood opposition, or when people question the very possibility of independence from "Hollywood" in today's world of media conglomeration. These contestations open questions of the ideological nature of the discourse, and I will explore some of them later in this chapter.

One more point should be made about this approach through language and "texts." John Caldwell has written extensively about "industrial reflexivity" in Hollywood, about the fact that Hollywood is endlessly reflecting on, representing, and celebrating itself (2008). This is done through various media—through award ceremonies, through "making of" documentaries, and most importantly, for my purposes, through films. Films about filmmaking constitute a kind of auto-ethnography of Hollywood—in Clifford Geertz's famous phrase, "a story they tell themselves about themselves" (1973a: 448). The world of independent film is not exempt from this kind of self-representation and self-celebration, though they often do it with more irony than is common in Hollywood. In any event, as part of the work of this and other ethnographic chapters, I examine not only how independent films look at the world (as "cultural critique"), but how independent film people look at themselves.

The Discourse of Independence

Bob Rosen, former Dean of the UCLA School of Theater, Film, and Television, was one of the founding board members of IFP/West (Independent Features Project/West, now Film Independent), in which they tried, in the early years, to hammer out—amidst "prolonged and heated debate"—a definition of what made a film "independent." They came up with four criteria: that the film be "risk-taking in content and style," embody a "personal vision," be funded by "non-Hollywood financing," and embody the "valuation of art over money" (interviews, July 25, 2006 and November 10, 2008). Would-be and practicing independent filmmakers are encouraged/liberated to make "personal" films, in which they tell the stories they want to tell, in the ways they want to tell them. As Hollywood is famous for controlling directors and the contents of their films, "non-Hollywood financing" is meant to ensure that the filmmaker is truly independent.

The value of independence from Hollywood (and ultimately from the necessity for pleasing an American public that has been programmed with Hollywood values and expectations) is repeated over and over in the public representations of the independent film community. One site in which it is particularly audible is at the annual Independent Spirit Awards, hosted by Film Independent. At the 2007 awards ceremony, a short film was shown at the beginning of the ceremony. As I wrote in my notes:

Film Independent staged a competition for a short film about the idea of "independence." The winning film, called *Independence*, was really pretty good, starring a homeless guy [standing amid his junk, including a TV with no screen]. He just sort of raps along in a funny way about the upsides and the downsides of independence. On the one hand, nobody can tell you what to do. On the other hand, your TV set doesn't have a screen. It ended with the guy saying, of course, in order to be independent you needs lots of other people. (Field notes, February 24, 2007)

The last point is important. "Independence" does not mean isolation; it means being part of a community of people who share the value of being independent from the mainstream represented by Hollywood.

More generally, the term "independence" must have been repeated a hundred times in the course of the awards event. As I wrote in my field notes while watching,

People went on and on and ON about the value and meaning of "independence," and how everyone in this room shares this ultimate value.... The foreign directors seemed especially passionate about it—the Mexican cinematographer [Guillermo Navarro] who took best cinematography for *Pan's Labyrinth*, and the German director [Florian Henckel von Donnersmarck] who took best foreign film for *The Lives of Others*. One got the feeling from them that the ultimate horror is to have to bow to the views of others, and the thing about independence is really just following your vision without interference. . . . The German filmmaker said, the best way to have independence is to lower your budget. He made *The Lives of Others*, which [went on to win many prizes], for $2 million. He said "people are not in this for the money." (Field notes, February 24, 2007)

Another major site for the public reiteration of the discourse of independence is at the Sundance Film Festival, which I attended in 2007. I have a large-format (11″ x 16.5″) brochure about the Sundance Institute that I think was handed to me as part of my packet when I picked up my pass, or perhaps was just lying around among the volumes of free literature at the festival.[1] The front of the brochure has the word "INDEPENDENT" in all caps and very large font. Above the word it says "Free the Artist," and below the word it says "Free the Audience." We open the brochure and see the

"Free the Artist" spread, which asks, "What if the question, 'How will your film . . . make money?' were never asked? Then only two questions remain: 'Is this the story you want to tell?' and 'What is the best way to tell it?'" (3). The idea of artistic independence is then given an urgent political spin: "What's ultimately at stake—the creative use of freedom in an open society —is far too important to trust to economic or political forces, or to the whims of fashion" (Robert Redford, quoted on 5). As with Film Independent, but less strongly emphasized, there is an invocation of a balance between celebrating the artistic independence of the filmmaker and situating the filmmaker in a collaborative community: "Here, the tenuous coalition between independence and productive collaboration strives to achieve surprising results" (7).

At the same time, there is much greater emphasis on reaching and indeed creating the audience that will appreciate these films. We first read the following: "When independent artists, free from the constraints of the marketplace and political pressures, find their own truth, audiences are freed to experience new truths within themselves. The affect [sic] is intoxicating, addictive, and life-sustaining" (5). The brochure seeks to conjure an audience that is not merely open to the kinds of films these filmmakers will make, but actually thirsting for them: "The Institute continually explores innovative ways to put the voice of freely expressed ideas before audiences that crave originality, diversity, and authenticity" (7). All of this comes together at the film festival, "where independent film meets independent audiences" (11).

"Independence" is the core value for the world of independent film. But it is very hard, if not impossible, to sustain all four criteria of independence listed by Bob Rosen. In particular, it has been difficult to stay away from Hollywood money if/when it becomes available. More on this below.

The Discourse of Passion

In *The Field of Cultural Production*, Pierre Bourdieu (1993) provides a theoretically sophisticated exploration and analysis of the world of "art." Opposing both reductive social interpretations (e.g., linking specific kinds of works to specific social groups) and reductive "charismatic" interpretations (vesting the value of the work of art in the creative genius of its creator), Bourdieu develops the concept of the "field of cultural production," a social field in which artists and a large cast of supporting players vie with one another for recognition and prestige, in the course of which specific values—of what counts as "art," and of what constitutes good and bad artists, genres, and works—are constantly created, maintained, and transformed.

At the base of the field of cultural production is the fundamental opposition between art and commerce. The world of art as a whole sets itself off from the wider social and economic world as what Bourdieu calls "an anti-economy" that "is so ordered that those who enter it have an interest in disinterestedness" (1993: 40). More importantly, the art/commerce opposition structures the relationships between different kinds of art *within* the field of cultural production: "The opposition between the 'commercial' and the 'non-commercial' reappears everywhere. It is the generative principle of most of the judgments which, in the theater, cinema, painting or literature, claim to establish the frontier between what is and what is not art, i.e., in practice, between 'bourgeois' art and 'intellectual' art [or] between 'traditional' and 'avant-garde' art" (Bourdieu 1993: 82).

In certain parts of his discussion, Bourdieu divides the field of cultural production into two subfields, a "field of restricted production" and a "field of large-scale production." The field of large-scale production is the more or less commercially and/or popularly oriented zone of the field of cultural production, producing for large/mass audiences. On the other hand, the field of restricted production at its most extreme is one in which cultural producers produce only for the recognition and approval of other like-minded cultural producers, and not for more widespread recognition (Bourdieu 1993: 53 and passim). The opposition between large-scale and restricted fields obviously maps reasonably well onto the Hollywood/indie opposition, and I will return to it later. Here I want to explore a particular manifestation of the art/commerce opposition in American independent film, the opposition between money and "passion."

From the point of view of the indie world, independent films are made from passion, from the filmmaker's intense personal commitment ("personal" is another keyword here) to tell a particular story in a particular way. Passion is the opposite of a commercial sensibility; the heat of passion is opposed to the coldness of cash.[2] Passion is also the opposite of a mechanical filmmaking sensibility; a film emerges from the filmmaker's personal vision, as opposed to (in the worst case) the formulas and franchises and mechanically stamped out "cookie cutter" movies of Hollywood. Filmmaker Richard Linklater wrote about going to a commercial casting agency when he was casting *Slacker*: "The place smells so much like the business side of filmmaking we run in horror. We're now determined more than ever to avoid these industry types *who have no passion* for cinema. We'll find ALL of our people elsewhere and do the film a full 100% against the industry way" (Linklater 1992: 4, emphasis added).

Passion talk can be heard everywhere in the film world; "passion projects" are virtually synonymous with independent films. Ursula Jackson*, a partner in an independent but studio-oriented production company, had this to say: "A really good friend of mine just won one of the Nichols contests [for a film set in Bosnia], which is the screenplay contest that is run by the Academy. And everything that wins that is *so much a passion piece*, almost a documentary, the films are so involved in true life and all that" (interview, December 2, 2005).

For another example, Cherien Dabis (*Amreeka*), a young Palestinian-American independent filmmaker, spoke about doing two kinds of filmmaking: "My career is such that I have *my passion projects* that I want to write and direct, and those are really mostly Middle Eastern stories, and then I also have this commercial sensibility, like writing on *The L Word* [where she is a staff writer], things I feel like I need to do to pay the bills, things I think are fun, that I would like to see made" (interview, April 4, 2006).

Or Fred Irving*, the head of a specialty division of a studio, was talking about why producers would take risks investing in certain independent films:

> There are *movies of passion* and the people putting up the money realize it's a huge risk, a bigger risk [than backing studio films]. It's like buying junk bonds instead of buying high quality municipals or something. You know what your return is going to be, or you think you do, on a movie with Tom Cruise in it . . . or with certain subject matter. But other movies [like *Brokeback Mountain*] about gay cowboys, you sort of would say you'll be lucky to make your money back. Everybody does this for the love of the movie; that's the only reason you're doing it. (Interview, March 27, 2006)

In all of these examples, independent films as passion projects are contrasted with studio or commercial films: passion projects are personal

(Dabis's Middle Eastern films; Jackson's friend's film about Bosnia), and they are made first and foremost for love, not money (commercial films are things that "pay the bills," that generate big "returns on investment," and are "good business").

The quality of *being passionate* in turn is seen as important to a filmmaker as a personality in the independent world. Passion is often felt to be a necessary ingredient in making a strong film; independent filmmakers are people who are passionate about their ideas and their projects. While it often comes up in casual conversation, I found an excellent illustration of this point in the HBO television documentary series *Project Green Light*. The series focused on a competition for funding for independent films, with the winner getting $1,000,000 from Miramax Films to make his or her movie. The judging panel consisted of actors Matt Damon and Ben Affleck, as well as producer Chris Moore and several Miramax executives.[3]

The contest was launched by a script competition on the HBO website. The panel received something like 2,200 entries, and the number was eventually reduced to ten. The ten contestants were sent kits containing a camera, film, and other necessary material and asked to shoot a scene from their movie. All of them were then invited to New York, where the TV series was being filmed. The ten were cut to three, but then the panelists found it impossible to make a choice among the three. At that point they invited the three, one by one, to come back and meet with the panel to make the case for why s/he should be the winner. Here we need to tune in to the dialogue and listen for the rhetoric of "being passionate":

> Producer Chris Moore [to the camera]: What was being looked for in a winner was somebody who would deserve and live up to the fact that we gave them a break. And *did they have enough passion to fight the battle? The passion was something big that we were looking for.*
>
> Ben Affleck [to finalist Pete Jones]: In your mind, when you got into this thing, what did you think would be the basis for the decision-making? There is no right answer. . . .
>
> Pete Jones [very emphatically and, yes, passionately]: It's about making the *best film.* . . . It's about you guys screwing the studio system and saying, let's make the *best film.* Market the film? Fuck you. Who cares? We are making the *best film.* We are putting out a million bucks. I don't have a million bucks. But studios have some money and a million dollar

budget won't crush them. So let's make the *best film* that we can make and obviously, I'm biased. I think my movie's the best film to make. My film probably wouldn't get made by a studio. By a big studio. You know? I think that "Greenlight" is the kind of project that would make a film like this.

[Jones leaves the room.] . . .

Jon Gordon, executive vice president of Miramax [to the group]: I was really bowled over when he walked out of the room and when he did that I really in my heart, I knew he was the guy.

Billy Campbell, president of Miramax TV [to the group]: *He is articulate, fun, passionate.* It's a very open story that people all over the country can appreciate.

Jon Gordon [to the group]: The guy had a lot of heart when he came in here and if he puts that into making that movie he can make a good movie. I feel like Rocky just walked in here and if Harvey [Weinstein] was sitting in the room right now. . . . *This is a company that responds to passion in filmmakers.* . . .

In the end it was on this basis that Pete Jones won $1,000,000 and the chance to make his film, *Stolen Summer* (2002), and have it be guaranteed distribution by Miramax.

The discourse of passion as against the coldness of commercialism and of formulaic filmmaking is one version of the art/commerce opposition in the world of independent film. Another is the discourse of staying out of the studios, where the commercialism of the studios represents the death of creativity.

Trying to Stay out of the Studios

"Hollywood" is often represented as a dangerous place for a filmmaker with vision and integrity, and many filmmakers believe that it is important to stay out of the Hollywood studios entirely in order to maintain their artistic independence. The ideal of filmmaking independence is symbolized, even mythologized, in the very low budget film. The "no-budget, DIY [do-it-yourself], down-and-dirty, whatever-it-takes filmmakers" (Adam Fish, personal communication) who manage to put the film together with grit, ingenuity, and their mothers holding the lights, are the heroes of independent filmmaking. Kevin Smith, who worked in a convenience store in Red Bank, New Jersey, and made *Clerks* (1994) for $27,575 by maxing out all his credit cards, is one such indie hero. So is Mark Borchardt, hero of Chris Smith's documentary *American Movie* (1999), who had no job, scrounged money from relatives, and cast his entire family in a little horror film called *Coven* (2000). John Cassavetes, who is one of the ancestors of the contemporary indie movement, made very low budget films on his own in the 1950s and 1960s, outside of studio control (e.g., *Faces, A Woman under the Influence*). The Independent Spirit Award still has a category called the John Cassavetes Award, given to films with budgets of $500,000 or less.

Some filmmakers who have yielded to the temptation to make a film in a studio felt they have been badly burned by the experience. Kevin Smith talked about his bad experience with *Jersey Girl* (2004), which was made by Miramax/Disney, which involved expensive stars (especially Ben Affleck and Jennifer Lopez), and got mostly very bad reviews:

> I had to actually listen to studio notes. . . . So there were changes made to the movie. . . . I never want to go through this shit again. I don't want to work with fucking really famous people. It got me to a point where I was like, "I don't want to fucking work with a lot of money, because that means that the studio is going to make you do whatever you can to make it more palatable to the masses" (in Horowitz 2006: 279).

Or here is Guillermo del Toro talking about a bad experience making his film *Mimic* (1997), speaking during a Q&A after a screening of his new film *Pan's Labyrinth* (2006):

> **Moderator:** "Let me ask you about your relationship with studios."
> **Del Toro:** [He said] "This film [*Pan's Labyrinth*] was completely independently financed." He said he had had a bad experience with Miramax, for his film *Mimic*. "It turned into a cockroach movie. Hollywood is not like a tidal wave, it is like mildew, fuckin' fungi. It was a very shocking experience. The way they do marketing is obscene." (Field notes, November 6, 2006)

Steven Soderbergh (e.g., *sex, lies, and videotape, The Informant!*) similarly yielded to the studio temptation and found it a bad experience when he made *Ocean's 11* (2001) for Warner's:

"For me, *Ocean's* made no sense," he says. "It was the hardest thing I ever did. It's a movie about absolutely nothing. I found it just brain crushing. I never felt fluent, never felt comfortable. Every day I was hanging on by my fingernails. . . . About two weeks into it, I was feeling like, I want to do a little, a guerrilla movie. I just need to wash this out of my system." (in Biskind 2004: 416)

And finally, when Florian Henckel von Donnersmarck, director of *The Lives of Others*, received his Academy Award for that film, he brandished the statue and exclaimed, "Filmmakers, the only way you can make the films you want is to remain independent! Lower the budget! Stay out of the studios!" (field notes, February 24, 2007). Insiders will be quick to point out some of the ironies forecast earlier. Despite his strong comments, Soderbergh went on to make more "Ocean's" films for the studio, although he is famous for using the money to finance the more challenging indies that he also continued to make. Von Donnersmarck seemed passionately sincere at the time of his Academy Award about exhorting filmmakers to stay out of the studios. Nonetheless, he went on to make a big commercial film called *The Tourist* (2010), starring mega-expensive stars Angelina Jolie and Johnny Depp, which incidentally flopped both critically and at the box office. And there are other examples one could name. But it is important to recall that we are talking about a discourse, a kind of accepted vocabulary of terms and tropes and ideas that makes ongoing sense within a particular social world even when it is violated by individuals.

Discourses are maintained in many ways: through reiteration at the level of talk, through at least some level of behavioral conformity in practice, but also, and importantly, through the kinds of reflexive representations discussed earlier—for example, films about filmmaking. Thus the idea that the studios are dangerous places for an independent filmmaker has been dramatized in several independent films, in which the message is beamed back to the indie community in living color on the big screen. Let us look briefly at two here: a relatively small film called *The Big Picture* (Christopher Guest, 1989), and Robert Altman's classic *The Player* (1992).[4]

As noted earlier, my discussion will remain largely at the level of story in the films. While I am not uninterested in close textual readings (I will offer one in chapter 8), for the most part I am not pursuing questions of how texts work but of what they say—socially, culturally, politically, historically. I am concerned with the ways in which these films are grappling with the epochal transformations going on in the United States and globally, as discussed in the introduction. In the present chapter, the issue is the broad critique of Hollywood as a vehicle for the long-running hegemonic culture, before we get to more historically specific moods and themes of the emerging order. In the case of the two films to be discussed here, I will look at the stories as morality tales, warning against the temptations and seductions of Hollywood.

In *The Big Picture*, Kevin Bacon plays Nick Chapman, a naïve young independent filmmaker whose first film wins a prestigious student film award. As a result, he is swarmed all over by insincere agents and ruthless studio-based producers who want him to make another film, this time in the studio context. He has another movie he wants to make, something that reflects his own personal vision, but the narcissistic studio producer keeps coming up with random alternative suggestions, which would change the film beyond all recognition. Nick at first resists, but in the end he caves in to virtually everything. (A second plot line reproduces the same dynamic at the level of sex and relationships. Teri Hatcher plays a gorgeous woman who seduces Nick away from his current girlfriend and basically breaks up his life.) The movie that finally gets made is a mess, and it flops.

In the film, "Hollywood" is mercilessly caricatured—its falseness, its lack of taste, its irrationality. At the same time, we understand that it is seductive, both literally and metaphorically, and we are given an object lesson in what "Hollywood" can do to the naïve and unwary young independent filmmaker. As Nick gives in to "Hollywood," he loses his artistic integrity, his ability to make the kind of good film he had made before, and indeed even his moral compass as a human being.

In *The Player*, Tim Robbins plays Griffin Mills, a studio producer who hears dozens of pitches a day and falsely tells everyone who pitches to him that he'll get back to them, but then never does. He begins to be stalked by one of these disappointed writers; he tries to figure out who it is and winds up confronting and killing the wrong writer. Detectives are on his trail, but when he is asked to participate in a police lineup, the witness picks out the wrong man and Griffin goes free. This is the main story line.

But the secondary story line concerns a film within the film. Griffin hears a pitch from a writer with a grim script about a woman who has been framed for the murder of her husband and is sent to the gas chamber. The writer is the embodiment of the indie ethos—he tells Griffin there must be no stars in the movie; he also says the woman has to die, that there must be "no fuckin' Hollywood ending." Griffin promises. But Griffin in fact thinks it is a terrible script and hatches a plot to unload it on his rival at the studio, hoping the film will fail and his rival will be destroyed.

Toward the end of the main film, we see a screening at the studio of the film within the film (called *Habeas Corpus*), and we see that it has been completely Hollywoodized. The cast has been loaded up with stars—Julia Roberts plays the condemned wife who goes to the gas chamber, and Bruce Willis plays a district attorney. As the gas fills the chamber, Julia's head slumps, but just then the music surges up and Bruce Willis comes running down the hall to save her. He breaks the glass of the chamber and carries her away in his arms. The lights go up in the screening room and everyone is applauding, including the writer. The writer has sold out and the studio wins.

Much could be said about both of these films—both, for example, have interesting layering of multiple stories; both have ironic, over-the-top happy endings—but my purpose is not to analyze them as texts. Rather, I am interested in the way in which the films can be seen as dramatizing, at the level of public culture, the discourse of "staying out of the studios" that we heard at the level of everyday talk. The same can be said about the *Project Green Light* series discussed earlier, in relation to all the everyday talk of passion. The films/program turn the key messages of the indie world—good films are made from passion, not money; stay out of the studios or they will eat your soul—into morality tales, full of drama, pathos, irony, and humor, and with real (at least within the films) material consequences.

In the second half of the chapter, I will discuss the more positive ambitions of independent filmmaking, the ambition to be not only different from Hollywood but, in senses to be discussed, better. Before getting to that, however, I need to address several critiques of the assumptions underlying the preceding discussion.

Independence Is Dead, Long Live Independence

In an important article, media scholar Michael Curtin (1996) explores what he calls "the neo-network era" in television and related trends in other culture industries. He argues that while television professionals still seek to reach a national audience, at the same time the industry has been increasingly restructured to seek, and to take advantage of, niche markets, markets that may be smaller in size but that generate greater "intensity" in their audiences (1996: 197). He notes in particular the growing interest of the industry in oppositional cultural forms:

> One of the consequences of this new environment is that groups that were at one time oppositional or outside the mainstream have become increasingly attractive to media conglomerates with deep pockets, ambitious growth objectives, and flexible corporate structures. As the channels of distribution have grown more diverse, the oppositional has become more commercially viable and, in some measure, more closely tied to the mainstream (Curtin 1996: 197).

Although Curtin does not explicitly discuss the relationship between Hollywood studios and independent films, it is clear that his argument would map well onto the Hollywood/indie case.[5] Starting in the late 1980s, the Hollywood studios began creating or beefing up "specialty divisions," divisions of the larger studios dedicated to making lower-budget, more "independent-style" films. The details will be presented in chapter 3, but here we may simply note that the studios were behaving exactly as Curtin describes, seeking access to the emerging indie audience/market by producing films that had some degree of indie look and feel, what indie people (and Curtin) call "edge."[6]

The fact that Hollywood began to make its money and other resources available to some independent filmmakers in the 1990s has generated a range of positions on the question of "independence." In some quarters it lent itself to a discourse of dismissal of all claims of independence: indies had become a Hollywood "brand." From a more moderate point of view, the specialty divisions offered a positive opportunity for independent filmmakers. If Curtin is right that the culture industry began to take a positive interest in oppositionality, indie producers and filmmakers could in theory exploit this to their advantage, without giving up their independence. As Austrian (and very independent) filmmaker Michael Haneke said, "Of course I'm a critic of the studio system. . . . But that doesn't mean that one can't work within that system" (in Wray 2007: 47). But finally, a significant sector of the indie community has continued to feel that this is a dan-

gerous compromise, and that the only way to maintain artistic independence is to keep one's distance from Hollywood. My own position is that
all of these positions have been true in one or another context, and I will
explore each of them briefly here.

THE DISCOURSE OF DISMISSAL

It would be absurd to argue that independent film was not changed by its
growing relationship to the studios and its growing commercial success.
Although various scholars and observers would set the time frame differently and would characterize the changes differently, virtually all would
agree that independent film has evolved significantly from the 1980s to the
present. But there are stronger and weaker versions of this position. The
strong version, which I will look at first, argues that indies are, in one way
or another, "dead," as a result of their (partial) embrace by the studios. As
we have seen in the discourse of trying to stay out of the studios, many
indie filmmakers themselves fear the studio embrace as the kiss of death.
But in addition, many outside observers look at the landscape of independent film today and dismiss the whole idea of independence as by now
nothing more than a particular kind of Hollywood product. Where, from
Michael Curtin's point of view, the studios were hoping to buy and market
indie "edge," the view here is that, in the course of buying it, they inevitably
destroyed it.

This position can be traced back in part to the work of Horkheimer and
Adorno in the 1940s, about the insatiable and irresistible power of the
culture industry within capitalist society ([1944] 2006). Horkheimer and
Adorno insisted on the ways in which the culture industry (which, for
many parts of their discussion, is almost directly translatable as "Hollywood") is able to wholly dominate modern thinking. Even when certain
cultural products appear to, or claim to, differ from others, the differences
are illusory. As Horkheimer and Adorno say, "Sharp distinctions like those
between A and B films, or between short stories published in magazines in
different price segments, do not so much reflect real differences as assist in
the classification, organization, and identification of consumers. Something is provided for everyone so that *no one can escape*" ([1944] 2006: 43,
emphasis added). A few pages earlier, discussing the planned housing
developments of the era, they write of the ways in which these "subjugate

[people] only more completely to their adversary, *the total power of capital*" ([1944] 2006: 41, emphasis added).

Although few if any media studies scholars work with an explicit Horkheimer/Adorno (hereafter H/A) perspective, there is no question that it still has a great deal of force. Thus, as early as 1989, a year many observers take to be the beginning of the contemporary independent film movement, filmmaker Jon Jost (e.g., *All the Vermeers in New York*) published an article in *Film Comment* called "End of the Indies" (Jost [1989] 2005). Jost's main point is an almost perfect echo of the H/A position:

> Except in the most venal of senses, little of [the] American indie wave staked out anything that could legitimately claim any kind of independence from the Hollywood aesthetic model, its motives, or the preponderance of lawyers, deal-makers, and money talk which fills those seminars dotting the film world landscape. . . . The "independent" wrapping is but a subterfuge, a PR angle for the dim wizards of the press, asserting a difference that is not there (Jost [1989] 2005: 55).

Film scholar Justin Wyatt comes to similar conclusions. Following a consideration of industry marketing strategies that is very similar to Michael Curtin's, Wyatt discusses the ways in which Ang Lee's film *The Wedding Banquet* (1993) was marketed as an independent film but in fact had moved significantly toward the ideological and commercial center. He concludes, like Jost, with a sweeping dismissal of so-called independent film: "[B]y the midpoint of the [1990s], independent cinema was largely an illusion. Even supposedly groundbreaking and iconoclastic 'indie films' were firmly located within the safe domain of dominant ideological and commercial practice" (Wyatt 2001: 71).

And for a final example, let us look at a long online article called "After the Indie Revolution" (Timberg 2004). The author begins by quoting various enthusiasts for independent film but then turns to the critics who one way or another dismiss indie claims of "independence," especially compared to earlier eras of independent filmmaking. In particular, he quotes *Nation* film critic Stuart Klawans several times. Comparing the indies of the 1980s and 1990s to those of the 1950s and 1960s, Klawans concludes that "the term 'independent film' . . . is mostly nostalgic" (2000). At another point, echoing the industrial arguments of Curtin and Wyatt, he says, "What the 'movement' is about is a commercial reconsolidation of the film industry." And in his strongest statement he says, "We're at a moment when 'independent film' has become part of a brand name."

The dismissal of independent film as a kind of Hollywood "brand" and a marketing ploy represents the most negative take on the exchange of resources between independent film and Hollywood in the 1990s. I should note that it is quite widespread. Nearly every time I give a talk about this project, someone raises their hand and voices some version or other of this view. There is, of course, some truth to this position, for Hollywood is after all still very powerful. But there are also other views to be considered.

CHALLENGING THE BOUNDARY

In the discourses discussed earlier in the chapter, about independence versus Hollywood, about passion versus money, and about "staying out of the studios," there is an assumption of a relatively clear-cut boundary between the world of independent film and the world of Hollywood studios.[7] Social theorist Pierre Bourdieu has pointed out that the idea of such a boundary is an ever-reproduced effect of the underlying structure of any field of cultural production, the oppositional duality of art and commerce. Bourdieu has argued further that the boundaries of a field of cultural production, in the sense of both its outer limits and its internal divisions, are always sites of struggle:

> The *boundary* of the field is a stake of struggles, and the social scientist's task is not to draw a dividing line between the agents involved in it by imposing a so-called operational definition, which is most likely to be imposed on him by his own prejudices or presuppositions, but to describe a *state* (long-lasting or temporary) of these struggles and therefore of the frontier delimiting the territory held by the competing agents (Bourdieu 1993: 42).

Many people in the world of independent film would agree with Bourdieu that the boundary between "indies" and "Hollywood" is a kind of structural illusion. Two major figures in this world, Geoff Gilmore and James Schamus, have in different ways argued this position (see also Vachon 2006: 15).

Geoff Gilmore, formerly head of the Sundance Film Festival and currently head of the Tribeca Film Festival, said in an interview that the idea of some kind of sharp divide between indies and Hollywood is "part of the mythology that has grown up" around independent film, and that it was important to recognize instead the continuities between these two supposedly distinct worlds:

> **GG**: A lot of people in the independent arena would really argue that the independent arena doesn't exist.
> **SBO**: Really? In the sense that—
> **GG**: That it's part of the broader film world. That it's part of the industry, that the independent film industry is only and always has been part of the broader community. (Interview, May 25, 2006)

Gilmore wasn't actually saying that there is no difference between the (stereotypical) studio film and the (stereotypical) independent film. But he wanted to emphasize, among other things, that while in general the dichotomy between indies and studios can be mapped onto the dichotomy between passion and commerce, nonetheless both kinds of films do get made in both worlds:

> There's an argument that independent film is largely creatively driven, that independent films get made because of the passion of their producers and their art, and one certainly would not argue that about the archetypical studio film. You don't make *Mission Impossible III* because you're dying to create an artistic accomplishment. . . . [But] it is not a hard-and-fast distinction, and it certainly doesn't suggest that there are not creatively driven studio films or commercially driven independents. (Interview, May 25, 2006)

This argument was taken further by producer and studio executive James Schamus. Schamus has been, and continues to be, one of the key figures in the independent film world, starting out as an independent producer in partnership with Ted Hope in their now-legendary production company, Good Machine. After several twists and turns, Good Machine was bought up by Universal Pictures and transformed into its specialty division, Focus Features, with Schamus at its head. Many would agree that Focus Features in turn has successfully sustained a record for producing high-quality, independent-spirited feature films, despite being inside the studio gates (e.g., *Traffic* [Steven Soderbergh, 2000], *Brokeback Mountain* [Ang Lee, 2005]).

Like Gilmore, Schamus critiques the notion of drawing a boundary between the world of independent films and "Hollywood." But he casts his argument in a more historical frame. He implies that there was once a good reason for independent film to organize itself and think of itself as a separate entity, outside the gates of the Hollywood studios. By now, however, many outstanding independent-spirited films have been made in the specialty divisions of the major studios, and it is time for independent filmmakers to stop "pretending to be storming the castle when in fact 'we' are well inside it" (Schamus [1999] 2001: 256).[8] He goes on to say that film people working both inside and outside of the studios "share simply a genuine sentiment that we like films that say something to us, films that are meaningful in some way, and that such films can now be found both within the studio system, within the mini-majors and major independents, as well as 'outside' the system" ([1999] 2001: 254–55).[9]

Gilmore and Schamus (and others from whom we will hear in later chapters) thus view the specialty divisions and mini-majors, dedicated to financing the production of films that might otherwise have been made outside the studios, not as a threat to independence but as an opportunity for the flourishing of independence. The specialty divisions provided extraordinary resources—production and marketing funds, distribution networks—while at the same time offering filmmakers a significant amount of creative independence.

This position, like the others, is true up to a point. I would agree that many excellent independent-spirited films have by now been made within the specialty divisions of the studios. I also consider that the specialty divisions and mini-majors have been enormously important in moving independent film into a much more central location in American public culture. At the same time, it is clear that there is a whole range of truly edgy/difficult/challenging films that simply could not get made in those contexts. This brings us to the third position on the possibility of "independence," the importance of what indie producer Ted Hope has called "Truly Free Film."

"TRULY FREE FILM"

The third position on the possibility of filmmaking independence today, in an era when it is hard to resist Hollywood money, might be called the "hard core indie" position. This view begins, like the first view above, from an H/A assumption: that the culture industry is indeed very powerful, and that it is highly unlikely that a filmmaker can work within any kind of Hollywood-related or studio-type context and retain his or her independent spirit. Here is a rather despairing statement to this effect by Hope in the 1990s:

> Today's new media giants are embracing the independent film but as a marketing concept only; every day they bring more and more of the production, distribution and exhibition apparatus under their control. Although we celebrate our independent "spirit," the logic of the studio film—its range of political and social concerns, its marketing dictates, and even its narrative aesthetic—is slowly colonizing our consciousness. The screens are controlled by the studios and sooner or later every filmmaker winds up working for the studios. (Hope 1995)

But Hope's response to this situation is not, as in the first position above, to dismiss the whole idea of independence as some kind of niche marketing strategy. Rather, it is to fight ever harder for what he calls "truly free film," and to come up with ever more creative strategies for independent filmmakers to not only make their films but have them circulated and seen. Through important speeches to the indie community, and through his very influential blog "Truly Free Film," Hope continues to push for new ways for independent filmmakers to make the films they want to make, without interference from "Hollywood."

In 2008, Hope gave the keynote address to the Filmmaker Forum in Los Angeles. For various reasons to be discussed in later chapters, financing for both making and distributing independent film began to shrink severely starting in 2007. Voices within the indie community were saying that "the sky is falling" for independent film (quoted in Bilsborrow-Koo 2008) and that (once again) indies are dead. But Hope argued that the difficult new climate should be seen as creating the conditions of possibility for a more truly independent filmmaking world. In particular, he argued that filmmakers must give up on the hope/dream/fantasy of finding a distributor (a mini-major or a studio) and start self-distributing their films: "Can we banish the dream of golden distribution deals, and move away from asking others to distribute and market for us? Can we accept that being a filmmaker means taking responsibility for your films, the *primary* responsibility, all the way through the process? That is independence and that is freedom" (Hope 2008: 1).

The development of DIY distribution strategies that Hope is promoting, mostly involving creative use of the Internet, is meant to guarantee that independent filmmakers will be able to continue making the films they want to make and having people see them.[10] Moreover, it is meant to guarantee that independent films made in this defiantly independent way will be protected from Hollywoodization. And in fact, willy-nilly, the DIY strategy is becoming more widespread. As film critic Manohla Dargis wrote in 2010, "For [filmmaker Jon] Reiss and other do-it-yourselfers, the most important thing is to reach their audiences, any which way, niche by niche, pixel by pixel, in theaters or online. 'This is the other voice of film,' Mr. Reiss said with urgency, 'and if this dies, all we're left with is the monopoly'" (Dargis 2010a: 3).

While Hope has worked with specialty divisions, he was always much more skeptical about the possibility of retaining creative independence in those contexts. Now that studio money has become scarcer since the financial downturn of the late 2000s, Hope sees a silver lining in the new financial climate, an opportunity to return to the truly independent filmmaking that prevailed in the era before the specialty divisions came to dominate the landscape.

Finally, then, there is truth to Hope's position, as there is to the other two. As I noted earlier, although the specialty divisions have turned out some excellent, independent-spirited films, there is clearly a limit to the range of work they are willing to support. Producers like Hope, as well as his friend and ally in the New York indie scene, Christine Vachon, have consistently made films that push against and go beyond that (dare we say) boundary. While the specialty divisions have represented an opportunity in some cases, they have also operated as a serious barrier to independence in others. To the degree that independent producers and filmmakers became dependent on studio resources, they relinquished, in Hope's view, some degree of their artistic freedom. Now they have the opportunity to take it back.

Telling the Truth, Showing the Real

What then makes independent films different from, and ideally better than, your stereotypic Hollywood movie? If one listens to the discourse, in conjunction with watching the films, the short answer is something like this: independent films seek to tell the truth about contemporary society.

Where Hollywood films seek to provide escape and fantasy, independent films seek to tell realist or hyper(bolic)-realist stories about the world as it really is, in all its ugliness and cruelty, or all its weirdness and strangeness, and if this makes audiences uncomfortable, so be it. In order to get to these points about truth and realism, I need to work through the discourse of pleasing/not pleasing the audience.

INDEPENDENT FILMMAKERS AND THEIR AUDIENCES

Independent filmmakers often have a prickly and somewhat adversarial relationship with the imagined audience, that is, the mainstream American audience schooled in Hollywood movies, presumed to want only to be mindlessly entertained. Hollywood-oriented screenwriters and/or film-makers like John Hamburg (e.g., *Little Fockers*) have found themselves looked down on because they cared about pleasing the audience: "[I was making] a comedy in film school. And at NYU, there weren't a lot of guys doing comedy. There were a lot of movies about homeless people in Washington Square Park. . . . I remember getting into arguments with people who were like, 'Oh, you just care about the audience'" (quoted in Horowitz 2006: 107).

Many independent filmmakers, by contrast, make films to please only themselves and a small handful of people who share their tastes. In "The Good Machine No-Budget Commandments," producer Ted Hope and his business partners set out a list of dos and don'ts for making independent films. Point 8 is, "Write for a very limited audience—your closest friends. Do not try to please anyone—crowd pleasing costs" (Hope 2010a). Screen-writer/filmmaker Charlie Kaufman (e.g., *Synecdoche, New York*) is quoted as saying, "It's never my goal to win an award or to write a screenplay *that people will really enjoy*. It is about a subject that I am exploring and to do it in a truthful way" (in Muñoz 2008: 5, emphasis added).

Independent filmmakers hope their films will find an audience—they certainly have to persuade their financial backers that their films will find an audience—but ultimately they are ready to say to hell with the audience if necessary. Filmmaker Rodrigo García has made films like *Things You Could Tell Just by Looking at Her*, which he described as "practically a thesis on what an uncommercial movie is" (interview, July 14, 2006). I asked him about the degree to which he thought independent filmmakers do or should listen to the advice and feedback of others. He replied,

I think it [varies from] movie to movie. I have a script right now that I've written that I want to make. It touches on a lot of things that I want to make a movie about. . . . Not many people say to me it's bad, but a lot of them say "what is this?" So I'm not listening [to them]. Or I'm listening but I think there's just some movies you have to make the way you see them. This will be one of them and I may make it and crash and burn and it will never see the light of day but screw it. (Interview, July 14, 2006)

And here is a more extended example, from the screening of a documentary called *Kabul Transit* at the 2006 L.A. Film Festival. The film, showing Kabul as a heartbreakingly ruined city but its people as survivors, is presented with no narration, no story, and no—as they say—throughline. It is simply a series of striking and beautiful scenes that follow one after the other. After the screening, anthropologist/director David Edwards and his codirectors Greg Whitmore and Meliya Zulfacar took Q&A:

Q: Somebody starts out saying admiringly that the film is really cool, all fragmented as it is, he wants to congratulate the filmmakers.
David: Yes, there is no single story, no single character. . . . And anyway that's the way it is, Kabul is really very fragmented.
Q [approvingly]: Non-western films and European films are like this, they don't "mollycoddle the audience."
Q [from a woman who seemed to know she was swimming against the tide of the previous comments]: But I think it was too fragmenting, you didn't provide enough context, I couldn't make sense out of the film.
Meliya: The situation *is* very fragmented.
David: Some people like the way the film is made, and some people get frustrated. [EMPHATICALLY:] *We made a decision.*
[spontaneous applause in favor of this position and against the previous question.] (Field notes, June 28, 2006)

As we were walking out, David was approached by someone with a press badge from *Variety*.[11] He commented to David about the low level of sophistication of American audiences who want simple stories. He blamed it on TV. As he was walking away, another man walked up and congratulated David on a brilliant film. I asked David if he would compromise the film by adding narration or other signposts, since that might enhance the possibility of getting a TV contract. He said, "Absolutely not, I'd rather put it on Google Video" (field notes, June 28, 2006).

All of this is very much in the vein of Bourdieu's arguments about the field of "restricted production," noted earlier. We hear artists who hope people will see and like their films, but who will not compromise their artistic values, shared with a relatively small group of cognoscenti, in order to please the audience. From Bourdieu's point of view this performance of an "interest in disinterestedness" is a kind of posture that seeks the highest possible level of prestige within the field of cultural production as a whole, at the furthest remove from an interest in commerce and money. I am sure there is some element of truth to this; independent filmmakers are certainly not immune to the calls of the ego.

Yet I would argue that a purely Bourdieusian reading of these kinds of statements, at least in the world of independent film (and perhaps in general), is simply too thin, too focused on the prestige effects of this positioning, too cynical about the ideals behind this attitude. For behind the negative stance toward the (mainstream) audience are a number of positive values related to the critical function of independent film. One has to do with the idea of telling the truth about the world around us, showing it "as it really is." The other has to do with disturbing or shaking up the complacent or passive audience so that people will become aware of these realities.

REAL VERSUS FAKE

I indicated earlier that some independent producers and filmmakers can get quite angry about what Hollywood films are doing and saying. When they are explicit about what makes them so upset, the issue almost always revolves around things like truth versus lies, and reality versus fakery, with independent film on the side of truth and the real. Of course, truthfulness is not necessarily the same thing as realism. One can tell all kinds of truths in non-realist modes—through fantasy, poetry, abstraction, and so forth. But in practice in the world of independent film, truth talk tends to be intertwined with reality talk at the level of discourse, and it translates much of the time into an ethic and an aesthetic of realism or hyper(bolic)-realism (I will discuss that distinction later) at the level of film.

For the purposes of the present chapter, we remain at the level of discourse. For example, indie screenwriter/filmmaker Charlie Kaufman said, "I hate *movies that lie to me*. Should I sit there thinking my life sucks because it's not like the ones on the screen, and I'm not getting these life lessons? My life, anyone's life, is more like a muddle, and these [Hollywood] movies are just dangerous garbage" (quoted in Waxman 2006: 155, emphasis added). Independent filmmaker Harmony Korine (e.g., *Kids*, *Gummo*) said, "I can't stand plots, because *I don't feel life has plots*. There is no beginning, middle, or end, and it upsets me when things are tied up so perfectly" (quoted in G. King 2005: 59, emphasis added). Similarly, Ted Hope said later in the interview quoted above,

> Looking at the crap Hollywood was turning out when I was 20, I was like, nobody is making a movie for me and I am just this normal kid from the suburbs. . . . Really all I wanted was a story of a normal person with normal problems because at the end of the day that is what I thought made movies really work. It was not so much even what you saw, but what you were able to talk about afterwards. And that is not often the story of alien invasions, but the *story of real life problems.* (Interview, March 15, 2006, emphasis added)

What Hope means by "a story of a normal person with normal problems" is not necessarily what the average filmgoer might envision by the word "normal"; Hope has produced films like *American Splendor* (2003), about the underground cartoonist Harvey Pekar, who was physically unattractive and chronically depressed. But that is clearly Hope's point—that most "normal" people are not beautiful and happy, and certainly not all the time.

Closely connected to the question of truth in independent films is the question of endings. Hollywood feels compelled to deliver the happy ending, while independent filmmakers feel that such endings are usually false, far from the realities of life. Director Brian De Palma started his career as an independent filmmaker and always remained something of a maverick in Hollywood. We learn from an account of the making of *Bonfire of the Vanities* that De Palma was worried about the ending: "He understood audiences wanted catharsis, some way to synthesize everything they had just seen. . . . He understood that one reason people went to the theater and movies was for the chance to experience the kind of satisfying endings they rarely found in life . . . [but] such moments seemed elusive to him, and false" (Salamon [1991] 2002: 373–74; sentence order rearranged).

Similarly, Danish filmmaker Susanne Bier discussed the non-happy ending of her film *After the Wedding* (2007) at a screening in Los Angeles. Here is an exchange between Bier and various audience members during the Q&A:

> **Moderator:** I read a quote from you, to the effect that the world is a hurtful place.
> **SB:** I am a happy person. But there is a lot of pain in life.
> **Audience Member:** Americans want happy endings.
> **Another Audience Member:** I'm Scandinavian. Most Americans like happy endings. But life is not about happy endings.
> **SB:** Happy endings are not truthful. (Field notes, February 26, 2007)

A few quick notes are in order here on the appearance of foreign films and filmmakers in this book. First, I take Brian Larkin's point that a particular social film world is organized not only by the films people make but by the films they watch (2008). International films constitute a significant percentage of the films that circulate on the American indie circuits, watched by both ordinary audiences and the filmmakers themselves. Closely related to that is the second point, which is that many if not most international films share the anti-Hollywood, or at least un-Hollywood, ethics and aesthetics of American independent film. Indeed, much of what counts today as the indie aesthetic was inspired by European films in the first place, including (among other things) the so-called neo-realism of post–World War II Italian films. Thus, we can hear from European and other international directors some of the same kinds of critique of Hollywood that we hear from American independent filmmakers, as well as the same kind of insistence on truthfulness and realism. Finally, in this era of globalization of filmmaking and film viewing, the distinction between American (independent) and foreign films can get very blurry indeed.

Returning to the Americans, then, most independent filmmakers and producers are committed to a kind of realism in their films that represents a commitment to tell the truth to their viewers. As one young filmmaker recently blogged about his new film, about to open in a theater, "If it speaks with honesty, people will listen and respond" (Porterfield 2011). Filmmaker Rodrigo García discussed honesty and realism (again, the two are always very closely tied together) in an interview:

He went off at some length about how bad Hollywood movies are, how fake—that was the difference, between fakeness and honesty. . . . When he was talking about what he valued in filmmaking, he kept using the word "naked," trying to look at something *as it really is*. He also kept using the phrase, "taking a truthful look." He said you could make a film about anything, the important thing was looking at it as nakedly as possible, taking a completely truthful look at whatever it was. (Field notes, July 13, 2006)

Or take Christine Vachon, another of the major independent producing pioneers: "I built my company on a rebellion against conventional taste, against the no-rough-edges, film-by-consensus style [of Hollywood]," she said. "At Killer [Films] we don't believe that people make the right choice, and then the wrong choice, then fix everything with minutes to spare" (2006: 4, 12). And then she goes to the reality issue:

The most dangerous movies Killer [Films] has made are the ones that reflected the real world back with the least amount of artifice: *Kids, Happiness, Boys Don't Cry*. I wouldn't call these films "realistic;" nothing on screen is. What they are are stories without clear heroes or redemptive "arcs." People may or may not get what is coming to them, and those plots spook an industry premised on wish fulfillment and getting the girl (2006: 75).

If we look back at many of the comments disparaging "Hollywood" or "American audiences" quoted earlier for other purposes, we can see in them too that the issue is one of truth and/or realism. Thus, we heard Charlie Kaufman say that his goal in filmmaking was not to please audiences but to explore particular subjects "in a truthful way." Or we heard David Edwards and his codirectors defending the fragmented and hard-to-understand nature of their film about Kabul by saying that fragmentation was the reality of Kabul as a city today. Or we earlier heard Hollywood-oriented producer Ursula Jackson (condescendingly) describe independent films as "almost documentary, . . . so involved in true life."

Film critic A. O. Scott has dubbed this trend in independent film "neo-neo-realism." Discussing a number of contemporary independent films in this realist mold (*Wendy and Lucy, Man Push Cart, Ballast*, and others), Scott locates them in a lineage that begins with Italian neo-realism during and after World War II (the iconic example being Vittorio de Sica's *The Bicycle Thief* [1948]). He describes the art of these films as lying "in their discovery of a mysterious, volatile alloy of documentary and theatrical elements" (2009: 40). Although he, like the filmmakers, does not use the language of "cultural critique," he recognizes the critical function these films serve: "To counter the tyranny of fantasy entrenched on Wall Street and in Washington as well as in Hollywood, it seems possible that engagement with the world as it is might reassert itself as an aesthetic strategy. Perhaps it would be worth considering that what we need from movies, in the face of a dismaying and confusing real world, is realism" (2009: 40).

There is one final piece to this reading of independent film as setting itself up against the cultural hegemony embodied in Hollywood movies. We have already seen that many independent filmmakers refuse to try to please the audience. In fact, many go further than that and actively seek to make audiences uncomfortable to one degree or another. This is often put in terms of making people "feel something." For example, filmmaker Karen Moncrieff (e.g., *The Dead Girl*) said, "I'm interested in movies that make people feel something, and that's what I gravitate toward. I like to be pushed off my center when I go to the movies. I like to be invited to feel and think" (Moncrieff n.d., ca. 2006). Rodrigo García, in the interview discussed earlier, made similar comments about "how a film needs to make demands on you, and throw you off balance." He went on to say that "art is not supposed to make you feel good, it's supposed to question things, hold up the mirror, take you somewhere you won't or would rather not go in real life." He also used stronger language about the kind of impact he sought from a good film. Talking about how Americans are conditioned by Hollywood movies to want "entertainment" and a happy ending, he said "he just can't stand it, for him a film is only worth something if it really 'beats him up'" (field notes, February 10, 2007).

This urge to disturb the audience will be explored further in the next chapter. I see it as part of the larger project of cultural critique behind the independent film movement, which I have tried to frame and forecast in this chapter. Without using the language of "cultural critique," independent film people (producers and filmmakers) seek to challenge the dominant culture, as embodied not only in Hollywood but also in the mainstream audience. How they go about this will be explored in the chapters to come, through a consideration of a range of major and minor independent films.

One final point before moving on. As discussed earlier, skeptics have challenged the discourse of "independence" as at best false consciousness and at worst self-serving ideology. The same question might be raised about (my) taking the rhetoric of honesty and truthfulness at face value. The argument can be made that the harsh realism and disturbing representations of at least some independent films are more about shocking the older generation than about telling the truth about contemporary society. Young independent filmmakers who make particularly shocking or unpleasant films are sometimes portrayed as bad boys or girls who are just seeking attention. As with the arguments about the discourse of "independence," there is no doubt some truth to these charges. But to follow out that point would be to write a different book. My purpose throughout is the ethnographer's purpose anywhere—to maintain a critical eye and ear, yes, but at the same time to take what people say seriously and see where that takes us.

We turn next to the first film chapter, where I will seek to understand what is perhaps the most prominent feature of many independent films: their darkness, or what indie people call their "edge."

CHAPTER 2

Dark Indies

From the beginning of this project, I immersed myself in independent films. At first I was somewhat mystified. While many of them were compelling, many of them were also quite dark and, in one way or another, disturbing. They were clearly "not Hollywood." This generated the first question of my research beyond the purely ethnographic: what was this all about? In Part I of this chapter, I tackle this general question of "darkness" and propose to understand it in terms of the generational positioning of a new breed of filmmakers, the first post-boomer generation usually known as Generation X. I argue further that "Generation X" represents not a particular cohort that ended at a certain point in time, but an ongoing and open-ended social entity that is bearing the brunt of the massive economic transformations called "neoliberalism."

In Part II of the chapter I then turn to specific sets of films that directly or indirectly address the conditions of life under neoliberalism in America. These include films classically associated with "Generation X" (*Slacker*, *Reality Bites*, and others), concerned primarily with the misery and/or insecurity of work in the neoliberal order. But they also include much darker films by/about immigrants struggling to survive not only in a neoliberal economy but in the long shadow of 9/11.

Part I: The Darkness of Independent Film

From early on in my viewing, I was struck by the extreme darkness (of mood, of tone, of look, of story) of many independent films.

Many of them range from very gloomy to "pitch-black" (Ansen [2007a: 65] on *Se7en*). *Newsweek* film critic Ramin Setoodeh recently complained that between 2005 and 2009 "roughly three fourths of all the films [nominated for Academy Awards] fixated on death" and described many films as "piling on the pain" in what "is starting to feel like Misery Porn" (2009: 70). David Denby of the *New Yorker* described a recent indie as "grating, almost punitive" (2010, on *Margot at the Wedding*). Hollywood-oriented producer/director Jennifer Farmer described independent films in general as "dark, dysfunctional, heavy, violent, twisted, alternative kinds of things" (quoted in Stubbs and Rodriguez 2000: 28).

Correspondingly, there is an assumption among many independent filmmakers that it is not necessarily a bad idea to make audiences feel uncomfortable, disturbed, and depressed. Gregg Araki, director of *Mysterious Skin,* said "he set out to create a movie that would devastate his audience" (in Hernandez 2004: 2). Filmmaker Rodrigo García, director of *Nine Lives,* said in an interview (field notes, February 10, 2007), that for him a film is only worth something if it really "beats him up." Austrian director Michael Haneke is quoted as saying, "I've been accused of 'raping' the audience in my films, and I admit to that freely–all movies assault the viewer in one way or another" (in Wray 2007: 47). As with some of Haneke's films, there may be extreme physical violence, and there is always a great deal of emotional violence. There is rarely a happy ending. While not all independent films are dark, disturbing, and depressing, so many are that I daresay this kind of film has, almost from the outset of the indie movement, defined the genre as a whole.

Of course, one can also find comedies in the world of independent film. But first of all, there are many fewer of them than of the dark and devastating sort of film. And second of all, the comedies themselves are infected with the prevailing darkness. There is no such thing as a straightforward comedy in independent film. At the most innocent end, a comedy must at least be describable as "quirky" (e.g., *Little Miss Sunshine* [Jonathan Dayton and Valerie Farris 2006]). Ratcheting the darkness up a notch, it might be described as "edgy." For example, what is generally taken to be the founding film of the contemporary indie movement, *sex, lies, and videotape* (Steven Soderbergh, 1989) is described on its poster and DVD box as "an edgy, intense, comedy." At the far end of the spectrum of dark independent comedy is a film like the Coen brothers' *A Serious Man* (2009), about which critic Ramin Setoodeh wrote, "I had to get up and leave in the middle, it's so depressing—and it's a comedy" (2009: 70).

The darkness comes in several varieties. There may be emotional misery and depression, usually related to impossible relationships in which the characters are trapped. There may be extensive physical violence, sometimes embedded in those impossible relationships, and other times random and psychopathic. There may be deeply perverse sexual desires and relationships, such as pedophilia, sado/masochism, or incest; pedophilia alone is so prevalent in independent films that I will devote a whole discussion to it in chapter 4. All of these, singly and often together, add up to what is meant by some of the favorite vocabulary of independent film: dark, twisted, edgy.

I need to take a moment here to talk about the idea of "edge," as it is one of the key terms of this discourse. First let us look at some usages and then try to figure out what it means. Hollywood-oriented producer Sheila Hanahan Taylor described independent films as "edgy, envelope-pushing, cutting edge, slice of life pieces" (e-mail, November 11, 2005). Former Miramax executive Jack Lechner talked about his disagreements with Harvey Weinstein: "[Miramax] was becoming more of a studio. I wanted us to do *Election*. It's a very edgy movie, an old Miramax movie," presumably meaning the kind of movie Miramax used to make before it lost its edge (quoted in Biskind 2004: 323). Similarly, vice chairman of Lionsgate Productions, Michael Burns, talked about Lionsgate's celebrated decision to distribute Michael Moore's *Fahrenheit 9/11*: "Smart, edgy, sophisticated fare—it's our sweet spot" (quoted in Roberts 2004: 42). Or here is independent producer Christine Vachon writing about the kinds of films she likes to produce: "I've got a reputation for 'edgy,' 'dark' material—the kind of movie where you're maybe rooting for the bad guy" (Vachon 2006: 4). Or finally, here is actor George Clooney talking about his friend, independent filmmaker Steven Soderbergh: "I think Steven is reluctant to be a successful director, and that's why he stayed independent so long. . . . [I]t's a fear any independent director has: that early on they're edgy, but when they get fat and happy, the edge goes away" (quoted in Waxman 2006: 103).

The idea of "edgy" not only applies to films and filmmakers but extends to all aspects of the independent film world, in contrast to Hollywood. Thus, Diana Zahn-Storey, executive producer of the Independent Spirit Awards show in 2009, talked about the "look" of the show: "We don't want to be the Oscars or the Golden Globes. You won't see a glitzy look. . . . Ours is more edgy and slightly hipper" (Muñoz 2009: 9).

What then does "edgy" mean? If I had to translate it with a single word, I think I would choose the word "off"—off-center, off-balance, off-moral, somehow or other not quite right. The idea of edge seems closely bound up with the idea noted above, that a good independent film should make the viewer uncomfortable, disturbed, destabilized. There is no single way to be edgy; there is edgy-dark, edgy-dangerous, edgy-perverse, edgy-disgusting, and so on. The common thread is that viewers should not be easy—whether with the story, the look, the music, or some other aspect. If, as film scholar Linda Williams has famously argued, different genres of film have different bodily effects (melodrama makes us weep, horror films make us scream, etc.; L. Williams 2003), perhaps one could say that the edgy independent film is meant to make us squirm. Of course, there is a spectrum of edge, from the kind of light and playful edge of the Independent Spirit Awards decor to the much darker edge of many of the actual films.

Some of the films are darker than others. In some cases the filmmaker will give the audience some humor to relieve the darkness (the Coen brothers are a case in point); in some cases music is used as a counterpoint (Altman especially comes to mind); and in a few cases, such as *Precious* (Lee Daniels, 2009), the filmmaker actually gives us, at the end of a long harrowing story, a semblance of a happy ending or a satisfying resolution. These details and variations matter a great deal when one is experiencing and thinking about any particular film. But in aggregate there are simply a lot of very dark and disturbing movies out there on the indie circuits.

The darkness of so much of independent film set up for me the opening questions of this project. Where was this impulse to make depressing, emotionally violent, and/or sexually perverse films coming from? And how to understand the fact that these films—many of which may range from unpleasant to difficult to almost impossible to watch—found a significant national audience in commercial theaters from the late 1980s on? One clue is to be found in the generational positioning of the new breed of independent filmmakers that emerged on the scene, starting in the late 1980s.

INDEPENDENT FILMMAKERS

Independent filmmakers see themselves first and foremost as creative artists. They consider themselves individual *auteurs*, each with his or her own story to tell. They see themselves as passionate about their work, deeply committed to making films of quality and significance as opposed to the empty and false fare of Hollywood.

Sociologically speaking, independent filmmakers do not like to be pigeonholed in terms of identity categories, class locations, generational niches, or any other classifying or collectivizing set of terms. Filmmaker Gregg Araki, hailed as (among other things) a pioneer of the "new queer cinema" in the 1990s, put it this way:

> I like to be thought of without any kind of adjective attached to it. A gay filmmaker, a Gen-X filmmaker, an Asian-American filmmaker—I'd just like to be thought of as a filmmaker. . . . I approach films in the way a musician approaches music. It's just my means of expression, my chosen medium. . . . I'm an artist, not a politician. (in Hays 1997: 1)

At one level—at the level of understanding that an artist would hope for individual recognition purely on the merits of his or her work—I am completely sympathetic to this position. At another level, however, we must recognize that artists produce their work within particular locations within particular cultures/societies/histories, and they embody—for the most part unconsciously—the spirit of those times and places. Without in any way denying the individual creativity, or lack thereof, of particular artists, my interest is situated at this cultural and historical level.

Turning then to the sociological profile of independent filmmakers, it is part of the ideology of the indie world that diversity matters, that the voices of women, minorities, and people from other countries and cultures importantly expand and complicate the mix of films available to American audiences. The degree to which this diversity is actually achieved is of course variable. I have not seen any reliable data on racial diversity in the independent film world; impressionistically the indie community may be slightly more racially diverse than Hollywood, but we don't really know. I do have some data that indicate a better representation of women among independent filmmakers than Hollywood directors; that will be discussed in chapter 7. I also have some interesting data about class diversity among independent filmmakers; this will be relevant to discussions of the contrast between filmmakers and producers in chapter 5. For present purposes it is probably fair to say that the majority of independent filmmakers come from basically middle-class backgrounds.[1]

Of central importance to the present chapter are issues of generation. As noted in the introduction, the vast majority of independent filmmakers were born within the parameters of "Generation X." Born starting in the 1960s, Generation X was the first generation to collectively feel the harsh economic effects of the new neoliberal order and to feel the darkening of the national mood represented in the idea of "the end of the American Dream." Without suggesting any conscious intentionality on the part of most (but not all) independent filmmakers, I argue that these filmmakers are both channeling and confronting, in myriad ways, these new and dark conditions in their films.

Other scholars have drawn attention to the connection between Generation X and the new wave of independent film. Peter Hanson, in *The Cinema of Generation X* (2002), and the contributors to the special volume of *Post Script* (L. King 2000) on Gen X films all touch on a range of issues that will be central to this book, including jobs, family, and politics in the lives of Generation X. A very interesting and astute book by journalist Jesse Fox Mayshark called *Post-Pop Cinema* (2007) also surveys the work of a range of independent filmmakers who emerged in the 1990s, most of whom will be looked at in the present book as well. Without using the phrase "Generation X," Mayshark interprets their work within a generational framework, arguing that they collectively represent a move away from an earlier postmodernism and toward a search for "a sort of self-conscious *meaningfulness*" (2007: 5). Finally, I want to single out an article by Julian Crockford, within the *Post Script* volume noted above, as being especially relevant to the arguments of this book. Crockford picks up on the early literature on neoliberalism, before the term was in general use, which emphasizes the shift of American capitalism to a "service economy." He situates Generation X within this shift, as I do, and he productively reads the Gen X film *Reality Bites* (Ben Stiller, 1994), which I will discuss later in this chapter, against a backdrop of the film *Wall Street* (Oliver Stone, 1985). Crockford shows how *Wall Street* was both a story about a different economic moment and a foreshadowing of the economy that will define the lives of the characters in *Reality Bites*.

MORE ON GENERATION X: THE END OF SECURITY

Generation X—and again the referent here is mostly middle class—was born into the relative comfort and security of the post–World War II

American economy.[2] As they grew up, however, the economy began to turn down. As they moved into their twenties, they began to be told, via journalism and other channels of the public culture, that they were the first generation since the Great Depression that would not do better than their parents. As they moved into the workplace, they began to experience concretely what that might mean—jobs beneath what they might have expected, given both the experience of the preceding boomer generation and their own hard work throughout years of schooling. Worse, as the job market worsened, they had to worry about getting and/or keeping any job at all, no matter how deadly it might be.

Not surprisingly, many Gen Xers had a certain amount of attitude about jobs they felt to be beneath them. Many were able to coast on parental support for extended periods of time, while they waited for better opportunities (see especially Ortner [1998] 2006c). This phenomenon was the basis of the "slacker" stereotype that has been embraced by some Xers, as we will see later in the chapter. But it is deeply resented by the vast majority of Xers who work hard and yet are unable to build economically comfortable lives in the present and economic security for the future.

Profound economic insecurity, then, is at the center of the Gen X worldview. But as we see in both the popular culture and scholarly studies, economic insecurity is often linked to a seemingly unrelated set of anxieties, mainly related to bodily integrity and bodily damage—crime, socially transmitted disease, environmental degradation, war. This linkage between economic insecurity and fears of bodily danger was picked up in scattered sources starting in the 1990s, including in Mike Davis's discussion of "Fortress L.A." (1990) and Michael Moore's film *Bowling for Columbine* (2002), as noted in the introduction. In anthropology, it was explored cross-culturally in Jean and John Comaroff's important collection *Millennial Capitalism and the Culture of Neoliberalism* (2001; see also Larkin 2008), and for the United States in the recent Gusterson/Besteman collection of anthropological essays, *The Insecure American* (2010). To this very valuable body of work I want to add some previously unpublished ethnographic data that show essentially the same patterns.

In the mid-1990s, I was doing some research on a group of young adults, grown children of classmates with whom I had graduated from high school. (I call them collectively Children of the Class of '58 or CC58.)[3] Like the independent filmmakers, almost all of these young people had been born within the official demographic time frame of Generation X, roughly between the early 1960s and the early 1980s, so I was reading the Gen X literature, trying to get a general sense of what I might expect. I circulated a questionnaire by mail, which included short questions about, for example, CC58's education, jobs, and marital status, but also an essay question at the end: "Do you think the world has changed much since your parents' time?" to which I received about 140 responses. At that point I was not yet tuned in to the dark worldview of Generation X, and I remember being somewhat shocked by the responses.

First and foremost were the economic anxieties and fears that are at the core of the Gen X worldview. Jeff wrote, "I will probably be worse off than my parents when I reach their age." Robin wrote, "The possibility of doing better than our parents, financially, is not great. I think many of us will be lucky if we can even equal our parents' economic status." Jessica wrote, "A college education no longer assures one of a good job, and even a professional degree will not always help." And there were many more comments of this sort.

In addition to the theme of economic anxiety, there was a theme of bodily fear and danger that very much surprised me at the time. Most of these young people had grown up in fairly sheltered and comfortable middle- to upper-middle-class homes. Moreover, most of them were from intact families, which is to say that their fears were not necessarily stemming from personally disrupted situations. Yet there was a real feeling of threat and danger in the world around them.

Quite a few of them mentioned AIDS. Sheri wrote, "[The world] is different. Socially—we have AIDS, so instead of sex being simply 'morally' wrong, as it was in the 50s, now we fear for our lives." Rachel wrote, "AIDS is a part of our generation—a reality and fear that my parents didn't know." Dana listed a number of differences from her parents' time; the following was first on the list: "AIDS: When my parents were my age, venereal disease (most of which could be treated) and pregnancy were the most serious consequences of sex. Today, if promiscuous, as many are, sex is often a dangerous act."

The AIDS issue in turn was part of a larger sense of a more dangerous and violent world (and this even before 9/11/2001). Sheri wrote, "And how do we ever feel totally safe? Violent crime seems to be a daily issue we experience. We do not have the secure feeling to walk where we want or to feel safe alone, as our parents did." Kenneth wrote, "Crime and violence have become more and more of a threat to everyday life. Cold war is over but terrorism/3rd world nuclear power is the new enemy." Andrea wrote, "The crime rate is much higher. . . . The world is not as safe as it used to be, and it is scary to contemplate a future that may only get worse."

Most disturbing perhaps were the texts where economic anxieties, intimate dangers from sex and AIDS, and large-scale, and even global, dangers are all intertwined. Here are a few out of many examples, and look for the linkages between the intimate and the large-scale. Josh wrote,

> The profusion of media images, from Vietnam, to Watergate, to increasing levels of violence, divorce, have made our generation more scared and less hopeful.

Rachel wrote,

> AIDS is a part of our generation—a reality and fear that my parents didn't know. Technology has leaped forward. We can do so much in so little time—but we can also destroy the world many times over. I have experienced no world wars but horrible wars are happening all over. Wars that no one side can win.

Diane wrote,

> As an educated person in my mid-twenties, I clearly see the extreme violence in the movies, newspapers and on TV daily, plus there is the traumatic spread of the AIDS epidemic and the abundant drug scare (just to name a few). . . . I recently have been considering marriage but my real concern . . . lies with the challenge of raising a family of my own in the 90's. There are definitely certain considerations that are apparent now such as child-care, the necessity of dual income, inflation, rising health care, and an all-time high crime rate, which will bear heavy weight on my decisions to come in the future.

And finally, Andrea wrote,

> The world is a more dangerous place today than it was for my parents. Women are at greater risk of sex and violent crimes being perpetrated against them. The effect this has on my life can be summed up with one word—FEAR. I have a far greater awareness of what might be dangerous

than my parents needed to have. . . . We are working longer hours for less material gain. We are also in a more precarious position due to: revolving credit, the global economy, staggering health care costs, benefits that only benefit the insurance companies, environmental degradation and rape and a smorgasbord of other social ills.

In these and many of the other mini-essays these young people connect the most intimate and the most global fears, often in a single phrase or sentence: increasing violence and divorce, AIDS and global warfare, AIDS and health care costs and violent crime, environmental degradation and rape.

One might pause to ask how realistic these anxieties were. It varied a great deal. The economic anxieties of course were and continue to be quite realistic. The anxieties about the violence of the global order—of war and environmental degradation—were and continue to be quite realistic.

Concerns about AIDS are more complex. The AIDS epidemic was very frightening in the 1980s and 1990s, before effective drug treatments were developed (AIDS was first identified in 1982 ["So little time . . ." 2007]).[4] But the chances that the young people answering my questionnaire— mostly white, (upper) middle class, and heterosexual—would be in a position to contract AIDS were very small (see also Watney 1987).

As for violent crime, which was probably the single most frequently expressed anxiety, this seems to be the least realistic fear. Sociologist Barry Glassner opened his study of *The Culture of Fear* (1999) with the following paragraph:

> Why, as crime rates plunged throughout the 1990s, did two-thirds of Americans believe they were soaring? How did it come about that by mid-decade 62% of us described ourselves as "truly desperate" about crime—almost twice as many as in the late 1980s, when crime rates were higher? Why, on a survey in 1997, when the crime rate had already fallen for a half dozen consecutive years, did more than half of us disagree with the statement "This country is finally beginning to make some progress in solving the crime problem?" (1999: xi, with footnotes referencing the sources of his figures).

Glassner primarily blames the media for creating and perpetuating irrational, counter-reality fears.[5] Yet media representations clearly resonated with people's own subjective anxieties. The young adults answering my questionnaire in the 1990s clearly believed deeply that their world was a much more dangerous place than it had been in the (somewhat idealized) time when their parents (my generation) were growing up.

In sum, we hear in these texts a range of dark feelings—a sense of insecurity about the future, a sense of physical and bodily dangers (realistic or not), a sense of relative helplessness and hopelessness, and finally a fair amount of anger about all that. Thus, without seeing Gen X filmmakers as in some sense conscious spokespersons for their generation, I am suggesting that the darkness of so much of independent film emanates from the same deep generational anxieties we hear from cc58 and other "natives." Indeed, as we will see below, at least some independent filmmakers have explicitly embraced the Gen X identity. But that is not important for this argument, nor is it important that every filmmaker who makes a film embodying these moods or themes actually be of the correct chronological age. Many people can relate viscerally to the Gen X worldview without being chronologically Gen X themselves. The point is simply that there has been a massive sea change in the culture, and Generation Xers are at the epicenter of it, whether they are simply leading their lives in the New Jersey suburbs or making independent films anywhere in America.

But there is an important difference between ordinary people and people who make films or other major contributions to the public culture. People on the ground, like the Children of the Class of 58, or the people of "Pleasanton," New Jersey, with very similar insecurities and feelings of anger (Newman 1993), try to make the best lives they can within the problems of the world as they see it. At best this involves a lot of improvising, adapting, and adjusting in their lives and those of their families. At worst it involves more actively defensive maneuvers like the kinds of things documented in *The Insecure American* (Gusterson and Besteman 2010)— moving to gated communities, walling out immigrants, giving up civil rights in exchange for "security," and so on. They exert a lot of agency, but mainly to shore up and protect their own immediate lives. This is not a criticism; this is how most of us survive.

Filmmakers, on the other hand, make films. They draw on the world as experienced in many different ways—as themes, as moods, as "structures of feeling." They put some version of that world up on a screen and make us move beyond our own lives and into worlds "out there." They create "public culture" and invite us, or even—recalling some of the more aggressive language of filmmakers—force us, to engage with it. Now let us look at some films.

Part II: Representing Neoliberal America

Throughout this book, I will treat independent film as a form of "cultural critique." I adapt this idea from George Marcus and Michael Fischer's valuable work *Anthropology as Cultural Critique* (1986), in which they argue that one of the promises of social and cultural anthropology has been "to serve as a form of cultural critique for ourselves. In using portraits of other cultural patterns to reflect self-critically on our own ways, anthropology disrupts common sense and makes us reexamine our taken-for-granted assumptions" (1986: 1). Michael Fischer later extended this point to films, especially films set in other cultures (1995). The point can also be made, with little adjustment, about the ambitions, if not always the achievements, of American independent film in general. In telling harsh or strange or otherwise disturbing stories about other people's lives, they seek to "disrupt common sense and make us reexamine our taken-for-granted assumptions" about our lives and the world around us.

Cultural critique is not full-fledged political critique. Political critique, which will be discussed in later chapters, is ideally a call to action, while cultural critique is a call to see/think/feel in reflective and critical ways. But that is no small thing in itself.

Cultural critique works primarily through representation. As discussed in the last chapter, independent films seek to create truthful, usually meaning realist, representations of the world. Although independent filmmakers often deny political intent (we heard Greg Araki say, "I'm an artist, not a politician"), from the point of view adopted here, the commitment of independent film to truthfulness and realism should be seen as a kind of political act. The view of realism as an unsophisticated form of artistic expression fails to appreciate the political significance that sheer representation can carry.

Within the world of independent film, there is a particular rhetoric of why one should make a film. This is the idea that a filmmaker should have a story that he or she urgently wants to tell. The difference between a (stereotypical) director-for-hire and a serious filmmaker is that the filmmaker's story comes from within—it is, as we heard in the last chapter, "personal." The desire to "tell one's story" is, within the ethic of the indie world, the only reason to make a film.

But where do these stories come from? While the stories are surely "personal" and come from the inner life and personal circumstances of the filmmaker, again the filmmaker or other artist does not live in a social and cultural vacuum. Here then I want to propose a model of the art and work of independent filmmaking as one of intervening in, and "talking back" to, the stories that are already out there in the public culture, including but not limited to the stories coming out of "Hollywood." The urgency to "tell one's story," I suggest, comes from a sense of needing to counter other stories, to correct them, to debunk them, to tell the truth.

For the long Generation X, starting in the 1980s and continuing into the present and foreseeable future, the story in question is the story of the American Dream. The idea of the American Dream, that anyone could achieve a reasonable level of economic security and social respect in American society if they worked hard and lived properly, dominated American public culture for virtually the entire twentieth century. (Again, the one rarely acknowledged limiting factor was race.) The American Dream may be understood here as the folk version of one of the great master narratives of modernity, the idea of universal progress and betterment of life for all.[6] For a long time this "dream" corresponded with reality for large numbers of Americans. But for the first generation since the Great Depression that will not do better than its parents, and that faces the real possibility of sliding back down the ladder, this "dream" has begun to appear as a cruel lie. It is the exposure of this lie and the exploration of its consequences that we see in a range of independent films of the 1990s and 2000s.

SOME NOTES ON DISCUSSIONS TO FOLLOW

First, I acknowledge again that I will be looking at the films primarily in terms of their stories. While I fully understand that films are very complex textual assemblages, working at multiple levels of meaning and impact, and involving multiple aesthetic and technical strategies, for my purposes here—the cultural and, broadly speaking, political interpretation of films —the stories must be the primary focus of my interest.

Second, while my primary focus is on independent films, I remind the reader of the fuzzy boundary between the indie world and the rest of the industry. In the discussion that follows I sometimes invoke and discuss films that arguably embody the "independent spirit" but for one reason or another were made in a Hollywood studio (often by a filmmaker who had made a successful independent film before). I also include in the independent category many films that were made in that large intermediate zone that includes specialty divisions of studios and so-called mini-major studios like Miramax or Lionsgate. And finally I sometimes bring foreign films and filmmakers into the discussion; although my primary focus is on the American independent film scene, foreign films actively circulate alongside American films on the indie circuit. And as Brian Larkin has argued with respect to the circulation of Indian Bollywood films in Nigeria, for at least some purposes a film scene can/should be defined in terms of not only films being made but films being watched (2008: 187).

Third, coming from a Geertzian background, I take it for granted that films not only "represent" whatever it is they represent but also—when they work—shape the consciousness of their audiences in particular ways. As Geertz wrote in discussing the Balinese cockfight, "Art forms generate and regenerate the very subjectivity they pretend only to display. Quartets, still lifes, and cockfights are not merely reflections of a pre-existing sensibility analogically represented; they are positive agents in the creation and maintenance of such a sensibility" (1973b: 451). On this point I am very much in tune with certain strands of film studies scholarship that look at ways in which films shape subjectivities. As used throughout this text, the idea of "representation" is not simply a matter of putting images out there to be contemplated objectively, nor is it simply a matter of getting people to "feel something" (although that is very important too). At its most ambitious, it is a matter of conjuring in audiences' worldviews, subjectivities, and structures of feeling.

That being said, I am also deeply concerned with the relationship between films and a preexisting real world. I take it that the world does consist of certain hard realities; the question of "representation" here is always a question of selection—of what is shown (and not shown) and how what is shown is presented and represented. Here I have found the work of Vivian Sobchack particularly enlightening and useful (1998, 2003). Sobchack tackles the perennial question, often dismissed as a form of "reflectionism," of a film genre's "relation to its historical and social context" (1998: 147). Writing of film noir, for example, she argues that this relationship is "not metaphoric but . . . synecdochic and hyperbolic." That is, "noir represents concrete parts of the whole landscape of American wartime and postwar culture—but its synecdochic selectivity and partiality result in a hyperbolic textual exaggeration of aspects of that context's actual life world" (1998: 148).

The same may be said of much of independent film in general.[7] Indie filmmakers think of themselves as making realist films, not so much in a naturalistic sense, but in the sense of stripping away falsely pleasant and perfect exteriors and showing the underlying reality of things. The effect is often more hyperbolic than realistic, worse than the real thing, or at least worse than the kinds of real things middle-class people would normally experience. Sobchack's view of noir, and perhaps some other genres as well, as operating by selection and exaggeration from a real lived world, rather than standing metaphorically for some other, and often more abstract and general, set of meanings, informs many of the film interpretations to follow.[8]

Finally, I need to say a few words about how films were selected for discussion in this and later chapters. As noted earlier, I watched a large number (currently about six hundred fifty) of mostly independent films in order to get an overview of the whole spectrum of work in this "field of cultural production." I tried to be as open-ended as possible in my film viewing throughout the project, because I wanted to be receptive to emerging patterns within the genre, beyond or behind the intentionalities of individual filmmakers.[9] As in the interpretation of discourse, it is the patterns that are of interest, for once you realize that you have seen, say, eight or nine films with pedophiles in them, you know you must begin to think about what is going on. In practice there was a kind of back-and-forth process between allowing the patterns to strike me (the darkness, to be discussed in this chapter; the pedophiles, to be discussed in chapter 4) and more proactively posing questions to my large pool of films. For the present chapter, for example, I did go actively looking for films that had explicit associations with "Generation X." But having looked at them, I realized there were issues concerning the American Dream, which in turn reminded me that I had been seeing (without focusing on) this theme in quite a few films about immigrants, which then led me to look at the body of "immigrant films" that I consider in the last section of this chapter. Throughout this process I added to, but never subtracted from, the pool in general or any given subset of films in particular.

And so at last to the films.

Four films came out in the 1990s that were specifically set in the context of the new economy, were made by filmmakers who were born in the official Gen X time frame, and explicitly embraced the Gen X identity, or at least were seen by Xers as speaking to their lives. The films were *Slacker* (Richard Linklater [b. 1961], 1991), *Reality Bites* (Ben Stiller [b. 1965], 1994), *Office Space* (Mike Judge [b. 1962], 1999), and *Fight Club* (David Fincher [b. 1962], 1999).

This particular group of films is more heavily weighted toward the studio end of the spectrum than most of the groups of films to be discussed in this book. While *Slacker* was a micro-budget ($23,000) independent film, *Office Space* and *Reality Bites* were relatively low budget ($10 million and $11.5 million, respectively) studio films. *Fight Club* is the confounding case. It was made in a studio for a relatively large budget ($63 million), yet it is always seen as one of the classic "indies" of the 1990s, presumably because of its dark themes and Fincher's very anti-Hollywood attitude. It is one of six films that Sharon Waxman discusses in *Rebels on the Backlot* that were greenlit by studios in the 1990s despite the fact that their directors "shared a collective disdain for [the] studio system" (2006: x). For the purposes of the present section, I am less concerned with whether the films were technically "independent," or even "semi-independent," than with the fact that they have been defined in various ways as Generation X films.

All four films revolve around the unhappy nature of white-collar work under neoliberal capitalism.[10] As seen in the earlier discussion of "McJobs," the picture of work in the new economy is increasingly grim. The "good job" is getting harder and harder to find and/or keep. We get a picture of people laboring in sterile cubicles, with difficult bosses making arbitrary and unreasonable demands. People are often asked to work overtime and on weekends with no additional compensation; any unwillingness to do so marks one for firing in favor of a more willing worker. There is a culture of downsizing even when it has not been shown that this would increase profitability. It has been shown that managers who let more people go make more money than managers who let fewer people go (Ehrenreich 2005: 224).[11] Anyone can be arbitrarily fired at any time, and much as one may dislike one's job, one has to live in fear of losing it. Higher-priced workers are more tempting targets than lower-paid ones, and thus a promotion or a raise is often a bittersweet thing (2005: 217). The job market is perpetually tight, and the older one gets, the harder it is to find the next job. Beyond a certain age, every new job pays less than the last one. Many older workers (and "older" is a very relative term; in advertising one may be over the hill by 30 [Sennett 1998]) cannot find any jobs at all (Sennett 1998, 2006; Newman 1999; Ehrenreich 2005).

I will run through the films individually first, highlighting the work issues. At the end I will consider them as a group as interventions in the public culture on the emerging neoliberal order.

Richard Linkater's *Slacker* consists of a kaleidoscopic series of vignettes, by turns funny, disturbing, or cruel, of mostly young people in Austin, Texas. Virtually no one has a job. People sometimes try to make money through little enterprises, as in the case of some little boys who have figured out how to get free cans of soda from a machine; they then sell them to other people. (One of the guys who buys a can calls them "little capitalists.") Throughout the film, most people don't talk about work at all. They talk about their various other obsessions, from UFOs to JFK conspiracy theories to the now-legendary Madonna pap smear. But occasionally the subject of work comes up. One guy says he's still unemployed and that the band he plays in has just changed its name to "The Ultimate Losers" (Linklater 1992: 54). ("Loser" is a long-standing jargon term for a [middle-class] man who doesn't work, doesn't have any ambition, and/or can't seem to get ahead.) Another is asked by the video interviewer what he does for a living, and he erupts with a surprisingly Old Left speech about work: "You mean work? To hell with the kind of work you have to do to earn a living. All that does is fill the bellies of the pigs that exploit us. Hey, look at me . . . I'm making it. I may live badly, but at least I don't have to work to do it" (1992: 79). A little later he adds to the video camera, "To all you workers out there: every single commodity you produce is a piece of your own death" (1992: 80).

Linklater has specifically allied himself with the concept of Generation X; Douglas Coupland, the author of the novel *Generation X*, wrote the foreword to Linklater's book *Slacker* (1992). Linklater always insisted that from his point of view the idea of slacking was not about laziness, but about a kind of principled resistance to the kinds of work one is expected to do in the new economy. As he said in an interview, "It's not that everyone in

Slacker is unemployed, it's just that their little slave job isn't what's motivating them in the world" (quoted in Ortner [1998] 2006c: 103).[12]

Let me turn next to the more Hollywood-oriented *Reality Bites*, which again both is viewed as and identifies itself as a Gen X film. This is clear from the opening sequence, in which Lelaina (Winona Rider) is giving the valedictorian speech at her graduation, all about how her class has inherited the ruined world left by the boomers. Here is just a bit of what is quite a long speech: "And they wonder why those of us in our 20s refuse to work an 80-hour week, so we can afford to buy their BMWs. . . . The question remains, what are we going to do now? [The viewer sees a shot from above of a graduate's cap, on which is written in tape, 'Will work 4 food.'] How can we repair all the damage we inherited?" Lelaina gets a job at a TV station but makes a mistake. Her boss says to her, "I can fire you and find an intern who'll do your job for nothing." Meanwhile at home her roommate Vicki (Janeane Garofalo), who works at the Gap, brings home a friend, Troy (Ethan Hawke), who is temporarily out of work and needs a place to stay. Lelaina resists, saying that he will turn their apartment "into a den of slack," but Troy moves in, settles in on the couch, and begins to fall in love with Lelaina.

Lelaina meanwhile has been making a documentary about her roommates, and in the course of this she meets Michael (Ben Stiller), a TV producer, who also falls in love with her. Michael is clearly a baby boomer, as is indicated in part by the fact that he is a workaholic: "I think I'd be working even if I weren't paid." He is of course the antithesis of Troy, whom Lelaina continues to berate about not working. Troy finally explodes, saying, "What is it that you want from me? . . . You want me to get a job on the line for the next 20 years until I'm granted leave with my gold-plated watch and my balls full of tumors because I surrendered the one thing that means shit to me? Well honey you can just exhale cuz it's not gonna happen, not in this lifetime." Leaving aside the slightly anachronistic notion that anyone could get to stay in a job for 20 years nowadays, Troy refuses to cave in about getting a real job, and in the end Lelaina chooses him and the film comes to a romantic happy ending.

There are a few workplace scenes in *Reality Bites* (Vicki at the Gap, perfectionistically folding sweaters or insincerely flattering customers; Lelaina at the TV station, being chewed out by her obnoxious boss), but most of the action takes place in the apartment or in other locales away from the workplace. The other two films in question here are much more heavily based in the workplace itself, and the displeasures of the workplace centrally motivate the action.

Office Space is about a man named Peter who is being driven mad by his work at "Initech." Peter works in a little cubicle with a boss who keeps dropping by with picky criticisms about his work (he forgot to put a certain blue cover sheet on a report) and unreasonable demands for overtime and weekend labor. At one point Peter says to his friends, "Much more of this and I'm gonna [he imitates spraying the room with machine gun fire]." His fiancée insists that they go to a couples therapist, where he says, "Since I started working, every single day of my life has been worse than the one before it."

But the therapist hypnotizes him, after which he stops caring about his job performance and does what he wants at work. Echoing Linklater about the slacker attitude, he says, "It's not that I'm lazy, I just don't care." Once he stops caring, his bosses suddenly decide that he is one of them, and they take him into their confidence as they target people for layoffs. They mention that they are planning to fire his two friends, Michael and Samir, saying that the company will "bring in some entry-level graduates, farm some work out to Singapore, the usual deal."

Peter tells his friends and then tries to get them involved in a deal to defraud the company. Samir—representing some kind of indeterminate South Asian or Middle Eastern immigrant—doesn't want to do it, saying he has to get his résumé ready. Peter says, "For what? So you can get another job where they'll fire you for no reason?" Samir says, "I'm not going to do anything illegal." Peter says, "Illegal? This is America! You came here looking for the land of opportunity. This is it!"

Peter prevails and they run the scam, but contrary to the plan, what they did is very obvious and they decide they have to pretend it was a mistake and return the money. Peter sneaks in and returns the money, but when they show up for work the next morning the building is on fire, clearly having been set by another disgruntled employee. In the next scene we see workers cleaning up the rubble after the fire. Peter is part of the cleanup crew. His friends come by and offer to get him a job in another tech company, but he declines, choosing downward class mobility over the misery of the cubicle. As the credits run, we hear Canibus performing "Take This Job and Shove It."

The final film in this series is *Fight Club*, easily the darkest of the set. The films just discussed all represent work in neoliberal capitalism via comedy with varying degrees of irony and painful edge, but *Fight Club* plays it as a violent, life-or-death reality. Like the others, *Fight Club* embraces the Gen X identification (see the brochure that comes with the DVD, pp. 3, 13, 14). It was panned very heavily (e.g., "a witless mishmash of whiny, infantile philosophizing" [Kenneth Turan, *Los Angeles Times*, also quoted in the brochure, p. 4]), in large part for its extreme violence, but also because that violence was justified in the film by what appeared to be a kind of phony social/political rationale. I must say I somewhat agreed with Turan's critique the first time I saw the film, but as I watched it again, particularly tracking the question of work in neoliberal capitalism, I found it to be much more serious.

As in *Office Space*, the Narrator (Edward Norton), who is never named, works in a miserable office with a miserable boss. He hates his job and suffers from intolerable insomnia. He works largely to consume (mostly IKEA furniture); the consumerism and the work form a vicious cycle. On one of his business trips he meets Tyler Durden (Brad Pitt), who is in the soap business, on an airplane. When he goes home, he finds his apartment on fire, and he goes to stay with Tyler. Tyler works at various "shit jobs" because they offer him "other interesting opportunities." He works as a movie projectionist where he splices pornographic frames into family films; he works as a banquet waiter where he pees in the soup; we learn later that his soap is made from human fat gathered from the dumpsters outside a liposuction clinic. Tyler says, "It was beautiful. They were selling rich women their own fat asses back to them."[13]

One night outside a bar Tyler suddenly asks the Narrator to hit him. The Narrator refuses, but eventually they fight and the Narrator realizes that it makes him feel better. For example, when he goes back to the office, we see his boss nagging him, but there is no sound: "After fighting, everything else in your life got the volume turned down." Or later he says, "When the fight was over, nothing was solved. But nothing mattered either." Finally, Tyler makes a speech in which we come to see what this is all about:

God dammit, an entire generation pumping gas, waiting tables, slaves with white collars. . . . We're the middle children of history, man, no purpose or place. No Great War, no Great Depression. Our great war is a spiritual war, our great depression is our lives. We've all been raised on television to believe that one day we'd all be millionaires and movie gods and rock stars, but we won't. . . . We're very, very pissed off. (DVD, chap. 20)

Other men show up for fights for the same reasons, and the fighting becomes institutionalized in clubs that start springing up all over the country. Tyler's plans for the clubs also become more grandiose, and they start evolving into a kind of paramilitary organization, with strong hints of Nazi-style fascism (the human fat-based soap; everyone required to wear black shirts; a very blond Germanic-looking young man who becomes Tyler's new favorite). They undertake terrorist-style operations around the city, finally planning to blow up the buildings of the credit card companies.

By this time the Narrator has had it. It is all too violent and immoral for his sensibilities, and he tries to stop Tyler. They fight and in the course of that the Narrator comes to realize that Tyler is his own alter ego, his own worst self split off and run amok. There is a showdown in which the Narrator says, "I don't want this." And Tyler says, "What do you want? You want to go back to the shit job, fuckin' condo world, watch sitcoms?" The Narrator realizes he has to kill himself to kill Tyler and shoots himself in the mouth. Tyler dies but the Narrator lives, but it is too late to stop the buildings of the credit card companies from exploding and collapsing as he watches.

Now let us step back and think about the films in terms of the issues of cultural critique raised earlier. First, and perhaps most importantly, the films collectively announce a state of affairs: the neoliberal economy is here. They take the fragmented experiences of ordinary life (bad jobs, no jobs, relentless insecurity) and put them up on the screen in stories that are one way or another compelling—funny, violent, or weird. In the films, work in the neoliberal economy has no intrinsic pleasure, nor does it lead to security, happiness, or success. Rather, work today is something that eats your soul and destroys your life. This view was more common in the lower levels of the working class in an earlier incarnation of capitalism.[14] In the films just discussed, on the other hand, the characters are educated people in white-collar jobs who historically could expect to be on the way up but actually are on the way down. The films say to middle-class viewers, with varying degrees of explicitness, that there is a general and systemic problem here. On the one hand, this means that it is not your fault. On the other hand, this means you need to wake up and see what's going on.

Closely related to the problems of work is the idea of the slacker. We have heard Gen Xers say, both inside and outside of the films, that slacking is not the same as laziness; slacking is about not caring about and not investing in the kind of deadening work that is available in the new economy. The idea seems to be that a lazy person is personally defective, while slacking represents a principled, even political, choice. Since capitalism depends on a disciplined and committed workforce, slacking in this sense is indeed subversive; Tyler Durden simply carries this subversive view of anti-work to its destructive extremes.

Yet the solution is not clear. Slacking will surely lead to downward mobility, but observers of neoliberal capitalism would say that hard work is no longer a guaranteed defense against downward mobility either. This conundrum generates the fact that these films are full of arguments about work. Perhaps the clearest example is in *Reality Bites*. Lelaina argues with the slacking Troy as we have seen. But she also argues with her roommate Vicki, who is not slacking. Vicki works at the Gap in a relatively demeaning job, pandering to customers who need incessant flattery. Nonetheless, she is happy to have the job and even happier when she is promoted up a level to some kind of managerial position. When Lelaina loses her job at the TV station, Vicki offers to hire Lelaina for a part-time job at the Gap at $5 per hour. Lelaina makes disparaging comments about the job and refuses, whereupon Vicki is insulted and walks away. What is the right answer?

Two of the films also involve the proposal of illegal and immoral activities as alternatives to, and revenge against, low-pay, soul-destroying work. In *Office Space* Peter proposes a computer scam that would defraud Initech of money that he and his friends would split among themselves. In *Fight Club* Tyler Durden develops Project Mayhem to commit terrorist acts against property. In both cases again there are arguments. In *Fight Club* the Narrator starts resisting on moral grounds the increasing escalation of violence on the part of Tyler's project and eventually kills Tyler. In *Office Space* Peter is bombarded with moral judgments because of his scheme to defraud the company. His girlfriend Joanna tells him that, despite his circumlocutions about his scheme, it is outright stealing and it is wrong. His friend Samir says, "You are a very bad person, Peter." He also has a dream in which a judge says, "You're a very bad person." Those of us with relatively standard moral equipment are heartened by all these clear-cut condemnations of illegality and immorality. Yet again the movies end equivocally. Although Peter gives the money back in *Office Space*, the final scene shows the disgruntled employee who set the fire relaxing on a beach somewhere in the Caribbean. And after the Narrator kills Tyler Durden in *Fight Club*, he stands with his girlfriend watching the buildings blow up, telling her that everything will be all right. But it is not at all clear what that means.

Finally, there is the question of the films "talking back" to the dominant culture. For the most part I mean "talking back" metaphorically, in the sense that all the films by the very nature of their stories "talk back" to the dominant ideology about work and the American Dream. But it is also the case that, at some point in every one of the films, a character literally makes a speech railing against work in the contemporary economy. In *Slacker* we heard the Old Left character say, "To hell with the kind of work you have to do to earn a living." In *Reality Bites*, we heard Lelaina's valedictorian speech against the 80-hour work week and Troy's rant against the metaphorically cancerous nature of work ("my balls full of tumors") in today's economy. In *Fight Club* we heard Tyler Durden's rant about "an entire generation [wasted] pumping gas, waiting tables, slaves with white collars." And finally, in *Office Space* we hear Peter yell at Samir for being a sucker, for wanting to play it straight when the American economy itself is a morass of illegality: "Illegal? This is America! You came here looking for the land of opportunity. This is it!"

Peter's ironic inversion/perversion of the American Dream in his speech to the naïve (from Peter's point of view) immigrant Samir brings us to the other major set of films to be considered in this chapter, films made by and/or about immigrants to America in the early twenty-first century. For after all, the American Dream was always as much about immigrants coming to America as it was about people in America seeking to rise up the class ladder.

Global X: Immigrant Films

The Gen X films we have been looking at are set in the middle class. Indeed, the whole idea of Generation X is a middle-class idea—it is about middle-class educated young people who expected to do well but have been faced with a new set of economic realities. Immigrants coming to America in the late twentieth and early twenty-first centuries face the same neoliberal order, but from a much more disadvantaged position. In addition, they come as racial "others," facing racial discrimination on top of an economy with greatly shrunken opportunities. If the American Dream has receded for white, middle-class Gen Xers, it has become an even crueler lie for many immigrants. The "immigrant films" I will consider here are uniformly darker and more violent than the three comedies discussed in the last section, and in some ways even darker than *Fight Club*, in that *Fight Club* was a kind of fantasy, while these films are all very much in a realist mode. In addition, they are all much more overtly critical of "America," not only because of the hardships imposed by the neoliberal economy, but for a wider range of negative characteristics: racism, violence, surveillance.

Actually there is a relatively clear break between the immigrant films of the 1990s and those made after 9/11/2001. Let me begin with the films in the 1990s. One would not call most of them particularly "dark." None of them contain any of the markers of darkness discussed earlier—violence, depression, perversion—and indeed most of them have happy(-ish) endings. Most of them revolve around tensions between immigrant parents and their Americanizing children: *The Wedding Banquet* (Ang Lee, 1993) was a comedy about two gay male lovers, one of whom (Wai-Tung) is Chinese American, who fake a marriage to placate Wai-Tung's traditional parents; *The Joy Luck Club* (Wayne Wang, 1993) follows four Chinese women who survived harrowing experiences in China, examining their relationships with their very assimilated American daughters; *Mississippi Masala* (Mira Nair, 1992) portrays the family tensions that arise when the daughter of an immigrant Indian family falls in love with an African American man. This genre of family-focused immigrant film, with generally happy endings, continues into the first decade of the twenty-first century with films like *Jump Tomorrow* (Joel Hopkins, 2001), a comedy about a Nigerian man who manages to evade an arranged marriage, or *The Namesake* (Mira Nair, 2007) and *Amreeka* (Cherien Dabis, 2009), both of which are slightly darker but nonetheless retain the happy/hopeful ending. In all these films the characters suffer certain difficulties, including a hint of racism, but on the whole "America" implicitly appears as a reasonably good place, a place where people are free of stultifying traditions and can marry whom they choose, or in some other way achieve a certain happiness.

Around the turn of the twenty-first century, however, a much darker strand of films by/about immigrants begins to appear. The lighter films do not disappear, as we have just seen. Side by side with them, however, we begin to see films in which the America immigrants must deal with is a dark place, violent, extremely racist, even fascist. In part this new strand of dark immigrant films can be explained by the events of September 11, 2001, and I will spend some time on the explicitly post-9/11 films. But not all of these films are constructed as responses to the events of 9/11. Rather, I think we are seeing the same effects I have been discussing for independent film more generally: the end of the grand narrative of American culture, the so-called American Dream. It is no longer credible that if one comes to America and works hard one is likely to succeed. And as with the narratives of my Gen X informants, the collapse of this "dream" is accompanied by a sense of danger and violence.[15]

THE 9/11 FILMS

I begin with the 9/11 films. One film, called simply *September 11*, is a compendium of eleven short (eleven-minute) films commissioned by a French producer (Alain Brigand) from an international spectrum of filmmakers (2002). Among these is a film by Mira Nair (*11'09"01*) about a Pakistani immigrant family in Queens whose son is initially among the missing, and who is suspected by the FBI of being one of the terrorists. FBI agents invade the house and begin going through the desk drawers and papers. It turns out, however, that the son died near the towers. He was a certified paramedic and was apparently rushing in to the towers to help people. We begin to feel the fear—of racial profiling, unreasonable search and seizure, invasion of one's life by authorities—that suffuses most of these films. A second film, *The Visitor* (Tom McCarthy, 2007), involves an illegal Palestinian immigrant who suddenly disappears in the course of the film. The film takes the point of view of an older American college professor who had become attached to the young immigrant, and we follow the professor through stony-faced bureaucracies and sterile detention centers as we try to find out what happened to the young man. Again the emphasis is on the sudden and arbitrary nature of the security apparatus, the sense that an immigrant (and especially, as in this case, an illegal immigrant) in the United States today may literally have no civil rights.

A third film in this explicitly post-9/11 framework explores the pathology of the racism that blossomed after those events. *Sorry, Haters* (Jeff Stanzler, 2005) is about a Syrian/Muslim cab driver in post-9/11 New York City named Ashade. Ashade is shown to be a good man, taking care of his sister-in-law and her son after his brother was detained by Homeland Security. The Muslim community is also shown to be decent and moral, raising money among themselves to help him in his effort to free his brother. Into this picture steps Phoebe (Robin Wright Penn), who basically invades his life. At first she seems to be upset about the breakup of her marriage, but it gradually emerges that she is really quite crazy. At home she obsessively works on a collage of the burning towers on 9/11; she claims that her boss has stolen her family, but it is not her family; and throughout the film she makes shocking racist comments with no self-awareness about doing so.

And she will not leave Ashade alone. She steals his money. She tries to engage him in a plot for some hazy goal of "retribution." In the end she slips an explosive device into his coat pocket and pushes him down the subway stairs. As the bomb explodes she walks away and pastes a picture of him on the wall outside the subway. While the logic of the film is not entirely clear, it seems to be saying that 9/11 triggered her racist madness, as indeed it triggered so much racist madness after those events.

And finally, a film called *The War Within* takes yet another dark angle on the fallout of 9/11 for Muslim immigrants in America. I want to spend a little more time on this film, as it is the only one that explicitly contrasts the post-9/11 harassment of Muslims with the idea of the American Dream that attracted these immigrants to America in the first place. The film opens with a young Pakistani man named Hassan being kidnapped and tortured in some undefined location by American security forces, even though he is innocent. They also show him a photograph of the beaten dead body of his best friend, implying that they did that too. In prison Hassan is befriended by a devout Muslim, who turns him from his current secularism toward Islamic orthodoxy and also recruits him to a terrorist organization. He goes to America with the intention of engaging in acts of terrorism, including the bombing of Grand Central Terminal in New York City.

Hassan goes to stay with another man with whom he had been good friends growing up, Sayeed, living with his family in suburban New Jersey. The family is living the American Dream—the immigrant who made good, the house in the suburbs, the children in nice multi-culti schools, and so on. Sayeed is unaware of Hassan's plans, but he is puzzled by the changes in him—the new Islamic orthodoxy, and the hostility toward America. The film then unfolds as a dialogue between Sayeed and Hassan about America. Early in the film, as Sayeed first picks up Hassan's antagonism toward the United States, Sayeed looks puzzled and says, "It's a beautiful country. Nice people." Later there is an extended exchange at a barbecue in Sayeed's backyard, between some of Sayeed's friends on the one hand and Hassan on the other. One man, holding his son, says, "This is a great country, where he [the son] has a chance to make a good life, without worrying about corruption and violence." But another man angrily disagrees and makes a fairly long speech that ends with, "This government only cares about one thing: tyranny, murder, and domination." The first man again attempts to defend America, but then Hassan sharply cuts in, saying, "Poverty is real, dying is real, not some discussion to be had at dinner" (DVD, chap. 13). Later, Sayeed makes one final attempt to bring Hassan around. They are in a restaurant and Sayeed says, "I know things are not perfect here. . . . [But] look around you. . . . There are Jews, Christians, Muslims, everyone sitting eating comfortably, safely, peacefully. Going to school together, businesses together. What's wrong with that?" (DVD, chap. 13).

Yet in the end it is all a disaster. Hassan's terrorist cell is rounded up and their bomb factory is dismantled. Hassan is forced to begin making bombs in Sayeed's basement. Sayeed discovers this and, good citizen that he is, with faith in the American system of justice, he calls the police. Hassan leaves, goes to Grand Central Terminal, and follows through with his plan to explode the bomb and himself. The FBI respond to Sayeed's call but, not believing his honesty and his sincere intentions, they arrest him as a terrorist and take him away.

At one level all of these films must be taken literally. They are about all-too-real events and the fallout of those events for innocent people. Because the lead characters are Muslim men, and because the films are explicitly positioned within a post-9/11 framework, the American viewer is asked to take the logic of the films at face value. A specific kind of insecurity for Muslim men in America, no matter how innocent and assimilated, has emerged in the wake of 9/11. Their lives are in danger; at the very least, their worlds can be upended at any moment.

At the same time it will be productive to situate these films within a broader set of films about the immigrant experience in America in the twenty-first century. The film *The War Within* provides a bridge between the two sets, insofar as it sets up the contrast between the American promise of material success and the new realities of anti-immigrant racism. Thus, I want to look at another group of immigrant films that, in a sense, tell the same story without the 9/11 framework. I want to show that these films embody the same general darkness we have discussed with respect to independent films in general, a sense of both sadness and danger in the collapse of one of the great master narratives of modernity, the American Dream as both myth and reality.

DARK IMMIGRANT FILMS

In the interests of space I will give a very compressed sketch of four more recent films about immigrants that came out in the United States in the period 2004–7.

In *Man Push Cart* (Ramin Bahrani, 2005), a Pakistani immigrant works as a street-food vendor in New York City. He is depressed throughout the movie and never smiles. We learn that his wife has died and his in-laws will not let him see his son. He is helped by a successful Pakistani immigrant but later dropped by him. His food cart is stolen, possibly by the man who sold it to him in the first place.

In *The Motel* (Michael Kang, 2006), a Chinese immigrant woman and her thirteen-year-old son live in a motel; the father is gone. The boy sees all kinds of cheap sex and low-life people and hates his life. A handsome young Korean American man starts to teach him the ropes of becoming a man, like how to get a girl to have sex with him. The boy then attempts to rape his friend, a young Chinese American girl who works in her family's restaurant.

In *Padre Nuestro* (Christopher Zalla, 2007), a teenage Mexican boy named Pedro comes to the United States illegally to find his father. He is transported in a tractor trailer with many other people, including a young man named Juan. Juan steals Pedro's bag with all the papers he needed to find his father. Juan then goes and finds the father, a dishwasher in a French restaurant, and pretends to be the son. Eventually the two boys meet and the false son Juan kills the real son Pedro. The father is arrested for deportation.

In *Take Out* (Sean Baker and Shih-Ching Tsou, 2004), we meet Ming, a young Chinese immigrant man who works as a delivery boy for a Chinese restaurant in New York City. The smugglers who brought him to the United States, to whom he is in debt, beat him up and threaten worse if they do not get their money. His friend at the restaurant is optimistic—"It will all pay off"—but Ming is very depressed and miserable. His buddy offers to let him take all the deliveries and all the tips for the day. He does it and makes a lot of money, but then he takes one more delivery and gets mugged by two black teenagers in an elevator, who take all his money.

In all these films, the events of 9/11 are absent or pushed into the background. Instead, the films are organized around the more general misery of the immigrant experience. Of course, it has always been difficult to be a poor immigrant. But with the American Dream, there was a sense that the hard work and miserable life would eventually pay off. This is not what we see in these movies.

We first of all see everyone working hard. As with some of the Gen X films, it is noteworthy that virtually all of these films are set in workplaces rather than homes. There was the taxi driver in *Sorry, Haters*; many scenes in the movie take place in the cab. We see the food vendor pushing his cart over and over again through the streets of New York in *Man Push Cart*. In *The Motel*, the Chinese American boy and his mother both live and work in the motel. In *Padre Nuestro* we see the father working hard in the kitchen of the French restaurant. In *Take Out* we see Ming delivering food again and again, riding his bicycle through the rain in the streets of New York. And at the end of all this work, there is no happy ending. Instead, other people steal the poor immigrants' means of livelihood (Ahmad's food cart) or their hard-earned money: Phoebe steals Ashade's money in *Sorry, Haters*; Juan cons the father out of his money in *Padre Nuestro*; the muggers take all of Ming's money in *Take Out*.

We also see that no one has any kind of "normal" family situation. Unlike the immigrant family films, where families were largely intact and where the biggest problem was intergenerational conflict over "tradition" and "modernity," the protagonists in these dark immigrant films all have some kind of broken family situation. In *Sorry, Haters*, the protagonist Ashade is a single man who lives in some kind of male dormitory. The destructive Phoebe claims to have had her family stolen from her; this is what sets the plot in motion. In *Man Push Cart*, Ahmad's wife has died and his in-laws will not let him visit with his son. In *The Motel* the father is gone and the boy and his mother have a bad relationship. In *Padre Nuestro*, Pedro and his father are never united. In *Take Out*, Ming reveals to his friend that he has left a wife and child back in China.

Indeed, in those films where the characters achieve a "normal" family, it is taken away from them. In *Sorry, Haters* we meet the wife and child of Ashade's brother, but the brother has been arrested. And most spectacularly, in *The War Within*, Sayeed lives happily with his family in the New Jersey suburbs, telling his old friend Hassan what a good country this is, but in the end FBI agents come to his home and arrest him, handling him roughly as his wife and children look on.

And finally, I want to call attention to the violence in these films. In the relatively lighter immigrant films, one rarely sees physical violence. But all of these darker films contain at least one major violent act, and sometimes more.

Here I will separate the explicitly post-9/11 films from the others. It is not surprising that we see a lot of violence in the post-9/11 films, as the violence was in a sense the whole point. Moreover, most of those films are overtly "political," in the sense that they articulate a fairly explicit critique of the American state. In relation to immigrants, for example, we see an implicit critique of the Homeland Security apparatus invading people's lives and arresting mostly innocent people (*The Visitor*, *The War Within*, Mira Nair's contribution to the *September 11* compendium). Other contributions to the *September 11* compendium, which I have not had time to discuss, draw connections between the violence committed against America on 9/11 and the long history of U.S. violence abroad.[16]

But I want to look more closely at the films in which the 9/11 connection is not central, in which poor immigrants are simply trying to make a living, and in which they or others close to them come to be subjected to relatively extreme, and sometimes fatal, violence. We saw the thirteen-year-old boy trying to rape his friend in *The Motel*, Juan killing Pedro in *Padre Nuestro*, and the black teenagers mugging the Chinese delivery boy in *Take Out*. I would also include *Sorry, Haters* in this discussion, in that Ashade is killed by Phoebe in the course of events that unfold out of his innocently driving his cab.

I have been suggesting that all of these films are telling another version of the story of the end of the American Dream. But what is the relationship between the end of the American Dream and the appearance of greater levels of physical violence? It will be recalled that we have seen this linkage before in film (Moore), published literature (Davis, Comoroff and Comaroff, Gusterson and Besteman), and the essays of the Children of the Class of '58. I noted in that discussion of the essays that cc58's fears of violent crime appeared to be relatively unrealistic, and their fears were thus somewhat puzzling. On the other hand, for the poor immigrants, as for all poor people, there is a close and real connection between poverty and physical violence. This is heightened in the present American context by post-9/11 fearmongering campaigns about terrorists among us. Thus, immigrants, like most poor people, have good reason for their fears.

But that still leaves open the question of representation: who is telling these stories, and why now? Again I think the answer to the puzzle lies in the positionality of the filmmakers themselves. With few exceptions, the immigrant films are not made by poor immigrants; they are made by young and in many cases educated filmmakers within the broad parameters of the long Generation X I have been discussing here.[17] Some are immigrants, some are children of immigrants, and some appear to be Americans whose immigrant ancestry is much farther in the past. All are making their films within the contemporary American context, with their own lives and those of other members of their communities coming under the greatly increased economic stringency induced by the neoliberal order. All are responding to those real conditions.

In addition, all of the films can be read as enacting that peculiarly anthropological form of cultural critique identified by Marcus and Fischer, in which the representation of others allows and even forces us to hold up a mirror to ourselves. Immigrants in America make for a particularly powerful representation of the brutalities of the neoliberal order. Neoliberalism pits rich countries against poor countries, rich people against poor people, and poor people against each other. Stories about immigrants failing economically, being abused legally, and being harmed physically tell the story of the end of the American Dream at least as powerfully as, if not more so than, stories of downwardly mobile middle-class kids.

The films discussed here and throughout the rest of the book are (with occasional exceptions) part of the emergence of the independent film movement that took shape in the late 1980s and flowered in the 1990s and 2000s.

They constitute a zone of "cultural critique" in a period in which problematic changes were taking place in the American political economy, but in which there was relatively little awareness of what was going on, and even less overt political action. In the next chapter I tell the story of how that movement took shape "on the ground," as we like to say in anthropology, creating the conditions of possibility for making these often-challenging films in the first place.

CHAPTER 3

Making the Scene

This chapter is about how the contemporary indie scene came into being, starting in the late 1980s. A "scene" has usefully been defined as, among other things, "all the places and activities which surround and nourish a particular cultural preference" (Straw 2002: 7).[1] The world of independent film is precisely a scene in this sense, a trans-local "community of taste" (Straw 2002: 6) that has constructed itself against the aesthetics and economics of "Hollywood."

The idea of a "scene" maps reasonably well onto Pierre Bourdieu's concept of a "field of cultural production" (1993). Both concepts are attempts to grasp the whole space, both abstract and material, within which a particular kind of art is produced, transacted, and consumed. But there are a number of significant differences between the two. For one thing, Bourdieu's "field" is primarily a theoretical or "etic" construct, conceptualized from the point of view of the theorist, while "scene" is primarily an "emic" construct, conceptualized largely from the point of view of the participants. This division is not absolute, and both concepts have both emic and etic dimensions, but relatively speaking, that is how they line up. Secondly, the two concepts differ in terms of the social vision behind them. For Bourdieu, the field of cultural production is a space in which artists vie—"struggle"—with one another for recognition, in the course of which the relative prestige of whole genres may shift over time. A "scene," on the other hand, is more—we could say—Durkheimian, that is, more a space of collectiveness, of mutual pleasure and mutual recognition. Of course, there is plenty of competition in any real-life scene, and one could always look at any given scene as a Bourdieusian field, in terms of the struggles and stakes in play. But the *idea* of a scene is the idea of a positively shared social and cultural world, "a community of taste," and that is how I will look at the scene of independent film in this chapter.

The indie scene consists in part of an infrastructure with a range of institutions: production companies, professional organizations, festivals, film schools, magazines, and so forth (on infrastructure see also Levy 1999; G. King 2005). Some of these existed before the 1980s and were expanded and transformed; others were brought into being as part of the new movement. I will tell the story of the creation or transformation of these institutions primarily through the personal, retrospective narratives of some of the movement's key participants. The narratives convey the thinking behind people's actions, the networks of personal relationships in play, and the excitement and energy of that time. At the same time I set these insider accounts in counterpoint with (compressed) larger histories of the Hollywood/indie relationship, and with a sketch of the political economy of the United States in the 1990s, when the independent film movement was starting to flower.

A Brief Overview

Virtually from the beginning of the movie industry, there were issues about the fact that the studios exercised a tremendous amount of control over writers, directors, and actors. Thus, from early on one saw the phenomenon of breakaway independent film companies, most famously the creation of United Artists by Charlie Chaplin, D. W. Griffith, Douglas Fairbanks Jr., and Mary Pickford in 1919 (Balio 1976; see also Merritt 2000; Mann 2008). At the same time, there has been a long line of directors, including, for example, Frank Capra, Sam Fuller, Alfred Hitchcock, and Nicholas Ray, who managed to make films with a distinctive and "personal" vision while remaining within the studio system (see especially the documentary *Edge of Outside* [Shannon Davis, 2006]).

"Hollywood" itself has gone in cycles, sometimes exerting more and sometimes less control, and thus allowing less or more "independence" within the studios at different times in its history. Robert Sklar has argued that the studios made much more interesting and provocative movies in the first half of the twentieth century. Their spirit was in a sense broken by many factors, but especially, Sklar argues, by the Communist witch hunts of the 1950s that made the studios fearful of offending both the cultural mainstream and the political authorities (Sklar 1975). As a result the 1950s and 1960s saw the production of the bland and vacuous fare that came to stand for all that was wrong with "Hollywood movies." But then came the so-called Hollywood Renaissance of the 1970s, which gave us a new generation of independent-minded directors, including Francis Ford Coppola, Robert Altman, Woody Allen, and Martin Scorsese, again operating (mostly) inside the studio system (Mast and Kawin 1992).

But again there was, for reasons too complex to pursue here, a reaction, and the studios began to reassert control over their "product." Beginning in the mid-1970s, and accelerating after 1980, they increasingly committed themselves to the strategy of making blockbusters—huge, expensive, and exciting but not very mentally challenging films (*Jaws* [Steven Spielberg, 1975] is generally taken as the first blockbuster). This has meant looking for lowest-common-denominator films that will please the largest possible numbers of people and offend, if possible, no one. It has also meant looking for formulas, "franchises," the idea that if something is a hit the first time, then the best thing is to do it again. It is in this context, with the rise of the blockbuster and the fairly rapid exhaustion (with, of course, individual exceptions) of the creative energy of the 1970s, that the contemporary indies movement was born (Biskind 1998, 2004).

The independent film movement that begins in the late 1980s has its own prehistory, specifically highlighting filmmakers who worked outside of the studio system.[2] Most accounts of this prehistory begin with the work of John Cassavetes in the 1960s and 1970s; Cassavetes made intensely "personal" films, largely based in the white working and middle classes, focusing on complicated and fraught interpersonal relationships. Other key independent films of the 1970s include David Lynch's *Eraserhead* (1977), Charles Burnett's *Killer of Sheep* (1978), and John Hanson and Rob Nilsson's *Northern Lights* (1979) (Levy 1999).

We may also think of this prehistory in terms of the different scenes of independent filmmaking, rather than in terms of individual films and filmmakers. An account of several of the scenes was very usefully outlined for me by Bob Rosen, former dean of the School of Theater, Film, and Television at UCLA. The first included "the intense avant-garde film scene(s) in New York and San Francisco, marked by risk-taking radical women directors such as Shirley Clark, cultural activists promoting independent exhibition and distribution such as Jonas Mekas, [and] innovative filmmakers rooted in an emerging gay subculture in the arts such as Andy Warhol and Kenneth Anger" (e-mail, January 31, 2011). A second scene was primarily centered in Los Angeles and included a number of minority filmmakers who "embraced themes of ethnic and racial diversity and strove for realistic depictions of life in their communities" (ibid.). In his comprehensive study of the "history and geography of minor cinemas in Los Angeles," David E. James has an excellent chapter on this L.A.-based scene of minority cinema starting in the 1950s and taking off in the 1960s and 1970s, including work by Native American, African American, Chicano, and Asian American filmmakers (2005: chap. 8).

Film scholar Douglas Kellner called attention to a third important scene in that period, namely, the scene of left/radical filmmaking (Kellner, personal communication). This included the 1973 founding of the collective that called itself "Newsreel," which split up very quickly over political issues but whose several factions produced four films before dissolving (Nichols 1978). It also included the founding of the journal *Jump Cut* in 1974. In its opening editorial, the editors explain that the journal is "committed to presenting and developing film criticism which recognizes theories often unfamiliar to Americans, such as structuralism, semiology, and Marxism," and further that the aim of the journal is "to develop a political film criticism . . . which does not accept as binding the bourgeois idea that art is somehow separate and detached from the social life of women and men" (Editors 1974; see also Steven 1985).

At a broader level in this time period, the space now occupied by independent cinema was largely occupied by "foreign," mostly but not entirely European, films. Foreign films would inspire many of the 1970s American "movie brats," who were exposed to them in film school. In addition, Harvey Weinstein, cofounder (with his brother Bob) of Miramax Films, famously had the epiphany that changed his whole approach to movies when he saw François Truffaut's *The 400 Blows* (1959). The mention of Harvey Weinstein then brings us to the story of the birth of the contemporary independent film movement.

Starting in the early 1980s, a number of very important films were made outside the studios and began to get more widespread attention than the purely art-house or midnight cult-classic films of the 1960s and 1970s.

Richard Ferncase (1996) surveyed the independent films of the decade and showed how much was going on before the "big bang" of Steven Soderbergh's *sex, lies, and videotape* in 1989, including John Sayles's *Return of the Secaucus Seven* (1980), Jim Jarmusch's *Stranger Than Paradise* (1984), the Coen brothers' *Blood Simple* (1984), Spike Lee's *She's Gotta Have It* (1985), David Lynch's *Blue Velvet* (1986), and Errol Morris's *The Thin Blue Line* (1988). In the middle of the decade Robert Redford took over the little-known U.S. Film Festival (which wasn't renamed "Sundance" until 1991) and began expanding the fare of independent films shown there. The Weinsteins had founded Miramax Films in 1979 as a production company, but again around the middle of the 1980s they started moving toward the model that became so successful for them, and so important for the independent movement: shopping for cheap but interesting independent films, finding good distribution deals for them, and marketing them aggressively, both for audience and for awards.

In Peter Biskind's account, the event that really launched the movement was created by the intersection of Miramax Productions and the U.S. (Sundance) Film Festival in 1989, around the screening of *sex, lies, and videotape*. The film was a huge word-of-mouth hit at the festival and won the Audience Prize. The Weinsteins decided that they wanted it, and they went after it aggressively, paying $1 million for the film and guaranteeing another million for publicity and advertising (P&A) (Biskind 2004: 65). Ultimately Miramax in fact spent $2.5 million in P&A, but the film made $24.7 million domestic gross and another $30 million worldwide (Biskind 2004: 82). *Sex, lies, and videotape* became the first indie "blockbuster," but more importantly, Miramax demonstrated that there was a wider audience for indies; to some degree the Weinsteins even could be said to have played a major role in creating that audience. At the same time they demonstrated that there was significant money to be made from such smaller, quirkier, "personal" films.

Starting with the banner year of 1989, then, American independent cinema moved into a period of exuberant artistic creativity, audience growth, and financial success. In part this can be seen from the numbers: whereas in 1985 about fifty independent films were made in the United States, by 1998, the number was estimated to be around eight hundred (*Independent's Day*, Marina Zenovich, 1998) or "more than 1000" (Levy 1999: 44).

More important than the numbers was the striking originality of the films. A list of indie hits in that immediate post-1989 period would include Michael Moore's *Roger and Me* (1989), Jim Sheridan's *My Left Foot* (1989), the Coen brothers' *Barton Fink* (1991), Richard Linklater's *Slacker* (1991), Mira Nair's *Mississippi Masala* (1992), Neil Jordan's *The Crying Game* (1992), Tarantino's *Pulp Fiction* (1994), and Kevin Smith's *Clerks* (1994). Many other major independent films from the 1990s and 2000s will be named and examined in the course of later discussions.

Starting in about 2007, as part of the run-up to the near crash of the stock market in 2008 and the recession that followed, the resources for independent film began to shrink considerably. As we heard in chapter 1, there is a lively debate in the indie world about whether independent film is "dead" and, whether it is or not, where to go next. I will take up this discussion in the conclusions of the book. The main period covered by the book is the heyday of the 1990s and 2000s when independent film was most successful in both getting films made and reaching relatively large audiences.

Why the 1990s?

Why did the indie scene break out in the 1990s? There are obviously multiple answers, at multiple levels of scale. The simplest explanation is technological: the 1980s saw the proliferation of cable TV channels (one of the earliest being HBO, specifically devoted to movies), the expansion of the number of screens in theaters, and especially the astronomic growth of the home video market. All of these created a demand for "product" that the studios could not fulfill. Many independent filmmakers were able to capitalize on this demand to raise money for production costs; for example, Steven Soderbergh presold the home video rights to *sex, lies, and videotape* to finance the making of the film (Biskind 2004: 30–31).[3]

At a larger level we must consider massive changes in the culture industry as these affected the Hollywood studios. On the one hand, the old studios, which were private, freestanding corporations, were all bought up by large media conglomerates in this period (see table 2).

At the same time, as discussed in chapter 1, the studios did not fail to note the new commercial success of independent films in that period. Thus, all the studios began beefing up existing "specialty divisions" (originally formed primarily for the acquisition and distribution of foreign

TABLE 2

Purchase of Studios by Conglomerates

YEAR	STUDIO	PURCHASED BY
1985	20th Century Fox	The News Corporation
1989	Columbia Pictures	Sony
1990	Warner Bros.	Time Warner
1994	Paramount	Viacom
1997	Universal	Vivendi
2004	MGM[a]	Sony and others

[a] MGM struggled financially throughout the 1980s and 1990s. It was taken over by a consortium headed by Sony Corp. in 2004 and declared Chapter 11 bankruptcy in 2010. It is currently being run by executives of the independent production company Spyglass Entertainment (Wikipedia, "Metro-Goldwyn-Mayer").

films), or acquiring new ones, for the purpose of getting into business with independent(-style) films (see table 3).

A complete exploration of the relationship between these two developments is beyond the scope of this book, but a few notes are in order. It is generally agreed that the conglomerization of the studios ratcheted up the need for studio divisions to show a particularly strong bottom line and thus reinforced the blockbuster tendency that had started in the 1970s. At the same time, the opening of the specialty divisions was clearly a play for an audience segment that indies were successfully exploiting and indeed expanding, an audience of more sophisticated (and also in many cases more affluent) viewers. The two seemingly contradictory trends were part of a single story, the story of the diversification of studio production and marketing practices in an effort to capture both mass and niche audiences (see chap. 1).

The specialty divisions would become a major source of funding for many independent films, as we shall see in a moment. It is relevant here to recall the earlier discussion of whether "independence" is possible in the shadow of Hollywood, and especially within the studio gates. In that context I agreed in part with key figures in independent film such as Geoff Gilmore and James Schamus that the commercial motives behind the opening of the specialty divisions do not necessarily negate the artistic and idealistic motives (and achievements) of the independent filmmakers who worked

TABLE 3

Creation of Specialty Divisions by Studios

YEAR	STUDIO	SPECIALTY DIVISION
1991	Sony/Columbia	Sony Pictures Classics
1993	Walt Disney Company	Miramax
1994	20th Century Fox	Fox Searchlight
1996	Warner Bros.	New Line → Warner Independent (2008)
1997	Universal	October Films + Good Machine (2002)
		→ Focus Features
1998	Paramount	Paramount Vantage

within them. Extending that discussion further, from the point of view of independent filmmakers and producers, the specialty divisions represented a significant opportunity, and they took advantage of it when they could.

But there was in some sense always a struggle over the degree to which a filmmaker could take the specialty divisions' money and yet retain control of the film. Independent producer Albert Berger, for example, was quite clear-eyed in an interview about the relationship between independent filmmakers and specialty divisions. "It is a complicated dance," he said. "Obviously the studios are there to make money and are not altruistic. I wouldn't describe them as being tremendously embracing of the kinds of films we produce, but they devote a certain portion of their business to it and we have been the beneficiaries of that [business model]" (interview, December 30, 2005, word order slightly reorganized).

He and his producing partner, Ron Yerxa, have pursued a strategy, successfully for the most part, of exploiting the resources of the divisions without trading away the independence of the filmmakers with whom they are working: "We found an interesting niche so far [with the specialty divisions] and I am always worried that the jig is about to be up, but the idea is finding strong source material, connecting with personal filmmakers, with a real voice, who these studios want to be in business with, and being left alone to make the movie" (ibid.).

Returning then to the "why 1990s" question, the third and most inclusive level of explanation would look at the larger shape of the American economy in the 1990s. Here I need to pick up the neoliberalism discussion once again, but I direct it toward the upper levels of the class structure. The economy of the 1990s was very contradictory. On the one hand, as Robert Brenner has discussed, there was the "long downturn" starting in the late 1970s (Brenner 2003). The "long downturn" is crucial to the story, begun in the last chapter and to be continued throughout the book, about the dark worldview of Generation X. But although those deteriorating conditions have continued to this day, the second half of the 1990s also saw the first of a series of economic "bubbles," that is, artificially inflated markets—first in telecommunications, later in information technologies ("dot coms") and (beyond the point of Brenner's article) in real estate (Brenner 2003; see also Brenner 2002). The bubbles produced a great deal of wealth for some individuals, at least until they burst, as they all eventually did.

The people who made big money in the 1990s were, of course, Big Capital, the owners of the means of production. In addition, however, there was a very significant enrichment of the Professional Managerial Class or the PMC, at the next level down in the class structure. In fact, the PMC was undergoing significant changes in this era, and I need to spend a little time on that here.

The PMC was importantly brought into focus in the late 1970s by John and Barbara Ehrenreich (1979). As the name suggests, it is composed of the managers within the capitalist economy, as well as the professionals who provide specialized knowledge and expertise. It steadily gained in importance, as well as wealth and power, throughout the twentieth century, and its character also evolved. Education was always important to PMC occupations and statuses, but it became increasingly so as the more advanced capitalist economies increasingly became organized around knowledge and information. Its members are sometimes called "the cultural elites" (Ehrenreich and Ehrenreich 1979: 12), "the knowledge class" (Frow 1995; Traube 1996: xv), or the educated "information age elites" (D. Brooks 2005). More than any previous elite in the United States, the PMC's status and power are based on this unique combination of material and cultural capital, or wealth and education.[4]

At the same time, this stratum divides, as the bourgeoisie has always divided, into two broad fractions. As Pierre Bourdieu has discussed at length (1993), the two wings divide up as the world of commerce versus the world of art, as inclining toward relatively conservative versus relatively progressive politics, as relatively un- or even anti-intellectual versus the intellectualism of the "knowledge classes," and so forth. In other words, until recently there tended to be a direct correlation between wealth, politics, and culture. Wealthy people tended to be conservative on political and social issues, to vote Republican, and to (stereotypically) have little interest in culture, the arts, and the life of the mind. The correlation was not perfect, and there were, of course, always exceptions (especially in the sponsorship of "high culture"—opera, museums, symphony orchestras, etc.). But that was the general pattern.

Moreover, the wealthier, more conservative, less intellectual/artistic wing of the PMC (think investment bankers) was, until recently, what Bourdieu called "the dominant fraction of the dominant class," while the less wealthy, more politically progressive, and more intellectual/artistic wing (think college professors) was, although still part of the PMC elite, nonetheless "the dominated fraction of the dominant class" (1984: 469).

With the new generation of people who started making big money in the 1990s, however, a different configuration began to emerge. Although some followed the traditional pattern, a new configuration also appeared in this class, a hybrid post-1960s breed that combined big money with relatively progressive politics and often some interest in less mainstream culture. This new class configuration was picked up in the public culture as "yuppies" (young urban professionals, with the acronym echoing the "hippies" of the 1960s), "bourgeois bohemians" or "bobos" (D. Brooks 2000), and "the liberal rich" (Callahan 2010). All these terms call attention to the hybrid nature of this new class fraction, combining money with progressive politics and an interest in less conventional areas of the arts and culture.[5] And while one would not argue that this new fraction has collectively overtaken the investment bankers and hedge fund managers as the dominant fraction of the PMC, it has certainly become a much more powerful and influential segment of the PMC than it used to be (see especially Callahan 2010).

The emergence of this expanded and reconfigured wing of the PMC is very important to our story. It is important, first, in terms of creating a new breed of investor. Specifically, a number of key individuals who made money in the dot-com or other bubbles, and who identified with this more progressive wing of the PMC, became major investors in independent film. More on them later in the chapter.

The reconfiguration of the PMC is also important in terms of audience. We do not actually have any hard data on the social composition of audiences for independent films. Nonetheless, it is not difficult to make some highly plausible guesses about who constitutes this audience, based on the nature of the films themselves. Indie films are meant to be thought provoking rather than entertaining, "difficult" rather than easy and comfortable. Along with edgy features, indies also include foreign films and documentaries. All of these genres demand/address a relatively sophisticated audience, willing to be made to think, willing to read subtitles, and willing to sit still for the relatively academic style of many documentaries. I suggest—and without data can only suggest—that it was the expansion and reconfiguration of the PMC in the past several decades that has delivered the enlarged audiences (including both boomers and Xers) that made it possible to bring independent film out of the art houses.

We turn then to the making of the independent film scene in the 1980s and 1990s, looking first at New York City and then at Los Angeles. We will hear many of the key players tell the stories in their own words, and we will get a sense of the extraordinary energy and excitement of the time. We will see a cultural movement literally take shape, as people put their dreams and their bodies to work to make it happen.

Production Companies and the New York Indie Scene

Companies for the production of independent film started to proliferate in the late 1980s. Peter Biskind (2004) has given us an excellent account of the evolution of the larger independent film production companies in New York in the 1980s, especially Miramax under the Weinstein brothers and the Fine Line Features division of Robert Shaye's New Line Cinema. Miramax in particular played an enormous, even defining, role in the emergence of the independent film scene, as noted earlier. Here I will concentrate on some of the smaller but also very important production companies that opened in the period between the late 1980s and the mid-1990s. A list of such companies would include Mirabai Productions (1988), The Shooting Gallery (1991), Killer Films (1995), Forensic Films (1995), and many more. The one I have the best information on is Good Machine (1990), and I will tell that story here.

Good Machine was a partnership between Ted Hope (later of Thisisthat Corporation, and now with Double Hope Films) and James Schamus, now president of Focus Features. The following is based on a long interview with Ted Hope in March of 2006.

After Hope graduated from film school at NYU in 1985, he was reading scripts and writing "coverage" (summaries/critiques) of scripts on a freelance basis around New York City. On the basis of a fairly theoretical critique that he wrote of some script, the story editor suggested that he might like to meet James Schamus, who was working on a PhD in English and was known as an intellectual. They met in a coffee shop in the East Village around that time. Hope said about the meeting, "I remember James was carrying some obscure French novel which impressed me; to this day he wears bow-ties. He had no production experience but he had this incredible gift of gab and I was shy and it felt like a good marriage." They discussed collaboration but did not start the company at that time. Meanwhile Ted went to work for Hal Hartley, an independent filmmaker who started working in the 1980s. Ted produced several films for Hartley, including *The Unbelievable Truth* (1989), which they made for about $150,000. They took it to the Toronto Film Festival and sold it to Miramax for $250,000, and it came out and played in theaters in 1990. This was a breakthrough moment for Hope: "The success of *Unbelievable Truth*, and the fact that it actually came out in theaters—it was distributed by Miramax, we were on the rise with them at the same time—made it feel like things could start working" (interview, March 15, 2006).

While working for Hartley, and in conversations with Schamus, Hope was developing a vision of making films that addressed subjects that simply weren't being addressed by Hollywood because they were either taboo or not commercial or both. The key was to make the films on very low budgets, so that it would be feasible to raise the money outside the commercial movie system:

> You saw that you could just put your nose to the grindstone and figure out a way to make a movie for $100,000, which meant that you had a range of subject matter that was now available to you. And that was something James and I started talking about—the whole underserved audience, the fact that there were these people whose hunger must be huge because they have been deprived [of seeing and/or making good movies] for so long. (Interview, March 15, 2006)

Part of Hope's inspiration came from crossing paths with independent filmmakers all over New York City. Although I said earlier that a "scene" may be delocalized and in a sense trans-spatial, New York City's compact geography (as well as many other aspects of New York) played a significant role in making it the epicenter of the indie movement in the 1980s and 1990s:

> When I moved here I remember in that first year or two I went to my first New York Film Festival [in 1985] and had the cheap seats in the second row. I went to see [some] movie and when I got there I noticed that the director, and the star, and the producer were these guys and a woman that I saw every night at 11 o'clock in the 24-hour grocery store. And it was the Coen Brothers and Fran McDormand. And I was like, oh my. And then I went to see [Jim Jarmusch's] *Stranger than Paradise* which was playing across from Lincoln Center at the same time. And when I walked in there was this black guy who says, "Come see my movie, it is going to be here next." And you walked into the theater and sat down and there was a trailer of the same guy in front of the theater selling socks, and it was Spike Lee. And when I went home after seeing that movie I walked past Jim Jarmusch on the subway. It was like all of a sudden I was really kind of driven by the do-it-yourself aesthetic. It felt like this world was actually really small and these people were just really getting it done. (ibid.)

Eventually, and this is a long story that I don't have space to tell, Hope and Schamus formed the company Good Machine in 1990. Hope saw it as part of a linked series of production companies being formed, all more or less at the same time, and all by an interlinked set of players, in New York City:

> So James and I decided to form a company and that was the start of Good Machine. Larry Meistrich joined up with Bob Gosse who was Hal Hartley's non-cousin cousin, who lived down the block, and they formed a company called The Shooting Gallery. And Christine Vachon teamed up with Tom Kalin, who had been the director of *Swoon*, a film that James executive produced, and they formed a company, [KVP Films, which later morphed into] Killer Films. And this was the start of three producer-driven, low budget, indie film companies that came

from a very incestuous, collaborative group, everyone had been partners with each other [on other projects]. (Interview, March 15, 2006)

One of the keys to Good Machine's early success was producing Ang Lee's
The Wedding Banquet in 1993. Lee had won a writing prize and had $300,000
to make a film. A friend recommended Good Machine as a place to make a
low-budget movie, and Lee simply walked into the office one day. After
completing the film, Hope and Schamus showed it to two different foreign
sales distributors. "They both looked at it and said this is a Chinese gay-
themed comedy of marriage and there is no audience whatsoever for this.
And we were like, we made a completely un-commercial film and we had
$2,000 left in our bank account." But the film had been accepted into the
Berlin Film Festival main competition, and they decided to spend the
$2,000 to take the film to Berlin and try to sell it themselves. "James and I
had backpacks, shared a hotel room, took the film there. At the first screening for the film, everyone stood up on their seats and applauded. We ended
up doing $3 million worth of business on the $750,000 film."

Hope's story shows us how the New York indie scene was taking shape
starting in the mid-1980s, with the proliferation of small production companies (along with the bigger ones like Miramax and New Line/Fine Line)
happening all over the city, and with producers and filmmakers practically
tripping over one another at various sites in the city. Hope also mentioned
the New York Film Festival, and I will say more about festivals below. But
there is one more practical element of the way in which the scene crystal-
lized in New York and that had to do with people working on each other's
films. Christine Vachon emphasized this very strongly: "Now when people
reminisce about the 'independent film' scene in the 1980s, they're dreaming. There was no scene. It was the movies themselves that brought people
together. You would go work on a low-budget indie, like *Parting Glances*
(Bill Sherwood, 1986), and other people who were there would have
worked on something small with Jarmusch. The collective consciousness
came from the work, not the bars or screenings or festivals" (2006: 28).
Indeed, most of the people in the New York indie scene got their start by
hands-on work on other people's films. Ted Hope, as we saw, started his
career as an assistant director on one of Hal Hartley's films and went on to
become a producer in Hartley's company before founding Good Machine.
Lydia Dean Pilcher, who owns an independent production company called

Cine Mosaic, Inc., worked her way up the ladder from a lowly position assisting a location manager:

A lot of my friends [from film school] had started to work on this Scorsese film called *After Hours* (1985). It was in pre-production; a friend of mine was the location manager and he kept calling me saying "I really need help, this movie is nine weeks of night [shooting] and nobody wants to commit to nine weeks of nights." First I said no, and then he called me back in a couple of weeks and I think he caught me right at that moment when I [was fed up with my job], and I decided that I was out of my mind not to quit and go work for Scorsese. So I did and it was fantastic . . . I just kept working in production in New York, . . . it's an apprentice business, you network and one job leads to the next. (Interview, March 29, 2006)

Given the highly social and collaborative nature of independent filmmaking in 1990s New York City, you could also turn Pilcher's last point around: if networking generates more jobs, jobs generate more network, part of the making of the scene.

Specialty Divisions, Production Companies, and the L.A. Indie Scene

The Los Angeles story has to begin differently, with the proliferation of the specialty divisions of the major Hollywood studios. As discussed earlier, by the early 1990s the independent film scene had become quite visible, in terms of both a reasonable level of box office success and, more importantly, a high level of critical success. Indies were successfully accessing, and even playing a role in creating, a particular upscale and educated market that was attractive to the studios as part of their diversification strategies. Some studios already had specialty divisions from an earlier era, mainly for the acquisition and distribution of foreign films, and these were redirected toward independent(-ish) film production. Others bought existing independent production companies, while still others developed their own specialty divisions from scratch (see table 3 above).

Outside of the studios were the smaller independent production companies, scattered around Los Angeles. Most of them are in the business of putting together projects that are Hollywood oriented and would primarily be of interest to the big studios, but some were founded in the late 1980s and the 1990s for the purpose of making independent films. Some of these may be similar to the ones in New York just discussed, making very low budget films and operating with a strong DIY ethic in order to maintain strict independence. But most indie-oriented independent production companies in Los Angeles put together projects that would be of interest to the specialty divisions of the studios. One of the most successful of these—moderately successful financially, highly successful in garnering critical esteem—is Bona Fide Productions, a partnership between Albert Berger and Ron Yerxa. Berger and Yerxa generally work more within a Hollywood aesthetic (especially in terms of using stars) than many of the New York indies, and they also do a lot more with comedy. At the same time they always use material that is slightly off-balance or off-kilter— edgier, or, in one of their favorite words, "subversive"—and they describe themselves as making "left-of-center Hollywood films." Like the companies in New York, Bona Fide came together in the late 1980s, and I will again tell the story primarily in the words of the producers.

Albert Berger graduated from film school at Columbia University in 1983 and then moved out to Los Angeles. He began his career as a screenwriter and met Ron Yerxa in the course of trying to sell his first script. Ron at the time was a studio executive at CBS Theatrical. Albert tells the story:

> Ron and I developed a friendship over the years, and eventually I became more and more frustrated as a screenwriter. And he was such an unlikely film executive. He is a guy that is very dignified-looking and seemingly conventional but is very much an anarchist at heart. And he was in this environment at the studios and he looked the part but he was anything but. And clearly it wasn't going to work for him as a studio executive, he had somehow managed to stay afloat and succeed in that environment but his heart was much more towards producing as well. And we decided that maybe we would partner up and become producers together. (Interview, December 30, 2005)

They went to the Sundance Film Festival in 1989 with a book (*This Boy's Life*, by Tobias Wolff) that they were interested in seeing made into a movie; they were shopping for a filmmaker who would be interested and good for the project. (This is still their standard mode of producing— finding a book or script that interests them, and putting together the package, including the writer and director, or writer/director, on the one hand and the financing on the other.) As with Ted Hope and James

Schamus at the Berlin Film Festival, they were young and poor: "So, the first Sunday night of the festival, we were staying together in a little room, Ron and I, and we went to a party and we couldn't get into the party because we only had one ticket, and we tried this thing where one of us got our hand stamped and tried to rub it on the other's hand." It didn't work and they didn't get into the party, so they went across the street to see a movie.

> It was 10 o'clock on a Sunday night and the movie was *sex, lies, and videotape*. It was the very first screening of that movie. We hadn't heard of it. It was in a 200- to 300-seat theater and there were 50 people. And we sat down and started watching the movie and we were both sort of stunned because we had never heard of the guy and never heard of the movie, first time it had ever been shown, and it was so accomplished and so clearly the work of a filmmaker that we were sort of beside ourselves. (Interview, December 30, 2005)

They went up and talked to the director, Steven Soderbergh, afterward and made a date with him later in the week to discuss the possibility of his directing *This Boy's Life*. It emerged that Soderbergh had a book that he himself was interested in turning into a movie and directing, *King of the Hill*, and he asked them to produce that instead. Of course, they agreed. "And all of a sudden Ron and I had this project and Steven went on to win the Cannes film festival and Universal immediately gobbled up *King of the Hill*, and we had a project with him." That was their first film together, and they formed Bona Fide Productions in 1991 in order to produce it. Ron Yerxa joked about the beginnings of the company. He said that "at first the business was a very small and minimal operation. It was just the two of them, working out of Albert's house. He said he liked to joke that they worked out of the back of a vw van on a card table" (field notes, February 4, 2006).

For the first five or six years they did not have a deal with a studio/specialty division. A deal in this sense means that the studio has the right to have a first look at any project they generate, and in return the studio pays for the overhead of the production company and sometimes an advance against a future producing fee. Operating without a deal meant they were more in the position of the New York independents, having to raise money on a film-by-film basis. It also meant that they were continually broke. Yerxa said, "There were just periods where I had absolutely no money, I just lived beyond credit card debt" (interview, March 12, 2006).[6] But eventually, on the basis of some early successes, they were able to negotiate deals with various studio specialty divisions, and these arrangements sustained them until well into the 2000s.[7]

Bona Fide Productions is, as I said, one of scores of small production companies dotting the landscape of Los Angeles. The L.A. film world (including Hollywood) is not a huge community, and probably most producers—certainly those on the independent side of things—know one another, or at least know of one another. Despite the sprawling nature of Los Angeles, compared to the compact nature of New York City, most of these people run into one another in a variety of contexts, from popular restaurants to organized events. Organized events range from panels, screenings, and festivals that take place in and beyond the city throughout the year, up through the great Independent Spirit Awards extravaganza in a tent on the Santa Monica beach in February.

The Social and Cultural Infrastructure

I have been discussing the nuts and bolts of the formation of the independent film scene in the late 1980s, in terms of the proliferation of production companies geared toward making independent films. I have broken down the discussion in terms of the differences between the "scenes" on the East and West Coasts, but I need to emphasize that there is a tremendous amount of interconnection and crossover between the producers and filmmakers on both coasts, and the contrast is in no way absolute. Differences apart, however, my emphasis so far has been on production companies as constituting the most fundamental element of the independent film infrastructure.

It is partly through the practices of actually making films that the people involved come to be aware of themselves as a social universe—a network, a community, a scene. Christine Vachon, in a passage quoted above, emphasized the actual work of filmmaking as the most important factor in producing and reproducing a "collective consciousness." In addition, however, there is a large set of interlocking institutions that play a major role in the further constitution of the scene. These include film schools, film magazines, film organizations, and film festivals with their associated awards. All of these serve practical functions—film schools and film organizations provide education and training; magazines, including especially *Filmmaker*, provide information and tips for filmmakers, as well as opening up the indie world to the lay reader; festivals give awards that are important for the futures of particular films and also operate as markets in which film deals can be made. In addition, the film schools, organizations, and festivals are major sites for the never-ending social networking that keeps the scene alive on the ground.

Furthermore, all of these institutions perform what might be called cultural functions, defining what independent film is, constituting an independent film public that includes both the filmmakers and their audiences, and creating and sustaining particular identities for filmmakers and audiences alike. Film schools, *Filmmaker* magazine, and the Independent Spirit Awards are forever defining the very nature and value of "independence" and forever positioning filmmakers as simultaneously independent and collaborative within a larger world of independent film. The cultural processes of subject and community formation in the indie world are complex and will be dealt with elsewhere. Here I stay with the practical question of how these institutions were literally made, or in some cases transformed from an earlier state, in the 1980s and 1990s. Once again I will do this mainly through personal narratives.

FILM SCHOOLS

At the most practical level, film schools train students in how to make films. The larger ones also offer students various interning, exhibiting, and networking opportunities, to try to help them get jobs, sell their screenplays, and get recognition for themselves and their films. Extensive research on film schools was beyond the scope of this project, but they are an important part of the story, and I will make a few brief comments here.

The importance of film schools has been expanding at least since the 1970s. The "Hollywood Renaissance" of the 1970s was primarily launched by the so-called film school brats—Coppola, de Palma, Lucas, Scorsese, Spielberg, etc.—who had been steeped in film history and in European film traditions; these directors reinvigorated Hollywood itself rather than going independent. Film schools took another big jump, in both numbers and importance, in the 1980s, presumably as both cause and effect of the

growing independent film movement: in 1980, 35 percent of first-time directors were graduates of film schools, but by 1992, the figure was up to 72
percent (Levy 1999: 34).

Bob Rosen, long-time dean of the UCLA School of Theater, Film, and
Television, talked about his career and about his sense of the film school
phenomenon. Rosen has a PhD in history from Stanford and began by
teaching in the history department at Penn in the early 1970s. "Within a
year he had created a course called 'Film as Social and Intellectual History.'
He said he had to teach his colleagues that film was a legitimate thing to
study; they thought of it as something you bring in to supplement your
courses, 'AV aid.'" He said he "came to UCLA in 1974 to give 10 lectures and
never left" (field notes, July 25, 2006).

In a later e-mail he wrote about how the school has evolved over the
course of his time there:

> [It began as] a free-form place for independent spirits, radical thinkers
> and ethnic minorities to have access to the means of production, and
> the freedom to take risks and make movies outside of the Hollywood
> mainstream. Over time it evolved into being a film school with a co-
> herent program that strives to train real professionals without sacrific-
> ing the spirit of independence and risk-taking. Can you successfully mix
> oil and water? Look at the Oscars, Emmys and Guild Awards going to
> our graduates, overwhelmingly for movies with an edge. (E-mail, No-
> vember 28, 2009, revised by Rosen January 31, 2011)

ORGANIZATIONS

Another important component of the indie infrastructure is the network
of organizations that devote themselves to furthering the cause of independent film. The first, an organization called the Independent Feature
Project (IFP), was founded in 1979 by a producer, Sandra Schulberg. According to Emanuel Levy, it began as a "collective" and was "a project born
with a post-1960s spirit: 'Let's all get together and have a voice'" (1999: 47,
48). According to Peter Biskind, "IFP conducted a series of seminars about
working outside the system—how to raise money, how to produce, how to
distribute yourself—it was like inventing the wheel" (2004: 16).

Part of reinventing the wheel involved defining what an independent
film is. Bob Rosen was involved in early meetings at the IFP that estab-

lished an initial set of criteria for what constituted an independent film: that (as we heard in the last chapter) a film must be "risk-taking in content and style," that it must embody a "personal vision," that it be funded by "non-Hollywood financing," and that it embody the "valuation of art over money" (field notes based on untaped interview, July 2006). But agreeing on the criteria was less difficult than deciding whether any given film actually fit: "What you had was a lot of deeply felt soul searching as to what constituted independence and how it should be defined, so you ended up with passionate arguments about purity. We even had a purity committee at one point, you know, what is a REAL independent film? . . . Well, that was a terrible game but it was a great group" (interview, November 10, 2008).

Rosen was an early member of the board of IFP/West, which was founded in Los Angeles in the late 1980s, as was Barbara Boyle, chair of the Department of Film, Television, and Digital Media at UCLA. (For the remainder of this section I will concentrate on IFP/West [later renamed Film Independent] as it is the organization I came to know best.) Boyle was an entertainment lawyer who, among other things, worked for many years as a business partner with legendary B-movie independent filmmaker and producer Roger Corman. One part of her job consisted of going to Europe to shop for foreign films, so important to the art-house scene in the 1970s. As the independent film scene emerged in the 1980s, Boyle became involved in the founding of Film Independent and served on its Board of Directors from 1988 to 2000. Within that time, she served as president for five years. As she said, "In the Los Angeles office Film Independent is jokingly referred to, and maybe not so jokingly referred to, as The House That Barbara Built" (interview, November 23, 2005).

But the organization was struggling financially in the early 1990s. Dawn Hudson was a young dancer and aspiring actress in Los Angeles who took a part-time job at the IFP/West office in 1990. Hudson describes herself as having been very radical in college: "When I was majoring in government at Harvard it was because I wanted to overthrow the government and change the world." She had tried working as an intern for various politicians and concluded that it was "very tough to make an impact in politics, . . . to change people's consciousness . . . so I became more interested in the arts" (interview, February 3, 2006).

Shortly after Hudson was hired, however, IFP/West ran out of money and everyone was fired. She recounts,

A couple of months later the president of the board called me and said would you come work with us, help us out of this hole really, we are in trouble. And I said, well my check has bounced, you still owe me $700, and I worked a lot for very little, it was a tough gig and I really would rather keep up with my magazine writing or something else. And [the president] said, can we just have a meeting? And I had a meeting with one of the board members and he wrote me a personal check for the amount of money they owed me. And he said, could you just come out and help us get on our feet, and I was hired kind of on a temporary basis that way. (ibid.)

Hudson protested that she

had no ambition to be a filmmaker or to run an organization. [But] they said, all these professional non-profit administrators haven't helped us so much and we would love to have somebody who is passionate about film . . . I really wanted the life of the artist. I really felt that was where one would have an impact in the world. But I also found my skill set suited to running this, because I think it has to do with not just skills but a real deep passionate belief that film can change the world (ibid.).

Hudson became the executive director of Film Independent, and her achievements in building the organization have been extraordinary. It now has about four thousand members, hosts the annual Independent Spirit Awards, and took over the L.A. Film Festival in the year 2000. According to its website, it also raises about a quarter of a million dollars in grant funding every year to support "emerging filmmakers" through a wide variety of programs.[8]

FILMMAKER MAGAZINE

Filmmaker is the "magazine of independent film." It was founded in 1992 as a publication of the New York–based IFP, and it has a circulation of over sixty thousand readers (www.filmmakermagazine.com). Published quarterly, and focusing primarily on upcoming independent films about to be released in theaters, it includes articles and interviews, as well as editorials from the editor-in-chief of the magazine, Scott Macaulay. It (along with Macaulay's weekly e-newsletter and ongoing blog) is an indispensable element of the public culture of the independent film world.

The founding of *Filmmaker* magazine in 1992 was very much part of the coalescing of the indie scene in New York City starting in the late 1980s, and it begins again with a James Schamus connection. Both Macaulay and Schamus were involved in alternative theater work in New York in the 1980s, and they became friends through that. (Macaulay was working as the director of programming at a well-known performance space called "The Kitchen.") But in addition to their theater interests, both were interested in getting involved in filmmaking. Schamus asked Macaulay to produce an independent film with him called *The Golden Boat* (Raoul Ruiz, 1990), with Schamus as producer and Macaulay as associate producer, which they did. Later, Schamus was reading scripts for New Line Cinema, and when he quit, he recommended Macaulay for the job, which he took. Somewhere in all this Schamus and Ted Hope formed Good Machine, and they had a film project that they asked Macaulay to produce (*What Happened Was...*, written and directed by Tom Noonan, 1994), which Macaulay coproduced with his partner Robin O'Hara, and which won the Grand Jury Prize at Sundance.

But finally, to get to *Filmmaker* magazine, Macaulay tells another James Schamus story:

> The IFP published a magazine called the *Off Hollywood Report* and they were turning it around and needed a new editor. They asked James. So James called me and said, do you want to do it with me? I said sure. I was the co-editor and James was the editor and we did several issues together. And then James, who had just started the production company Good Machine, said, "I don't really have time to do this anymore. Why don't you do it?" So I started editing the magazine while I was still working full time at The Kitchen. I had this full-time job and . . . I was writing and editing on nights and weekends. (Interview, March 15, 2006)

To provide some idea of the value of the magazine to the scene, here is one among many testimonials from its website:

> *Filmmaker* is bar none the best magazine covering the world of American Independent Film. Beyond being informative, revelatory, and daring, it's an inspiration. Each time it arrives in the mail I'm excited to find the story of another Fitzcarraldo-like effort by a new filmmaker and, in reading such stories, I'm once again challenged to make my own films.

The magazine is a steadfast reminder of the pure and desperate urge from which good filmmaking arises. What better thing for a publication to offer its readers than courage? (Steven Shainberg, Writer/Director/Producer, *Secretary*, *Fur*; www.filmmakermagazine.com)

FESTIVALS

The final element of the "making of the indie scene" that I will sketch here is film festivals. Film festivals showcase previously unreleased films; they operate as competitions for awards and honors; and they operate as markets in which the films might find buyers and distributors. Like everything else in this story, there was an explosion of film festivals throughout the United States, and indeed throughout the world, starting in the mid-1980s (see especially Turan 2002). I will concentrate here on the most important one in the United States, Sundance.

The Sundance Film Festival started life as the U.S. Film Festival. It was taken over in 1985 by Robert Redford's Sundance Institute and renamed the Sundance Film Festival in 1991. It was directed for many years by Geoff Gilmore, in many ways one of the most powerful people of the independent film world. Gilmore had majored in history and social theory as an undergraduate at the University of Pennsylvania, where he took Bob Rosen's course "Film as Social and Intellectual History." Gilmore was inspired by Rosen's teaching and calls him to this day his "mentor and friend." At about that time, Rosen took the job at UCLA, and Gilmore enrolled in the UCLA film school PhD program. While at UCLA, as he said in an interview, "I also did a lot of other things, I got very involved quickly with UCLA Film and Television Archives and I got very involved with the exhibition part, running a cinémathèque showing films and doing a lot of different exhibition programs, which I did from the first year that I got here."

Although Gilmore came close to finishing the PhD, he began to have doubts about a future as an academic: "I started at some point getting restless about the academic world and I felt that what I was doing was very esoteric and I remember feeling that I could talk to about 200 people in the world about what it is that I do in a serious way." And then a major opportunity came along:

I was entering my 30s and wondering where I was going to go and what I was going to do and I got a call from a woman who was running the

Sundance Institute. At the time [a key person was] leaving the Sundance film festival, and he said there was only one person to recommend for the job and that was me. The reason he recommended me for the job was because I was one of the few people who never called in to ask him how to do anything or ask him for information, I just kind of did it on my own, which is true. (Interview, May 25, 2006)

We can pick up the next part of the story from Peter Biskind's account in *Down and Dirty Pictures*. Despite the success of *sex, lies, and videotape* in 1989, the Sundance Film Festival was foundering badly under what Biskind portrays as Redford's "passive aggressive" personality. The previous head of the festival, Tony Safford, resigned in 1990, but—as Gilmore tells us above—suggested Gilmore as his replacement. "[Tony] Safford was a gifted programmer, but paradoxically, his most significant contribution may well have been recruiting Gilmore as his successor" (Biskind 2004: 84).

With Gilmore's arrival, the culture of the film festival (which at that time bore the traces of its 1960s counterculture origins) began to change. In 1991, the name of the festival was changed to the Sundance Film Festival, and the programming was very strong, including "Richard Linklater's *Slacker*, Hal Hartley's *Trust*, John Sayles's *City of Hope*, Julie Dash's *Daughters of the Dust*, Matty Rich's *Straight Out of Brooklyn*, and Todd Haynes's *Poison*" (Biskind 2004: 105–6). *Poison*, "homoerotic and violent," won the Grand Jury Prize for features, while Jennie Livingston's "ode to transsexuals," *Paris Is Burning*, won the Grand Jury Prize for documentaries (Biskind 2004: 106). Gilmore did not actually do the programming for that year, which was done by Alberto Garcia (Biskind 2004: 105). But the winners, and the selections more generally, signaled a shift to the edgier fare that became the hallmark of the Sundance Film Festival under Gilmore's leadership, and that set Sundance on a course of growth in size, excitement, and prestige.[9]

All of the institutions discussed in this section (film schools, independent film organizations, *Filmmaker* magazine, and film festivals) perform practical functions: teaching, informing, selecting, awarding, creating markets, and more. All of these entities also perform social functions, bringing people together in events that provide both networking opportunities and a sense of collective endeavor, of being part of a community or scene. And finally, although I have not been able to discuss this here, all of these

entities perform what might be called cultural functions, establishing definitions and values (remember IFP's purity committee), and at the same
time constituting participants as particular kinds of subjects, minimally, as
believers in and connoisseurs of the special value of independence in
filmmaking.

Indie Financing and the New Investors

The final piece of creating and sustaining the infrastructure of the indie
scene involves developing a range of sources of financing for the films.
Since independent films are not made by the studios, indie producers must
always raise their financing on their own. I will say a few words about
general financing strategies but then focus particularly on a new breed of
investors who have emerged around the independent film scene. These are
people who bring not only money but, as I came to learn, progressive
ideals to the making of independent films.

There are many ways of financing an independent film, and indeed
being creative about finding financing is one of the positive challenges for
indie producers and filmmakers. There is, of course, the very low end, DIY
model—borrowing from relatives, maxing out one's credit cards, and extracting free labor from friends and family. This kind of "micro-budget"
filmmaking is still the stuff of legend in the indie world. But there are only
so many times that one can do that, and beyond that most independent
filmmakers must seek less personal forms of financing.

The classic East Coast model was, until recently, to presell the foreign
rights in Europe, which guaranteed a certain amount of money to make
the film, and also showed that the film was of interest to an audience. One
was then in a good position to seek a private investor. If one was successful
in finding an investor, in turn, one might then seek a bank loan to round
out the package. This strategy became much less common after the con-
striction of the market, starting in about 2007, but it was one of the
primary strategies of the 1990s and early 2000s. A variant of this model
involves preselling video/DVD rights, as discussed earlier.

The classic West Coast model is the one we heard about earlier from
Berger and Yerxa: one hopes to interest one of the studio specialty divisions in one's film. In the best-case scenario, they agree to finance the film
and one's money troubles are over. Often, however, they do not agree (or

they only partially agree and want others to share the risk), and then the L.A. independent producer and/or filmmaker is in the same position as his or her New York counterparts, selling foreign rights and/or DVD rights, seeking bank loans, and, especially, seeking private investors.

Here let us focus more closely on these investors. Once upon a time, there were relatively few individuals interested in financing high-risk independent films. But as a result of the reconfiguration of the PMC discussed earlier, in which one sees a new linkage between money and progressive politics, the independent film scene was able to attract a different kind of individual to investing, people who were drawn to the counter-hegemonic values of the indie world.

I would first mention Charles Ferguson, who wrote, produced, and directed the widely acclaimed documentary about the Iraq War, *No End in Sight* (2007), which was highly critical of the Bush administration. Ferguson, who has a PhD in political science from MIT, made a lot of money in software in the mid-1990s. He founded Vermeer Technologies, "which created the first visual Web site development tool, Front Page. In early 1996, [he] sold Vermeer to Microsoft for $133 million" (Wikipedia: "Charles H. Ferguson"). He subsequently launched a production company, Representational Pictures, and fully financed the making of *No End in Sight*, which, as already mentioned, won the Special Jury Prize at Sundance in 2007 and was also nominated for an Academy Award.

Ferguson's progressive politics became even more visible with his next documentary, *Inside Job* (2010), an exposé of the illegalities in investment banking that brought about the near crash of the stock market in 2008. The film won the Best Documentary Oscar, and when Ferguson came to the podium to accept the award, he first commented that, despite the multiple frauds behind the crash, not a single one of the apparently guilty parties had been brought to trial. Making this kind of political statement at the Academy Awards is risky, as many in Hollywood—even those who might agree with Ferguson—do not like to see explicit politics introduced into the event (see chap. 8).

A second example of a progressive investor is Marc Turtletaub, head of Big Beach Productions. I first heard about Marc through Albert Berger and Ron Yerxa, who produced *Little Miss Sunshine*. *Little Miss Sunshine* had first been sold to Focus Features, but Focus sat on it for some time.

Turtletaub had been interested in being in business with Berger and Yerxa, and he decided to buy *Little Miss Sunshine* back from Focus Features and finance it himself, which he did to the tune of $7 million. I met him on the set of a later investing/producing project, *Sunshine Cleaning*, and asked him about his background. He said

> he's from Perth Amboy, N.J. . . . He went to the Wharton Business School at the University of Pennsylvania and also took a law degree. He took over his father's business, The Money Store, was very successful, made a lot of money, and then sold it six years ago for many millions of dollars and went into the film business which is really his passion. (Field notes, March 20, 2007)

I asked him if he has any particular focus for his choice of productions.

> He described himself several times as a child of the counterculture. Said he only wants to make films that have some kind of redemption, wants to "touch people," "change people." He's not interested in just entertainment; he wants to entertain but it has to be something more. He said he is lucky that he has the wherewithal to wait until the right script comes along. He said there is just a handful of producers who are similar to himself; they have the money and they also want to use it to do good. (Field notes, March 20, 2007)

Turtletaub went on to mention Jeff Skoll, who is probably the most active and well known of the wealthy investors interested in supporting socially and politically progressive films. Skoll, who has an MBA from Stanford, cofounded eBay in 1996. He retired from eBay in 2000 at the age of thirty-five "with an estimated $2bn in his pocket" (Wood 2006: 4). In 2004, he founded Participant Productions (later Participant Media) with the "express purpose [of making] movies that will help to change the world" (Wood 2006: 3). Through Participant Productions, Skoll has made major investments in films like *Good Night and Good Luck* (George Clooney, 2005), *Syriana* (Stephen Gaghan, 2005), *An Inconvenient Truth* (Davis Guggenheim, 2006), *The Visitor* (Thomas McCarthy, 2007), *The Soloist* (Joe Wright, 2009), and many others. Moreover, Participant Productions does not simply make films: "Skoll saw that the films he loved didn't have much 'follow-up in the real world' and decided to provide an infrastructure that would allow movies to make a difference far beyond the cinema.

Participant Productions creates partnerships with activist groups [and] organises an action campaign around each movie" (Wood 2006: 3).

Other individuals might also be briefly mentioned. Lisa Maria Falcone, a New Yorker of Latina background married to a wealthy hedge fund manager, has also set up a production company to finance independent films. I met her on the set of one of her investments, *Mother and Child* (Rodrigo García, 2010), and asked her how she chose projects to invest in. She replied in language similar to Turtletaub's, about wanting to make films of social value, but additionally with a philanthropic model similar to Jeff Skoll's: "She said she is interested in films that have some sort of social value. . . . She said she is forming a company where she invests in a film, and then donates 10 percent of the profits to the cause that is the theme of the film, in this case to agencies that deal with adoption issues. Eventually she hopes to have a foundation that both invests in independent films and supports related causes" (field notes, February 13, 2009).

In addition, director John Singleton (*Boyz n the Hood*, 1991) and actor Forest Whitaker (*The Crying Game*, 1992) are known for investing in, and in other ways helping and supporting, films by African American filmmakers.

In this chapter I have told the story of the making of the independent film scene in the 1980s and 1990s. After an initial historical overview, I spent some time situating the emergence of the scene in relation to changes in the American economy and class structure that had begun in the late 1970s and began to make themselves felt in the late 1980s and the 1990s. The remainder of the chapter was taken up with a kind of map of the scene in terms of its primary institutions—production companies, film schools, film organizations, festivals—and an oral history of the ways in which these things were brought into being or transformed by the energy and idealism of real individuals. Then-young would-be producers like Ted Hope, Christine Vachon, Lydia Dean Pilcher, Albert Berger, and Ron Yerxa were excited about the possibility of making something happen, breaking with "Hollywood," and doing something new. Dawn Hudson took over Film Independent with the explicit belief that independent film could change the world, and a whole new breed of investors emerged with a similar hope that this new kind of filmmaking had the possibility of fostering social change.

I will consider explicitly political films in chapter 8. In the next chapter I return to the films as embodiments of other aspects of the dark and complex worldview of Generation X. For ultimately the point of all this infrastructure was to create the conditions of possibility for making films that could/would not get made in the Hollywood studios, that made demands on viewers to see the world in whole new ways.

CHAPTER 4

Moral Ambiguity

In an important article, "Melodrama Revised," film scholar Linda Williams argues that melodrama is "the foundation of the classic Hollywood movie" (1998a: 42). Williams is picking up a thread begun by literary critic Peter Brooks in his work on nineteenth-century theater and fiction (1995) to the effect that melodrama as a literary genre has played a central role in the formation of modern consciousness. Central to melodrama as a genre/mode in both fiction and theater in turn is "the indulgence of strong emotionalism" and also "stark ethical conflict"; a melodrama is "an intense emotional and ethical drama based on the manichaeistic struggle of good and evil" (P. Brooks 1995: 11, 12). Film studies scholars have brought Brooks's arguments to bear on Hollywood movies, with respect to so-called family melodrama (Elsaesser 1987) and "women's film" (Gledhill 1987), but Williams is arguing that we should see melodrama as underwriting and structuring Hollywood movies as a whole.

There are a variety of definitions of melodrama. Williams defines it as "a modality with a high quotient of pathos and action" (1998a: 51). In addition, all that pathos and action are generated by the engagement between characters who represent pure good and pure bad—Brooks's "stark ethical conflict." Thus, one of the most basic Hollywood movie formats is simply the good guys against the bad guys, often in a visually and musically spectacular setting, with the good guys winning out in the end. Indeed, the happy ending of the classic Hollywood movie may be seen in part as tied to the melodramatic structure: evil is punished, virtue is rewarded.

To get right to the point of this chapter, all of this is precisely what independent film is not. I will not risk trying to say what independent films generically *are*, but it seems clear that, at almost every level, they are not melodramas. In the first place, they generally eschew strong emotionalism, both at the level of acting and at the level of the mise-en-scène (i.e., the total visual, musical, etc., setting of the action). They resist, for example, "some symphonic score, lacquering over every scene, telling you what to feel" (Vachon 2006: 270). Second, there are few clear-cut good guys and bad guys. Major good guys—"heroes"—are largely absent. What we might have taken to be bad guys are often rendered as complicated persons so that the viewer is discouraged from judging and condemning them and from taking an unambivalent moral position. And finally, the good guys rarely triumph over the bad guys at the end; insofar as "good guys" are present, they are often marginal characters. Indeed, with the absence of a clear good/bad contrast, there cannot be such an ending. Just as the darkness of many independent films puzzled and provoked me and motivated chapter 2, so did the moral ambiguity of many independent films puzzle and provoke me similarly and motivate the present chapter.

Moral ambiguity may extend to virtually any subject in independent film. I count at least seven films watched in the course of this project in which someone literally gets away with murder.[1] But for reasons to be explored, a lot of the moral relativism seems to surround the subject of children. For example, in *Citizen Ruth* (Alexander Payne, 1996), the lead character Ruth Stoops, a woman with a serious drug habit, abandons her four children and walks blithely away from the final scene, smiling, as part of an upbeat ending. *Citizen Ruth* was billed as a comedy (critic Janet Maslin [1996: 1] called it "hilariously brazen" and Laura Dern's performance "sidesplitting") and was nominated for a Grand Jury Prize in the 1996 Sundance Film Festival.

Probably the largest group of films in this category revolves around acts, or suspected acts, of pedophilia. Men molesting or raping children or teenagers, or suspected/accused of doing so, were central figures in nine independent films that I saw in the course of the research, and offstage but crucial figures in several more. The number itself is noteworthy and raises the question of why we are seeing so much of this phenomenon in independent films of the 1990s and 2000s. But beyond the numbers is the moral ambiguity question. In three of those nine films, the filmmakers take a relatively clear position that the sexual molestation of children is wrong and criminal, and that a moral person or a moral institution should not in any way condone it. But in the other six films the situation, which is to say the filmmakers' point of view, is much more ambiguous.

In this chapter I want to look at these "pedophile films" at both levels. In the first part of the chapter I ask—as many others have done—why the subject of pedophilia has become such an insistent issue in American public culture in the late twentieth and early twenty-first centuries. Further, while much of the popular culture represents pedophilia as a danger coming from outside the home (satanic cults, preschool teacher sex rings, released convicted pedophiles residing in the neighborhood, etc.), the films almost entirely present pedophilia as a danger within or close to the family. For this part of the discussion, then, I will explore the films in relation to issues of the family in contemporary America, as seen again through the eyes of "Generation X."

But in the second half of the chapter I will return to the moral ambiguity question. What could it mean to be ambivalent, morally unclear, about pedophiles molesting children? Why are we seeing so much of this relativism in these films? In what sense could we understand this—or not—as part of "cultural critique"? Here I will step back from the specific subject of pedophilia and return to the broader question of moral relativism in contemporary public culture, situating these and other films both within and against the "post-moral" culture of neoliberalism.

Moral Positioning in the Pedophile Films

In this section I both introduce the films in question and look at the ways in which the filmmakers construct the pedophile, through plot and other mechanisms, as a morally ambiguous character rather than clearly bad. I begin, however, with those three films in which the filmmaker does in fact take a clear moral position against pedophiles and against institutions (especially the Catholic Church) that enable them.

In two documentaries about the pedophilia epidemic in the Catholic Church, *Twist of Faith* (Kirby Dick, 2004) and *Deliver Us from Evil* (Amy Berg, 2006), the filmmakers establish a clear position that priests who molested children under their care committed morally unacceptable, and in fact criminal, acts and should be held accountable. To the extent that the Church condoned, or turned a blind eye to, those acts and allowed them to continue it too was acting similarly and should be held accountable. Similarly, in Mira Nair's feature film *Monsoon Wedding* (2002), one of the plot lines involves an uncle who had molested his niece when she was a child. As the uncle was a long-supportive relative of the family of the bride, there was some tension about whether to cover up this issue in the interest of peace in the family. In the end, however, the father of the bride makes a speech saying that such behavior was unacceptable and casting the uncle out of the wedding and out of the family.

But the other six pedophile films are much less straightforward on this question. I start with two films that are, as we learn from interviews, quite explicit and self-conscious in creating an atmosphere of ambivalence and ambiguity about the pedophile—the documentary *Capturing the Friedmans* (Andrew Jarecki, 2003) and the feature *Little Children* (Todd Field, 2006). In both films, the dramatic strategy is to shift the emphasis of the story away from the figure of the pedophile and on to the question of the social paranoia and hysteria surrounding pedophilia. At the same time there are various moves in the film that cast doubt on whether the abuse ever happened, and/or if it did, whether it merits such a strong reaction.

In *Capturing the Friedmans*, first, the filmmaker positions himself, and seeks to position the viewer, on the side of the supporters (mainly the oldest son) of Arnie Friedman, the convicted pedophile. A great deal of footage is devoted to various individuals (several parents; an "expert" of some kind) claiming in effect that the police coerced the testimony of some, or maybe all, of the children. The film thus manages to suggest that nothing may have happened at all, or that whatever happened has been blown out of proportion.

Another way in which the question of abuse is rendered ambiguous in *Capturing the Friedmans* is that the film gives almost no screen time to the victims. Whereas the two documentaries about the epidemic of pedophilia in the Catholic Church basically start from, and stay with, the victims and show us their continuing pain, this film shows only one adult victim, who is filmed with his face in the dark, and who speaks very flatly and offhandedly about the abuse. This is not to cast doubt on his credibility; it is only to say that virtually nothing is done in the film to draw the viewer's sympathy toward this individual or the other victims. Indeed, during one of the filmed Q&A sessions shown in the bonus material on the DVD, the lead detective tries to defend herself against the charges of bad police work and asks the filmmakers, "Why didn't you talk to the victims?"

In an interview also available in the bonus material, the director Andrew Jarecki confirms the ambiguity that has appeared in the film. He refuses to hazard a judgment as to whether the father Arnie was guilty and indicates that he thinks the convicted son Jesse was almost certainly not guilty. Perhaps he is right; the American justice system has certainly been known to make terrible mistakes. Yet the film is not set up primarily as a critique of the justice system. Rather, it seems to be using the fallibilities of the justice system as part of a larger strategy for making the case ambiguous. Jarecki says about Arnie and Jesse Friedman, "Whatever you believe about their guilt, you feel for them, they are real human beings. . . . There are so many gray areas, when a good person does bad things" (bonus interview on DVD).

The feature film *Little Children* takes a similar tack. The previously convicted pedophile Ronny is portrayed as a slimy human being. He clearly still has sexual issues—he takes a woman out on a date and forces her to watch him masturbate. But we never actually see him prey upon children in the film, and in fact the focus of the film is on the hysteria of the townspeople about his presence in the community. He is made a sympathetic figure in several different ways. For one thing, the only intentionally funny scene in the movie is when he goes for a swim at the public pool. When the parents realize he is in the water, they scream in unison and pull all their kids out of the water, looking foolish and hysterical when the man was just taking a swim. Second, a man in town takes up a crusade against him, painting vile things on his house and rendering him a victim of vigilante justice. Finally, at the end, unable to control his urges, Ronny castrates himself. At that point even the vigilante is overcome with pity and carries him to the hospital.

The director, Todd Field, makes it clear in an interview that he was specifically trying to create ambiguity about Ronny. He says, "It was an important thing that we never know for sure what he has or hasn't done. . . . All we know about him for sure is that he's been charged with indecent exposure to a minor. Now, he could have dropped trou[sers] in front of a 17 year old girl, which would have been legal in some countries" (in Macaulay 2006). As in *Capturing the Friedmans*, the question of whether the pedophile actually committed abuse against children is put in doubt, and the pedophile rather than the children is rendered the victim.

Again, we do not know whether Arnie Friedman was "really" guilty, and partly because he took a plea, we do not know whether a jury would have found him guilty. In the case of Ronny in *Little Children*, there is no question of whether Ronny is "really" guilty of anything, because Ronny is a fictional character and he has been written precisely to be ambiguous. (Although I must say the filmmaker plays with the audience. We are given enough reason in the film to think Ronny is some kind of nasty sex offender, but then we are implicitly chastised [via the pool scene] for jumping to conclusions and falling prey to "moral panic.") But my point here is precisely that the filmmakers do not ask us to think about questions of guilt or innocence, good or evil. Rather, they set out to make films about the inherent ambiguity of their subjects' deeds.

There is an extensive literature on the idea of "moral panic," about how people scapegoat certain types of individuals (often pedophiles) for social problems that lie elsewhere, and how the media feed these scapegoating frenzies (see, e.g., Lancaster 2011). It is important to recognize the moral panic issue, and I will be looking at the pedophile as a displacement of, and scapegoat for, other social problems later in the chapter. Nonetheless, for present purposes I am interested in the question of "real," and genuinely predatory, pedophilia and the various ways in which it is represented in the films, morally and dramatically.

Looking then at three of the remaining pedophile films (I set aside one—*Doubt*—for discussion later), the ambiguity about pedophilia is created in other ways. *Mysterious Skin* (Gregg Araki, 2005) is about two boys, Neil and Brian, who were abused by their baseball coach when they were seven or eight years of age. When, in a flashback, Neil's mother takes him to the baseball diamond and turns him over to the coach who will soon seduce him, Neil is shown to flirt with the coach. The scene thus poses the question, is the abuse really abuse if the child apparently invited it?

Interviewer Terry Gross questioned the director Gregg Araki on this issue in an interview on *Fresh Air*:

Gross: In the actual novel, the character thinks, remembering back to this moment, "desire sledge-hammered my body." Does that make the coach's actions any less reprehensible to you, the fact that the boy is actually attracted to the coach?

Mr. Araki: Yeah . . . that was one of the things about the book . . . what makes the book for me such a powerful kind of experience. (NPR Transcript, May 25, 2005: 9)

The discussion continues with more in this vein. Araki maintains, among other things, that many victims of abuse actually have certain positive memories of it, as well as guilt about those memories. This may well be true, and it is an interesting point. But it does not address the moral ambiguity created by the film, in which the child's flirtation seems to legitimate the coach's actions.

A final strategy for creating moral ambiguity may be seen in the features *Happiness* (Todd Solondz, 1998) and *L.I.E.* (Michael Cuesta, 2001): portraying the pedophile as a likable character. In *Happiness*, we know from early in the film that the father Bill has violent murderous nightmares. We also know from fairly early on that Bill is drugging and sodomizing his son's friends. Yet at the same time he seems in many ways to be one of the more "normal" people in the film, especially compared to the deeply sexually screwed up Allen (played by Phillip Seymour Hoffman). Bill is portrayed as a good husband and father. He and his son Billy have a warm, loving relationship in which Billy feels comfortable talking to his father about anything, including sex (Bill is a psychiatrist). Well acted by Dylan Baker, Bill comes across as a decent human being.

There are other ways in which the film lets Bill off the hook. As Joan Hawkins has pointed out, we are never shown any actual sex between the pedophile and the children (although this is true in most of the pedophile movies). Further, since Bill drugs his victims and they have no awareness of the act, they presumably do not have the kinds of traumatic memories victims of abuse usually have (Hawkins 2005: 101).

I have found a lot of interviews with director Todd Solondz, but in none of them does he discuss this question at length. His general position vis-à-vis his critics, however, is clear: that—and here is the realism point again—nothing in his films is as morally outrageous as the real world: "I think that certainly there's nothing in . . . anything I've done really that I think is as troubling as what one sees in real life. Real life is much harsher and certainly here we are in the days of Terri Schiavo [a young woman who was held in an extended coma while the family publicly fought over whether to pull the plug]. You can't get more obscene or grotesque than what life has to offer" (in Frank and Bond 2005: 3).[2]

Finally, *L.I.E.* also uses the strategy of making the pedophile character appealing, even "normal." Early in the film we see the pedophile "Big John" cruising the Internet for porn photos of little boys. He also has a teenage boy living with him in his house. When the lead character Howie's father is arrested and Howie comes to stay with him, Big John puts a porn movie on the video player, puts his hand on Howie's thigh, and starts to engage in verbal seduction. Yet Big John is also portrayed as a very likable character. We are first introduced to him at his own birthday party, happily singing songs and dancing with his aged mother. We are shown that he served in the Marines in the Vietnam War and received medals of valor. The viewer is especially invited to like him when he makes a decision not to have sex with Howie, but rather to care for him like a father. He takes Howie to visit his (Howie's) real father in jail. He becomes nurturant and loving. Once again the viewer is led away from the moral issue and drawn into liking and caring about the character. Moreover, he is shot and killed at the end; as with Ronny's castration, the pedophile has become the victim.

In the director's commentary on *L.I.E.*, Michael Cuesta talks about the Big John character: "You need this to understand the complexity of the guy. He's not a two-dimensional monster, he has a life like you and me." At one point in the film, Big John says he likes girls (appropriate girls, not little girls). Howie looks confused. Big John says, "I know, it's confusing." And then Cuesta says in the commentary, "That's the point of the whole movie, sex is confusing, it's one big gray area." Then he expands the point: "It's important for me to explore the gray areas of every character. Not the black, not the white, but the gray. To take one of the darkest figures in modern society, to show him as a human being, a three-dimensional character, creates great drama, great contradiction."

Failure to Protect[3]

It would not be too much to say that the pedophile films are as much about the dysfunctions of the (white, middle class) family as they are about the dysfunctions of the pedophile. In two cases the danger is internal to the immediate family (Arnie Friedman, Bill in *Happiness*), although in both of those cases it is explicitly denied that the father molested (Arnie Friedman) or would have molested (Bill) his own son.[4] In the other cases the danger is external to the family: Catholic priests, the baseball coach, the uncle in *Monsoon Wedding*, Ronny, and Big John. Yet all the films represent the real locus of the problem (and of the film's moral judgment) as the family. Literally all of the films invoke a theme of what I am calling "failure to protect." That is, their stories tell us that the sexual abuse of the child took place not only because of the pedophile's compulsions, but because one or the other parent, and sometimes both, not to mention in some cases the Catholic Church as a whole, failed to protect the child.

In all of these films, one or both parents are in some ways "absent." We start with mothers. In *L.I.E.* the mother has been killed in an accident on the Long Island Expressway. In *Little Children* the mother is simply uninterested in her child; she either ignores the child or handles her roughly when the child doesn't immediately cooperate. In *Mysterious Skin*, by contrast, the mother is excessively seductive; she loves her son but in an inappropriate and confusing way. In *Happiness* one of the boys, age thirteen, who is sodomized by the pedophile had been left alone while his parents went away for the weekend.

Two of the films actually have a more complex structure concerning mothers. In *L.I.E.*, the boy's mother is absent (dead), but the pedophile has a loving mother who calls him every day and worries about his health. And in *Little Children*, the innocent child's mother is emotionally absent, while the pedophile has a loving mother who tries to protect him from the self-appointed vigilante in the town. In both cases then the literal or emotional absence of the innocent child's mother is highlighted by the emotional presence and supportiveness of the pedophile's mother.

Turning to the documentaries, in *Twist of Faith*, the mother appears simply as cold and unfeeling; she refuses to support her son Tony in his crusade against the Church.[5] In *Capturing the Friedmans*, the mother represents herself on screen as emotionally alienated from her family, and in fact she was the one who urged the father Arnie and the son Jesse to take a plea agreement with the prosecution.

In most of the films, the father is literally or emotionally absent as well. In *Mysterious Skin*, there are two central young male characters, both of whom had been abused by their baseball coach when they were boys. For one of the young men, the parents are divorced and the boy lives with his seductive mother while the father is never seen; for the other, the father appears early in the film, mainly to call his son a sissy; he then disappears and we learn later that he left the family. In *Little Children*, the husband/father has become enthralled with a porn star on the Internet and spends most of his time at home masturbating in his study. In *L.I.E.*, the father is arrested and jailed for illegal business practices. In *Happiness*, the father of one of the children takes a vacation with his wife and leaves his thirteen-year-old son home alone to be raped by the pedophile.

It is not only in the pedophile films that there is a link between absent parents and disturbingly sexualized children. Among the independent films that I watched in the past few years there was also a set of films in which young girls make sexual advances to much older men. In *12 and Holding* (Michael Cuesta, 2006) a twelve-year-old daughter of a therapist attempts to seduce an older man who is one of her mother's patients. In *Half Nelson* (Ryan Fleck, 2006) a girl who we are told is thirteen or fourteen years old flirts actively with her middle school teacher, and in *Election* (Alexander Payne, 1999) a girl of about sixteen seduces her high school teacher. In *Towelhead* (Allen Ball, 2007), a girl of thirteen flirts with her neighbor's husband and he eventually rapes her, and in *American Beauty* (written, like *Towelhead*, by Allen Ball, but directed by Sam Mendes, 2000), a sixteen-year-old girl comes on to her neighbor's husband, though he stops when he learns she is a virgin. In *Hounddog* (Deborah Kampmeier, 2007) a girl of eleven dances seductively, although with apparent innocence, before various men at various times in the film. (She is eventually raped.) There was also a French film, *Léon: The Professional* (Luc Besson, 1994), that made the American indie circuits, in which a girl of twelve attempts to seduce an older man who has been serving as her mentor. And finally, there was a documentary, *Roman Polanski: Wanted and Desired* (Marina Zenovich, 2008), about Polanski's notorious escapade of what he claimed to be consensual sex with a thirteen-year-old girl.

The issues with these seductive-girl films are somewhat different from those in the pedophile films, and I will not attempt to discuss/interpret them within the confines of this chapter. I only want to point out again the apparently inescapable connection between absent parents and problematically sexualized children, in this case young girls who are represented as coming on to older men. In every one of the films just described, there is a significantly absent parent. In *12 and Holding* the therapist mother is divorced; in *Half Nelson* the girl's father is gone and the mother has to work long hours at her job; in *Election* the girl is said to have grown up without a father; in *Towelhead* the parents are divorced, and the mother, learning that her boyfriend had helped her daughter shave her pubic hair, sends the girl off to live with her father; in *Hounddog* and *Léon: The Professional*, the mother of the girl has died; and finally, in the Roman Polanski case, the girl was said to have been sent to Polanski by her divorced mother.[6]

In sum, these films set up a structure in which a child is left vulnerable to the predations of a pedophile because one or both parents failed to protect the child. At one level, issues of dead, missing, or inadequate parents are long-standing themes of American, if not global, folklore (*Cinderella*, *Bambi*, etc.). At another level they are quintessential themes of the 1990s (and beyond): the destabilization of gender roles and of the family. As anthropologist Jean Comaroff, also writing about the epidemic of pedophile scares at that time, put it, "The category of 'abuse'—of violating juvenile flesh—is expansive and imprecise. It collapses, into one carnal sign, diverse sources of angst about an endangered mode of domestic reproduction; about the breakdown of the nuclear family and the commercialization of bodies, procreation, and child-care; about sharp shifts in a gendered division of labor" (1997: 15). We turn then to this issue.

The Family from Gen X's Point of View

Family breakdown is a major theme, almost an obsession, in the literature on, as well as by, Generation X. Many Gen Xers, and in particular many of those who write books reporting from the trenches of their generation, clearly believe that Generation X has collectively gotten a very raw deal from its parents. Geoffrey T. Holtz, for example, pulls together a lot of data to argue that the parents of Generation X, strongly supported by the wider culture, were collectively "anti-child," and indeed that was part of why the birthrate went into decline in the first place. He spends a lot of time on the rise in the divorce rate and in the number of children being raised by single parents. He then draws heavily on a range of negative scholarship to catalogue the many ways in which children of divorced parents and children raised by single mothers show a range of very negative effects, from poorer grades to higher rates of poverty to higher suicide rates (Holtz 1995; see also Howe and Strauss 1993).

A high proportion of independent films are set in the contemporary family.[7] And a high proportion of those—even before we get to the pedophile films—tend to portray families that are deeply dysfunctional, often in multiple ways. A few examples would include *The Ice Storm* (Ang Lee, 1997), *Rachel Getting Married* (Jonathan Demme, 2008), *Margot at the*

Wedding (Noah Baumbach, 2007), *Relative Evil* (Tanya Wexler, 2004), and *The Royal Tenenbaums* (Wes Anderson, 2001). As Todd Solondz, director of *Happiness,* said, "We are the nation that suffers isolation and alienation more than any other. . . . Much of this is because of our fractured families. . . . We talk about family values because the family isn't there" (in Feinstein 1999). Or as independent producer Lydia Dean Pilcher said, "The whole idea of the nuclear family is being blown apart" (interview, March 29, 2006).

In many of these films children are put at risk, and in some of them children die. Stoltz's point that the parents of Generation X were anti-child sometimes seems literally portrayed in the films, singly and collectively. At the 2007 Sundance Film Festival, I saw *Hounddog,* noted above, in which an eleven-year-old girl was raped; I intentionally did not see *An American Crime,* in which a teenager is held captive in a basement and tortured to death "by a surrogate mother and some unbridled kids" (McCarthy 2007: 6). As journalist Todd McCarthy, reporting from the festival, wrote, "Children get a very rough ride in pictures on view in this year's festival" (McCarthy 2007: 1).[8]

Clearly what is being represented in these films, as well as in other literature written from a Gen X point of view, is a widespread sense of family "breakdown." For whatever reason—death, divorce, desertion, or simply emotional absence—parents are seen as "failing to protect," and children are represented as being in danger of molestation or even death.

The question of the state of the contemporary family is very heavily contested. On the one hand, there is a clear set of new, real conditions. Family historian Stephanie Coontz summarized them as follows:

> The rate of divorce tripled between 1960 and 1982, then leveled off to a point where 50 percent of first marriages, and 60 percent of second ones, are likely to end in divorce within forty years. Between 1960 and 1986, the proportion of teenage mothers who were unmarried rose from 15 percent to 61 percent, while the total number of children growing up with only one parent doubled, to a full quarter of all children under age eighteen" (1992: 3).

The question is, what do these numbers mean for individuals, for "society," and especially for children? There have been studies purporting to show that children of divorce and/or children raised by single parents have often been very damaged by their experience. Even Coontz, whose mission as a family historian is to show that families have always been quite messy, says that "some of the most disturbing [contemporary] problems are those involving youth" (1992: 2). But the notion that children have been damaged has also been heavily ideologized. It has become the center of a right-wing campaign for "family values," for the restoration of some form of the traditional patriarchal family that, many would argue, caused its own forms of quite extensive damage for women, children, and even many men (see especially Stacey 1996).

I have no expertise in family sociology or child welfare and will not attempt to say anything definitive as to whether children are damaged or not, or if so, in what ways, and which children. To the extent that the statistics are correct, I find them quite disturbing. At the same time, I am also very aware of the ideological issues just noted and feel cautious about accepting the statistics. Yet even if the idea of "damage" is being greatly overstated, it is hard to imagine that such extensive changes in intimate life would not have had some kind of significant impact on the experience, the emotional lives, or at the very least the imaginations of children growing up under such turbulent conditions. Whether any given Gen X filmmaker experienced parental divorce or other forms of destabilization of family life while growing up is not the issue; the idea of radical family instability became in that era simply part of the zeitgeist.

But there are a number of reasons why Generation X might have felt these changes particularly strongly. It may be noted first that the period of particularly rapid change, as seen in Coontz's numbers, was precisely the period in which the originally designated Gen X was growing up—from the 1960s into the 1980s. Second, I call attention to class issues in the numbers. I have already indicated that "Generation X" is really about the middle class, a class that had just been through two decades of family stability and economic security. Single and/or divorced and/or working mothers were much more common in poor families; what was new and dramatic for that era was that these patterns were moving into the middle class. And third, we must tie all this back to the issues of neoliberalism that are central to this book. Most children of divorced parents stay with their mothers, and most of those mothers experience economic downward mobility; this is simply a legacy of patriarchy that has not gone away. But the 1970s saw the beginning of the "long downturn" in the neoliberalized economy, amplifying the effects of changes in family finances and family fortunes. The rising insecurity in the family and the rising insecurity in the economy moved into a positive feedback loop, in which each factor makes the other factor worse.

All in all, it seems reasonable then to argue that Generation X was particularly hard hit by the changes in question, and this is at least part of what we are seeing in all those dark and disturbing films about vulnerable children and dysfunctional families. This suggests that we should look at these films at least in part from the child's point of view, which is very different from the "moral panic" point of view. We must consider the possibility that, from the child's point of view, the pedophile occupies the space of the missing parents. One way in which he occupies this space is as a predatory monster who has been let loose by the parents' failure to protect. But another way in which he occupies this place, at least in some of the films, is as a somewhat positive substitute for the missing parents. Looked at in this way, we begin to understand that what appears as "moral ambiguity" may have, at least in some contexts, another kind of logic.

A certain psychological argument would have it that children in dysfunctional families and/or families with absent parents are starved for love and attention from parents, and more generally starved for a sense of family as a supportive group of people on whom one can rely. This argument has been made about the television programming created for Generation X, including centrally sitcoms that portray nonstandard but nonetheless happy "families" ("My Two Dads," "Two and A Half Men," "Party of Five") and sitcoms based on "friends as family" ("Friends," "Melrose Place") (Owen 1997: 11–12). The same general arguments have been made about Gen X films like *Reality Bites*, discussed earlier, or *Boogie Nights* (Paul Thomas Anderson, 1997); Peter Hanson devotes a whole chapter to "the essential Gen-X concept of the importance of surrogate families" (2002: 53). Similarly, film critic Jesse Fox Mayshark looks at a group of well-known Gen X independent filmmakers (Richard Linklater, Todd Haynes, Paul Thomas Anderson, and others) against a backdrop of (among other things) the unraveling of the nuclear family and reads their films in terms of a "search for meaning" and especially a "yearning for connection" (2007: 8 and passim).

Some version of these arguments can reasonably be applied toward understanding the moral ambiguity operating in some of the pedophile films. There is a sense in several of these films in which the boy's need for his father's love overrides the father's (or "father's") acts as a pedophile vis-à-vis other children. In *Capturing the Friedmans*, the son David clearly loves his father. Most of the time he completely denies all the charges against his father, but at one point, in the middle of a speech about how great a father Arnie had been, he asks in anguish, "So what if he slipped?" suggesting that he is aware of his father's weakness but values his love above that. In *Happiness*, when the son Billy learns that his father had been sexually molesting Billy's friends, Billy's primary (though not only) concern is to establish the solidity of his own relationship with his father. And finally, in *L.I.E.*, although Howie knows that Big John is a pedophile, he understands that Big John cares about him. He thus does not condemn Big John and in fact comes to tease him affectionately about his predilections.

In all of those films, the father(-figure) does not molest his own son, but in other cases he does and he is still forgiven. I saw an episode of the television series *Law and Order* ("Captive," May 4, 2007) that was clearly adapted from the film *L.I.E.* but made certain changes that bring out this point. The Howie character is found dead at the beginning. The Big John character is played as a likable figure, and he says believably that he loved the dead boy. As in the movie, "Big John" is living with another boy. For a while "Big John" is a suspect, but eventually the case is solved with the other boy having killed "Howie" out of jealousy. We learn at the end that the killer boy's father was not his real father but a stepfather, and moreover that he beat the boy. The message seemed to be that people's families are so messed up that even a pedophile, if he is a loving "father," is preferable.

And finally let us look at a scene from the movie *Doubt*. In *Doubt* a nun (Sister Aloysius, played by Meryl Streep) who is the headmistress of a Catholic school comes to believe that one of the priests (Father Flynn, played by Philip Seymour Hoffman) might be abusing one of the boy students. The boy, Donald Miller, is the only black student in the school. Although Sister Aloysius is unable to get any corroboration for her suspicions, she goes to the boy's mother (Viola Davis) and tells her that she believes that Father Flynn is molesting her son. But to her shock, Mrs. Miller refuses to be disturbed about this:

SA: I am concerned about the relationship between Father Flynn and your son.
MM: . . . What do you mean concerned?

SA: That it may not be right.

MM: Well, there's something wrong with everybody, and even that soul got to be forgiven . . .

SA: I am *concerned,* to be frank, that Father Flynn may have made advances on your son.

MM: May have made?

SA: I can't be certain. . . .

MM: Then maybe there's nothing to it. (scene 12)

Sister Aloysius and Mrs. Miller continue to parry back and forth. Mrs. Miller gradually reveals that she thinks Donald is homosexual, and that his father beats him, probably for that reason. It becomes clear that she sees Father Flynn's interest in Donald, whatever the nature of it might be (and again we never know), as being in the boy's best interest:

> My boy came to your school cause they were gonna kill him in a public school. His father don't like him. He comes to your school, kids don't like him. One man is good to him—this priest—and does the man have his reasons? Yes. Everybody does. You have your reasons. But do I ask the man why he's good to my son? No. I don't care why. My son needs some man to care about him, and to see him through the way he wants to go. And thank god this educated man, with some kindness in him, wants to do just that.

Both the TV program and the film thus set up a structure in which the real father is bad and the abuser is, if not "good," at least not bad, or at least offers the love and protections the boy could not get from his real father. In this context, then, what seemed like moral ambiguity vis-à-vis the pedophile turns out to have a fairly clear emotional logic, in relation to the problems of the father in (or not in) the contemporary family.

Of course, any good Freudian would tell us that fathers are always problematic, and that the father-son relationship is always highly fraught. But for the generation growing up in the middle class in the second half of the twentieth century, "the family" was an increasingly confusing and difficult place, putting unprecedented, and often contradictory, psychological demands on children. In this interpretation, the figure of the pedophile, both feared and, in a very confused way, desired, condenses into one symbolic form this complex state of affairs.

But this is a very partial interpretation. I said earlier that the moral ambiguity that we see in the pedophile films is only one example of a more widespread moral relativism seen in many other contexts. Here then I want to leave both the pedophile (although we shall hear from him again) and the family to consider this more general phenomenon, and specifically to explore the ways in which it articulates with the advance of neoliberal capitalism.

The Discourse of "the Gray Areas"

I begin with a panel discussion I heard among a group of documentary filmmakers in a public arena. The panel was very interesting, in part because so much of the discussion was taken up with ethical issues: how documentary filmmakers feel about using reenactments in the absence of footage from the events in question; how documentarians feel about paying money to subjects who appear in their films; and finally, how they feel about making films about morally problematic individuals like murderers or pedophiles.[9]

> **Moderator Lisa Leeman (*Out of Faith*, 2006) [to the panel]:** Let's talk about making films about problematic people, who have done difficult things to live with.
> **Stacy Peralta (*Crips and Bloods: Made in America*, 2008):** I do it just to find out what drove them.
> **Moderator Leeman:** There's a fine line between honoring their humanity and [I didn't get this exactly, but something like "endorsing their acts."] Is it our job to cast judgment?
> **Jessica Yu (*Protagonist*, 2007):** [No.] You have to leave the door open for the audience.
> **Joan Churchill (*Aileen: Life and Death of a Serial Killer*, 2003):** [No.] Nothing is black and white. There is a humanity here.
> **Marina Zenovich (*Roman Polanski: Wanted and Desired*, 2008):** [No.] It's not for me to judge. I'm interested in exploring the journey. (Field notes, March 27, 2008)

This discussion is interesting for a number of reasons. It is interesting that the moderator kept pressing the moral issues around making these kinds of films, and even more interesting that the panelists kept setting them aside: virtually every panelist took some version of the position that "it's not for me to judge." But the nonjudging is justified in a variety of ways. Both Stacey Peralta and Marina Zenovich said they are not interested in judging because they are just trying to understand, and communicate to audiences, what makes these problematic individuals tick. They are saying in effect that it is an ethnographic problem, a problem of knowledge, rather than a problem of ethics. (This is not unlike the position I am taking in this chapter about the nonjudgmental filmmakers themselves.) Jessica Yu says, "You have to leave the door open for the audience," an instance of a discourse we will hear more of in chapter 8 with respect to filmmakers not taking sides on political issues. The idea here is that it is an insult to audiences to tell them what to think; the filmmaker presents the facts and allows the audience to draw their own conclusions. Finally, Joan Churchill takes the position of realism: "Nothing is black and white," life is ambiguous, good people ("there is a humanity here") do bad things, and it is the filmmaker's job—at least the independent filmmaker's job—to record this truth. The world is messy; we will not paper it over (like Hollywood) but will tell it like it is.

Although all three of these versions of "it is not for us to judge" can be heard throughout the independent film world, I want to concentrate here on the statement that "nothing is black and white." We may call this the discourse of "gray areas," and we have already heard two examples of this. We heard Andrew Jarecki invoke the "gray areas" when explaining why he refuses to pass judgment on whether Arnie Friedman might be guilty or not. Even if Friedman is guilty, Jarecki seems to be asking for some compassion and understanding from the viewer: "There are so many gray areas, when a good person does bad things." We also heard Michael Cuesta invoke the "gray areas" with respect to Big John: "It's important for me to explore the gray areas of every character. . . . To take one of the darkest figures in modern society, to show him as a human being, a three-dimensional character, creates great drama, great contradiction." His point here seems to be similar to Jarecki's, in trying to get the viewer to see Big John with some humanity; he also stresses (since this is a fictional feature film) the dramatic intent behind this choice, the intent to shake up viewers' standard moral assumptions.

I give two more examples of this discourse of the gray areas here. As I was working on an early draft of this chapter, I saw an interview in *Film-*

maker magazine with Hilary Brougher, who wrote and directed the film *Stephanie Daley* (2007), about a high school girl who gives birth to a baby in a bathroom stall. What happens next is not entirely clear, but Stephanie either waits until the baby dies or suffocates it (later she says "I killed her with my mind") before rejoining her friends. In discussing the scene, Brougher first notes that "the forensic evidence is often ambiguous" in these cases, as to whether the child was stillborn or was smothered (in Van Couvering 2007: 35). She then goes on to talk about how the young Stephanie character is relatively passive and not practiced in making decisions like this, saying, "I'm not trying to judge passivity but I am interested in the mechanisms and the repercussions of it. I'm not interested in making big moral statements about what's right and wrong; I'm interested in the gray areas" (2007: 36). Further on she points out that young girls in Stephanie's situation often give birth like this, alone in some isolated place, "in kind of altered states for a while and in intense pain" (2007: 37). She continues, "So do these girls even know what happened? Our judicial system isn't really set up for that. We're set up for black and white; we're not set up to deal with the gray" (2007: 37).

As with the directors in the other two examples, Brougher is calling for a more sympathetic understanding of a person who has apparently committed a crime even more heinous than pedophilia: baby killing. But she is also making a point about the difficulty of anyone—the coroner, Stephanie herself—knowing what actually happened, and thus the difficulty of judging. (Nonetheless, the film does not go all the way with relativism. In the end Stephanie takes a plea and says she will serve a sentence of five years with the possibility of parole in six months.)

As a final example, let's look at *The Dead Girl* (Karen Moncrieff, 2006), which I will talk about at greater length in chapter 6. *The Dead Girl* is about a girl named Krista who gets murdered by a serial killer and about the repercussions of that event for people who are connected to it in different ways. The film is in segments, and one segment concerns a middle-aged couple, Ruth and Carl. It gradually becomes clear to Ruth and the viewers that Carl is in fact the serial killer who has been in the news and who killed Krista. Ruth starts to take the evidence, mostly clothing of the victims, to the police but then decides not to. When she burns the evidence, she also strips off her own clothes and throws them in the fire, as if they were polluted by the crimes and the blood. What is she thinking? The filmmaker talks about this at length in an interview:

> I think it's a really terrible choice. . . . In creating the character I . . . worked backward from a detail that I read about a woman who made a similar choice and dumped evidence in a landfill from her husband who was a serial killer. In writing this I thought to myself, "Who is this person? Who must you be that that choice seems like a viable one?" To most of us, it's probably horrifying. Her life and how it's constructed requires that she make that choice. In a certain way, she doesn't have lots and lots of options. (The NYC Movie Guru 2006; nycmovieguru .com/karen&mary.html)

It then emerges that there was another scene, after the scene in which Ruth destroyed the evidence, that got cut: "After the end of [Ruth's] vignette, there was another little section which is no longer in [the film]. To me," says Moncrieff, "it's still not over. Even when it's over, it's still not over. She will continue to struggle with this decision into the future and I think it's entirely possible that, as time goes on, she might [here she is interrupted]" (ibid.). Moncrieff does not use the language of gray areas, but we are clearly in the same moral territory.

I find this discussion—a dialogue between Moncrieff and the interviewer, but also between Moncrieff and herself, and even between the fictional Ruth and herself—about whether to judge and how to judge some horrible and heinous criminal absolutely fascinating. What is so interesting is the way in which Moncrieff goes in and out of the relativistic mindset. At one level she has a clear sense of what I take to be the normal reaction to serial killers ("To most of us, it's probably horrifying"). At the same time, she is deeply challenged to understand how a real woman somewhere else made the other choice: "Who must you be that that choice seems like a viable one?" And although she wrote the script one way this time, she says (merging herself and her character), "To me it's still not over. Even when it's over it's still not over. [Ruth] will continue to struggle with this decision into the future and I think it's entirely possible that, as time goes on, she might. . . ." It is even appropriate that Moncrieff was cut off and could not finish the sentence.

The discourse of "gray areas" is, as I said, a discourse of realism. The filmmakers who use this language are asserting, one way or another, that this is reality. Life does not fall into clear categories of good and evil, but rather is full of murky moral situations that one has to learn to deal with however one can.

Moral Ambiguity in the Neoliberal World

Moral ambiguity as an issue recurs in the literature on/by Generation X.[10] The characterization has been both applied to the generation and embraced by some who have put themselves forth as its spokespersons. Douglas Rushkoff, editor of *The Gen X Reader* (1994), refers to what he calls the "post-moral understanding" of Generation X, and Peter Hanson, in *The Cinema of Generation X*, refers to Generation X's "telling aversion to moral absolutes" (2002: 2). Yet these are fragmentary comments, and I have not seen any extended and/or coherent discussion of the subject in the literature. Thus, I will pursue the examination of moral ambiguity in the films not directly through the lens of Generation X but rather through a more general consideration of the relationship between the films and certain aspects of neoliberalism. Gen X remains as a subtext, and I will return to it at the end of the chapter.

Moral ambiguity in the public culture extends well beyond independent film. Everywhere one turns, one finds characters with major moral deficits whom we are invited to like. In the Hollywood film *Mr. Brooks* (Bruce A. Evans, 2007), for example, Kevin Costner plays Earl Brooks, a handsome and charming man with a lovely family and a thriving business who is also a serial killer. We are especially invited to sympathize with him when we learn that he is attending Alcoholics Anonymous and is trying in this and other ways to master his urge to kill. The TV series *Dexter* is more complicated. Dexter is also a serial killer, but his compulsion to kill has been channeled into killing people who are themselves killers, and thus given moral justification. He is also portrayed as lacking any normal feelings and thus as having to perform being a friendly and genial person. But he does this very successfully, and over the course of the series he is increasingly humanized. Again then the viewer is drawn into liking the character and is even offered a dubious moral justification for his actions.

And then, of course, there is Tony Soprano, surely the most successful morally ambiguous hero of them all. Tony is a thug and a killer; we see him beat, kick, strangle, suffocate, and otherwise harm and kill with his bare hands a very large number of people over the course of the many episodes of the series. But Tony is also extremely charming and psychologically vulnerable, and he is a (mostly) good husband to his wife Carmela and a loving father to his kids. Michael Cuesta's earlier comments about Big John apply almost perfectly to Tony: to show this violent thug "as a human being, a three-dimensional character, creates great drama, great contradiction." Not only was *The Sopranos* hugely successful in attracting viewers over the course of its six seasons; it garnered numerous awards and was praised as, among other things, "the best-written dramatic series in the history of television" (Biskind 2007: 9) and "the richest achievement in the history of television" (Remnick 2007: 29).

The dramatic and/or philosophical endorsement of moral ambiguity does not go entirely unopposed or uncontested. We may recall first that three of the so-called pedophile films took a clear moral stance against pedophilia and those who would condone it. It is also worth noting that the television series *Law and Order: Special Victims Unit*, which focuses on "especially heinous" sexual offenses like child molestation, is never morally ambiguous, and the perpetrators are always caught and punished in the end. *Law and Order: svu* has certainly not received the critical acclaim that *The Sopranos* garnered, but it has, on the other hand, run a great deal longer than *The Sopranos* did.

Even within the programs or films in which the dominant tone is morally ambiguous, characters will occasionally give voice to the more clearcut moral position. Take, for example, a film called *The Reader* (Stephen Daldry, 2008). This is a film about a woman who had been a guard in a German concentration camp in World War II. Eventually she is caught and is brought to trial with the other women involved. A law professor takes his students to observe the trial, and one of the students asks in some disgust why they are wasting their time doing this. Another student says, "We are trying to understand." The first student says, "Six women locked 300 Jews in a church and let them *burn*—what is there to understand? . . . Tell me! I'm asking! What *is* there to understand?" (chap. 1).

For another example of a character asserting clear moral condemnation, consider a conversation in season 1, episode 8 of *The Sopranos*, between Dr. Jennifer Melfi, Tony Soprano's therapist, and her ex-husband. Dr. Melfi is being suitably (given her role) nonjudgmental about Tony, and at some point her exasperated ex-husband explodes, "You call him a patient—the man's a criminal, Jennifer. And after a while, finally you're going to get psychotherapy with its cheesy moral relativism. Finally you're going to get good and evil. And he's evil." Yet it must be acknowledged in this case that these lines were voiced by a marginal character with an almost invisible role in the series as a whole. Tony Soprano dominated the series, and the series dominated so-called quality television for six years. It is clear that moral relativism has come to play an accepted, and perhaps admired, role in a media world once dominated by the more clear-cut good/bad, black/white binaries of classic Hollywood morality.

In order to understand this striking phenomenon, I propose that we return first to the discourse of gray areas. I said above that the discourse of gray areas is meant to be a discourse of realism. Here then one must ask again, what is the reality being represented?

Sticking for a moment with stories of pedophiles, filmic or otherwise, some authors have argued that these are allegories of real harms done to (mostly poor) children through what we would now recognize as effects of the neoliberal agenda: the drastic cutbacks of funding and other support for federal and state programs that would help them. For example, cultural studies scholar Henry A. Giroux argued in the 1990s that

> the central threat to childhood innocence lies not in the figure of the pedophile or sexual predator but can be found in the diminishing pub-lic spheres available for children. . . . Far from benefiting children, many of the programs and government reforms proposed by Clinton and enacted by the Republican-led congress represent what Senator Ed-ward Kennedy has called "legislative child abuse" (1998: 266–67; see also Scheper-Hughes and Stein 1998).

Following but broadening this point, I want to suggest that the fuzzy morality of so much of American public culture, including significant areas of independent film, mirrors the fuzzy morality (or worse) of neoliberal capitalism. I postpone until the end of the chapter the question of whether this mirroring constitutes a kind of buying into the new cultural order, or a critique of it, or both.

Capitalism in its basic form is a fundamentally amoral system, in which the only goal is making a profit. Throughout most of the twentieth cen-tury, this amorality was counterbalanced by regulations that restrained corporations and banks from doing almost anything they could get away with to make greater and greater profits. As discussed earlier, starting in the 1970s, in line with neoliberal theory, most of those regulations have been systematically removed. Moreover, the removal of regulations that restrained profit making within certain ethical and legal frameworks was accompanied by a discourse that celebrated the pursuit of profit without any concern for human impact whatsoever. Indeed, such concerns were despised as weak and sentimental. Instead, we came to have a fundamentally post-moral market, caricatured (but not by much) in the movie *Wall Street* (Oliver Stone, 1987) and portrayed in chilling detail in the documentary *Enron: The Smartest Guys in the Room* (Alex Gibney, 2005). In both cases we are introduced to persons/characters for whom all ethical constraints on business behavior have been abandoned, and for whom, as Gordon Gecko says in *Wall Street,* "greed is good."

Within the neoliberal economy, in turn, one may say that moral ambiguity, if not outright immorality and illegality, rules, at both the level of the workplace and the level of the actual business of the corporations. Looking first at the workplace, sociologist Richard Sennett (1998) writes of the ways in which success in the contemporary corporation has less to do with the actual performance of the job and more to do with the performance of the self. Managers practice the skills of "deep acting" and learn to maintain the "masks of cooperativeness" (1998: 112). The same point is made by anthropologist Elizabeth Traube in an interpretation of the Hollywood film *Ferris Bueller's Day Off* (John Hughes, 1986). Ferris is a cheerfully amoral high school student who sets out to play hooky from school, to recruit his friends into the endeavor, and to completely fool and/or thwart the adults who might stand in his way. Traube describes Ferris as "a creature composed entirely of surfaces, the product of the multiple masks he assumes" (1992b: 76). Like Sennett, she links this to conditions of work in the new economy, which requires "a self who resides in the shifting surface of a carefully staged personality" (1992b: 74).

The question of (im)morality in the workplace was also central to both *Fight Club* and *Office Space*, discussed earlier. In *Fight Club*, Tyler Durden's rage against work in the new economy becomes so extreme and destructive he has to be killed. As for Peter in *Office Space*, his proposal of a scheme to defraud the company sets off a torrent of condemnation, including not only his friends initially refusing to participate and his girlfriend telling him that his plan is nothing but theft, but a rather puzzling dream sequence in which a judge appears and tells him several times that what he is doing is wrong. This excess of condemnation actually makes more sense when one recognizes that the issue is not merely the bad social relations of work (the picky boss, etc.), but the very (im)morality of the new regime of work itself, "where they fire you for no reason."

But the moral ambiguity of the workplace is as nothing compared to the actual practice of business in the neoliberal economy. As anyone who reads the papers, not to mention the academic literature on neoliberalism, knows, corporations get away with grand theft all the time (see especially Martin and Shohat 2003). They defraud clients, cheat competitors, don't pay taxes, and reward themselves handsomely for doing these things. All of this has been well documented in films like *Enron: The Smartest Guys in the Room* (Alex Gibney, 2005), *Walmart: The High Cost of Low Prices* (Robert Greenwald, 2005), and *Inside Job* (Charles Ferguson, 2010). Indeed, when it comes to health- and energy-related businesses, they could even be said to get away with murder, as seen once again in the daily papers, as well as in recent films like *Capitalism: A Love Story* (Michael Moore, 2009), *Gas-Land* (Josh Fox, 2010), and *Mann v. Ford* (Maro Chermayeff and Micha Fink, 2011).

In short, the world of neoliberal business is a world in which amorality, immorality, and often illegality have come to seem "normal." The workplace is a dog-eat-dog world where everyone wears a mask of geniality and stabs the next person in the back at the earliest opportunity. The world of business deals is a world in which literally almost anything goes, as long as the company doesn't get caught, or even when it does. Turning back to the public culture, it is hard not to read the moral ambiguity in representations of serial killers, mobster thugs, and pedophiles as a kind of spreading infestation of the moral disintegration we see in the neoliberal economy. And yet that makes no sense when one thinks of the real people one knows who write TV shows and make independent films.

I can only conclude as follows: These filmmakers and TV producers are obviously not endorsing pedophilia and murder, nor are they embracing the dehumanized post-morality of the neoliberal economy. What they do seem to be saying is that the world is a very morally messed up and confusing place, and that we cannot go back to the white hats and black hats of the Hollywood melodrama. We need to be shaken up and disturbed by this state of affairs. It is relevant to recall here the statement by Todd Solondz, who made the film *Happiness*, about an apparently decent middle-class husband and father who was drugging and sodomizing his son's friends. Needless to say, the film created quite a flap when it came out. Solondz was accused of being a childish bad boy making an extreme film just to get attention. But Solondz's reply was about the moral mess of the real world: "I think that certainly there's nothing in . . . anything I've done really that I think is as troubling as what one sees in real life. . . . You can't get more obscene or grotesque than what life has to offer" (in Frank and Bond 2005: 3). In the best interpretation, Solondz and others who make these challenging films that make us uncomfortable are trying to get us to think about that.

In the next chapter I return to my ongoing ethnographic account of the world of independent filmmaking, specifically to look at producers. Because many independent films are "difficult" in the ways discussed in the last two film chapters—dark, pessimistic, morally complex—the independent producer's job is especially challenging. I focus on both the practical aspects of the producer's job and the more intangible process of producing "value" for films whose value is not always self-evident.

CHAPTER 5

Making Value

Films are of course made by many people. Since at least the 1960s the standard view has been that the most important figure in making a film is the director. This view continues in the independent film world, where directors usually write their own material (or writers direct their own films); the writer-director is specifically called the filmmaker. Almost as important, but much less visible, are the producers, the individuals whose job it is to create and sustain the conditions for a filmmaker to make a film. Some observers have noted the critical role of independent producers in the emergence of the indie movement: for example, film critic Emanuel Levy noted, "Young filmmakers know that a fearless producer can make all the difference, particularly in the early phases of their career. Along with 'hot' directors, a new breed, the gutsy indie producer, emerged" (1999: 19).

What do indie producers do?[1] Their creative contributions must be noted first, as outsiders are often unaware of this aspect of the producer's role. Thus it is the job of the independent producer to find the most interesting and creative filmmakers, with the most interesting stories to tell, and help them make the best film they can. (A less common model is finding a book or script first and then finding the best director to make the film.) The language here is often that of helping the filmmaker realize his or her "vision." As producer Joana Vicente said about herself and her business partner (and husband) Jason Kliot, "We are creative producers, we are very communicative people, we want to help the directors to really fulfill their vision and achieve what they set out to do" (interview, March 29, 2006). Ted Hope talked about his decision in film school to become a producer in similar terms: "It became clear to me that at least at that time everybody at film school [wanted to be] either a director or a cinematographer, but I really understood that people needed somebody to help them facilitate their vision" (interview, March 15, 2006).

In practice, this is an enormously complex, multidimensional job. Christine Vachon works primarily with filmmakers who come to her with their own scripts-in-progress: "When I'm asked what producers do, I say, 'What *don't* they do? I develop scripts [working with the filmmaker]; I raise money; I put together budgets; I match directors with cinematographers, cinematographers with production designers, production designers with location managers; I make sure the shoot is on schedule, on budget, on track; I hold hands; I stroke egos'" (Vachon 1998: 2).

James Schamus started out as an independent producer and moved on to become CEO of Focus Features, a specialty division of Universal Studios. In many of his comments, and not surprisingly given his position, Schamus tends to blur the distinction between indies and studios, and his comments here apply equally to studio and independent producers:

> Great producers are people who spawn ideas, work with writers and develop material; they put talent together, bring in the director, bring in the appropriate cast and then they also hire and organize the film shoot. They are the people who are primarily responsible for the creative package as well as going out and raising the money or dealing with the studio and overseeing the film "from soup to nuts" meaning from the original idea, all the way through at least consulting with the studio on marketing and distribution plans. (Schamus 2006: 2)[2]

Finally, actor Joseph Gordon-Levitt and filmmaker Gregg Araki made similar comments talking about Mary Jane Skalski, producer of *Mysterious Skin*:

> **JG-L:** I've been doing this for a really long time now, I started acting when I was six, and I never really knew what a producer did. . . . It's like they come around and schmooze and eat. . . . Mary Jane was the first time where I started to understand, "Oh, I get how we couldn't be doing this without her."

GA: They basically do everything. (from the "director's commentary" on the bonus track of the DVD)

The centrality and high value of the producer in the world of independent film are publicly recognized at the Independent Spirit Awards, the annual award ceremony of the indie world. In the Academy Awards, the Oscar for Best Picture is awarded to the producer(s), but there is no more general award for a producer's achievements. The Spirit Awards, on the other hand, have a specific Producer's Award, which is awarded not for any particular film but for a distinguished body of work an independent producer has produced.[3] "The award recognizes an individual who demonstrates the exceptional creativity, tenacity, and vision required to produce quality independent films, despite highly limited resources" (IMDb.com 2010).

This is not to say that independent producers always feel appreciated by the filmmakers with whom they are working. On the contrary, one producer wrote to me about the "truly undervalued, overlooked, misunderstood (because of financing and credit confusions), even disrespected position of producers in film, whether indie or Hollywood" (e-mail message, December 27, 2010).[4] The job, as we shall see, is difficult, and the producer is often the easiest person to blame for difficulties and failures. Nonetheless, as the Independent Spirit Producer's Award indicates, and as most observers agree, a strong and supportive producer is one of the absolutely indispensable conditions for a successful, or even simply a completed, independent film.

In this chapter I want to look at how independent producers produce not only the films but also the value of the films. I will begin by showing that the young men and women who became independent producers in the 1980s and 1990s and beyond display a distinctive sociological profile, and I will link that profile to certain social and economic conditions that prevailed in that period. I will then go on to ask about the production of value in both the Bourdieusian sense—let us call it "symbolic value"—and in a more substantive sense.

The Sociology of Producers and the Neoliberal Economy of the 1990s

The independent producers who are part of this project are mostly within the age range of the filmmakers, Generation X, born between the early

1960s and the early 1980s. Some are a bit older, and most fall at the early end of the Gen X range, but on the whole there is not a major age/generation gap between the producers and the filmmakers. This is relevant in the sense that the producers and the filmmakers would share the worldview and the general aesthetic behind the independent films they make together. Beyond this, however, there are some interesting differences.

First, gender: As we will see in the next chapter, women form a relatively small percent of directors and filmmakers. But it is a striking fact that women constitute almost half of the ranks of producers. In 1974, the Producers Guild of America (PGA) recorded that 8 out of 3,068 members were female, or 0.3 percent (Abramowitz 2000: 65). According to Vance Van Petten, executive director of the PGA, currently about 45 percent of its members are women (interview, December 13, 2007).[5]

Next, class: It is an equally striking fact that independent producers tend to come from relatively high capital backgrounds and collectively are clearly part of the Professional Managerial Class or PMC. Many come from upper-middle-class families with significant amounts of money. Even if they are not all members of the PMC by virtue of money, they are almost uniformly so by virtue of higher education. I note first that all of them at least completed an undergraduate degree. This might seem unremarkable except that it is not always true of the filmmakers whose work they produce. Further, most of these individuals went to private colleges and universities, and many of them went to very prestigious colleges (Tufts, Amherst, Antioch, Wesleyan, Brown, Smith) and universities (Columbia, UC Berkeley, University of Chicago, Stanford). Beyond the bachelor's level, more than half of them have advanced degrees.

The high proportion of independent producers with elite educational backgrounds stands out against a significant number of independent filmmakers with little or no higher education at all. Examples include such well-known figures as Quentin Tarantino (who never finished high school), Steven Soderbergh, Kevin Smith, Spike Jonze, David Fincher, Paul Thomas Anderson, and Richard Linklater. This is not to say that all filmmakers should be seen as in some sense "low capital" compared to producers; on the contrary, the profile of filmmakers is extraordinarily diverse in class terms, covering a wide range of economic and educational backgrounds, and complicated further in some cases by artistic parents fostering a creative habitus even in the absence of money and/or education. But the fact that one can list seven well-known independent filmmakers with little or no higher education does underscore the fact that 100 percent of independent producers completed at least a BA, that a significant number of those went on to higher degrees, and that a significant proportion of all those degrees are from elite institutions.

Both the gender and the class demographics make sense when situated within the context of the 1990s and beyond. The improvement in the representation of women in the ranks of producers starts from nearly zero in the 1970s, at the time of the ("second wave") women's movement, and grows steadily to the present figure of nearly 50 percent. It is clearly one of the payoffs of the movement.

As for class, in chapter 2 I discussed briefly the contradictory economy of the 1990s, in which the general trend of the economy for most people was downward, but in which some people, in certain booming areas of the economy (mostly in the finance, high technology, and knowledge/information industries), were able to make spectacular amounts of money. The downward trend, for the middle and working classes, had actually begun in the 1970s, but only fully registered starting in the 1990s, when the public culture began telling young people ("Generation X") that they would be the first generation since the Great Depression that would not do better than their parents.

As for the much smaller number of people who did well and moved into the upper tier, I discussed in chapter 3 the very interesting development in which, for a certain sector of the PMC, there was a reconfiguration of the traditional relationship between wealth, politics, and cultural interests. In the traditional configuration, wealth tended to go with conservative politics, and with an interest in "high culture" or else no cultural interests at all. While there was always a more politically and culturally progressive wing of the PMC, it tended to be less wealthy and powerful, what Bourdieu called "the dominated fraction of the dominant class." In the new configuration, on the other hand, there has emerged a certain hybrid fraction that has both significant wealth and progressive political and cultural interests, what David Callahan (2010) called the "new liberal rich."

I discussed this shift with respect to investors in independent film, and I now bring the point to bear on producers. In aggregate producers are not as wealthy as the investors, but most come from situations of clear financial security if not great wealth. More important for thinking about producers in class terms is education. As noted above, a large majority of producers come from elite educational backgrounds. Callahan, among others, has called attention to the close connection between wealth and education in the new economy, which has been called "the knowledge economy": "When the Forbes 400 list was first published in 1982, it was dominated by oil, manufacturing fortunes, and old-money families. . . . By 2008, nearly half of the billionaires on the Forbes list . . . derived their wealth from financial services, technology, and media or entertainment" (2010: 22).

When I have spoken with producers about my "finding," that is, the high-capital profile of contemporary independent producers, I have encountered a certain resistance. Some questioned the finding itself and wondered about a possible skewing of the sample. It is true that the sample is small and I cannot offer any robust statistical claims for representativeness. Yet the high proportion of independent producers with blue-chip educations is striking, not only in comparison with the more mixed profile of filmmakers but also in comparison with past patterns in Hollywood. For example, a biographer of independent producer Walter Wanger, who was active in the industry in the 1930s and 1940s, notes his college degree at a time when "articulate, college-educated producers were unheard of" (Bernstein [1994] 2000: xiii) and goes on to say that "[t]hrough the late 1970s, the prevalent view of the producer . . . was [as] an uncultured philistine" ([1994] 2000: xiv).[6]

Others, however, acknowledged that independent producers may indeed be more likely to come from wealth, in the sense that producing requires a certain cushion of resources to underwrite both financial risk taking and dry periods when there is no money coming in. But when I suggested that the producers' high educational capital (as well as the money) might play a role in their success, I again encountered some resistance. Ursula Jackson,* partner in a production company that makes studio-oriented films, had this to say: "It doesn't matter where you went to college or anything. . . . Here, it is such a crapshoot. The kid who was the dumb one in the mail room is next thing running the department. It is ridiculous. There is such a vagueness as to what the future holds; it allows for the dreamers to dream. It allows for the weird, fluke anomalies to hit" (interview, November 12, 2005).

The idea that one could be catapulted from the mailroom to the head of the department (or from the drugstore ice cream counter to stardom) is a very old and enduring idea in Hollywood. There is probably still some truth to it, because the system is in some ways very free-form and kind of crazy, and canny self-promotion without official credentials can indeed get one quite far in some cases.

But it is precisely my point that times have changed—the 1990s are not the 1950s—perhaps with people not quite noticing, or not noticing its implications. I also had several conversations with independent-oriented producer Ron Yerxa about this. At first he too denied the relevance of the high-class education factor: "Really, producing you don't need anything, there is no license, no college degree, no one respects a college degree necessarily. I mean, once in a while saying that you went to Yale or Harvard counts somewhat, but most of the time it would be more interesting to hark back to the early moguls and say you came up in some seat-of-the-pants kind of a way." But then Yerxa checked himself: "As a producer I might be saying something contradictory because it is certainly a much more Ivy League time than ever before" (interview, April 5, 2006).

Pierre Bourdieu would not have been surprised to find that independent producers tend to come from high-capital backgrounds. Like my informants, he points to the necessity for a financial cushion, especially in the more risky zone of the field of cultural production, such as is occupied by independent film: "The propensity to move towards the economically most risky positions, and above all the capacity to persist in them (a condition for all avant-garde undertakings which precede the demands of the market), even when they secure no short-term economic profit, seem to depend to a large extent on possession of substantial economic and social capital" (1993: 67). Although Bourdieu is writing in this passage about the artists themselves, he makes the same point in an earlier discussion about art gallery owners (1993: 40), whose role in the art world is analogous to the role of independent producers in the film world.

It will be useful before going on to restate what might seem to be the confusing connections between the neoliberal economy, the changing class structure, and the generational shift that I am working with in this book. Neoliberal economic policies starting in the 1970s favored a combination of deregulating American business and finance and cutting back on state-supported public services. The effect has been to create a polarization of the American class structure, with a few people moving up into, in some cases, rather spectacular wealth, and the large majority of the middle and working class either sliding down or hanging on by their fingernails. Generation X was the first generation to feel the effects of this economy. Technically, of course, Generation X refers to everyone born starting in the early 1960s, but in reality it was a class-specific term referring to young people in the now precarious and insecure middle class. Independent filmmakers tend to come from that class/generation location, and I have argued that many of their films speak from and to the anxieties of that time and place in the class structure. Independent producers are on the whole also demographically part of Generation X, but most of them come from the more successful part of that class location, the handful of the (upper) middle class that made it up through what might be thought of as the neoliberal funnel. The breakout of independent film in the 1990s may be seen in part as a product of a productive synergy between these two elements of the newly configured middle class in neoliberal America, more versus less successful, more versus less secure.

The Producer's Habitus

Independent producer Louis Drubner* was kind enough to sit for a long interview over breakfast one day. I was delighted to learn that he had a completely worked-out theory of the "elements" that go into making a good or great independent producer. I will list some of his points briefly here and then return to them in greater detail throughout the chapter. (All quotes are from interview transcript, March 23, 2007.)

Drubner's first major item was "taste," the ability to find the highest-quality material and/or to back the highest-quality filmmakers. Taste matters, he argued, much more in the world of independent film than in the studios, where one's talent as a producer is based first and foremost on one's ability to make financially successful films, rather than films that garner some kind of artistic appreciation and respect.

His second major element is what he called "relationships." By relationships he meant not so much a large network of people one can call on, although that is important too, but specifically the importance of being someone with strong people skills; a good producer needs to be able to talk comfortably to anyone about anything. "It is your ability to go out and be a friendly good person, to be able to have good conversations, to be able to understand creative people and talk about other movies with them and other things they like to talk about."

The final element is, as Drubner put it, the "ability not to take no for an answer, to be one of those people who is really good at convincing people to say yes." But at this point we were running out of time and he did not elaborate further. However, the point was articulated more fully by PGA executive director Van Petten: "Producers are movers and shakers by nature. . . . They are the most idealistic, most entrepreneurial, most independent people you could imagine in our business" (interview, December 13, 2007).

In Drubner's view, having good taste, having a good personality and a knack for "relationships," and having a lot of personal drive/forcefulness/perseverance (what social scientists often call "agency") are the core elements one needs to be an effective and successful independent producer.[7] I want next to suggest that all of these are closely tied to the high-capital backgrounds—whether material or educational or both—of independent producers.

TASTE

One cannot overestimate the importance for a producer of being viewed by one's peers as having good taste; it is one of the major forms of cultural capital in the business. Producer Ted Hope has been described as "an unparalleled spotter of new talent" (Mandelberger 2009). And an article in the *Hollywood Reporter* about independent and independent-oriented producers describes Bill Horberg as having "a reputation for impeccable taste" (A. Thompson 2005: 37).[8] A producer's reputation for good taste in the independent film world may not translate into much money, and in fact rarely does, but it does translate into that sometimes more valuable form of capital, respect by peers. The *Hollywood Reporter* article just mentioned opens with the following subhead: "These producers painstakingly develop, assemble, sustain and push through the daring, difficult, not obviously commercial movies that no one else wants to make. It can take forever. After many years of cajoling investors, talent and distributors to bet on their movies, these veterans might not be millionaires, but their stellar track records have won them something much harder to come by in this world: respect" (A. Thompson 2005: 36).

Taste was the first item on Drubner's list of qualities needed for someone to be a good/great independent producer. He illustrated his point with reference to producers Albert Berger and Ron Yerxa, who produced, among other things, *Election* (Alexander Payne, 1999) and *Little Miss Sunshine* (Jonathan Dayton and Valerie Faris, 2006):

> There is taste. Ron and Albert are producers who have excellent taste, who I think have excellent taste, everyone thinks they have excellent taste. Being able to know what is good—that can't be underestimated. . . . On the independent film side, you *are* your tastes, much more than on the studio side. On the studio side you can get away with making *X Men 3* and make a lot of money, nobody cares. On the independent side, if you found a *Little Miss Sunshine* or you found an *Election*—those guys understand a voice, they understand a point of view, they understand a vision, they understand that creative side of it. (Interview, March 23, 2007)

Producer Ted Hope echoed Drubner's point that, in independent film, "you *are* your tastes." Hope posted a blog on his forum "Hope for Film" called "Why Producers Are Valued." Taste with respect to both "picking [and] crafting" films was high on his list as well (Hope 2010c).

Taste plays a role at every stage of making a film, but it is most significant in the initial stages of choosing to work with a particular project. Producers themselves rarely use a language of taste in relation to choosing projects; rather, they use a language of some kind of spontaneous attraction to certain works or directors. Producer Albert Berger uses a language of love: "I always had a great love for literature and it was always neck-and-neck between wanting to be a writer and wanting to be a filmmaker. I spent a lot of my late teenage and college years reading voraciously and most of the projects that we have developed have come from books." Berger then lists a number of movies he and his partner have produced and says, "Most of these were based on books and they were all things I read that I really loved in one way or another" (interview, December 30, 2005).

Producer/specialty division head James Schamus uses a language of attraction, of being "drawn to" certain works: "Generally speaking, no matter what the film, no matter what the genre, I'm still drawn to films that you might say have a signature; when the director or the creative team have a very particular outlook on the material so that it's not just processed cheese. . . . We're really looking for the filmmakers who have individual voices and have the need to speak in those voices" (2006: 4).

As these quotes suggest, not only do good producers have (what is viewed as) good taste, but they have, and have to have, a certain confidence in their own tastes. In the quote presented above, Albert Berger went on to say that his film projects were all based on books "that I really loved in one way or another and thought, this is something I am interested in, and for better or worse I have always proceeded with that." "To do what I do," writes Christine Vachon, "I have to believe that the films I produce will be so vital that they will find their audience, or will create one of their own" (1998: 16). Or Vachon again, "One of the things all great producers have in common is the courage of their convictions" (1998: 7). Producer Joana Vicente, who partners with her husband, Jason Kliot, talked about this at some length: "Whenever one of us has a very strong feeling about doing the project, or very strong feeling about not doing it, even if it is just a gut thing, just didn't like the director, or there is just something off, we learn that really the best thing that we have is our instincts and we just learn to trust our instincts because every time we made mistakes it was a time there was something [off] and we didn't do something about it" (interview, May 11, 2006).

Where does taste come from? In his monumental work *Distinction: A Social Critique of the Judgement of Taste* (1984), Pierre Bourdieu argues against the view that is widespread in the world of the arts that taste is in some sense natural or spontaneous. He calls this view "the ideology of charisma" and argues instead that taste emerges from social background: "Whereas the ideology of charisma regards taste in legitimate culture as a gift of nature, scientific observation shows that cultural needs are the product of upbringing and education: surveys establish that all cultural practices (museum visits, concert-going, reading, etc.), and preferences in literature, painting or music, are closely linked to educational level . . . and secondarily to social origin" (1984: 1). Obviously not all high-capital people have what would be considered good taste; far from it. But people who are seen as having good taste are more likely to come from backgrounds where they have been exposed to things already validated as "good," and where they absorb as a kind of "second nature" a tacit sense of what goes into high-quality cultural goods. Without positing some simple-minded connection between the high-capital backgrounds of independent producers and the quality of the films they (choose to) produce, it is clear that they collectively embody that resonance between taste and class that Bourdieu has emphasized.

Louis Drubner, Vance Van Petten, and just about every producer on the planet agree that a producer needs to have a lot of what social scientists call "agency." The idea of "agency" in social science jargon comprises a number of interrelated ideas revolving around self-confidence, around the idea of being able to make things happen in the world, around activity rather than passivity, around energy and will. Drubner earlier described it as a kind of forcefulness, as being "one of those people who is really good at convincing people to say yes." Van Petten earlier called it "individualism, entrepreneurialism and independence." Other producers speak of it in other terms. Christine Vachon calls it "fearlessness": "I think producing is about being fearless" (2006: 10). Lynda Obst calls it "nerve": "Unfortunately, nerve, not talent, is the one necessary and sufficient trait for success" (1996: 143). Barbara Boyle asked her class in the Producers Masters Program at UCLA what was the most important characteristic of a producer, and then she wrote on the blackboard, in large capital letters, "PERSEVERENCE" (field notes, December 4, 2004).

Producers talk about other producers in terms of their (again variously labeled) agency. Van Petten calls producers in general "movers and shakers by nature" (interview, December 13, 2007). Laura Ziskin was described in terms of her "prodigious amount of energy" (Ziskin 2002: 16). One producer said about another one, who jumped into producing a major feature film at a very young age, "Wow, he's got a lot of *chutzpah*!" (a Yiddish term in wide circulation meaning, basically, "nerve"; interview, March 15, 2006). Author Rachel Abramowitz said about former president of Columbia Pictures Dawn Steel, "Dawn thought she could do anything" (2000: 229), and quoted former high-ranking studio executive Paula Weinstein as saying, "I never knew any other way than to assume that everything was possible and go after it" (2000: 20).

Producers tell stories of their own agency. Some of these are about successfully handling crises during production, but I will save those for the production chapter. Here are some others. Several people talked about how they got jobs in the business through forcefulness and resourcefulness. Ted Hope talked about getting his first job in film: "Although I wanted to be in production, I had read a casting notice in *Backstage* magazine, and I learned very quickly that I couldn't just send in my résumé. I had to show up and I went with a pitch on why they should hire me"; he got the job (interview, March 15, 2006). Jason Kliot pushed his way into his first job in film: "I forced my way in there, I just wouldn't stop talking until the guy said, yeah, ok, you can work on it" (interview, March 19, 2006). In her interview, Keri Selig repeatedly described herself as "having no fear." "She told a story of seeing a Production Assistant get fired on set, and she walked right up and asked for the job" (field notes, April 14, 2007). One producer described how she got a script to a director by overriding the resistance of the director's agent: "She called every day for something like 40 days and the agent would not return her calls. And finally the agent said, you are borderline stalking me, and the producer said, that's how strongly I feel about this script. And the agent said, I will show him the script just to get you off my back. And the director read the script and agreed to direct the film" (field notes, February 9, 2007).

Finally, Laura Ziskin said in an interview, "I know I have this reputation as being someone who's a fighter and aggressive and all that. And you know, I don't think of myself that way at all. I find that part of the process really stressful. I don't want to fight; I just want everybody to understand and agree with me" (Ziskin 2002: 20).

One interesting thing that emerged as I tracked the agency question across a large number of interviews was that producers were often contrasted with screenwriters on what might be called a scale of agency. Albert Berger started out as a screenwriter but became frustrated with the relative powerlessness of the role; he decided to move into producing, where he could take an active role in making projects happen (interview, December 30, 2005). Other writers talk about preferring writing precisely because one does not have to enter the fray. Like Berger (and probably most screenwriters, though I don't have much of a sample), Edward Ericson* was frustrated with his inability to sell his scripts. He said he thought about going into producing but said that "that is just not my personality." Since he seemed a shy and soft-spoken person in the interview, I presume he meant that he didn't have the kind of agency/aggressiveness needed for the job (interview, July 30, 2006). Similarly, a young screenwriter with experience in producing said, "Now that I understand what production is and entails [as she explained later, "a lot of managing"], I am even more clear that I don't want to be a producer. I definitely like the writing side of it" (interview, March 15, 2006; nonetheless, she is in fact producing).

Finally, producer Sheila Hanahan Taylor and MGM executive Stephanie Palmer wrote about the problem of working with screenwriters: Hanahan Taylor wrote, "I beg all [screenwriters] to remember that this is a business. . . . Even though you're inclined to sit at your keyboard and be a hermit, you need to be a business person a little bit and get out and mix with people." Palmer added, "You are the entrepreneur of your career" (Palmer and Hanahan Taylor 2005: 12). In a world that values a high level of agency, one can see why screenwriters, who are viewed as not having much, might be placed relatively low on the totem pole. Similarly, for high-agency people like Albert Berger, one can see why producing might be much more satisfying than screenwriting.

Agency is a highly charged concept. It is often associated with Americans (individualistic, entrepreneurial) as opposed to the rest of the world, with men (forceful, aggressive) as opposed to women, and, for my purposes here, with high- as opposed to low-capital status.[9] Bourdieu makes this connection when he writes of the habitus of artists who gravitate toward the riskiest kinds of avant-garde work, linking high-capital backgrounds with agency words like "self-assurance," "audacity," and "flair" (1993: 68).[10] As I have discussed elsewhere (Ortner 2006d), agency has associations with non-classed things like purpose and intentionality and "getting things done," and this is clearly what is explicitly valued in producers. But it also has associations with a sense of power and freedom to act, and with being used to getting one's own way, qualities more likely to be found among people with a lot of material and/or cultural capital.

RELATIONSHIPS

"Relationships" was the second of Louis Drubner's three essential elements that make up a good/great producer. In producer discourse, "relationships" as a concept has at least three different fields of meaning. One is in a sense quantitative and has to do with the idea of building up and maintaining a large network of relationships, people one can call on for help, favors, knowledge, contacts, and so on, and people for whom one might provide the same in turn. "Networking"—building up and maintaining this large pool of people with diverse forms of potential usefulness—is very important to a successful career in the (independent) film world; providing networking opportunities is one of the important functions of (independent) film organizations. In the absence of a studio structure, every independent film has to be made from scratch; a large network of varied relationships is crucial to the process.

The second field of meaning of "relationships" has to do with the ways in which, once committed to a film, a producer cares for, nourishes, and protects the film and its filmmaker from beginning to end. This is an intense relationship, very much about quality rather than quantity, and often with (female) gendered overtones, even when the producer is male. I will reserve a discussion of this kind of relationship until later in the chapter.

The third field of meaning is the one that Louis Drubner was particularly emphasizing: the importance of having a good personality and good "people skills." At another point in his interview, Drubner elaborated, "You have to be able to be real. I don't mean in a fake real way, but be a real person, and also be able to just be likeable, or whatever it is, so people want to work with you" (interview, March 23, 2007). The idea that a good producer needs to have good people skills is something one hears again and again in the world of producers. Ted Hope wrote in his list of "Why Producers Are Valued," in the item headed "Access & Relationships," "It's not just who you know but how much they want to pick up the phone when you call" (blog post, July 15, 2010). Speaking on a public panel, a producer named Barry Jordan* said, "There's a huge personality factor, you have to be able to get along" (field notes, November 13, 2005).[11] Finally, producer Ted Kroeber said, "I am very much a people person. I enjoy working with people" (interview, February 11, 2006).[12]

Being a "people person" is not necessarily gendered, but people skills can easily take a gendered and/or sexualized form. Barry Jordan talked about giving notes (what we in academia call comments) to a writer: "The producer shouldn't just dump all the criticism on the person at the start. It's like dating, you have to feel the person out" (field notes, November 13, 2005). Similarly, Lynda Obst wrote, "Reeling him in, be it the director, star, studio, is . . . akin to the lessons women learn in *Cosmo* like 'Getting your man to commit.' The process resembles aspects of the mating ritual" (1996: 69), and, "Flirting is an essential tool for surviving the gender gap. . . . A call about my deal never closes without my telling [my agent] I love him, and I giggle at the opening, 'Hiii, Jimmy,' like a high school cheerleader cooing at the captain of the football team" (1996: 177).

The issue of personality and people skills threads through every aspect of the work of a producer, from making deals to making films. But there is one site where it is actually institutionalized and ritualized: the so-called meet and greet between producers and (would-be) writers. I observed one "meet and greet" in which two producing partners met with a writer they thought they might be interested in working with. The ostensible point of the meeting was to talk about ideas for scripts the producers had and to see if the writer would be interested in developing any of those ideas. But it was also clear that the writer was being sized up as a personality, whether— in the commonly heard phrase—he was "good in the room," and whether he was somebody with whom they would enjoy working over the long term. I felt sorry for the screenwriter, who didn't seem terribly socially skilled; I don't know the outcome of the meeting. But another screen-writer, Cathy Rabin (*Before the Rains*), told me she hated meet and greets, calling them "hollow, going-through-the-motions" encounters. Not only was there a personality factor; there was also looks and age. "She said she doesn't do 'meet and greets' any more. She said it's an important 'ritual' in the whole process but she always hated it, was not good at it, and now she's a woman 'of a certain age' where her appearance would be a negative" (field notes, December 4, 2005). As a coda to all this, studio executive Stephanie Palmer "has opened a new service called 'Good in a Room,' which teaches creative professionals . . . how to present themselves and their ideas so their projects will get purchased and produced" (Palmer and Hanahan Taylor 2005: 12).

As Stephanie Palmer's service would have people believe, good people skills can be taught and learned. It is also likely that some people are simply inherently better at this than others. On the whole, however, and as with "agency" (to which it is not unrelated), one is more likely to have the kind of people skills Louis Drubner was talking about—"to go out and be a friendly good person, to be able to have good conversations"—if one comes from a background relatively high in capital, and especially educational capital.

I have been emphasizing the fact that many independent producers come from relatively privileged backgrounds, in terms of money, education, or both. I have further been emphasizing that the kinds of qualities a successful producer is thought to need—good taste, a sense of personal agency, and good social skills—are the kinds of qualities that are more likely to be found among people with those kinds of backgrounds. All of this fits well with Pierre Bourdieu's theories of the ways in which artistic value—what counts as good art from the point of view of discerning audiences—is created. That is the next question.

The Production of Value

We return here to the work of Pierre Bourdieu. Bourdieu is only the most recent in a long line of sociologists and anthropologists who have argued for the social production of value in the arts, but his take on the subject is at this point the most sophisticated. Bourdieu argues that the creation of value of artistic works takes place in what he calls a "field of cultural production." Within the field, what is created is a discourse of value; such discourse is "one of the conditions of the production of the work" (1993: 35):

> Given that works of art exist as symbolic objects only if they are known and recognized, that is, socially instituted as works of art and received by spectators capable of knowing and recognizing them as such, the sociology of art and literature has to take as its object not only the material production but also the symbolic production of the work, i.e., the production of the value of the work or, which amounts to the same thing, of belief in the value of the work. (1993: 37)

In this final part of the chapter, then, I want to look at the ways in which the various aspects of the producer's role create value in Bourdieu's sense, that is, other people's belief in/recognition of value, or what might be called "symbolic value." But while I agree that in the final analysis there is no such thing as real—natural, inherent—value, I find Bourdieu's emphasis entirely on the production of "discourse" and "belief" somewhat limiting, particularly with respect to the kinds of labor producers do. To get around this limitation, I will thus also have recourse to a notion of "substantive" value, related primarily to inputs of social and mental labor that actually make things better (within an internally defined framework of what counts as "good" and "better").

It all begins when a producer chooses to, or agrees to, produce a particular film. When a producer with a reputation for good taste does this, there is an almost automatic production of value for the film by the sheer act of the producer making that choice. This is especially the case for first-time filmmakers who do not yet have their own reputations for quality with which to infuse their new project.

But the decision to produce a particular film is only the beginning of an extended relationship between the producer and the filmmaker (and the film) in which value, as an almost material quality, is transferred from the producer to the filmmaker intensely and continuously. This value always has the double aspect just noted, a kind of performance for others that we may think of as symbolic value, and many kinds of substantive value, via mental and material labor, for the production of quality in the film. I will look first at the production of symbolic value.

The decision to take on a particular project involves making an enormous commitment, and the language surrounding it is always very intense. Such a commitment is sometimes couched in terms of "believing in" the project. Albert Berger said, "How could you shepherd something for a year and a half, or however long it takes, five years, if you don't completely believe in it?" He also used a language of faith, declaring (before the film came out), "I have a lot of faith in *Little Miss Sunshine*" (Berger interview, March 28, 2006). Lydia Pilcher used a language of excitement: "We have a [certain] novel that I'm really, really excited about" (Pilcher interview, March 29, 2006). Christine Vachon spoke of taking pride: "I can't be more emphatic: Throw your resources behind a script with which you're proud to be associated—and associated for a long time" (Vachon 1998: 20). She also used a language of strong emotion: "[A film is] a thing so fragile, a thing that requires imaginative leaps and an incredible emotional commitment" (Vachon 1998: 220). Or, of course, there is passion, as when Vanessa Hope declared, "I think producing requires being incredibly passionate about the material you are supporting" (V. Hope interview, March 15, 2006).

This initial passionate commitment is the beginning of a relationship that is invariably described in terms of great closeness and intimacy that lasts throughout the production of the film if not beyond. As Christine Vachon said about working with talented filmmakers in general, "you stick to them like glue" (2006: 10). She also made the analogy with a romantic relationship: "Typically, when new directors or producers come into Killer [Films'] office, we'll have a friendly lunch to check them out. Pam and I joke that we should give new directors a quiz to assess whether they can handle the job. It's really just one question: have you been able to maintain a long-term relationship in your romantic life?" (2006: 38). Lynda Obst used a language of marriage: "A producer must marry her director, no matter the gender" (1996: 214).

But by far the most common source of metaphors for the producer's relationship to the filmmaker—again regardless of genders—is the mother-child and/or parent-child relationship in its many manifestations. Almost all producers would agree with producer Deborah Hill's statement that "[making a movie] is like raising a child" (Hill 2000: 8). And as with all child rearing, the process involves a combination of loving and nurturing on the one hand and guiding/disciplining on the other. PGA director Vance Van Petten said in his interview, "Laura Ziskin and other members of the PGA have told me that they see producing as very similar to what a mother does in raising a family. Because you are dealing with creative people, you are nurturing but you are also focusing them and you have to discipline them toward a goal" (interview, December 13, 2007). Or here are my notes after a day on a movie set, noting (among many other things) some of the gender dynamics: "The director's assistant acts like the good and devoted *wife*. She said, 'I want to be where he can see me, in case he needs something.' She never lets him out of her sight. On the other hand, the female producer is like his *mother*. She will be a little bit firm; she won't exactly resist him, but she will present the other side, but then of course she will support him in the end and go to work on whatever he wants" (field notes, February 6, 2007). Again we see the mix of nurturance and support on the one hand and providing restraint (or trying to) on the other.[13]

The job of guiding/disciplining is important; a tactful but effective parent/producer knows how to set and enforce limits. Producer Lynda Obst wrote about this with respect to dealing with actors and crew during production: "A movie crew is like a family. I always think of myself as the mother and the director as the father, and when I'm working with a female director it's the same dynamic, but I degenderize it. Your actors and crew want strong parental leadership—just like kids" (1996: 213). Or Christine Vachon wrote of the importance of engaging the director in the budgeting beforehand, so the producer is not put in the position of being the parent who says no: "It's awful to tell directors they can't have what they want. Ideally directors should be complicit in the budgeting, so that you don't have to intone from on high: YOU CAN HAVE A CRANE. YOU CAN'T HAVE AN EXTRA DAY" (Vachon 1998: 41, caps in original).

But the parental guidance must always be embedded in a relationship of nurturance and protection. The language of "nurturing" tends to be gendered female/maternal, as in Van Petten's quote about women producers, or when Lynda Obst writes, "The maternal instinct is extremely helpful in the nurturing end of the business: producing" (1996: 185). But there is also a more gender-neutral language of "protecting," which is extremely widespread. And whereas the maternal language tends to be used primarily by female producers, the protecting language is used by men and women alike.

"Protecting the director" is seen as absolutely central to the producer's job, especially on the set of a movie in production. This involves in part solving technical problems, so that the director does not have to be distracted by them. It also involves solving human-relations problems and thus keeping peace on the set. (The anthropologist on the set may come under the heading of a technical problem, a human-relations problem, or both. At one point I was chagrined to realize that the director was probably being protected from me.)

It is almost impossible for a producer to talk or write about producing without at some point using the phrase "protect the director." Producer Christine Vachon writes that filmmaker Todd Haynes had had trouble with Harvey Weinstein at Miramax over *Velvet Goldmine* (1998) and was resisting working for Weinstein again on *Far from Heaven* (2002). She goes on, "We can't do it with Miramax because Todd is too angry. He feels too unprotected. If I get down on my knees and say to Todd, 'Look, I think we have to do it with Miramax and I will protect you,' He would say OK" (Vachon 2006: 159). Producer Joana Vicente talked about working on *Awake* (Joby Harold, 2007): "And then when I did *Awake* I was on set every day. Because the studios were involved so it is important to be there every day to protect the director" (interview, March 29, 2006). One producer explained the role of another producer on the set of one of the films I observed in production, saying, "She is [the director's] producer, . . . She is there to protect his back" (field notes, February 6, 2007). Finally, journalist Sharon Waxman wrote about the troubled production of *Three Kings* (David O. Russell, 1999). Director David Russell had a lot of trouble with George Clooney on the set, and Clooney in turn brought in the executives at Warner Bros. Line producer Greg Goodman said, "There was way too much pressure on David to 'perform' in the classic studio sense—'Don't fuck this up. You better do good on this.' We producers should have done a better job of protecting David so he could do his job" (Waxman 2006: 245).

Filmmakers in turn talk of having felt protected by their producers. Actor/director John Cameron Mitchell wrote about Christine Vachon, "During production in Toronto, Christine was very calming and soothing to my jittery nerves. She's also very protective" (in Vachon 2006: 149). Or at a panel on directing independent films, the moderator asked the panel, "'Did you feel protected by your producers?' Julian Schnabel, nominated for directing *The Diving Bell and the Butterfly*, said, 'John Killick produces all my movies. He always protects me.'"[14]

Finally, at the end of a project, there is pride in what has been produced, once again often rendered in maternal/parental language. Caroline Baron wrote about keeping creative control of her projects "so I can be proud of . . . what I've brought into the world" (Baron 2006). And Stephanie Allain wrote about successful directors whose work she had produced, "I look at John Singleton, Robert Rodriguez, . . . and Sanaa Hamri . . . and it . . . strikes a deep sort of mothering satisfaction in me to see them do so well" (Allain 2007: 15).

I have spent a relatively long time here on the intimate language of producing—of marrying and mothering and protecting directors, of nurturing films and filmmakers and careers—because I would argue that it is partly in this intensely described/experienced relationship that the production of value of the film (and the filmmaker) takes place. There is a sense of the producer staying extremely close to the filmmaker, literally and metaphorically, throughout and beyond the project. There is a quality of anointing the filmmaker with the high-quality elements of the producer's habitus, transferring it almost as a physical quantum from the producer's self to the director and the film.

And all this has, to return to the larger point about symbolic and substantive value, this double-faced meaning. On the one hand, it is an extended performance that says, over and over again throughout the life of the film, that this film and this filmmaker are important, full of great value and worth. Through this performance, value is produced in the eyes of others, and also no doubt in the self-perception (or, in stronger terms, the ego) of the filmmaker him- or herself. Producers are well aware of the performance value of their tremendous investment in a film. As Christine Vachon wrote, "The central discipline for a producer is a constant, inexhaustible enthusiasm. My job is to [both] discover talent and find a way for you to know about it" (Vachon 2006: 190, sentences reversed). Ted Hope said something similar. The first point on his list of "why producers are valued" is "validation" for the filmmaker him/herself, and beyond that in the eyes of others: "[The producer's] support of them means that the project is real (or at least they think it will mean that to others)" (Hope 2010c).

At the same time, we know very well from the discussion at the beginning of the chapter that producers invest an enormous amount of real labor in the production of a film. As filmmaker Gregg Araki said earlier, "Essentially they do everything," and producing (like parenting) is a tremendous amount of work. This work, I would argue, produces something we could call substantive value, as well as the symbolic value just discussed. In order to make this case, and to conclude this chapter, I want to focus in more narrowly on the producers' educations.

Education: The Question of Substantive Value

Thus far I have treated the producers' educations primarily as forms of capital. The degrees from fine schools have a reputational value. Even when other people are not aware of an individual's degrees, or deny that they matter, the credentials are there, submerged within the taste and self-confidence and social skills that insiders recognize as the qualities of a good producer. Yet if at one level education functions as symbolic capital, producing symbolic value, at another level we must see it as producing substantive value as well. One can tease out at least three levels at which this operates.

I would call attention first to the actual creative input that independent producers contribute to the films they produce. While there may be some creative producers in the Hollywood studio system, in the world of independent film all producers are creative producers. Virtually all producers work closely with screenwriters and/or filmmakers in developing the script. Many had been English majors. Many started out as writers themselves. Where the studio would just call in another writer, an independent producer rolls up his or her figurative sleeves and pitches in. This kind of creative input often continues throughout the life of the production, as the producer tries to help/enable the filmmaker to do the best possible job. As producer Joana Vicente said, "I think in every film we have done, we never gave up, and have really always tried to make the best possible film. Sometimes we stay in post-production for a long time; sometimes we need to do three shoots; but I think it is about just never letting go . . . it has to become the best it can be. . . . That is our philosophy" (interview, March 29, 2006). This commitment of time and genuine care is clearly not the empty play of cultural capital, but the artistic process as productive labor.

Another thing of substantive value that higher education ideally provides is a sense of, and an appreciation for, a wider world than the one in which a person grew up. At the very least, it broadens people's tastes. While some producers and filmmakers come from artistic backgrounds, most come from families with fairly conventional taste. College or film school is a place where young people often discover a taste for the arts and ideas that move them beyond whatever class habitus they came from. Specifically, for many of these individuals, it is clear that college and/or film school played a major role in turning them toward a taste for the particular kind of challenging object that is the contemporary independent film.

More generally, higher education opens up a sense of the diversity of lives in the world. I said earlier that indie screenwriters, directors, and writer/directors come from much more variable backgrounds than indie producers: they may come from different class backgrounds; they may be from racial or ethnic or sexual minorities; they may be from other countries; they may be more politically radical; they may be in more ongoing conversation with their own unconscious minds than the rest of us; and so on. They write from, and often about, those locations. In turn, indie producers develop a taste for figuratively going to those places with the director or filmmaker, in effect bringing their stories back to the more comfortable, usually white, mostly straight, folks of the professional managerial classes.

Finally, and perhaps most importantly, college is where young people ideally learn how to engage in critical thinking. It was striking to me that many producers and filmmakers talked or wrote about the importance of critical literary and cultural theory in their work. For example, documentary filmmaker Kirby Dick talked about becoming interested in conceptual art in school. He explained that conceptual art "is art that is very idea-based, very theoretical, often times very informed by critical theory and to some degree influenced by it." He said that an assignment to do a conceptual art project in a class radically changed his thinking and moved him decisively toward a commitment to the arts (interview, March 9, 2007).

Dick later went on to codirect (among other things) a documentary about French theoretician Jacques Derrida (*Derrida*, Kirby Dick and Amy Ziering Kofman, 2002).

For another example, screenwriter and producer Vanessa Hope talked about how she enjoyed discussing theory with a filmmaker with whom she was working:

> Of all the people I've met and dealt with in the business she's one of the more intellectual ones. She reads philosophers like Walter Benjamin and [Georges] Bataille, and she cares about that and integrates it into her understanding of the world . . . and she's partners with an artist . . . he knows [the theory too], we always talk about Žižek, Slavoj Žižek, they care about these philosophical ideas about the world." (Interview, May 20, 2006)

Similarly, Christine Vachon wrote about studying semiotics in college:

> As an undergraduate at Brown, I could study film only through the semiotics department, which meant an immersion in theory. I spent a year in Paris studying with Julia Kristeva and Christian Metz, and going to lectures by Michel Foucault. Did all that semiotics and structuralism have an impact on my producing? I don't know, but I did see some interesting stuff. (Vachon 1998: 5–6)

Indeed, there is a small subgenre of documentaries specifically devoted to social and cultural theorists. In addition to the documentary about Jacques Derrida noted above, there are films about Slavoj Žižek (*Žižek!*, Astra Taylor, 2005) and Pierre Bourdieu (*Sociology Is a Martial Art*, Pierre Carles, 2001). One documentary looks at a cluster of contemporary theorists, including Cornel West, Michael Hardt, and Judith Butler (*Examined Life*, Astra Taylor, 2008). I would also mention here the UCLA Critical Media Festival, which focused in part on films that take a more theoretically informed approach.[15]

At first I was puzzled by the interest of producers and filmmakers in cultural theory. I think of theory as part of academic work, rather than having to do with the practical work of filmmaking itself. One solution to this puzzle would be in terms of the cultural capital to be gained from theory name dropping. There is surely some of that going on, and people are aware of the impressive effect that a few choice theory terms, preferably in French, can have in certain contexts (see, e.g., Vachon 1998: 114). Yet I think there is something more serious going on as well. I propose that what is being signaled here is the ways in which theory work teaches one about the necessity for critical thinking of various kinds, and gives one tools for getting beyond the surface of things to ask about the structural and ideological premises behind what we see.

I never actually discussed this question with any of the people I spoke to, but I recently came across an interesting discussion of the impact of studying theory in college. The discussion occurs at the beginning of an article about feminism and film, and I will return to the article in the next chapter as well. The author begins by making a point about the kind of impact the study of literary theory in college makes on "an impressionable young person":

> Once you have engaged in enough feminist readings of "The Iliad" or performed close textual analyses of "Alf" or written papers limning the intertextual relationship between "Videodrome" and "Madame Bovary" —once, in other words, you've glimpsed the social, political, historical and ideological underpinnings of every text ever constructed—you'll never see stories the same way again. They'll shed their innocence and expose their dirty secrets and reveal the world as a darker, more dangerous place than it once seemed. (Chocano 2011: MM48)

The quote fits nicely with my earlier discussion of the darkness of independent film, and the sense of a more dangerous world that appears in both Gen X discourse and many independent films. But my point in quoting it here is to illuminate the substantive value of theory for generating the kind of critical sensibility that many producers bring to their work on independent film.

In sum, I have argued in this final section that we must take Bourdieu fully into account in understanding the social production of taste and artistic value. But at the same time we must be willing to talk about "substantive value" in the world of the arts, in this case in the making of independent films. This does not commit us to some naïve belief in good taste as some natural born gift, or good films as having tapped into some natural essence of quality and value. But it does force us to look at things— in this case education—as operating both symbolically (as "capital") and, within a certain preexisting value system, substantively (in this case as creative labor, as the source of wider worldviews, and as a basis for critical thinking).

This chapter has been part of the series of ethnographic chapters in which I have been exploring the conditions of possibility for the ongoing life of the independent film world and for the making of independent films. In the next chapter I return to the films themselves, in this case to consider the culture and politics surrounding films directed by women and addressing women's/feminist issues.

CHAPTER 6

Film Feminism

We return again to the films, and to the question of cultural critique. In the 1970s women had launched the most sweeping critique of culture and society since Karl Marx's critique of capitalism: the exposure of patriarchy as a deep structure of modern society, or perhaps all societies. Since then women have made enormous strides toward gender equality, in the United States and globally; the United States will continue to be my primary focus here.

As in many other fields, there has been a significant rise in the number of women working in the film industry, including as studio executives, producers (as discussed in chap. 5), directors, and filmmakers; I will provide some numbers below. In this chapter I am concerned primarily with women directors/filmmakers, and in some cases women screenwriters, making or writing independent films.[1] In the wake of the feminist movement, and in a time that many call post-feminist, what kinds of films are they making? Where is the feminist critique today? This chapter thus heeds Kathleen McHugh's call to take stock of "film feminisms in our contemporary moment, in which feminism has been declared dead" (2009: 113).

But women independent filmmakers are not only generationally post-feminism; they are also generationally X, born mostly in the 1960s and 1970s, just like their male counterparts. As Peter Hanson indicates in his roster of Gen X filmmakers, Sophia Coppola (*The Virgin Suicides*), Jodie Foster (*Little Man Tate*), Tamara Jenkins (*Slums of Beverly Hills*), Karyn Kusama (*Girlfight*), Kasi

Lemmons (*Eve's Bayou*), and Kimberly Pierce (*Boys Don't Cry*) were all born between 1961 and 1971 (Hanson 2002: 177–98); most of the women I will be discussing in this chapter were born in that period and on into the early 1980s.

In general the "Gen X" label tends not to be used when talking of women of this generation; just as the label is implicitly middle class, it is also implicitly male.[2] Yet the women no less than the men of this generation have been struggling with the epochal transformations of neoliberalism, and this will be seen to have significant manifestations in their films. Like so many indie films in general, women's indies portray the (neoliberal) world today as disturbingly dark and violent. And at the same time, adding a further dimension to the darkness, women filmmakers and/or their characters must also deal with continuing sexism/patriarchy, that is, with the unfinished business of the feminist movement of the preceding generation.

In the first part of this chapter I will explore the experience of women in the film world, in relation to the charges of "post-feminism." In the second part of the chapter, I will look at a range of films by women directors in terms of the complicated intersection between the feminist critique of the patriarchal order and the Marxist critique of neoliberal capitalism.

Women's Experience in the Film World
THE CHARGE OF POST-FEMINISM

In a recent article looking back at issues of women and feminism in films of the early 1990s, journalist Carina Chocano contrasts *Thelma and Louise* (Ridley Scott, 1991) with *Pretty Woman* (Garry Marshall, 1990). *Thelma and Louise* featured two strong women characters who challenged the patriarchal order, while *Pretty Woman* celebrated the lead female character as eye candy for men and shopper/consumer for the economy. At the time, Chocano wrote, "*Thelma and Louise* felt like a direct rebuke to the clueless throwback that was *Pretty Woman*, with its Paleolithic attitudes and its confusing agenda" (2011). By now, however, Chocano concludes that the significance of the two films has been reversed: "Revisiting *Thelma and Louise* recently, I was struck by how dated it seemed, how much a product of its time. And *Pretty Woman*, it turns out, wasn't a throwback at all. It was the future" (2011).

Starting also in the early 1990s, and even a bit before that, feminist scholars began identifying a condition they called "post-feminism" (Rosenfelt and Stacey 1987; Stacey 1990; Modleski 1991; Traube 1994; Hawkesworth 2004; Tasker and Negra 2007; McRobbie 2009; Faludi 2010). The gist of this literature is that younger women today have both incorporated the fruits of the earlier ("second wave") feminist movement and rejected the idea of, or the necessity for, continuing to pursue feminist goals. Put more strongly, younger women have come to view that earlier movement as embodying and advocating a style of femininity/femaleness with which they do not want to be associated: "[P]ostfeminism signals more than a simple evolutionary process whereby aspects of feminism have been incorporated into popular culture. . . . It also simultaneously involves an 'othering' of feminism . . . , its construction as extreme, difficult, and unpleasurable" (Tasker and Negra 2007: 4). This shift of consciousness, further, is viewed as having been actively fostered by the media, which have sought to refocus female identities on a self-pampering individualistic lifestyle by way of the acquisition of consumer goods, goods that provide both pleasures in themselves and ways to succeed with men (see especially McRobbie 2009).

Much of the literature on post-feminism has been based on readings of popular culture. For example, one of the prime culprits in the discussion has been the very successful television series *Sex and the City* (HBO, 1998–2004), which features four "liberated" young women who do nothing but shop, engage in their various relationships with men, and talk about the shopping and the relationships. I have no doubt that there are indeed young women today aspiring to be like the by-now-mythic Carrie Bradshaw (Sarah Jessica Parker) and her friends. As against this, however, I make two points. First, we have little ethnographic data on what "young women today" are actually thinking; we do not know which if any girls/women (class, race, age, etc.) are taking *Sex and the City* or anything like it as their model of grown-up femininity. And second, we shall see that the view of, and the politics surrounding, women's lives that we get from independent film is very different from the view we get from popular television and Hollywood movies.

I will be looking at the films in the second half of this chapter. Here I want to pull together some historical and ethnographic data on the situation of women in the film industry. Because questions of sexism and patriarchy affect all women, though perhaps somewhat differently in the studios and as independent filmmakers, I will look at women across the industry as a whole.

Perhaps the place to start is with the very visible success of a number of women who became heads of Hollywood studios, as well as presidents of production in studios, starting in the 1980s. Sherry Lansing was the first woman to become president of production of a major studio, 20th Century Fox, in 1980; Dawn Steel became the first president of a studio, Columbia Pictures, in 1987. Lansing went on to become president of Paramount Pictures in 1992. (For a fascinating account of the Lansing/Steel era of the 1980s and 1990s, see Abramowitz 2000.) At the time of the article "Hollywood's New Old Girls' Network" in 2005, four of the six major studios had women in the top creative decision-making roles, as Gail Berman became president of Paramount, joining Stacey Snider, who was chairman of Universal; Amy Pascal, who was chairman of Sony Pictures; and Nina Jacobson, who was president of Walt Disney Company's Buena Vista Motion Pictures group (Hass 2005).[3]

Next, producers. We saw in the previous chapter that, between the 1970s and the 2000s, the proportion of women in the Producers Guild of America jumped from 0.3 percent to 45 percent. We have no way of knowing what proportion of these women producers are more studio oriented and which are more independent oriented, but in any event there has clearly been a dramatic increase in the number of women working as producers of films in the industry as a whole.

Finally, I note the improvement in the number and percentage of women working as directors, the most prestigious role in the industry. In 1974 there were 2,343 men and 23 women listed in the membership of the Directors Guild of America (DGA), which works out to 1 percent (Abramowitz 2000: 65).[4] Today, however, it is around 7 percent (Martha Lauzen, quoted in Dargis 2010b). While this is not a huge number, or a large percentage, it does represent a significant improvement.

Turning specifically to independent film, I have not been able to find any figures on women directors. But I can make an estimate based on an indirect measure, namely, the percentage of women directors in my filmography, which is 18 percent. Since I was watching mostly independent films, since I was not actively seeking out films by women directors, and since, finally, the statistic is based on what sociologists call a relatively large "*N*," or sample, it seems reasonable to accept this as at least a rough approximation of the number.[5]

As interesting as the numbers for female directors of independent films is the emergence of a new pattern, the codirecting of films by woman-man partnerships. Fourteen of the films I watched in this period were codirected by a male/female partnership (in various senses of the term), seven documentaries and seven features. Four of the features were well received in the indie community (nominations, awards, etc.) but garnered relatively small audiences. The other three, however, were among the more successful (financially and/or critically) independent films of the period of my research. One was *Little Miss Sunshine* (2006), a quirky comedy about a dysfunctional family that manages to pull itself together to support the young daughter when she is accepted into a child beauty pageant. It was directed by the husband-wife team of Jonathan Dayton and Valerie Faris. The second was *Half-Nelson* (2006), a dark story of an idealistic high school teacher with a serious drug habit who loses control of his life. The director is listed as Ryan Fleck, with Anna Boden getting credit for the script. The two are a couple, and Fleck joked in an interview that he "stole" the directing credit from Boden (Fleck and Boden n.d.). The two shared directing credit on their next film, *Sugar* (2008). And finally there was *Persepolis*, directed by the artistic team of Marjane Satrapi and Vincent Parronaud (2007), about a young woman in Teheran who had grown up in a progressive family and finds it impossible to live under the fundamentalist regime in Iran. As far as I know, these codirecting partnerships are almost entirely seen among independent filmmakers.

There are a number of reasons why the percentage of women directing or codirecting independent films would be higher than the number of women directing Hollywood movies. First, and somewhat abstractly, there is a notion in some quarters that independent films are by nature more like stereotypic "women's films" than most Hollywood movies. They are smaller, more intimate, more personal; many of them are focused on close personal relationships. Of course, this is a large generalization, and there are many indie films that would not fit this description. Nonetheless, there is enough of a tendency in this direction that, from a certain point of view, one could say that Hollywood is to indies as male is to female. One independent producer said as much to me, with some discomfort: "There is a sense—do not quote me as saying this—but a studio executive at one of the mini majors recently said to somebody I know that in the independent film business, [including] his company, they make movies for women. [He said,] the audience for independent films is women, which is interesting. That [people who make independent films] are trying to get at certain emotions, and a certain sensibility, and so thoughtful filmgoers tend to be for them women" (interview, March 23, 2007).

Similarly, independent filmmaker Rodrigo García said in an interview that he sees the audience for his films as primarily older women. He said, "Older women have had it with all the bullshit, they're ready to see it like it really is" (field notes, February 10, 2007).

Second, one might consider the difference in the social experience of directing a big Hollywood movie and a smaller independent film. A large Hollywood movie set is (among other things) a very male place. The director needs to maintain authority over a large number of mostly male workers, with varying attitudes, and it is not an easy task even for many male directors. Obviously some women are able to do this successfully; Kathryn Bigelow successfully directed *The Hurt Locker*, with not only the usual mostly male crew but also a virtually all-male cast, all the way to an Academy Award. Further, this suggestion that there are gendered authority issues on sets is somewhat contentious, and on the one production I observed with a female director (*Sunshine Cleaning*, Christine Jeffs, 2008), everyone was at pains to say that her gender was completely irrelevant. On the other hand, filmmaker Karyn Kusama has been quoted as saying, "I think it's a little disingenuous to say [being a woman director is] not a different set of challenges, because people are simply more comfortable with men behind the camera and running the show, literally and figuratively" (in Horowitz 2006: 173).

Finally, and most concretely, one of the major organizations promoting and supporting independent film, Film Independent, has an agenda of actively recruiting and supporting women (and also minority) filmmakers. They run a program called Project Involve, which holds competitions for grants for young women and minority filmmakers. In addition to receiving substantial awards in terms of cash and equipment, the winners participate in workshops over the course of a year and receive quite extensive and intensive mentoring from more experienced filmmakers.

In sum, women's presence in key roles in the movie and film world has increased enormously since the 1970s. And while the improvement in the proportion of women directors is more modest than in the other roles, there are nonetheless quite a substantial number of women now directing films in general and independent films in particular.

It is a major point of the post-feminism literature that younger women find second-wave feminism irrelevant to today's world, a world in which virtually all occupations are open to women, in which women—like the studio heads noted earlier—have been very visibly successful in many endeavors, and in which many men have been sensitized to the need for egalitarian relations between the sexes. Moreover, in this view, younger women see second-wave feminists as having more or less abandoned an interest in attractive femininity in the pursuit of gender equality; younger women reject this de-feminization and refuse to identify with the older feminist generation and often with the very term *feminism*.

The generational friction between second-wave feminists and younger women is the recognizable subtext of at least one very successful film, *An Education* (Lone Scherfig, 2009).[6] The film tells the story of a very bright young woman in secondary school, Jenny, who is poised to go to Oxford but meets an exciting older man, David, and decides to drop out of school. As she had been an excellent student, her teacher, Miss Stubbs, tries to dissuade her from dropping out, but Jenny is determined to pursue this new life. Miss Stubbs embodies both the views and the look of a (stereotypic) second-wave feminist woman in the guise of the classic "spinster." She is unmarried; she is also portrayed as physically plain, not so much through her natural looks (which are not unattractive) as through the way she puts herself together (skinned-back hair, no makeup, old-fashioned glasses). She and Jenny have a number of arguments over Jenny's decision, and throughout their arguments Jenny contrasts the life of sensual pleasure (good food, music, trips to Paris) she is having with David with the "boring" and "dead" life of Miss Stubbs and other women (e.g., her school's headmistress) who have chosen a professional career and/or the life of the mind.

Jenny represents another version of the *Pretty Woman/Sex and the City* anxieties of older feminists for the younger generation of women. And indeed there are surely many young women around who see the world as

Jenny (temporarily) does, who think sexism is a minor issue and feminists are killjoys. But my conversations with younger-generation women in the film world (both studio and independent) revealed that most were acutely aware of ongoing issues of sexism. They may not be politically active, but as against the charges of "post-feminism," they certainly do not see the issues of feminism as over. I will suggest that this contradiction or disjuncture between awareness and (in)action may be relevant for understanding some of the films.

I interviewed only one woman who denied that there were continuing issues of sexism in the contemporary movie industry. This woman, Irene Nesbitt,* was an independent producer who produced Hollywood studio-oriented films. Irene insisted that she had never experienced sexual harassment, discrimination, or exclusion. She also insisted that the rise to power of female executives in the studios, discussed earlier, marked the end of an earlier era of sexism in Hollywood.

> **IN**: You know, I'll have to say, the truth of the matter is, I think sexism is not very rampant in the movie business.
> **SBO**: It's not?
> **IN**: I don't think so. I think Hollywood has actually one of the most impressive lists of women in power. There are a lot of studio heads who are women, I mean way more than the average in the Fortune 500. . . . In terms of power and decision-making, I think it's actually remarkably not sexist. (Interview, July 6, 2006)

But virtually all other critical observers of the Hollywood gender scene see it differently. Producer Lynda Obst (whom we met in the previous chapter reflecting ironically on how she coos to her agent "like a cheerleader") emphasized women's exclusion from the inner circles of Hollywood: "You can argue that being a member of the studio-head club makes you a member of the old boys' club, but Dawn Steel would tell you differently. A woman can rise to the top of the corporate hierarchy here, but the boys' club remains just that: the Boys' Club" (Obst 1996: 193). Journalist Rachel Abramowitz wrote about the pragmatic acceptance by women of the pervasive sexism of the industry: "Discussing sexism, indeed sexual harassment, in Hollywood was a little like discussing the fact that the sea was blue. It was just a fact of nature, keenly noted but largely accepted as the cost of doing business" (2000: xiv).

The pragmatic attitude Abramowitz points to does seem to be quite widespread and much more central to women's avoidance of the feminism label than any blanket rejection of feminism as a critique of the culture. People in both Hollywood and the independent film scene do not like to be seen as whining about anything, including sexism. For example, one (female) producer launched an angry tirade about a difficult (female) agent, describing the agent as a woman "who wanted to join the big swinging dick club." She turned to me at the end of the tirade and said, "Let's have a meeting and I will give you all the dirt about gender in this game" (field notes, February 9, 2007). But when we met, she more or less denied that she had invited me to have that conversation and deflected any attempt to engage the subject (field notes, April 14, 2007).[7]

These examples aside, many young women whom I interviewed were quite frank—and quite critical—about their encounters with sexism in the course of doing business. One young executive at a major studio said, "Gender is a big issue actually. I mean, it is a boy's world, especially at my particular studio. There are some studios that are run by women—Amy Pascal at Sony and Stacy Snider at Universal—but my studio is very male orientated and we [women] all really feel that. . . . I feel like I am being hazed at a fraternity" (interview, January 10, 2006).

She went on to say, "They decide that teenage boys see the most movies and so they make movies for teenage boys. So it makes sense to have boys, essentially large [boys] running the studios" (interview, January 10, 2006).

One young independent filmmaker recounted the following experience of a meeting in which she was trying to raise money from an investor:

It was kind of horrible. He ordered a three-course meal and then he ordered dessert at the end and he kept doing this thing where he would take my spoon and put ice cream on it and then hand me the spoon, like trying to feed me. . . . The ice cream he ordered came with a dish of toppings, and he took a cherry and held it in front of my mouth and said I've always wanted to do this to a woman. (Interview, April 4, 2006)

In addition, when this filmmaker told this story to her (female) producer, the producer said she had had identical experiences:

She started telling me stories about her meetings with private investors, and how it was the same thing. She was working with a female director at the time, and they had a meeting with investors where the entire time it felt like a double date and they weren't being taken seriously. At the end of dinner the investors wrote a check so at least something came out of that. But it was very degrading. (Interview, April 4, 2006)

For yet another example, a young independent screenwriter and producer talked about a very unpleasant job that she held for a while. The workplace was chaotic and the boss seemed to be corrupt. In addition, the men in the office were always telling dirty jokes and looking at magazines with nude women. She had a kind of political awakening: "That was the first time where I ever had a boss where I felt sexually harassed and I felt considered inferior because of my sex. I felt suddenly this huge empathy for every woman in the world who deals with that on a regular basis. I mean one way or another that's reality for most women in the rest of the world" (interview, May 15, 2006).

Let me also sketch here two very brief profiles of women independent filmmakers who are quite frank about their commitment to feminist issues, and who do not shy away from the "feminism" label. Mary Harron, first, has made several fascinating films about eccentric or marginal women. Harron made the early indie classic *I Shot Andy Warhol* (1996), about Valerie Solanis, a deranged young woman who founded the one-woman radical feminist organization S.C.U.M. (The Society for Cutting Up Men) and who, after being first noticed and then ignored by Andy Warhol, shot him. More recently Harron made *The Notorious Bettie Page* (2006), about a rather innocent young woman who left a background of sexual abuse in a southern family and became famous posing nude for bondage magazines in the 1950s. Harron is very frank about her feminist inspirations: "I feel that without feminism, I wouldn't be doing this. So I feel very grateful. Without it, God knows what my life would be. I don't make feminist films in the sense that I don't make anything ideological. But I do find that women get my films better. Women and gay men. . . . Maybe because they're less threatened by it, or they see what I'm trying to say better" (in Hornaday 2006: 3).

For another example, consider the films of Karyn Kusama. Like Harron, Kusama makes films about women who are in some sense marginal. Her first film, *Girlfight* (2000), was an independent film about a troubled teenage Latina girl who took up boxing as a way to deal with her problems. *Girlfight* tied for the Grand Jury Prize at Sundance that year and won many other awards as well. Kusama's next film, *Aeon Flux* (2005), was a Hollywood-sized science fiction story about a beautiful female martial artist who belongs to an underground political movement in the future. Although gender issues are never explicit in the film, the society we see is a kind of feminist utopia, with strong yet sexually attractive women and egalitarian gender relations. Most recently Kusama teamed up with screenwriter Diablo Cody to make *Jennifer's Body* (2009), a vampire film about two girl best friends, in which one of them is murdered and becomes a vampire and has to be destroyed by the other. Cody commented in an interview, "Karyn Kusama and I are both outspoken feminists. We want to subvert the classic horror model of women being terrorized. I want to write roles that service women. I want to tell stories from a female perspective. I want to create good parts for actresses where they're not just accessories to men" (in Kwan 2009).

In sum, as we listen to the talk of younger women in various roles and positions across the film industry, we do not hear echoes of *Sex and the City*. Rather, it seems clear that there is a fairly widespread awareness of ongoing issues of sexism and gender inequality. This awareness often dawns as young women leave relatively protected liberal environments (schools and families) and enter the real world in the form of the workplace and the job.[8] Yet the women (and we) must balance all that ("pragmatically") against the fact that they have now carved out a very significant place in the industry and are making more films than ever before. We need to look then at the films to see what they have to say, not only in terms of feminist issues but, as I indicated earlier, in terms of Generation X/neoliberalism issues as well.

The Films

I begin by noting once again that my viewing of (mostly) independent films was intentionally undirected. I watched films that came to my attention from a variety of sources—referenced in the published literature, recommended by friends, drawn from lists of nominees and prizewinners, and so on. I specifically had no agenda and wanted as much as possible to be open to whatever was distinctive about the films coming out of this self-defined world. I approached the subset of one hundred or so films by women filmmakers in much the same way.

Women filmmakers, of course, make all kinds of films, and not all of them are concerned with women or take a female point of view. The most visible case in point would be Kathryn Bigelow, who became the first woman to win the Academy Award for Best Director, for her film *The Hurt Locker* (2009). *The Hurt Locker* is a classic "guy movie," both in the sense that it has a cast with almost no women and in the sense that it is about a classically male subject, war. There was an interesting debate over this at the time of the Academy Award (see especially Dargis 2010b).

Along these lines there was also, in my filmography, a relatively large set of documentaries by women filmmakers on a wide range of not-about-gender political issues. A significant number of these films take on contemporary neoliberal capitalism, both in itself and in relation to environmental issues, and will be discussed in chapter 8. Others were concerned with race (*Tulia, Texas: Scenes from the Drug War*, Emily and Sarah Kunstler, 2005; *The Order of Myths*, Margaret Brown, 2008; *Trouble the Water*, Tia Lessin and Carl Deal, 2008; and *Heart of Stone*, Beth Toni Kruvant, 2009); with violence in other parts of the world (*Control Room*, Jehane Noujaim, 2004; *La Sierra*, Scott Dalton and Margarita Martinez, 2005; *The Prisoner Or: How I Planned to Kill Tony Blair*, Petra Epperlein and Michael Tucker, 2006); with what happens to prisoners exonerated by DNA evidence (*After Innocence*, Jessica Sanders, 2005); with 1960s political hero Daniel Ellsberg (*The Most Dangerous Man in America: Daniel Ellsberg and the Pentagon Papers*, Judith Ehrlich and Rick Goldsmith, 2009); and with the more complicated 1960s political figure William Kunstler (*William Kunstler: Disturbing the Universe*, Emily and Sarah Kunstler, 2009).

Thus, women filmmakers make films on a wide variety of subjects, and I do not mean to suggest that they are, or should be, all making films about women. Nonetheless, my interest in this chapter is specifically on the subject of women filmmakers representing women and/or issues of gender relations, with an eye to the question of "post-feminism." Within this focus, two general clusters of films stood out for me from my open-ended viewing. One was a fairly large set of films about violence against women. I will read these partly in terms of a continuing feminist agenda—an attempt to speak out about issues of domestic violence, rape, etc.—but also in terms of the more general darkness, including violence, which is part of the broader Gen X worldview. The second group was a set of films about lower-class women, poor mothers trying to support and protect their children under extremely difficult economic conditions. These too are very dark, and I look at them in terms of the intersection of class and gender in a world of neoliberal capitalism. What ties them all together is a kind of sympathy and respect for women (characters) that I take to be the minimal definition of "film feminism."

A word here about "politics" in film. As I will discuss at greater length in chapter 8, many filmmakers, both independent and Hollywood, explicitly take the position that one should avoid overt politics in film. There are some individual exceptions (George Clooney and Tim Robbins among actors; Michael Moore and some others in documentary filmmaking), but in general this is a widely accepted view. For example, we heard filmmaker Mary Harron say earlier in this chapter, "I don't make feminist films in the sense that I don't make anything ideological." Looking at the films to be discussed in this section, I would agree that most of them are not in any way "ideological," yet they seem to me to be infused with recognizable feminist concerns. In that sense they are indeed "post-feminist," that is, they have absorbed the concerns of the feminist movement and to some degree take them for granted. But this does not mean that the filmmakers do not see—and represent—the continuing urgency of those concerns in the contemporary world.

DARK INDIES, FEMALE STYLE

I begin with the violent films. Altogether there were ten films by women directors in my filmography, all of which came out between 1996 and 2009, in which women were abused, beaten, raped, and/or murdered by men. Violence against women has of course long been a feminist issue. Yet it was always part of a larger political agenda that included issues of economic equality in the workplace, social representation in the public sphere, division of labor in the household, and legal rights of various kinds. Of these issues, the struggle for representation of women in the public sphere has been very successful and the success has been, by definition, very visible. We now have many women in high places in both politics and the economy, the case in point for the present book being all those women heads of studios with whom I began this chapter. But this has had an unforeseen down side. For people like Eileen Nesbitt, quoted earlier, this creates the impression that issues of gender inequality have largely been resolved. In fact of course this is not true, and issues of economic inequality in particular have been stubbornly resistant to change; this will be relevant in the next part of the chapter. But if we ask why we are seeing so many films about violence against women in recent times, one possible answer is that such violence may appear to be the last remaining, and also stubbornly resistant, form of gender inequality.

I will run through the films briefly here. At the mildest level of violence, the woman is merely beaten. In *North Country* (Niki Caro, 2005), the lead character, Josey, is beaten by her husband in the early scenes of the film. She then leaves him to take a job in the mines of Minnesota to support her kids, but there she is severely harassed and at one point is aggressively roughed up by a coworker at the mine.[9] In *The Prizewinner of Defiance, Ohio* (Jane Anderson, 2005), a housewife enters and wins jingle-writing contests to supplement the family income. Her husband appears to be a decent man but beats her when he gets drunk. In *The Dead Girl* (Karen Moncrieff, 2006) a prostitute named Krista is found dead at the beginning of the film; the film is a reconstruction of her life and death. In one scene, Krista's lover, Rosetta, also a prostitute, is badly beaten up by a sex client.

Beyond beating, bad enough in itself, everything is much more extreme. There is first of all childhood sexual abuse: In *The Dead Girl*, we learn that Krista had run away from home and become a prostitute because she was being molested by her mother's husband. *The Notorious Bettie Page* (Mary Harron, 2006) is the story of a rather innocent young woman named Bettie who poses nude for bondage magazines in the 1950s; as a child she was molested by her father (and as a grown woman beaten by her husband). *Monster* (Patty Jenkins, 2003) is a fictionalized account of the life of Aileen Wuornos, "America's first female serial killer"; Aileen, called Lee in the movie, runs away because she is being both beaten and molested by her grandfather.

There is also rape: in *North Country*, the young Josey is raped by one of her teachers; in *The Notorious Bettie Page*, Bettie is taken to a remote place and gang raped by a group of men; in *Monster*, Lee is raped and tortured by a sex client. An additional film featuring a rape was *Hounddog* (Deborah Kampmeier, 2007); the film was about an eleven-year-old girl in a dysfunctional southern family who dances seductively (but with apparent innocence) in front of various men; she is eventually raped by one of the teenage boys of the town.

And finally—most finally—there is murder: In *Boys Don't Cry* (Kimberly Pierce, 1999) a young woman named Teena Brandon dresses and passes as a boy, Brandon Teena; she meets a young woman and they fall in love; her true identity is discovered by some men of the town and she is beaten and killed. In the vampire film, *Jennifer's Body* (Karyn Kusama, 2009), a high school student named Jennifer is abducted by a rock band and viciously murdered as a sacrifice to Satan. A series of young women are tortured and murdered by the psychotic investment banker/serial killer in *American Psycho* (Mary Harron, 2000). And the young woman Krista, who had left home because she was being abused by her mother's husband, is ultimately murdered by a serial killer in *The Dead Girl*.

A number of these films turn the tables, showing women enacting violence against men.[10] One not yet mentioned is the classic *I Shot Andy Warhol* (Mary Harron, 1996), based on a true story, in which a disturbed young woman comes to imagine that Andy Warhol is controlling her mind. She attempts to kill him and winds up at the end of the film in an insane asylum. Others already noted include *The Dead Girl*; in retaliation for the beating of her lover Rosetta, Krista goes out and beats up the man who did it, as well as trashing his car. A third and more complex example is the demon/vampire thriller *Jennifer's Body*. High school student Jennifer is abducted by a rock band and sacrificed to Satan, so that the band will become rich and famous. Because Jennifer is not a virgin, however, the sacrifice does not work properly, and Jennifer becomes a demon/vampire who then goes around killing boys. Eventually she is destroyed by her former best friend, Needy, but Needy in turn had become infected with Jennifer's demonic essence and is put away in an insane asylum. At the end of the film, Needy escapes from the asylum, goes and finds the rock band, and kills them all.

A fourth and even more complex example is the case of serial killer Aileen Wuornos. The case was made into both a feature film, *Monster* (discussed above), and a documentary, *Aileen: The Life and Death of a Serial Killer* (Nick Broomfield and Joan Churchill, 2003). Wuornos was severely abused as a child and kicked out of her home as a teenager; she eventually became a prostitute, picking up men by hitchhiking at night on highways. Wuornos killed her first victim after he tortured and raped her. She killed six more men out of a mixture of rage, self-defense, and a need for survival money for herself and her lover, Tyria Moore. In the end Moore turned

Wuornos in and testified against her. Wuornos was eventually executed in the state of Florida on the order of then-governor Jeb Bush.

Much could be said about all of these films, which are very emotionally complex and demanding. Here I make only one point, in relation to the post-feminism question motivating this chapter. How shall we read the women's violence against men? As anti-male rage? No doubt that is part of the story, certainly for abused women. But I also read them as stories opened up by the relative absence of organized feminist politics today. The viewer sympathizes with these women who are clearly poor, deranged, or powerless, but the films do not show any viable solutions to their problems other than retaliatory violence. The women are abused, the women are angry, but we see that there is no place to go with this damage and this anger. They take the law into their own hands and wind up in insane asylums or dead.

There is only one film among the ones discussed that actually moves the action from the level of personal rage to the level of political and legal action. This is *North Country*, which is based on a true story. The woman called in the film Josey Aimes was raped and harassed in the extreme. But (the real/fictional) Josey did not kill anyone. Rather, in a landmark case, she brought a class action suit against the mine owners, on grounds of harassment and discrimination, and won on behalf of the class as a whole. The film was made in a studio and has a Hollywood feel to it, with a cast of recognizable stars (Charlize Theron, Woody Harrelson, Sissy Spacek) and a happy ending as Josey wins the lawsuit. It is a sign of the times, as well as my absorption of the indie worldview, that I found the happy ending rather fake, even though it was true.

I take all these films as "feminist," both in their critique of a system that does not adequately condemn gendered violence, and in their fundamental sympathy and respect for women. But it is also important to remember that these films actually constitute a subset of the large number of dark/ depressing/violent films discussed in chapter 2 as embodying the dark worldview of Generation X more broadly. As noted earlier, the filmmakers discussed here are not only women but Xers, living in the midst of the neoliberal economy and all the pessimism and anger it has generated. It is worthwhile to recall that, in response to the question of how the world has changed since their parents' time, the Gen X Children of the Class of '58 expressed not only economic anxieties but a whole range of fears about, among other things, crimes of bodily violation—AIDS, assault, rape. The question of the neoliberal world brings us to the next set of films.

POOR WOMEN

The second group that emerged as a kind of mini-genre for me in the course of film viewing for the project consisted of films about poor (working-class and underclass) women: *Thirteen* (Catherine Hardwicke, 2003), *North Country* (Niki Caro, 2005), *The Dead Girl* (Karen Moncrieff, 2006), *Frozen River* (Courtney Hunt, 2008), and *Winter's Bone* (Deborah Granik, 2010). Although there are only five films, they have certain striking commonalities: all of the lead women are white, disallowing the usual cultural linkage between race and poverty; all center on women who have become, one way or another, single mothers; and all center on a theme of protecting the children. With the exception of Josey Aimes, who works in the mines in the 1970s, and who is thus part of the historical working class, the others all work at the lowest edge of the legitimate contemporary economy (part-time clerk in a convenience store, bingo parlor worker, hairdresser working out of her home) or below that edge (smugglers of illegal immigrants, [daughter of] backwoods drug cooker, prostitute). All are very poor, barely getting by. While there have always been poor, working-class and underclass women in capitalist society, I will take the appearance of a spate of these films between 2003 and 2010 as part of a more articulated critique of the neoliberal economy as it impinges on women in families.

I begin with some very quick plot summaries of the films. In *Thirteen* a divorced mother and recovering cocaine addict (Melanie) struggles to make a new life for herself and her teenage daughter. But the daughter becomes close with a very messed-up girl in her high school and embarks on a self-destructive path. In *North Country*, which has already appeared several times in these pages, a divorced woman (Josey) attempts to make a new life for herself and her children. She takes a job in the iron mines of Minnesota but suffers severe sexual harassment; she brings a lawsuit against the mine owners and wins. In *The Dead Girl*, the body of a young woman (Krista) is found in a field. Through flashbacks we learn that she came from a middle-class family but had run away because her stepfather was sexually abusing her. In *Frozen River*, two women (Ray and Lila) struggling in poverty join forces to make money by driving illegal immigrants across the frozen St. Lawrence River in winter. And in *Winter's Bone*, a seventeen-year-old girl (Ree) struggles to take care of her young siblings after the father disappeared and the mother became catatonic.

The (white) working/lower classes have always held a certain fascination for (white) middle-class Americans. For many, the working class is where they came from. For many too, even before the acceleration of downward mobility under neoliberalism, the working class (or lower) is where they fear they might wind up (see especially Ehrenreich 1989 on the middle class's long-term "fear of falling"). For many Americans, then, the working class can never be totally Other, or, at least, it is always part Other and part self. Unlike most other Others, working-class figures thus create very powerful possibilities for identification and dis-identification (see Ortner 2006b). The following discussion assumes this particular power of signification of working- and lower-class characters for middle-class audiences and, in the case of this set of films, for middle-class women.

What then are these films collectively saying about women, social class, poverty, and so forth, in the present moment? The first thing they seem very clearly to be saying is that life for many women in the twenty-first century is not like anything portrayed in *Sex and the City*. The women in that TV series have social lives full of charming men and seemingly inexhaustible money with which to buy an endless quantity of upscale consumer goods. In contrast, the lives of the women in these films are poor and chaotic, and men's places in those lives are mostly problematic. Consumer goods are scarce and, when acquired or desired, are primarily important for survival (several house trailers in *Frozen River*) or for sustaining relationships (presents for children in *Frozen River* and *The Dead Girl*), rather than luxury. The films are an implicit critique of a certain self-indulgent PMC lifestyle, and to the extent that it is also associated with the "post-feminism" of *Sex and the City*, they provide a critique of that lifestyle as well.

Beyond this I will argue that these films can be read as telling stories about the implications of the contemporary neoliberal economy not only for poor women but for many middle-class women who face the specter of downward mobility for themselves and their children. A bad economy is bad for everyone, but women/mothers face additional disadvantages, including both lower wages and usually greater responsibilities for child care and support.

Before I get to that discussion, however, I want to consider the ways in which the poor/working-class/underclass settings of the films in general recontextualize and resignify a variety of terms already in play in this discussion. Putting class in the picture does not simply add another "variable" to the mix, but shifts many things around.

HOW A WORKING-CLASS SETTING CHANGES THE PICTURE

In the first place, the working-class setting simply makes class itself visible. It is well known that Americans tend not to think very much in class terms. Most Americans self-identify as "middle class" and attribute most forms of difference or inequality to race and ethnicity (Ortner 2003, 2006b). Films in which white people are economically on the edge, or actually poor, make social class a visible reality. Representations of poor people of color may seem "normal," while representations of poor white people have the capacity to give middle-class whites second thoughts.

Second, the presence of lower-class-ness and poverty in the films changes the social/political meaning of "men." In the preceding section on films involving violence against women, there was a polarization of men against women and women against men. Such polarization was part of a stereotypical "feminist" perspective in relatively pure form, but from early on in the second-wave feminist movement it was criticized (correctly) as "bourgeois." Only white middle-class women, it was argued, had the luxury of seeing sexism and patriarchy as the preeminent social evils. Working-class women, poor women, and women of color have to deal with poverty, racism, and all their associated ills as well. When class and race are added into the mix, then, there tends to be much less categorical condemnation of "men."

We can see this clearly in these lower-class-based films. On the one hand, there are plenty of stereotypically bad (sexist, patriarchal) men. Indeed, all the films are launched by the fact that the men have, in one way or another, abandoned their families. But the "bad men" are counterbalanced in several ways. In several of the films there are women who are just as problematic as the men. There are the mothers who passively allow sexism (or worse) to happen and do not protect their daughters (Josey's mother in *North Country*, Krista's mother in *The Dead Girl*, Ree's mother in *Winter's Bone*). In a more active mode, there is Lila's mother-in-law who has stolen Lila's baby in *Frozen River*, and the three women who beat Ree up very badly in *Winter's Bone*.[11] In addition, some of the films have "good men" who counterbalance the bad husbands or fathers. There is the lawyer who takes on Josey's case against the mine owners in *North Country*. Melanie has a loving and understanding boyfriend in *Thirteen*. In *Frozen River* there is a concerned and decent state trooper who is supportive of Ray, and a kindly tribal policeman who steps in and lends a hand at key moments. And even apparently bad men may turn around in the course of the film, as in the case of Ree's uncle, who at first roughs her up and refuses to help her but in the end comes through.

Finally, the class factor may be seen to recontextualize the parent-child relationship. To see this, we need to look back at the pedophile films discussed in chapter 4. Although I did not underscore this at the time, most of those films were set in the middle class (*Capturing the Friedmans, Mysterious Skin, Twist of Faith*) or in several cases even the upper middle class (*L.I.E., Happiness, Little Children*). In that context I discussed the point that emerges from the Gen X literature that middle-class children, more used to stable two-parent families, seem to have felt particularly hard-hit (one might even say "abused") by the rising rate of divorce, of mothers going back to work, and of absent fathers. In that middle-class context I showed that virtually all of the pedophile films blamed one or both of the parents for the fact that the child was molested. The parents were seen as having failed to protect the children and were in many cases set up to appear at least as much to blame as the pedophile himself.

In contrast to the situation in those films, it is fundamental to the stories in all of the films set in the lower classes that the women (if not the men) actively seek to protect their children. In *North Country* all of Josey's actions are directed to supporting her children, after leaving her abusive husband. In *Thirteen*, Melanie struggles to support her kids both materially and, as the daughter spirals out of control, psychologically. In *The Dead Girl*, Krista is working as a prostitute and has had to put her child in the care of another family. But the entire plot is driven by the fact that it is the child's birthday, and Krista is intent on visiting the girl and bringing her a present. In *Winter's Bone*, all of Ree's actions are likewise directed toward supporting and caring for her younger brother and sister (as well as her mentally ill mother). She even tries to enlist in the Army in order to get the signing bonus, but the recruiter points out that she would not be able to take the children with her, whereupon she gives up the idea.

Frozen River, finally, actually has multiple plots about protecting children. First Ray, the white woman, tries to get a raise and thus some more income for herself and her kids, but then when that does not work out, she joins in the smuggling venture with Lila, the Mohawk woman.[12] Second, Lila turns out to have been married and to have had a baby, but the husband died, and the mother-in-law "stole" the baby from the hospital for reasons that are not clear. Lila gets involved in smuggling in order to make enough money to be able to reclaim and support the baby on her own. There is also a third plot in which a child is put at risk and then saved by the two mothers. On their final run across the frozen St. Lawrence River, the two women are ferrying a Pakistani couple carrying a large duffel bag. Ray thinks the couple might be terrorists, and the duffel bag might contain a bomb, so she puts the bag out on the ice and drives off. But the bag contains the couple's baby, and when Ray and Lila learn this, they go back to get it without a second thought, at considerable danger to themselves.

My point here is not that middle-class parents do not protect their children and that working-class mothers do, although that is how it appears when one surveys parents across the two sets of films. My point is that the contrasting class settings of the two sets of films alter the films' perspectives on parents. The pedophile films, set in middle-class (or higher) families, render the class factor relatively invisible to middle-class audiences, and in fact class plays no visible role in the stories. In that context, there is no sense of a larger political economy that is (enabling or) constraining the politics of family life, and the parents appear solely at fault. On the other hand, in these films set in the working or lower classes, the mothers' struggles to protect their children are rendered starkly visible. Even the bad behavior of fathers is, if not excused, at least contextualized within a larger picture of the scarcity of resources and the chaos of life in the lower classes. And in fact, despite all the bad things that happen in the films, and despite all the poverty and absence of resources, no children are ever harmed, at least not by predatory others as in the pedophile films.

In the foregoing discussion I have sought to show how the working-class settings of the these films "change the picture," making class in general more visible, reducing the polarization of the genders, and fostering recognition of the ways in which the parent-child relationship may be constrained by larger economic forces. I have spent some time on this issue because I think class is often given short shrift in discussions of social difference and inequality, which tend to focus more heavily on race and ethnicity. Under neoliberal capitalism, for unfortunate reasons, class is becoming much more salient.

MOTHERS AND CHILDREN AND DOWNWARD
MOBILITY UNDER NEOLIBERALISM

Needless to say, there is nothing new about poor women, single mothers, and so forth, in capitalist America. But two things about these films are significant in terms of relating them to the present historical moment. The first is the simple fact that the films appeared at this time, that is, the time when the terrible effects of neoliberal capitalism have become much more visible and tangible. The second is that most of the women characters are white. There is a long-term association in conservative American thought between black women and poverty, but not between white women and poverty. I suggest then that all of these films are speaking in part from and to the anxieties of (white) middle-class women at a time when the neoliberal economy is squeezing the middle class, and when middle-class families really need two incomes to get by. At the same time the rate of divorce and single parenting has skyrocketed for the middle class, and women still make less money than men. It is a perfect storm of economic and social threat for middle-class women with children (see especially Newman 1988).

In the past the "fear of falling" was largely an abstract possibility for the middle class, which seemed fundamentally secure. The point about people in lower-class positions, on the other hand, is not just that they're poor—have less money, less things—but that their lives are much more insecure. They have less margin of error and are much closer to some edge where their lives may start coming apart (see especially Ehrenreich 2001). All of this has become much more real, or at least more imaginatively real, for many middle-class women, and that is in part what we see in the films.

The films may be read as nearly physical embodiments of the relatively abstract idea of "downward mobility." And although we tend to think of downward mobility primarily in connection with middle-class people dropping down the class ladder, people in the lower levels of society can always drop down even lower, with even more disastrous effects. To show lower-class people sliding down thus creates even more powerful images of the potential devastation of downward mobility. In this final section then I want to explore the representations of downward mobility that we see in the films around four issues: poverty itself, consumer goods, social chaos, and loss of children. In the end all the films will come to some kind of shaky resolution, but once again these films are meant to be "realist," and happy endings are few and far between.

Let us begin with poverty itself. In two of the films, poverty is a virtual character. We see the poverty of the women in *Frozen River*, living in poorly insulated trailers in the freezing winter in upstate New York, Ray feeding her kids popcorn for dinner. The film is shot in the bruised colors of winter, with the weather announcer forecasting ever-colder temperatures on the sound track; the environment underscores the poverty of the characters. In *Winter's Bone* we see the poverty of Ree and her family, living in shacks in the backwoods of the Ozarks, running out of food, hunting squirrels for dinner, being helped just before the point of desperation by a kindly neighbor. Here too it is winter, and despite the green of the forests, the film has a cold and hungry look. In both films the physicality (and ugliness) of poverty is powerfully realized.

Second, there is the question of consumer goods, an issue that was central to the "post-feminist" mind-set of *Sex and the City*. In that context the loss of the ability to shop and consume is seen as one of the worst imaginable fates for a middle-class woman (see especially McRobbie 2009). In two of the films under discussion here, consumer goods play a central role. In *Frozen River*, Ray had been saving money to buy a double-wide trailer for her family. The plot is set in motion when the husband not only decamps at the beginning of the film but takes Ray's savings with him. The absent trailer continues to play an active role throughout the film. And in *Thirteen*, there are issues of clothes for the teenage daughter Tracy. The mother, Melanie, and Tracy have moved because of the divorce; Tracy is starting a new high school; Tracy does not have the necessary cool clothes; but Melanie has almost no money. Melanie takes Tracy shopping to buy secondhand clothes from a woman selling them from a van. Tracy seems fine with this, but that is before Melanie and Tracy's relationship starts to go downhill. Subsequently, Tracy teams up with the destructive Evie, one of whose major activities is shoplifting. Evie initiates Tracy into this activity and, like the absent trailer, the shoplifted clothes come to play an active role in the plot. For the women in both films, consumer goods are necessities—

things needed for physical and social survival. But they are also small luxuries, providers of relatively simple pleasures that seem always to be out of reach for poor people.

Third, there is a representation of poverty as chaos, as an inability to maintain order in, and control over, one's life, compared to the ideal life in the middle class. In *Thirteen* the chaos is embodied in the lower-class Evie, who is more or less completely out of control—lying, stealing, taking drugs, sexually promiscuous—and draws Tracy, formerly a good daughter, into her chaotic life. In *Winter's Bone*, it is embodied in the threat of homelessness. The father has disappeared, and unless he returns, the family will lose the house. The loss of the house is shown as a horrendous prospect; Ree says if they lose it they will be "turned out in the fields like dogs." And in *The Dead Girl*, the chaos takes the form of the inability to control people and things. Krista is trying to visit her daughter on her daughter's birthday. She does not have a car but gets her pimp/boyfriend to agree to drive her. However, he backs out at the last minute, and Plan A collapses. She then borrows a motorcycle, but the motorcycle breaks down, and Plan B collapses. Finally, she sticks out her thumb to hitch a ride. A man picks her up, but we realize it is Carl, who will kill her.

Next, all the films show what one understands to be the ultimate threat of poverty for mothers, the inability to take care of and protect one's children, and hence the possible loss of the children. The issue of the potential loss of children is the central engine of the plot in all five films. In both *Thirteen* and *North Country* the loss of the child is shown as taking place through alienation. In *Thirteen*, as Tracy gets more and more involved with Evie, she becomes more and more angry at, and hostile toward, her mother. And in *North Country*, as Josey is shunned by the townspeople for presumed sexual promiscuity, her son Sam is humiliated and becomes increasingly sullen and distant. Other films tell other stories about potential loss of children. In *Winter's Bone*, when it appears that Ree and her family will lose their house, a neighbor shows up and offers to take and raise the younger brother, with the implication that the boy will become a kind of servant in the neighbor's household. Ree, who is tremendously attached to the kids, replies angrily that the neighbor can go straight to hell, and that she and the kids would "die living in a cave before they would spend one night" with him. In *Frozen River*, although the bond between Ray and her sons is fairly solid, the specter of losing children runs through the entire film, as we have seen.

And finally, there is *The Dead Girl,* a brilliant film that constructs, through multiple episodes and a changing cast of characters, the most complex representation of a middle-class woman's fears about both downward mobility and the potential loss of a child. I would like to spend a little more time on it here. The body of the dead girl, Krista, is found at the beginning of the film. In relation to her mother Melora, Krista as daughter is the one exception to my statement that no children are harmed by predators in these films, since Krista is killed by a serial killer. But this is because the relationship between Melora and Krista is not a version of the protective mother-child relationship we are seeing in the lower-class women films. Rather, it is a replay of the mother-child relationship we have seen in the pedophile films, in which the stepfather was molesting Krista, and in which Melora was failing to protect Krista from the abuse.

Melora herself is very visibly middle class, in terms of her clothing and, as we eventually see, her house. Although her husbands are out of the picture, she does not appear in danger of downward mobility herself. Rather, the life and death of the daughter Krista condense both the specter of downward mobility—Krista becomes a prostitute—and the complete alienation of the child, as Krista cuts herself off from her mother and eventually dies without any reconciliation.

But Krista, in turn, had a daughter, and as the story shifts from the relationship between Melora and Krista to the relationship between Krista and her baby daughter, we shift to the terrain of the "lower-class women" films. As we know, Krista tries throughout the film to visit her daughter and give her a birthday present. Although she is separated from her, she is trying to maintain the connection. After Krista is killed, Melora finds the baby and takes her home. It is clearly an act of symbolically restoring her own lost child. But it is also an act of reversal of downward mobility, as she rescues the child from a poor household where the mother complains about the cost of caring for the baby, and takes the baby home to her own middle-class house.

I have been arguing that these films about poor/lower-class women can be read as allegories of the potential fate of any woman in the new social order, in which neoliberal policies, greater likelihood of divorce, and various patriarchal biases combine to render women particularly vulnerable to downward mobility. And although I have emphasized the anxieties of middle-class women, I want to return to the point once again that the films evince care and respect and even love for women in general, across lines of class and race. The films thus constitute a repository of political possibility, as I will argue about other political films in chapter 8.

We now turn to the final ethnographic chapter, about the actual process of (independent) film production. Although there are important ways in which film production has been affected by new technologies and by the neoliberalization and globalization of the economy, there are also many ways in which the process has remained surprisingly constant over the past fifty years, if not longer. In addition, most (but not, as we shall see, all) film people regard making movies as ultimately very rewarding. The chapter thus has a positive tone that will give the reader some relief, before we plunge back into the real world in the final film chapter.

CHAPTER 7

Making Films

There comes a time in every film's genesis when you have to stop talking about it and start shooting it. And therein lies the crux: As intimidating and overwhelming as making a movie is, it is more exhilarating than imagination or words can convey. Filmmaking is both beauty and beast.
Stubbs and Rodriguez (2000: 6)

One strand of the neoliberalism story has to do with the deteriorating conditions of work in the new economy. As discussed previously, the new economy is, among other things, "post-Fordist," which is to say that the system of explicit and tacit agreements between capital and labor that prevailed in the mid-twentieth century has been nearly dismantled, and the situation of American labor has deteriorated greatly. Decently paying working-class jobs have all but disappeared. Job insecurity is rife. The job prospects for the middle class are not much better. Young people with higher educations are often forced to take jobs far below their qualifications, and the jobs are both scarcer and more insecure as well. But my point about film production in this chapter is actually the opposite: the process of making a film remains a zone of relatively unalienated, or anyway less alienated, labor.

The movie industry has been enormously affected by neoliberalism, particularly in the sense that all the Hollywood studios have been bought by large corporations for which making movies is a small and somewhat disposable part of their enterprise. There is thus tremendous pressure on studios to make a profit; this is part of the background for the shift of studios to a blockbuster strategy, and this, in turn, is part of the background for the reactive emergence of the independent film sector. In this sense neoliberalism is behind this and every chapter of this book.

But when we look at production, at the actual process of making movies, there is a way in which the process can have a Fordist feel to it. In making a movie, people can feel collectively engaged in a project; people can feel bonded with those around them; people can feel that they shared in making something good at the end. They don't always feel that way by any means, but the conditions of the work are such that it is genuinely possible. One night on the set of *Sunshine Cleaning* I talked to producer Jeb Brody about how numbingly hard this work seemed to be, twelve or more hours a day, five or six days a week. Brody put it in perspective:

> He said yes, and while we [producers] get to take some time off when the picture is done, many of the crew immediately go on to another "show." But then he said, "But we are all creating something together, hopefully something good. How many jobs can you say that about? Maybe construction workers building a building, but how much else?" (Field notes, March 23, 2007)

Again, this is not to say that film production is some easy and happy-go-lucky process; far from it. A film production is a fragile thing. It is an enormously complex operation with many fault lines along which it can break down. The whole point of this chapter will be to take apart the production process, to look at both the weak points along which a production might come apart and the social mechanisms that, nonetheless, usually manage to hold it together. But I do want to frame that discussion in terms of this more positive general point.

The discussion that follows will make few distinctions between Hollywood films and independent films. In general, productions have the same general organization, the same general requirements, and the same general trajectories. But there are important differences, particularly in terms of the much lower budgets of independent films, which establish much greater constraints on what the filmmaker can and cannot do. Concerns about money can be quite overwhelming for independent filmmakers, and I need to spend a little time on that here.

Money

As was discussed at length in chapter 1, there are significant differences between Hollywood movies and independent films in terms of content and mood. In addition and related to that are differences of budget: Hollywood movies are expensive, because the studios hope to make a lot of money in return; independent films are made with small budgets so that independent filmmakers can avoid studio money and control and make the often-uncommercial films they want to make.

Small budgets in turn put a great deal of pressure on the production process, and independent producers and filmmakers have to worry intensely about money before, during, and after the life of the film. We can see this in the independent film *In the Soup*, which won the 1992 Grand Jury Prize at Sundance, in which filmmaker Aldofo (Steve Buscemi) spends the entire film trying to raise money for his film, to the point where the fundraising basically overtakes his life and he loses sight of the film itself. Eventually Aldolfo as narrator says, "I used to think there was more to making a movie than making money. I was beginning to see that there was more to making money than making a movie."

Even if a filmmaker and his or her producer succeed in raising a certain amount of money, there are always fears about running out, and making a very low budget film can be very difficult and stressful throughout the process. Filmmaker Doug Liman (*Swingers, Mr. and Mrs. Smith*) talked at length about this in an interview with author Josh Horowitz:

> **DL:** Making a movie for $200,000 requires a specific set of skills from the director. They better know how to DP [do the work of the director of photography]. They better know how to do every single job on that set. And when the money runs out, as it did on *Swingers*, the director is going to have to do every single one of those jobs that's left because there won't be any crew left. In *Swingers* every post-production sound was recorded by me with a DAT machine I bought from The Good Guys, used for twenty-nine days, and then returned with their money-back guarantee. I was insane. But I had to do what I had to. I had taken somebody's money. I had to finish the movie.
>
> **JH:** *You were also the DP of* Swingers. *How often were you behind the camera?*

DL: Who else would be behind the camera? I don't think you understand how small our crew was. There was almost no crew. The gaffer [chief electrician] was this guy known around L.A. as "Rod with a truck." You hire him because he comes with a truck with some lights in it. The majority of the lighting in that movie was done with lightbulbs I bought from Home Depot. (in Horowitz 2006: 197)

Making a film on $200,000 is almost impossible. But for many purposes even $2 million or $3 million is a relatively low budget, especially if there are stars with any kind of name recognition. Joe Carnahan talked about making *Narc* for a budget in that range, and the fear of not being able to finish: "If we had $3 million to make that film, I'd eat my hat, man. The crew was constantly being told there was no money and they were going to shut the film down. It created this powerful sense of dread and angst that if you're shooting a romantic comedy you're fucked, but the fact that we were doing this kind of heavy-duty melodrama, it worked beautifully. I would never want that kind of dread hanging over a project" (in Horowitz 2006: 9–10).

At the same time independent filmmakers will also talk about how having less money can also make one more creative. For example, filmmaker Karyn Kusama said, "I frankly find it a lot more creatively freeing to have a very limited budget. That's an exciting challenge to me. You start to really kind of hone what's crucial because you only have so many resources to go around" (in Horowitz 2006: 172). Similarly, we can hear Hollywood directors say that they had too much money and this was the cause of chaos and near breakdown in production. Francis Ford Coppola said of *Apocalypse Now*, "We had too many people, too much money, little by little we went insane" (on camera in *Hearts of Darkness*). Melanie Griffith commented about the endless delays in the shooting of *Bonfire of the Vanities*: "Sometimes . . . the more money they have to work with, the more fucked up things get" (in Salamon [1991] 2002: 226).

Leaving aside the money issue, however, the process of making movies is fairly standardized, and the following discussion contains examples from both kinds of films.

Filmmakers on Production

Filmmakers vary greatly on how they feel about the production process. Some love it, some hate it, and almost all agree that it is very difficult. I'll start with the improbable group of filmmakers who do not enjoy the film-making process, find it very stressful, but simply will themselves through it.

Here is an interview with Trey Parker and Matt Stone, on the making of *Cannibal! The Musical* (1996):

> **JH:** Was it fun to be shooting this bizarre musical while still in school?
> **MS:** No.
> **TP:** No. It's like making anything. You hate it. And anyone I've ever talked to that's worth their salt actually kind of hates the process. (in Horowitz 2006: 227)

And on the making of *Orgazmo* (1997):

> **JH:** Was it any more of an enjoyable experience than *Cannibal!* was?
> **TP:** Once again, it was miserable. It's always miserable. I have never had a good time on a set. I've never had a good time making an episode of *South Park* either. I always hate it, and I always say, "I'll never do it again." (in Horowitz 2006: 230)

Or here is Todd Solondz on production in general:

> The shoot, the actual production, is really the most stressful period for me. . . . It's always assaultive and physically draining, and fraught with all sorts of compromises that are part and parcel of the job. Some people have a directorial character. As for me, I don't think I was cut out to be a director. I'm not a director because I want to be. It's more that I don't want someone else to direct my stuff; if someone's going to screw it up, I'd rather screw it up myself. (in Tang 2002: 2)

And here is a little exchange between a director who dislikes production and one who likes it. Steven Spielberg visited Brian De Palma on the set of *Bonfire of the Vanities*. They were walking to lunch at the commissary, and De Palma commented that he never went to lunch there:

> De Palma said, "I go to my trailer and sleep."
> "I don't take a trailer, and I don't use it if I'm given one," said Spielberg. "I like to hang out with the actors on the way back to the set."
> De Palma rolled his eyes.
> Spielberg laughed. "I enjoy this process more than you do." (in Salamon [1991] 2002: 252–53)

Now let's hear from directors at the more positive end of the spectrum. Here's the view from filmmaker David Gordon Green: "When I'm in production, it's kind of an escape and a freedom—an exploration. We're all discovering things" (in Horowitz 2006: 86). Or screenwriter and director Callie Khouri said on a panel, "I'll bitch about writing all day long, but directing is so much fun, so exhilarating. . . . The worst day on a movie set is still the best day of your life. . . . It's a privilege. I love it. I'm happy to do it. Even when I'm having a temper tantrum" (field notes, February 27, 2008).

Or this from an interview with filmmaker Franc. Reyes. I asked him about his style of working on a set:

> I come from a big family, you know, I have seven brothers and sisters and I love the family idea. When I left home, . . . I left with a dance troupe so it was always a bunch of us against the world. That's the way I wanted my sets to feel. I love it when family members come to visit me or friends come to visit me. The people I choose to work with ideally have to be people who are collaborative people. I can't deal with people who are living in their own cult of personality and their own thing. I can't deal. We are making movies, for God's sake, there are people out there with real jobs. We're making movies, you've got to enjoy every step. (Interview, September 8, 2007)

But love it or hate it, everyone agrees that making a film is an enormously difficult job. Filmmaker Jim Jarmusch commented, "Shooting is enormously difficult and it takes the collaboration of many people and is very complicated" (from the bonus materials on the DVD of *Down by Law* [1986]). Mira Nair said, "[Filmmaking] is so hard and so obsessive and so much money is involved, it has to be totally possessing, otherwise I would rather be tending my garden and making a meal" (interview, September 3, 2007). Nair also said that "gargantuan energy is needed for movie making of any nature. It's so many personalities. It's so much [going on]." Or as James Mangold said on a panel, "There are so many worries. There is such a sense of chaos on the set. You're making decisions on a dime" (field notes, June 24, 2007). And Gregg Araki is quoted as saying, "I'd like to step away from the production—it's always so chaotic, so many people" (in Hays 1997).

Yet in the end most filmmakers are, and more or less have to be, pragmatic about the difficulties. Richard Linklater expressed that view: "People always talk about how hard and unnatural the process of making a film is. I've always worked toward a world in which making films is a very natural part of it. A lot of it is not looking at the inevitable problems as problems but as momentarily missing pieces of a puzzle" (Linklater 1992: 129).

The Director's Set

The set belongs to the director. The director has final authority and final responsibility. As Francis Ford Coppola said in the documentary about the making of *Apocalypse Now*, "A film director is one of the few dictatorial posts left in a world getting more and more democratic" (*Hearts of Darkness*, 1991). Or as Julian Schnabel said on a panel, "It is not a democracy when you're making a film. You have to be open when people bring you ideas. But ultimately the director is responsible for everything in the film" (field notes, February 21, 2008). The most common metaphors are military ones. Vilmos Zsigmond, the cinematographer on *Bonfire of the Vanities*, is quoted as saying, "The director is the captain of the ship. He's the general and you have to go along" (in Salamon [1991] 2002: 80). Bryan Singer, who had earlier made some independent films (e.g., *Public Access*, 1993; *The Usual Suspects*, 1995) and later directed *Superman Returns* (2006), expanded on the point: "If the ship goes down, you're the captain and you have to go with it. That's the loneliness of the job. They don't call it 'a Bryan Singer film' for nothing" (in Smith 2006).[1]

A set in production is always spoken of in the possessive case, relative to the director: it is his/her set. Richard Linklater, in a public interview, spoke about the importance of putting together a balanced crew: "It's good if the crew is all at the same level. . . . If you get some Academy Award winning DP [director of photography] or something, who's at a higher level than everyone, *it becomes his set*" (field notes, June 26, 2006). Or this from a letter from George Clooney to director David O. Russell during the *Three Kings* shoot: "You have an angry, frustrated set. You humiliate the script supervisor who's doing a miraculous job. . . . An extra has an epileptic seizure in the middle of *your* set. I'm on the ground with him and you go back to see replays of takes. This is your set. Even if you're not interested, fake it. *You* set the tone" (in Waxman 2005, end material, p. 9, emphasis in original).

I use this quote to say nothing one way or the other objectively about David Russell as a director; it is clearly George Clooney's point of view.

But the quote illustrates both the way in which, in local understandings, a set "belongs" to the director (*"your* set") and the fact that the director sets the style of work and social relations on the set (*"You* set the tone"). Some directors—Alfred Hitchcock, for example—famously ran a fairly tight ship (to continue the naval metaphor), storyboarding every scene in detail in advance (Ansen 2006). Similarly, asked in a public interview about experimentation during shooting, filmmaker Danny Boyle (*28 Days Later, Slumdog Millionaire*) replied, "We try to do most of the experiment at the script stage. It is too expensive to change things during shooting. I am very disciplined." Later in the interview, the interviewer asked him whether he allowed actors to improvise during shooting. Boyle answered, "Personally I don't like improvisation. I'm kind of a control freak" (field notes, June 29, 2007).

But other directors allow or even cultivate a certain amount of chaos on their sets and see it as contributing to the creativity of the filmmaking process. Here is a piece of an interview with Doug Liman (*Swingers, The Bourne Identity*):

> [Q.]: You have said in the past that you actually like an environment of chaos on a set.
> DL: Yeah. I usually find that my ideas in advance aren't as good as the ideas I come up with in the moment. So I like to have an environment that's thought provoking. . . . I really don't like wooden filmmaking. (in Horowitz 2006: 198)

Similarly, Mira Nair said, "What I love about shooting in India is to choreograph the chaos. . . . Here [in the United States] it's all so dreadfully competent and systematized—you have to create the electricity" (in Lahr 2002: 7). Steven Spielberg had a similar view: "I think the best performances—from filmmakers and from actors—have happened when there are whole stretches of tremendous instability about the process" (Smith and Ansen 2006: 65). And for the most famous example, take Robert Altman:

> Notoriously laid-back, in love with improvisation and multiple cameras, Altman was the director as party host, throwing a bash and letting the camera capture the results. He was once asked why he gave so few explicit instructions to his actors. "I'm looking for something I've never seen, so how can I tell them what to do?" (Ansen 2006: 69)

Regardless of personal style, however, the director's authority is theoretically final. A chaotic director (or an overly controlling director, for that matter) may be a prime cause of instability on the set. Nonetheless, everyone working in and on the film must adapt to the director's style and acknowledge his or her authority. This authority is repeatedly affirmed by all the technical workers—assistant director, heads of technical departments, editors. On the set of *Sunshine Cleaning*, for example, I was introduced to the production designer. We talked about the director using a real elevator rather than a set, even though it is more difficult to shoot. As I wrote in my notes, "He says solemnly, in a formula I have heard before, 'We are here to serve the vision of the director'" (field notes, March 19, 2007). Or here is Chad Beck, one of the editors of *No End in Sight* (Charles Ferguson, 2007), talking about the editing process: "I think the thing with [Ferguson] is that he had a tremendous amount of confidence and insight about telling the story of the entire occupation [of Iraq]. It wasn't too daunting and ambitious for him, and my job is to honor his vision. It is my job to make what he wants happen" (interview, February 3, 2007). Finally, the first assistant director (A.D.) in the satire on independent filmmaking *Living in Oblivion* intones early in the film, "I'm here to serve the vision of the filmmaker," and the DP in the documentary *Loop Dreams* says the same exact thing.

The Vulnerable Set

"When you're shooting, it's a very vulnerable time"
—Director Jason Reitman, speaking on a panel, February 20, 2008.

Ideally, and in principle, the director has full authority and control over his/her set and production. Yet there are fundamental fault lines in the social organization of film productions, lines along which the production can at any moment break down. Most films do not, of course, break down, but if we want to know why filmmaking is considered so difficult by many, one must look at both the fault lines and the social dynamics designed to override them.[2] I'll break the discussion into three general areas: relations between directors and crew, relations between directors and actors, and the material conditions of filmmaking.

DIRECTORS AND CREW

Any film is divided into so-called above-the-line and below-the-line personnel. Above the line consists of the creative team of the film: the director, producers, writers, and actors. Below the line consists of the technical people: the cinematographer or DP; the editor(s); the (first) assistant director (A.D.), who mediates between the director and the crew; the line producer, who deals with money and schedules and mediates between the production and the outside world; the heads of departments (electrical, sets, props, hair, makeup, wardrobe, etc.); and the actual workers in those departments.[3]

The above-the-line/below-the-line distinction is clearly and visibly a class divide. The crew members are largely working class; in the case of studio films they are all unionized and have a very strong working-class identity. As one producer said to me, "A movie set is a very blue collar place" (field notes, July 7, 2006). Similarly, I was talking to a cinematographer at a party at Sundance in 2007: "He asked me what my angle was for this project and I said 'class,' and he said that is perfect, it is totally right, and nobody is writing about it. He said all the producers and directors are from fancy educations, while everyone else is lower class" (field notes, January 28, 2007). And finally, as writer Julie Salamon observed, "The social stratification was the only certainty on a film set. The players were always different, but status was constant" (Salamon [1991] 2002: 114).

For super-cheap, usually first-time, independent films, the crew is often made up of friends of the filmmaker, and the class distinction may not be relevant, but even in those situations it is very easy for a crew member to begin to feel exploited. As filmmaker Chad Etchison said, "No matter how cool you are with your crew, there's definitely an us-against-them mentality that is unavoidable" (in Stubbs and Rodriguez 2000: 98).

In very low budget films, the crew may be inexperienced or incompetent. More often, however, film crews are extraordinarily skilled and professional. They take pride in their work and, especially if they like the director and the film, will throw themselves into the job heart and soul. More directors than not will rave about the commitment of the crew and the quality of their work. Crew members are willing to be accommodating, and to go the extra mile to help the director accomplish what he or she is trying to do. At the same time, they will not be taken advantage of and there are certain lines they will not cross. I'll give examples from two of the productions I observed, both of which involved meal breaks. I should note here that production days are very long and tiring, and meal breaks—which are structured into the contract—are very important.

The director gives orders to the crew via the first A.D., and the crew communicates its desires to the director in the same way. A good A.D. is critical to a smooth shoot; he or she can soothe crew dissatisfaction or amplify it. Here is an example from *Nameless Indie*:

> Before lunch Jack* [the director] was trying to get a certain shot and the Steadicam operator had to catch a plane. Plus it was getting late and the crew was due for lunch. The A.D. kept wanting to break and Jack kept saying, one more take. Finally the A.D. said this is the last take and when Jack said one more, he just said no and shouted out, "checking gate," which ended the scene. (Field notes, March 21, 2007)

And here is a very similar example from one of the other productions I observed, which for present purposes I will also disguise:

> Margie* the first A.D. comes in. She says, do we have to get the shot of the guys kicking in the door? The director Hal* says yeah, we have to get the shot. She says Harry* [the DP] doesn't think so. He says, well Harry's not directing this movie. She says Margie [herself] also doesn't think so. He says we need the shot. She says, getting angry, Hey man, it's 2:00 and [the crew haven't had lunch yet]. He says c'mon, and takes her away to the set. I assume he's getting the shot. (Field notes, February 21, 2007)

These kinds of problems are basically structural, and they can and do arise for virtually any director. But the problems are exacerbated when there are personality issues between director and crew. Some directors are simply not very organized, or don't want to be. Rodrigo García said that "he has worked as a cameraman and cinematographer on films where you just show up in the morning and the director waffles around trying to decide what he's going to shoot" (field notes, February 6, 2007). And we learn in the documentary *Hearts of Darkness* that Francis Ford Coppola was going through an enormous crisis of creativity and would show up on certain days on the set of *Apocalypse Now* without a plan for the day's shooting (E. Coppola, Bahr, and Hickenlooper, 1991).

I wrote earlier about how a director with an improvisational style may be a particular cause of instability on the set. This is reported to have been the case with David Russell during the shooting of *Three Kings*: "Russell wanted to work improvisationally, changing dialogue and devising new shots as he went along. The crew wanted more preparation and didn't know what to expect with Russell" (Waxman 2005: 237). They began to stage a kind of low-level resistance campaign:

> The crew began to form into a kind of anti-Russellian bloc. They thought the movie was strange, with its shifting dialogue and ambiguous morality. It had good Arabs and bad Arabs. It was confusing. They would mutter under their breaths, "What kind of crap is this?" and "This is insane. What movie are we making?"—comments that would filter back to the director. (Waxman 2005: 238)

Again I do not use this example to say anything specifically against David Russell, but only to illustrate the kinds of tensions that can arise, for whatever reasons, between a director and his or her crew.

Crew resistance evolved into full-scale mutiny in the case of a very low budget ($500,000) film called *Black Male*, as reported in the documentary *Loop Dreams*. The directors of *Black Male*, George and Mike Baluzy, are represented as being very difficult to work for. In addition, the line producer is represented as being extremely harsh with the crew. Meanwhile, the crew members, who are in any event making very little money, are being asked to work longer and longer hours, without any clear sense that they will be paid overtime wages. Finally, there is literally a mutiny of the crew, who threaten to walk off the film. One of the angry crew members says to the documentary camera, "People are trying to say that we don't care any more, but it's just that we're fed up about not being cared about. So just tell 'em to go to hell, basically. Screw the film" (scene 11, "Mutiny").

DIRECTORS AND ACTORS

The director/actor relationship is very delicate. On the one hand, directors have their views of what the movie means and how any given scene should be played, especially when they have written the screenplay themselves. On the other hand, actors have their own ideas about the role in general and the performance of any given scene in particular.

Directors vary in their feelings about actors as they vary in their feelings about filmmaking in general. Richard Linklater repeatedly expressed positive feelings about actors in a public interview: First he said, "I like working with actors who are really intelligent." Shortly afterward he said, "I love working with new actors." And then finally there was general enthusiasm:

"I just love actors. I love working with them" (field notes, June 26, 2006). In a public interview Danny Boyle remarked, "I started in theater. . . . It makes you love actors." But he went on to say, "Many directors hate or fear actors" (field notes, June 29, 2007). Other directors make the distinction between actors and stars, as did John Huston: "I hate stars. . . . They're not actors. I've been around actors all my life and I like them" (in L. Ross [1952] 2002: 16). Similarly, Brian De Palma is reported as having doubts about Bruce Willis's ability to play the role he was supposed to play in *Bonfire* . . . : Willis "wasn't an actor who could easily slip into somebody else's skin. He was a movie star more than anything else" (Salamon [1991] 2002: 119).

Implicit in the very idea of a star is a person who demands and expects special treatment and who feels entitled to act out and behave badly whenever so moved. Not all stars are like this, but accounts of stars' bad behavior go far beyond the mass market film magazines and can be seen in serious accounts of production as well. For example, Marlon Brando showed up overweight and unprepared for the shooting of *Apocalypse Now*. On one occasion he refused to come to the set because he didn't like the scene he was supposed to play (Coppola 1979: 138). At another point, when the production was running behind schedule, he threatened to quit the movie entirely and keep his $1 million advance (in the documentary *Hearts of Darkness*).

For another example, Morgan Freeman showed up unprepared for the shooting of *Bonfire of the Vanities*: "De Palma . . . was irritated that Freeman hadn't prepared. They'd kept shooting and shooting while the actor learned his lines. Meanwhile he had $30,000 worth of extras sitting around waiting. . . . He knew very well Freeman wouldn't dare pull this stunt with *Taming of the Shrew*. He wouldn't fumble his way through Shakespeare while ten actors were watching him" (Salamon [1991] 2002: 204). De Palma had even worse problems with Bruce Willis, who was unhappy with the way a scene was being played and began giving directions to the other actors himself:

As the camera was moved back into place, Willis suddenly spoke: "I think it should go twice as fast." . . . No one said anything, but that simple stage direction injected a queasy feeling in the air. The ruling order had been unbalanced. Actors were free to express their opinions to directors. This, however, was something else. Willis had circumvented the director's authority altogether. He was speaking directly to his fellow actors, telling them how to play the scene and doing it with the most casual assumption of power. (Salamon [1991] 2002: 249–50)

One would think the problem of out-of-control actors would be much less of an issue in the world of independent filmmaking. Independent filmmakers cannot afford big stars, and one would think that less exalted actors would have less sense of being entitled to behave badly. Yet in my limited observations on film sets, I did see one young actor—I'll call him Ricky—behaving badly in this self-indulgent way. First, he hadn't bothered to learn his lines well and kept flubbing them, throwing the other actors off, and causing the director to shoot more takes just because of him. He also left the set several times when he was supposed to be on call, and people had to go looking for him. Finally, he had a cocky attitude and a foul mouth; I overheard one crew member say to another that this was his second film with Ricky and that was two too many. In the end the filmmaker got his revenge. Since Ricky did not have a leading role, his scenes were not essential, and when I finally saw the film, all of his scenes were gone. His name was in the credits, but all we saw of him was the curve of his buttock.

In the satirical film *Living in Oblivion*, about the trials and tribulations of making a low-budget independent film, there are not one but two egotistical and problematic actors whose bad behavior threatens to sink the film. We first meet Chad Palomino (James LeGros), an actor who is incredibly full of himself, contradicts the director at every turn, and attempts to steal every scene from Nicole Springer (Catherine Keener), who is playing opposite him. Nick Reve (Steve Buscemi), the director, panders to Chad for a long time, and Nicole finally blows up. There is a brawl, and Chad is finally thrown off the set. Later we meet Tito (Peter Dinklage), a dwarf with a lot of attitude, who refuses to take direction. He grows increasingly hostile to Nick and eventually accuses the director of being prejudiced against dwarves and walks off the set. Although the film finally gets completed, the problems with these actors (as well as some lesser problems with the crew) threaten to destroy the film within the film entirely.

And finally, in the documentary *Loop Dreams*, not only did the filmmakers have serious problems with the crew, who, as we saw in the last section, threatened to mutiny, but there was also a young actor in a lead role who managed to create enormous problems for the film. On the night before the final day of filming, the actor went to a bar and, according to several crew members interviewed on film, was coming on to several women. A date or boyfriend of one of the women flew into a rage and beat up the actor quite badly, leaving him with cuts and bruises all over his face and a badly swollen eye. The next day's shooting had to be cancelled, thousands of dollars were wasted, and the directors were livid. They had to wait an entire week for the actor's face to return to normal in order to shoot the final day of the production.

MATERIAL CONDITIONS

Exacerbating the potential for breakdowns of relations, whether between directors and crew or directors and actors, are the material conditions of the filming. Difficult shooting conditions put stress on everyone, making it more likely for actors to feel underappreciated, crew to feel exploited, and directors to feel irritated with everyone.

The most common, and most widely publicized, poor material conditions come from shooting the film in a difficult environment. Director Mark Forster talked on a panel about shooting *The Kite Runner* (2007): "Sometimes there is real chaos. We were shooting on the Afghan/Pakistan border with almost no infrastructure, no toilets, no film stock. A director can literally go mad" (field notes, June 24, 2007). Director Hany Abu-Assad talked in a Q&A about the filming of *Paradise Now* in Nablus, Palestine, in the midst of the rubble of war. Somebody in the audience asked about what it was like to make a film under such difficult conditions: "He said, 'I'm sorry to answer that question.' He said it was terrible, that he would never do it again. Nablus was a horrible ruin of poverty and rubble and all of them [he and the actors who were also present] said they were terribly affected by the atmosphere of the city" (field notes, Q&A, January 2005).

Or take Eleanor Coppola's account of the filming of *Apocalypse Now* in the Philippines. For starters, it was extremely hot. The Coppola children got sick. The government was engaged in ongoing conflict with rebels in the hills and kept reclaiming the helicopters promised to the film. The production ran out of chemicals for the chemical toilets. There were giant cockroaches everywhere. There was a typhoon off the coast, with heavy rain and high winds for eight straight days. The sets were destroyed, and the production was shut down for six weeks. There is more, but perhaps this is enough to explain why Coppola had a near nervous breakdown in the course of shooting the film (E. Coppola [1979] 1992, passim).

And finally, for an example closer to home, take the filming of *Bonfire of the Vanities* in the Bronx. The first night of shooting at the Bronx location was chaotic: "By the time De Palma arrived, the scene was part block party and part incipient riot as the real residents of the area gathered near the ropes marking the boundary of the 'movie set' to watch this caricature of their lives being played out in front of them" (Salamon [1991] 2002: 116–17). As these comments suggest, the social environment of the filming was bad from the beginning: "As the night wore on . . . a few dispirited protesters shouted from the sidelines, 'No more stereotypes. No more stereotypes.' One of the policemen guarding the set was called away when, one block from where the cameras were rolling, a taxi driver was shot dead" (Salamon [1991] 2002: 119). On the last night of shooting in the Bronx, there was active aggression from the sidelines:

> People from the neighborhood crowded against the barricades and the rooftops of the stores lining the street to give the "Bonfire" crew a suitable sendoff. . . . The babble of the crowd and the blare of radios was punctuated by small, flat sounds. *Ping. Ping. Ping. Splat. Ping. Splat. Splat.* The spectators were pitching eggs and lightbulbs from the perimeters. (Salamon [1991] 2002: 224)

The producers had to enlist the help of a motorcycle gang, who were working as extras for the movie, to clear the area and stop the shower of eggs and lightbulbs.[4]

Obviously not all productions take place under such extremes of physical discomfort, violent environmental conditions, or hostility from the surrounding spectators. Yet even your average movie shoot is not a comfortable experience. The hours are often extremely long. Twelve hours a day is normal. Fourteen- and sixteen-hour days are not unheard of. (After twelve hours overtime kicks in for the crew, and after sixteen they get another very large hike. The money is thus quite good, but people are very tired.)

I did not know about the long hours before my first visit to a set (*Pas-*

sengers, in February in Vancouver). I recall starting to look at my watch as we passed eight, then nine, hours on my first day. Later I wrote in my notes: "So it was a very long day, 11 hours, and I was cold all day, had my coat on and my feet freezing the whole time. . . . Rodrigo [García] said 11– 12 hours is normal, standard. . . . I asked several times if he was tired, or if he found the schedule grueling, etc., and he kind of brushed aside these questions" (field notes, February 6, 2007).

As a completely nonessential person, I could have left any time I liked, but it was clear to me that the correct etiquette was to stay until the bitter end. On another shoot, after a frustrating and unproductive day, I decided to leave the set early (around 5 PM). As I wrote in my field notes the following day, "People noticed that I had cut out the night before, everyone was much friendlier and I had a lot of good conversations. I was thinking I would cut out again after dinner but it is so clearly not good etiquette, and people were being nicer, that I decided to put in the whole nine yards. Got back at 12:30 AM, but got a commendation from [one of the producers] for staying the whole time" (field notes, March 23, 2007).

Of course, the cast, crew, and director have no choice but to stay the whole time. The nature of shooting is such that there are long periods, mainly involved with setting up shots, in which nothing is happening for most of the people present. In a well-funded movie the top brass will have trailers, the middle-range people (including the anthropologist) will have chairs, and the crew will be sitting around on milk crates, which, as far as I can tell, they bring themselves. It is physically uncomfortable, it is boring, and on a low-budget movie the food will consist mainly of sweets: doughnuts, cookies, and high-sugar soft drinks. One can bring a book, although that is seen as somewhat highbrow; most people (above the crew) have laptops or smart phones and spend much of the day texting, doing e-mail, or (I suspect) playing games.

The long day is punctuated by intense flurries of activity when a scene is actually being shot. The practice of shooting long days is largely related to saving money; even with overtime it is apparently cheaper to keep the crew long hours in a single day rather than have more days.[5] But the specific length of the day is also related to whether the director has been able to "get the shots" s/he wanted, that is, to get any given scene shot to his or her satisfaction. This often requires many takes, and part of the frustration and irritation on the part of actors and/or crew comes when a director insists on doing what others feel are unnecessary retakes of the scene.

The cost of very long days can be very high. Cinematographer Haskell Wexler made a documentary called *Who Needs Sleep?* (2006) about a cameraman who, after several very long days in a row on set, fell asleep behind the wheel, crashed into a tree, and died.

Rituals of Production

I have tried to show some of the ways in which the process of film production can be difficult and complicated. There are structural divides between filmmaker and crew, and between filmmaker and actors, who are not all necessarily on the same page in terms of what the film should be and how to go about making it in the best possible way. These fragile relationships, in turn, are put under further pressure by the specific conditions of making the film—sometimes in radically uncomfortable locations, sometimes with very low budgets and few amenities, and always with long hours that generate boredom and fatigue.

Yet the film shoot must remain a relatively cohesive social system over the course of the shoot. People must do their jobs, must remain relatively cordial with one another, and must cooperate in such a way as to produce the final product, and hopefully produce it well. And here my anthropological antennae go up. One of the basic things anthropologists learn to see are the mechanisms by which fragile social systems are held together. Although anthropologists today are much more interested in exploring social instability and transformation than social stability and continuity, nonetheless we are all trained to observe the kinds of mechanisms that allow a given social arrangement to be held in place and allow the people living or working within that arrangement to feel a certain degree of solidarity with one another, if only for a limited period of time.

Part of the ordering of the process comes from the formal structuring of the schedule. The entire shoot is ideally planned out in advance, with a projected total number of days, and with a projected schedule of shooting of specific scenes for each day. In order to take into account any unforeseen issues that might have come up in a given day, the call sheet for the next day is not printed out until nearly wrap time the night before. I was chatting in the van one morning with one of the drivers on the way to the set of *Sunshine Cleaning*:

I have a chat with the driver on the way, an Italian guy originally from NY. He tells me he is a music promoter. He was a nice friendly guy, loves the work. Says he meets great people. Says you'd think movie people would be all full of themselves, lots of crazies, but they're not. I say that's kind of surprising. He says, oh no, it's very disciplined, like the army, there's a chain of command. He also says it's incredibly organized, just look at this call sheet, now in the music business you'd draw up a rough schedule for the day but half the time it didn't even get typed up. But *look at this*, he keeps poking the call sheet in his visor, everything is organized down to the "gnat's booty." (Field notes, March 20, 2007)

Or as independent filmmaker Heidi Van Lier wrote in her "list of things you can do to make people think you know what you're doing on your truly indie film, even if you don't. Be OVERLY prepared every day. And then overly prepared again. This is indie, you need to know your schedule and shot lists more than you would if you actually HAD money" (Van Lier 2009).

Beyond the formal planning and formal organization, however, there is informal behavioral etiquette. One has to learn how to behave on a set. As actress Helen Mirren said, "I was like a rabbit in headlights for years on film sets, not understanding who was doing what, and how you're supposed to behave. It's a terrifying environment, really" (in Smith and Ansen 2007: 58). One has to learn how to behave around stars. When Leonardo DiCaprio was a young actor, he was given advice about this by a senior director: "I didn't know how to conduct myself on a film set. The director, Michael Caton-Jones, really took me under his wing. He said things like, 'When you're rehearsing with Robert De Niro, you don't talk about what baseball cards you're collecting'" (Smith and Ansen 2007: 58). For myself, in one instance, I was simply told, "Don't talk to the stars."

There is also etiquette with respect to the relationship between above-the-line and below-the-line members of the production. As we lined up for lunch one day, producer Julie Lynn pulled me out of line and said, "I need to tell you some 'protocol,' we let all the people on hourly go through the line first so they get more time to eat" (field notes, February 8, 2007).

And finally there are rules of etiquette that basically express respect for the enterprise. One of them is staying the whole time, no matter how late it gets, which I mentioned earlier. Another, and a very important one, is being quiet and attentive during the actual takes. People not directly involved in the take, often including the director, are not normally in the space where the actual filming is taking place. The take is viewed through a monitor, and people gather around the monitors to watch. Producers and other key people, as well as the anthropologist and other special guests on the set, will have headphones so we can hear the sound of the action we are seeing on the monitor. Others are watching who do not have headphones and cannot hear the sound. Nonetheless, everyone watches silently and attentively. My first time on a set, with *Passengers*, I did not know the rule: "I accidentally spoke out loud during a take, and Julie [Lynn, one of the producers] shushed me, and I apologized and said I thought it didn't matter because the take—at the crash site—was so far from where we were sitting. And then she said, that may be true but it's also 'protocol' to be silent during the take because other people are listening. I had indeed noticed that; people are very respectful; that's what we're here for" (field notes, February 8, 2007).

I observed this again on the set of *The Ministers*: "Again there is a definite ritualization of watching the takes on the monitor. People get very quiet (of course they have to, but as Julie said, there's more to it than that) and they gather round the monitor and watch the takes very seriously, even though most of them do not have headphones, can't hear the dialogue, and often there is very little to watch" (field notes, February 20, 2007).

And then there is gift giving. Gift giving is endemic throughout Hollywood, probably since the beginning of the industry. Hortense Powdermaker commented on the exchange of expensive gifts "between stars and their directors, producers and executives, and often given by stars to their cameraman" (1950: 85). Lillian Ross describes an expensive saddle given to John Huston by "leading members of the cast" during the shooting of *Red Badge of Courage* and a gift of binoculars to Huston from the crew on the last day of shooting (L. Ross [1952] 2002: 138, 141). I did not get to see too much of this myself, as I imagine it takes place behind the scenes. But I did come across the producers of *Sunshine Cleaning* one night going through shopping catalogues. I asked them what they were doing, and they said they were picking out "wrap gifts" for the crew.

Powdermaker interpreted the gift giving as an expression of either ambition on the part of the less powerful or of power on the part of the powerful. She saw it as part of everyone trying to get ahead in this power-laden world (1950: 85). I'm sure there is something to this, but it is also worth noting how the gift giving moves across, and seeks to bind over, the major fault lines of production, between directors and actors, and between above-the-line and below-the-line personnel.[6]

Beginnings and endings are ritualized. Directors will start off a shoot with a gathering of the top cast members; more on this below. Every time a key cast member completes his or her set of scenes for the film, someone announces that that's a "picture wrap" for that individual, and everyone claps. In one case one of the producers broke out a bottle of champagne. At the end of the shoot there are wrap gifts for the crew as we saw, and there is usually a big wrap party.

There is also a general ethic of sociability on a set, although individuals vary in the degree to which they participate. According to Julie Salamon's account of the shooting of *Bonfire of the Vanities*, Tom Hanks was well liked because he liked to hang around and schmooze with other cast and crew members between takes, while Bruce Willis was disliked because he would retreat to his trailer between takes and socialize only with his "private entourage" (Salamon [1991] 2002: 148). For another example, I saw a screening of a film called *Stephanie Daley* (2006), starring Tilda Swinton and Amber Tamblyn. Tamblyn took Q&A afterward and talked about how some of the actors were very funny and kept everyone amused on set: "She talked about how some of the actors were just a scream, and Tilda was very funny and the guy who played her husband's friend was a scream, and they just kept everyone in stitches" (field notes, April 18, 2007). As the movie had been very emotionally disturbing, I found all this talk of hilarity on the set rather jarring, but in any event this is the sort of thing that is clearly viewed as positive sociability on the set. And for an example from my own on-set experience, a script supervisor came around one day offering everyone in the room cards containing upbeat messages of the sort one gets in fortune cookies, such as "Today you will get a pleasant surprise," or "Your hard work will pay off."

All of this takes place at the level of ordinary practice. The etiquette, the rituals, the everyday sociability go on with little or no intentional coordination. But there are two people whose job it is to more actively keep the set humming along: the producer(s) and the director.

In chapter 5, I discussed at length the producer's relationship with the director during production, in terms of the intimate dynamics of the producer-director bond. Here I want to look at the more general ways in which a producer operates on set to maintain the stability and cohesion of the production. Briefly, it is the role of the (independent) producer on the set to make sure everything runs smoothly. More than one producer said to me that they might appear to be doing nothing on set, but "there are always a million little things. What you are really doing is quality control" (field notes, Gail Lyon interview, July 7, 2006). Others use a language of "putting out fires" during the production. Lynda Obst mixed the firefighter metaphor with a medical one: "You put out the occasional fire, assert authority, reassure everyone. I have a Florence Nightingale kind of approach on the set and my most important function is often as medic" (Obst 1996: 203).

I will give three examples here of the kinds of things a producer might deal with on set, but in fact the producer might be called on to handle almost any problem whatsoever. In one case a child actor showed up with the wrong hair color. One of the producers swung into action, rushing the child over to "hair" and seeing to it that the problem was fixed in very short order, as everyone was waiting for the child in order to shoot the scene. In another case, the production was shooting in a residential neighborhood and there was a curfew of 11:00 PM. This was the last day of shooting at that location so the director was determined to get the shots, whether they ran over curfew or not. The line producer (not the same as the producer), whose production company was the local agency for the shoot, was trying to enforce the curfew. I was aware of what was going on and was wondering how it would play out: would the director and the line producer go toe to toe? But no, it was all handled by one of the producers. And for the final example, there was a disagreement between this same line producer and the cinematographer about whether they could get a certain shot. Words were exchanged, and things got a bit heated. Afterward the line producer went off in his own car while the cinematographer, the director, and one of the producers (as well as the lucky anthropologist) went off in another one. The producer spent much time in the car calming everyone down, talking about how everyone comes to a production with their own "paradigms," but how we all have to get over those things and get along.

Producers also play important roles in the social mix of the set. It was one of the producers who broke out the bottle of champagne for the picture wrap of one of the actors. A good producer will also make a point of getting to know members of the crew personally. I cannot resist one anecdote here, from the set of *Sunshine Cleaning*. During some stretch of downtime, I was approached by a crew member named Tim Pershing.

> He comes up and asks me about the project. I say it's about indepen-dent films. He says do you know [filmmaker] Mira Nair? I say yes, slightly, I know her husband, he was a colleague of mine [at Columbia]. He says, that's Mahmood Mamdani, he's a political scientist, I know because I'm a political scientist. Well you could have knocked me over with a feather. . . . And I said, what are you doing on this film? And he said, well, I'm the dolly grip, but I'm finishing my PhD in Political Science at Brandeis. I just do this to pay the bills. (Field notes, March 23, 2007)

I tell this anecdote because, as an academic, I love it, but its relevance to the present discussion is this: I mentioned the incident to producer Peter Saraf, without mentioning the crew member's name. But Peter already knew who he was. Peter had produced a film in Haiti and Tim Pershing had some academic interests in Haiti, and they had connected over that.

Producers may also play a useful social role in relation to the actors and stars. Actors and stars arrive as individuals and may not know anybody else on the set. The director will make an effort to be sociable and solicitous, but he or she is busy most of the time and does not have a lot of time to socialize. Some actors/stars may want to be left alone, but my impression was that most of them want to be involved in the social mix of the produc-tion. Producers, as we know from chapter 5, tend to have excellent social skills; they can make conversation with anyone about anything. Thus, when actors/stars are killing time on the set, waiting for their scenes, one will likely see one or more producers hanging around and schmoozing with them, keeping them happy and amused. As producer Lynda Obst said, "The producer's job is to make the star[s] happy" (1996: 217).

Ultimately, however, it is after all the "the director's set." As I said earlier, the director sets the tone for the entire production. Most directors actively seek to maintain a positive tone and to keep everyone relatively happy. Richard Linklater said, "I strive for a communal feeling on the set" (field notes, public interview, February 26, 2006). But every director has his or her own style of doing this. Mira Nair's style on set was described as follows: "At work, Nair is swift, clear, and good-humored. Even at the end of the day, after five failed attempts to coordinate her driver and the passengers in her car, Nair, with hands on hips, joked, 'There is a limit to democracy!' 'She has a kind of charmed humor,' [filmmaker Mitch] Epstein says, 'a way of making somebody feel good.' Sometimes she does it just by sidling up to a crew member and jostling him with her shoulder" (Lahr 2002: 7–8). Similarly, actress Amber Tamblyn talked about Hilary Brougher's directorial style on the production of *Stephanie Daley*: "She was all over the set, directing the actors, putting more strawberries on the pie, tending her baby daughter" (field notes, *Stephanie Daley* Q&A, April 18, 2007). Robert Altman, as we heard earlier, was "director as party host" (Ansen 2006: 69).

Along these lines, but on a much bigger scale, M. Night Shyamalan famously "worked at camaraderie." A crewman named Jimbo, who was also a "superb barman," set up an after-work bar on the set, which only opened occasionally. "Night [as he is called] always came, and he played Ping-Pong and shot pool and talked to everybody and stayed until Jimbo announced the last call" (Bamberger 2006: 198). Even beyond that:

> On Friday nights, a crew member's name would be picked out of a hat, and Night would award the winner an all-expenses-paid vacation for two to a European capital or Hawaii or some other lush place. Each week it got more elaborate, leading up to the biggest prize at the end: two weeks in the Far East. Night paid for the trips himself. It had nothing to do with Warner Bros., and it wasn't something other directors did." (Bamberger 2006: 198)

Every filmmaker knows that one of the most important things you can do to keep people happy is to provide them with good food. Even the smallest film set will have a table off to the side called "craft services." Christine Vachon explains:

> Craft service means the table that sits off to the side of the set with coffee, soda, juice, and snacks. You might think it's no big deal, but it is. If the coffee isn't ready in the morning, it will have a grisly effect on people's mood. Conversely, if you bring something special to the table —guacamole, brownies, pie, ice cream when it's hot or soup when it's cold—it's a great morale booster. (Vachon 1998: 85–86)

Similarly, filmmaker Heidi Van Lier writes, "On truly indie films people rarely get fed. If you just order some kind of take-out every day you already

look better than most of the indies your cast and crew have worked on. . . .
If you have someone make a Starbucks run once or twice a day for the
entire cast and crew, with specific orders, everyone feels really taken care
of, and you seem like you're aware of their exhaustion" (Van Lier 2009: 1).

With a bigger budget, a film shoot will have a caterer, and they have to
be good: "Nothing will upset your cast and crew like a terrible caterer,"
says Vachon (1998: 95). Like all directors, M. Night Shyamalan shared this
view: "One of his management philosophies was never to skimp on food,
in quality or in quantity. He knew it inspired loyalty and effort" (Bamberger 2006: 155).

If there is any kind of budget for it, a smart director will throw a party at
the beginning of a shoot, again at key moments along the way, and again at
the end. This has long been a tradition in Hollywood: "The start of shooting on *Hello, Dolly!* was marked by an exchange of gifts, notes of encourage-
ment and a small champagne and caviar party for Barbra Streisand, who
was playing the title role, in the office of director Gene Kelly" (Dunne
[1968] 1998: 221). Francis Ford Coppola threw a party for the huge cast and
crew of *Apocalypse Now* on his birthday, on the one-hundredth day of
shooting, and on the two-hundredth day of shooting (Coppola 1979: passim). But indie filmmakers will do it too, if they can afford it. In the
documentary about the making of the mini-budgeted ($500,000) movie
Black Male, we hear the directors talking about a wrap party, though we
don't see it on screen.

The question of maintaining a positive mood and tone on set, the
importance of providing some kind of decent food, and the importance of
throwing the occasional party—these are issues that affect everyone on the
set of a movie, cast and crew alike. But there is a set of issues that pertain
specifically to a director's relationships with his or her actors: the question
of getting actors to feel engaged with the group and with the project, and
the question of having actors feel cared for and protected.

In terms of getting actors engaged with the project, virtually every
director organizes some kind of community-forming event with the key
actors at the beginning of the shoot. Irwin Winkler talked about making
the Iraq War movie *Home of the Brave* (2006): "I gathered all the actors
together at the site where the army base was located [the film was shot in
Morocco] and just spent some time hanging out and developing a sense of
comradeship" (field notes, *Home of the Brave* Q&A, October 30, 2006).

Danny Boyle talked in a public interview about the shooting of the outer-space movie *Sunshine* (2007): "We had all the actors live together in student housing for a few weeks, for them to bond, and to develop a siege mentality. Every actor arrives in their own bubble, you need to pop their bubble, get them into *your* film" (field notes, June 29, 2007). Jonathan Dayton and Valerie Faris talked about the making of *Little Miss Sunshine*, a comedy about a dysfunctional family:

> **VF:** We only had one week, we didn't really rehearse scenes, we just got all the actors together and did things to get them used to being in this family.
>
> **JD:** We just did little exercises together. Like we asked everyone to write things about the other members of the family, or to write questions to put to the other family members. (Field notes, *Little Miss Sunshine* Q&A, September 25, 2006)

M. Night Shyamalan had various rituals for the making of the fantasy/fairy tale *Lady in the Water*:

> He felt all the actors should be available for a read-through, held a couple weeks before the first day of shooting. . . . To Night, read-throughs were holy. For *Lady in the Water*, the read-through would be the only time the whole cast would be together. . . . This was the agenda: a delicious buffet breakfast followed by an uninterrupted reading of the script, followed by a delicious buffet lunch. Food, work, food. Night knew from experience that the schedule worked. (Bamberger 2006: 155)

And finally, there is a notion in filmmaking culture that actors are vulnerable and need to be protected.[7] As Ang Lee remarked, "I have to assure the actors that they're in good hands" (in Smith and Ansen 2006: 65). Brian De Palma had a policy of not letting executives into rehearsal, because "the moment was too delicate, a time of tentative intimacy, as the actors—most of whom barely knew the director—revealed their interpretation of the material for the first time. His job was to protect these vulnerable creatures" (Salamon [1991] 2002: 120). And indie filmmaker Heidi Van Lier also used a rhetoric of protection: "Allow every first take to be considered a 'rehearsal' and it may make everyone feel more protected" (Van Lier 2009: 1).

In addition, directors will make a point of recognizing when actors are being pushed to do something difficult; they will be genuinely concerned that actors may be harmed or made ill in the course of performing their roles. Alejandro Gonzales Iñárritu talked about shooting *Babel* in the Mexican desert:

> Adriana Barraza is a fantastic actress. She is in poor health but is an incredible trooper. The shooting in the Sonora desert was very tough and she was suffering. I was worried about her health and offered to stop for the day. She said no, she knew we did not have much money and that would be costly, just went to the trailer, cooled off, took a shower, took a rest, and came back to work. She thought about how real Mexican illegals in the desert don't get a chance to go to a comfortable trailer. (Field notes, *Babel* Q&A, October 16, 2006)

Amber Tamblyn performed a scene in *Stephanie Daley* in which her character, Stephanie Daley, gave birth to a baby in a stall in a public restroom, in tremendous pain but prohibited from making a sound. It was a wrenching scene to watch and also evidently to perform. In the Q&A after the screening, she said the director, Hilary Brougher, "only shot three takes of the scene," and that she, Amber, "went to bed for a week after that scene" (field notes, *Stephanie Daley* Q&A, April 18, 2007). And one more example of consideration for actors doing difficult scenes, which I observed on the set of *The Ministers*: "They do an amazing scene in which the detective is tortured and eventually killed. The actor throws himself into it brilliantly, over and over, with every take. He looks wasted when it's all over. Franc. calls him in to see a replay on the monitor, and everyone claps when it's over. He looks surprised, pleased" (field notes, February 20, 2007).

Finally, the film is finished.[8] If it had been a troubled shoot, with many problems and with many people angry with or disliking one another, the word will be out and there will be negative publicity. But as filmmaker Kevin Smith said,

> I betcha if the movie had been a success all would have been forgiven. I mean, if you read stuff about *Jaws*, when they made it, everyone was at each other's throats, and when they made *Neighbors* everyone was at each other's throats and *Neighbors* tanked and they're still at each other's throats. *Jaws* was successful and everything was forgiven. (in Pierson 2003: 246)

But here I hark back to my opening comments about how film production can be—isn't always, but can be—a relatively non-alienating form of labor. For despite all the possibilities of conflict and pressure, many film productions work out well, with great feelings of solidarity and community among the cast, crew, and director. Valerie Faris said about *Little Miss Sunshine*, "We had a crew that all loved the film. You felt this kind of collective, group effort to get done and quickly, they were so supportive and interested and we were very appreciative" (interview, October 19, 2006). Similarly, Michael Showalter talked about the making of *Wet Hot American Summer* (David Wain, 2001): "The veneer . . . the baggage that everyone brought to this experience just sort of fell apart and I feel like there was so much camaraderie everywhere: cast, crew, just blending, and I think everyone's genuinely gonna miss each other when this is over" (bonus track, "Cast comments"). And finally here are some comments among the group who worked on the movie *One Last Thing* (2005). On stage for the Q&A were the director (Alex Steyermark), the writer (Barry Stringfellow), and two of the actors, Johnny Messner and the lead, Michael Angarano:

> Everyone starts with the ritualistic (but heartfelt, I think) comments about how great it was to work on this project with the other folks. The actors said how they loved working with the director because he was a real "actors' director," he took what they said seriously and then would give it some interesting tweak. They also said they loved working on this story because it was so compelling. . . . The director [in turn] said, "I love the cast, every single one." (Field notes, *One Last Thing* Q&A, April 19, 2006)

I have emphasized in this chapter what I called earlier the pre–post-Fordist quality of film production—the appreciation of skilled labor, the sense of participating in a collective project, the sense of productive achievement at the end—in part because it is a good story in bad times. But I also emphasize it in relation to the larger arguments of this book, specifically to point out (one example of) the uneven nature of neoliberal capitalism. For those lucky enough to get the dwindling number of good jobs like these, the work can be very rewarding.

The next chapter is the final chapter on the films, and the final substantive chapter of the book. I have been concerned throughout the film chapters to look at independent film as "cultural critique," as implicitly raising questions about the world we live in today—about the economy, the family, work, class, gender, and so forth. In the next chapter I look at films that are explicitly critical, explicitly political. Mostly documentaries, these films say what most other films only imply. The chapter will explore not only the politics in the films but the documentary form itself.

CHAPTER 8

Politics

"Hollywood" has been skittish about the representation of politics in film at least since the House Un-American Activities Committee (HUAC) hearings in the 1950s. With some important exceptions—mostly involving one or another contribution from Tim
Robbins or George Clooney—one rarely sees overtly political
films coming out of the Hollywood studios. The question of
politics in independent films is more complicated. That is what I
will explore in this chapter.

For present purposes I will define a "political film" as one that
is centrally and overtly concerned with exploring and critiquing
the dynamics of power, and more specifically, as one that in some
way "speaks truth to power." The famous Quaker phrase is particularly useful for my purposes here as I am interested in the
portrayal of relatively overt criticism, the idea that some individuals or characters actually give voice to critical points of view.

Of course, all films are political in some sense, and there is a
large body of literature in anthropology, feminist studies, and
cultural studies in which scholars seek to bring to light the politics
hidden in seemingly innocent "entertainment" (see references in
the introduction). This work is very valuable in terms of understanding the ways in which "Hollywood" often serves as a vehicle
for promulgating dominant ideological premises. My interest in
more explicitly political films, most of which come out of the
independent sector, is meant to complement that work.

Political films go beyond "cultural critique." They challenge
viewers not only to rethink and reconfigure their taken-for-

granted assumptions, but to actually—in the ideal case—move people to act for change in the real world. As Jane Gaines wrote of the political documentary (which will be our main genre for this chapter), these are "films that make audience members want to kick and yell, films that make them want to do something *because of the conditions of the world*" (1999: 90, emphasis in original).

In earlier chapters I paid particular attention to the politics of personal life: work and jobs, parents and children, gender and sexuality. In the present chapter I wish to focus on politics of the large scale: of capitalism, corporations, corruption; of national and global power, violence, race, war. Although my focus in this book has been on neoliberal capitalism, I will only return to that focus later in the chapter. In the early part I wish to look at "political films" dealing with a wide range of contemporary subjects.

Some of the issues in this chapter are similar to those in the feminism/post-feminism chapter. Contemporary political critiques have taken place at two levels: outward, against the bad political conditions of the world, and "downward," against the younger generation that is thought to have lost all political interest and will. Much of the discussion about the post-boomer generation's lack of politics originally took place in what might be called the "left (anti-)postmodernism" literature of the 1980s and 1990s, in which the older generation of left activists—most prominently Fredric Jameson—lamented the loss in the younger generation of a sense of history, of an understanding and appreciation of the radical past, and of any kind of political thinking for the present and future (see especially Jameson 1984a, 1984b; A. Ross 1988; Eagleton 1996).

The same set of issues, in slightly different language, has animated the literature on Generation X. Gen Xers (who may be taken for present purposes as embodiments of the "postmodernism" to which Jameson and others were referring) have been fairly straightforwardly accused of abandoning the activist politics of the 1960s and 1970s and of having become politically apathetic. Some Gen Xers have agreed with these charges:

> Millions of people in our generation don't get involved. We don't vote. We don't take a stand for our future. We don't get in the face of politicians to demand change. Instead we sit on the sidelines of our democracy, watching our taxes, crime rates, and tuition costs go up, while our quality of life, the value of our education, the health of our environ-

ment, and our chances of finding stable, high-paying jobs go down. (Nelson and Cowan 1994: xiv)

Others have reacted angrily to charges of political apathy, but they did not really disagree either. One character in the film *Slacker* holds up a now-famous sign that says, "Apathy is not the same thing as withdrawing in disgust." Or as Edward Norton, indie film star and card-carrying Gen Xer said, "It isn't just aimlessness we feel; it's deep skepticism. It's not slacker-dom; it's profound cynicism, even despair, even paralysis" (quoted in Hanson 2002: 62).

In this case there are actually some relatively concrete data supporting the charges. Starting from popular accounts, two political scientists began their study of the political life of Gen X with the observation that Gen X's "indifference to public affairs, withdrawal from participation, and general lack of awareness of things political [appears to be] unusually pronounced" (Bennett and Rademacher 1997: 22). The authors then apply an "apathy index" to the past several generations and conclude that indeed "gen-Xers . . . exhibit higher levels of political apathy than any of the other four [earlier] cohorts" measured in the study (Bennett and Rademacher 1997: 27).

But that was the late 1990s. At this point (2012) things have begun to change dramatically, with the launching of the Occupy Wall Street movement in September of 2011. Occupy Wall Street defines itself as being "against social and economic inequality, high unemployment, greed, as well as corruption, and the undue influence of corporations—particularly from the financial services sector—on government" (Wikipedia, "Occupy Wall Street," accessed January 4, 2012). In response to this message, people of all ages, but especially Gen Xers, have been experiencing a major awakening to progressive political action. After decades of political silence, the first hint that the so-called apathetic generation was waking up was the mass protests in Wisconsin earlier in 2011, against the conservative governor's attempt to outlaw collective bargaining for public workers.

Occupy Wall Street was not directly related to the events in Wisconsin and in many ways seemed to come from nowhere, but of course it did not. What I want to show in this final chapter is that, if one looks at American independent films, and especially at documentaries, the picture of political differences between boomers and Gen Xers looks quite different. While documentary buffs—and in some cases even the public at large—are aware of the major political documentarians of the boomer generation (Michael Moore, at the very least), few people are aware of the growing number of political documentarians in the next generation. These Gen Xers may not have been marching in the streets, but they were making powerful critical films that need to be recognized and discussed.

It is true that independent *features* have tended to emphasize "the personal" in ways that some would argue cuts the personal off from the political. While there are important exceptions to this point—for example, some of Steven Soderbergh's films, or many of the "immigrant" films discussed in chapter 5—many American independent features tend to focus relatively tightly on the dynamics of interpersonal relations, or on local worlds in which large-scale political structures and events are muted or invisible.

One response to this would be the great feminist slogan from the 1970s, "the personal is political." Even the most personal, relationship-focused independent film embodies some kind of social critique via the harsh realism of truth telling and exposure that has been discussed many times in these pages. In addition, there is a broad notion of independent film as "subversive," as doing/saying/showing the unexpected, the off-kilter, throwing audiences off-balance, and destabilizing people's assumptions about what is normal or ordinary or taken for granted.

But the other response must be that no film or film genre can do everything, and that we need to expand our focus to the larger field of independent film as a whole. Although the "personal" feature has tended to dominate and define the indie movement since the 1980s, the personal feature is the least "political" (in the large-scale sense specified earlier) of the independent genres. Here then we must turn to the documentary, where one of the major themes of the discussion will be precisely the question of integrating the personal and the political. Before we get to that, however, we need to look at the culture, as it were, of political filmmaking.

"This Is Not a History Lesson"

In this section I will show at some length that there is a fairly widespread (and also long-standing) view in the movie world that films, especially feature films, should not be too political. Just to be clear about my point from the outset, this is not a statement about people's personal politics, but a statement about how most people in the industry view the relationship between art and politics. At the personal level, "Hollywood" in general is known to be quite liberal/left/progressive, and the independent film world collectively is probably further to the left than Hollywood. Many of the people I interviewed—Ted Hope, Dawn Hudson, Marc Turtletaub—talked about getting into film in the first place because they wanted to "change the world." I also asked everyone I interviewed for a short answer about their politics, and 100 percent of them said something like "left," "very left," or "progressive." So again, I am not speaking of people's personal political views but a cultural discourse, almost an ideology, about the relationship between politics and film.

This is a discourse to the effect that political films, or anyway films that are "too political," are in some way or other problematic for (American) audiences and are to be avoided. There are several different histories/theories behind this view. One is surely a long-lingering effect of the Cold War of the 1940s and 1950s, in which the expression of progressive political views was basically dangerous (see Sklar 1975; Biskind 1983, 1998; May 1989). Another is an also long-lingering dichotomy in film-world culture between "entertainment" and everything else, the "everything else" including not only politics but educational, informational, and factual materials summarized in the phrase "a history lesson." Even in the world of independent film, where there is generally much less emphasis on "entertainment," some version of this dichotomy is in play. Filmmakers are nervous about being too didactic or political, certainly in feature films, but even to some extent in documentaries as well. In this section then I want to simply lay out the evidence for this point, which will form a backdrop for the rest of this chapter.[1]

Sometimes there is a straightforward expression of distaste on the part of the filmmaker for being "too political," too didactic. Producer of independent features Ron Yerxa said that "he didn't believe in hitting people over the head with politics in films" (field notes, February 4, 2006). Anthropologist and documentarian David Edwards said that "he got turned off by films that were too political" (field notes, June 28, 2006). Filmmaker Mira Nair said in an interview, "I cannot bear agenda" (interview, September 3, 2007). Most strikingly, the makers of two of the most political—by my standards—films that I saw in the course of this research both took pains to say in the Q&A that their films were "not political." Hany Abu-Assad directed a film called *Paradise Now* (2005), which I saw in a screening in Los Angeles, about two young Palestinian men who sign up to be suicide bombers in Israel. It was hard not to see this as a political film, but during the Q&A Abu-Assad said several times, "I don't believe in putting politics in movies" (field notes, January 2005 [missing exact date]). Similarly, director Charles Ferguson made a very critical documentary about the Iraq War called *No End in Sight*, which screened at the 2007 Sundance Film Festival. Ferguson spoke for a few moments before the film started, saying, among other things, "This is a film about politics and policy but it is not a political film" (field notes, January 26, 2007).

One can deduce that what people mean by "political" is "partisan." A political film, in this view, is one that takes a specific position and tries to convince the viewer of the rightness of that position. Some filmmakers are opposed to this in principle—the idea is that viewers are intelligent, and they should be allowed to make up their own minds. A slight variance of this point is that the audience would not sit still for this kind of politics in the context of what is supposed to be entertainment. The latter position was expressed by Michael Moore in a public interview at the 2007 L.A. Film Festival: "My first objective is to make a good movie. That's what I think first, not the politics. If you put the politics first nobody will want to see it. . . . Don't forget, it's a movie. It's not a sermon, not a diatribe. You are asking people to spend their money to see it. It is not a documentary, it's a movie" (field notes, June 26, 2007).[2]

Closely related to the denial of politics is the denial of other sorts of "message" or didactic intent. Stephen Walker codirected a documentary called *Young@Heart* (2007), about a chorus of quite elderly people who professionally sing rock songs to various audiences, including in schools and prisons. Part of the humor and pleasure of the film is that it is incongruous to hear eighty-year-old people doing very credible performances of, say, Jimi Hendrix or the Clash. Part of the drama of the film, on the other hand, is that some of these people are quite fragile and liable to get sick or die at any time. During a public interview at the 2007 L.A. Film Festival, Walker called in the chorus director, Bob Cilman, to talk about Bob's decision to cooperate with Walker on the film. Bob's first point was that "we didn't approach this as a social service. We thought of the art." Walker echoed his point: "It's not a social service, it is an artistic project" (field notes, June 28, 2007).

But probably the most common rhetorical move along these lines is to distinguish the film from a "history lesson." Let me start with some older Hollywood examples—for again, this is a long-standing pattern—the first one from an old journalistic account by Lillian Ross ([1952] 2002) of the production of the film *Red Badge of Courage*, based on the Civil War novel. The movie, directed by John Huston (1951), was a big Civil War costume drama starring the at-that-point-unknown Audie Murphy. While no one ever uses the phrase "this is not a history lesson," some of the same sentiments were clearly in play during the production. At several points in the book, Huston is quoted as worrying about whether the audience will be reading the movie too historically: "[Huston] told [producer Gottfried] Reinhardt that day, he was worried about the way the picture seemed to be turning into an account of the struggle between the North and the South in the Civil War" (L. Ross [1952] 2002: 108). Or later, Huston said to his cameraman, "[The] war in the movie must not appear to be a North vs. South war but a war showing the pointlessness of the Youth's courage" (L. Ross [1952] 2002: 117).

For a later example, writer Tom Wolfe is quoted as telling a funny story about being on *Nightline* in 1983 promoting the film of his book *The Right Stuff* (Philip Kaufman, 1983). Wolfe begins,

"The subject of the show was 'Movies and Propaganda' and on the show was [Constantin] Costa Gavras, the most totally propagandistic director ever to breathe the air. . . . [T]hey turn to Costa Gavras, who had just made a movie about the Israelis slaughtering the Arabs, and they turned to him and posed a question about politics and propaganda." Wolfe paused and assumed an accent meant to approximate the Greek filmmaker's. "Oh, I don't really know about such things, I just do entertainment." . . . Wolfe chuckled as he thought about Costa Gavras. "Entertainment. He kept using that word, *entertainment*, . . . and if he said it once, he said it forty times." . . . [Eventually Wolfe came to understand] that Costa Gavras knew exactly what he was doing. "He didn't want to turn anybody off his films by saying *they're going to get a history lesson* when they go to the theater." (quoted in Salamon [1991] 2002: 398–99, emphasis added)

Let's turn now to some more current examples. I actually first heard this in a class that Barbara Boyle, lawyer, former film executive, and now chair of the Department of Film and Television at UCLA film school, was teaching in the school's Producers Masters program. Boyle was teaching students about the art of the "pitch," the ability to boil down an idea for a film into a few catchy phrases, in order to sell the idea for the film to investors, studios, or what have you. Students had been assigned to find something—a news report, a work of fiction or nonfiction—that they thought would make a good film, and then pitch it to the class and to Boyle.

> The first pitch was based on a book which was a true story about a man named Scott McClung who was falsely arrested and imprisoned in Mexico and was almost murdered in prison but was ultimately released. Boyle interrupts immediately: "Is this a documentary?" The student says no. [Boyle expands her points about what a pitch is supposed to be and do—"to sell, not tell" the story.] . . . So the student starts again, trying to accommodate these points, but he keeps being too descriptive, too didactic. Boyle interrupts again: *Are you giving me a history lesson?* (Field notes, November 16, 2004)

Boyle actually doubled the question: "Are you giving me a history lesson? Are you giving me a political lesson?"

Most recently, I saw a documentary called *Chicago 10* (Bret Morgen, 2007), about the radical summer of 1968, and about the trial of the so-called Chicago 7. The film was made by a young filmmaker, Bret Morgen, who had not been born at the time these events took place, but had the idea of making a film that would carry the political message of "the sixties" to the younger generations. The film is not wholly committed to realist representational strategies, however, and occasionally does fairly strange things with the facts and realities of the era. In order to prepare the audience for what was to come, then, Morgen felt compelled to say in advance that, while the film was meant to capture the spirit and energy of the times, nonetheless "*it is not a history lesson*" (field notes, January 28, 2007).

It is not terribly difficult to tease out what "not a history lesson" means in these contexts. A "history lesson" focuses the viewer on the facts of the case and treats them as interesting or important in and of themselves, while a film—or presumably any other literary or artistic creation—sees those "facts" as of interest largely as a context within which larger understandings about the human condition emerge. We can see this in Boyle's further elaborations to her student: "Set up your framework, grab your listener! 'This is a drama about. . . . !' 'This is a comedy about. . . . !' " And the "about," though she never articulated this explicitly, is not the story of Scott McClung, but what she kept calling "the theme"—e.g., "a good man caught in a web of corruption" (field notes, November 16, 2004). Or as John Huston said about *Red Badge of Courage*, it is not about the war between North and South but about "a war showing the pointlessness of the Youth's courage" (L. Ross [1952] 2002: 117).

One effect of this view in some cases is to reinforce a boundary between feature films and documentaries, with the idea being that it is acceptable to have politics and "history lessons" in documentaries. Thus, after Ron Yerxa said to me that "he didn't believe in hitting people over the head with politics in film," he went on to describe with some enthusiasm a documentary he had just seen at Sundance, *Mardi Gras: Made in China* (David Redmon, 2005). The film focused on the plastic beads that are thrown and collected during the wild goings-on at Mardi Gras, including being thrown as rewards for girls flashing their naked breasts. The beads are actually made in a single factory in China, and the filmmaker cuts back and forth between, as Yerxa put it, "these frat boys cavorting at Mardi Gras and the 14-year-old girls slaving away at this factory" (field notes, February 4, 2007). Yet even documentary filmmakers feel the need to be cautious about being "political" and to avoid giving people "history lessons." Thus, we heard three documentarians—Charles Ferguson, Michael Moore, and Bret Morgen— all resist the political/"history" label, even when their films—certainly those of Michael Moore—would be seen as "political" by most viewers.

All of this seems to me, as I said earlier, a kind of overdetermined legacy, partly from the Cold War, when politics were dangerous; partly from the culture of Hollywood and its emphasis on entertainment; and partly (at the academic level) from a divide between the social sciences and the humanities, in which the (would-be) universality of art is opposed to the specificity and particularity of "history." It is also a legacy of a specifically *American* history (the Cold War, Hollywood) not shared by filmmakers in other parts of the world, so it is not surprising that we have always seen more overtly political (feature) films coming out of Europe than out of the United States.

Yet if American filmmakers make relatively fewer political features, they make a plethora of political documentaries, and in recent years they have been making more of them than ever. Moreover, some of these films have achieved extraordinary success at the box office, a fact that is related in part to important developments within the genre of documentary film as a whole. For the remainder of this chapter, then, I intertwine discussions of the evolution of the documentary genre with discussions of the recent florescence of specifically political documentaries.

The Classic Documentary

Film theorist Bill Nichols provides us with a useful set of definitions for what might be called the "classic documentary" (1991).[3] It will be relevant to the present discussion that the conventions of documentary filmmaking have undergone important changes starting in the late 1980s (see especially a documentary called *The Documentary's New Politics*, Eric Faden, 2005). The emergence of the "new documentary" is more or less contemporary with the emergence of the independent film movement as a whole, and I will discuss it later in the chapter. For now, however, I will simply summarize Nichols's account of how to think about the basic or classic documentary film.

Nichols begins by defending against the critique that has by now become a cliché, that "documentary is a fiction like any other," arguing instead that "*differences* . . . from fictional narrative are as crucial to the documentary as to the experimental film tradition" (1991: xi). He first defines documentary as one among many "discourses of the real," including "law, family, education, economics, politics, state, and nation," which together both represent and construct social reality (1991: 10).[4]

He then goes on to offer three more specific definitions of the documentary, one each from the point of view of the filmmaker, the text, and the viewer. Looked at from the point of view of the filmmaker, he calls documentary filmmaking "an institutional formation":

> Rather than proposing any ground or center outside the practices of documentary, such a definition [as an "institutional formation"] stresses how the field operates by allowing itself to be historically conditioned, unfolding, variable, and perpetually provisional, based on what documentarists themselves consider admissible, what they regard as limits, boundaries, and test cases, how boundaries come to exert the force of a definition, however loosely, and how the qualification, contestation, or subversion of these same boundaries moves from inconsequential anomaly to transformative innovation to accepted practice (1991: 15).[5]

Next, from the point of view of documentary as text, documentary can be seen as a film genre like any other, in which "various norms, codes, or conventions display a prominence missing from other genres" (1991: 18). For example, "documentaries take shape around an informing logic. The economy of this logic requires a representation, case, or argument about the historical world" (1991: 18). For another example, "Documentary relies heavily on the spoken word. Commentary by voice-over narrators, reporters, interviewees, and other social actors figure strongly in most documentary" (1991: 21).

And finally, Nichols considers documentary from the point of view of the relationship between the viewer, the film, and the world:

> The most fundamental difference between expectations prompted by narrative fiction and by documentary lies in the status of the text in relation to the historical world. . . . Cues within the text and assumptions based on past experience prompt us to infer that the images we see (and many of the sounds we hear) had their origin in the historical world. Technically this means that the projected sequence of images, what occurred in front of the camera (the profilmic event), and the historical referent are taken to be congruent with one another. (1991: 25).

And thus it emerges that "a central aspect of documentary" is after all "the 'history lesson'" (1991: 29). The idea that a documentary is fundamentally a "history lesson" is connected to Nichols's point that documentaries have an affinity with, in his powerful phrase, other "discourses of sobriety," including "science, economics, politics, foreign policy, education, religion, welfare. These systems assume they have instrumental power; they can and should alter the world itself, they can effect action and entail consequences" (1991: 3; see also pp. 29 ff.). Not surprisingly, then, political documentaries constitute a major component of the larger set of documentary films.

Political Documentaries

While not all documentaries are political films, most (American) political films are documentaries, and there is a close association between the two categories. Despite the widespread rhetoric against too-explicit politics discussed earlier, in practice the world of independent filmmaking is careful to always make space for documentary work in general and issues of political filmmaking in particular. Thus, for example, one of the film organizations in Los Angeles hosted a panel discussion among several documentary filmmakers, including cinematographer and director Haskell Wexler. During the Q&A, someone in the audience made a comment to the effect that "documentary is turning into agitprop, what with Michael Moore and all." Wexler stood up and said,

> I'm going to make my two-minute speech. What's called political? We're living in an insane time, unless we understand it. . . . Who's killing and torturing? Unless we take responsibility as artists [we are failing]. . . . [Our work must be] contrary to corporatized images. There are no jobs, our society is not organized for life and for people, it is organized for death and for profit. If we don't take that responsibility we are failing socially and personally. (Field notes, March 27, 2008)

Similarly at the 2007 L.A. Film Festival, there was a panel called "The New Action Movies: Filmmaking with a Cause," with three film people specifically discussing political and "socially conscious" filmmaking. The three panelists were actor Don Cheadle (*Crash, Talk to Me*) and filmmakers Kirby Dick (*This Film Is Not Yet Rated, Outrage*) and Davis Guggenheim (*An Inconvenient Truth, Waiting for "Superman"*). All of them spoke of the ways in which they became converted, as it were, to the position that one had to become more activist in one's filmmaking. Don Cheadle apparently became drawn into a more activist relationship to his subjects during the filming of *Hotel Rwanda* (Terry George, 2004); in discussing the possibility of making a documentary about Darfur, he said, "You hope to get people active" (field notes, June 27, 2007). Davis Guggenheim first said, "I'd always thought of documentaries as very cut-and-dried, sort of like eat your spinach." But then he had a conversion experience: "I had a career directing in TV, it became very rote. If I had an idea that I thought was exciting, someone would say, oh we shot it that way last week. Whatever you did was just another episode. [After making *An Inconvenient Truth* I realized that] there is no better high than doing [socially] important work" (field notes, June 27, 2007). Finally, Kirby Dick had an insight that moved him from the kind of implicit politics that many filmmakers feel is present in their films to a more explicit political stance:

> My films are political, even when you focus on a single person.[6] But when I got to *Twist of Faith* [an exposé of the child sexual abuse scan-

dals in the Catholic Church], I realized it was more. It was a very personal story, very traumatic, but when I finished I realized I had a political film. Since then I've decided to devote myself to more explicitly political films." (Field notes, June 27, 2007)

Political documentaries come in all shapes and sizes. I want to mention here several recent documentaries in the relatively "classic" mold that have received major accolades in the last few years. There was first of all *Enron: The Smartest Guys in the Room* (Alex Gibney, 2005), about the corporation that fraudulently manipulated its stock, cheated its employees, manipulated the electric power system of the state of California, and lined the pockets of some of its senior executives with billions of dollars. Although the film focuses on this one spectacular and horrifying case, the filmmakers are careful to situate the case within a larger culture of greed and deception that has become pervasive throughout large parts of the U.S. economy under neoliberal capitalism. A second film from 2005, *Why We Fight* (Eugene Jarecki), provides a terrifying account of the ways in which the defense industry has essentially infiltrated the U.S. government and plays a direct role in formulating and advancing U.S. policies of more or less permanent warfare. A retired lieutenant colonel, Karen Kwiatkowski, who is a major figure throughout the film, gets the last word: "When our young people go to war, they are not fighting for their country, they are fighting for the defense industry." The third film I want to mention here is called *No End in Sight* (Charles Ferguson), which came out in 2007. It is a stunningly detailed account of the steps by which Iraq was allowed to descend into social, economic, political, and military chaos after the U.S. invasion of Iraq. For reasons that are never entirely clear, in contrast to the situation in World War II when there were detailed plans in place for the U.S. occupation, in the Iraq case American troops were ordered to stand by and do nothing as all semblance of order and the rule of law disintegrated.

All three of these films work within what Nichols called a "discourse of sobriety"—providing the viewer with facts, with "history," with logical arguments, with appeals to reason and justice, with an intent to have an impact on the real world. I want to look a little more closely at one of these, *No End in Sight*, to illustrate the various mechanisms that construct the tremendous "sobriety" of the film. It is this "sobriety," in turn, that allows the filmmaker to transcend the "merely political," the "agitprop," yet at the same time to be wholly political in the sense defined here: speaking truth to power.

No End in Sight

The film "speaks" truth at every level. We have first of all the testimonies of the expert witnesses—military people, diplomats, and journalists—who emphasize over and over that they have been there, they have been on the ground in Iraq, they have seen and grasped the situation from observations and conversations in the immediate physical context. The immediacy of their observations—that Iraq is falling apart for lack of a coherent post-invasion plan and for lack of an adequate level of troops and equipment to maintain security—is supported at the level of visual evidence in the film: extensive footage of looting and general lawlessness at first, followed by the more coordinated "insurgency" that begins to take shape, with violent gun, mortar, and explosive attacks on U.S. troops and the UN headquarters.

The testimony of the people in the field is amplified by specialists in the United States—intelligence analysts, policy advisors, and academic specialists—who synthesize what they have gathered from the people in the field and organize it into reports and accounts that are transmitted to the administration in Washington. While some of these people have not spent time on the ground in Iraq, they take the point of view of those who have and try to communicate it to President Bush and the members of the administration, all to no avail. Their work goes unread and their views are dismissed.

Both groups emphasize that their reports are based on eyewitness experience, or on accounts of eyewitness experience. Both groups emphasize that the administration continues to make decisions (or to fail to make decisions) virtually without having set foot in the country, and thus without any firsthand experience whatsoever about what is going on. This dichotomy between having been there and not having been there then structures a more general dichotomy between knowledge and ignorance, which then organizes most of the footage we see of members of the administration speaking about Iraq. They are shown to be ignorant, to not know what is going on, and more frighteningly, to not care about what is really going on. Footage of President Bush making statements about the war shows him to be either confused or smirking or both. Footage of Secretary of Defense Donald Rumsfeld making statements about the war shows him constantly making wisecracks and evincing an extraordinary level of insensitivity (about the looting: "they seem to be losing a lot of jars in Iraq"; about reports that things are deteriorating badly: "it's all 'Henny Penny, the sky is falling'"; in response to GIS' complaining about not having armor on their Humvees: "You fight the war with the army you have, not the army you want").

In sum, good people speak truth to power; their veracity is supported by their status as eyewitnesses, by the multiplicity of individuals telling much the same story, by the footage of events on the ground, and finally, in what might be called a backhanded way, by the fact that those in power never even remotely defend themselves. Instead they show themselves to be ignorant about facts, duplicitous about their motives, and callous and uncaring about the suffering and destruction their policies are causing.

Yet as we will see when we get to the reviews, the film is never taken to be "politics" in the bad sense—propaganda bludgeoning the audience with partisan rhetoric. Rather, it is appreciated for its "sobriety," and I want to take a few minutes to consider how this sobriety is constructed.

The sense of sobriety in *No End in Sight* is constructed in part by the use of rhetoric and devices that will be familiar to any academic (which, in fact, is what the filmmaker is). Many of the interviewees are professors, and specifically professors at distinguished institutions. This of course provides them and the film with authority, but it also shapes their style of talking to the camera. One has the distinct feeling sometimes that one is listening to an academic lecture, albeit a good one, one that holds one's interest. Virtually all the interviewees are very articulate, and one of the aspects of their articulateness is that they say what they have to say in a very organized manner. Often speakers present their points in lists: points a, b, and c, or items 1, 2, and 3. There are also bullet-point lists presented visually on the screen, such as the mistakes that Ambassador L. Paul Bremer III made that played a major role in the descent of Iraq into chaos: (1) stopping the formation of an interim government, (2) de-Ba'athification, and (3) disbanding the Iraqi military establishment.

More generally there are title placards throughout. Some of these are descriptive, sometimes with one word—HISTORY or CHAOS—and other times with several lines of explanation. Other title placards show flow charts of relevant agencies in Washington, or of relevant agencies on the ground in Iraq. Yet another shows the various categories and amounts of expenditures adding up to what are clearly obscene amounts of money, yet appearing on the screen as an orderly and understated accountant's chart. The film clearly assumes not only a high degree of literacy on the part of the viewers, but a familiarity with the verbal and visual tropes of academic presentation.

Another aspect of the sobriety of the film is that interviewees speak in very moderated tones. Even when they are clearly quite angry, they never raise their voices. There is a little flare-up from former deputy secretary of state Richard Armitage when he thinks director Charles Ferguson is questioning his competence during an interview. There are also occasionally some exasperated looks and rolled eyes when speakers are expressing extreme frustration. By and large, however, there is tremendous restraint in the ways in which individuals render their accounts and make their points.

And then there is the look and sound of the film. Like many documentaries, the film alternates between scenes of the events under discussion—here, the disintegrating situation in Iraq following the American invasion—and speakers ("talking heads") commenting on and explaining the decisions that went into what we are seeing. I have already noted the restrained manner of the speakers. The same may be said of the footage of events on the ground. We see many kinds of disturbing clips—gunfire, bodies, explosions, people running in terror, arrests being made in the middle of the night, physically rough treatment of Iraqi persons, grieving survivors, burning cars, more gunfire, bodies, explosions. Yet the volume is often literally turned down. Explosions are relatively muffled if not completely silent. Instead of natural sound—yelling, screaming, gunfire, the roar of explosions—there is sometimes simply music: a muted piano or other instruments playing disturbing repetitive figures at low volume against a visual backdrop of fire and destruction.

And finally there is the narrative and moral shape of the film. At issue is the specific relationship between the analytic presentations of the speakers and the on-the-ground, almost entirely violent or otherwise emotionally provocative footage. What the film does, and indeed what most documentaries do, is wrap the emotionally provocative footage within the reasoned discourses of the talking heads. The sense of sobriety, of rationality and levelheadedness, of the film is created in part by this arrangement, in which the words and images of reason are made—visually, and hopefully—

to encompass the stupidity and irrationality of the policy makers as well as the madness and violence on the ground. The very last line of the film is given to the articulate Marine lieutenant Seth Moulton, who says, "And are you telling me that that's the best America can do? No. Don't tell me that, don't tell the Marines who fought for a month in Najaf that, don't tell the Marines who are still fighting every day in Fallujah that that's the best America can do." He pauses and gives a small shake of his head and looks down. "That makes me angry." It is the soft and controlled quality of that final utterance, "That makes me angry," that sums up the emotional tone of the film: anger controlled and appropriately directed by a consciousness in which rationality is uppermost.

Let us then turn to some reviews of the film, which was extremely well received by critics. It was on virtually every list of top ten films of the year. David Ansen called it a "powerhouse of a movie" (2007b: 12). Mark Harris called it "riveting, coolly intense, and unimpeachable," and later "mind-blowing" (2007: 1). Richard Schickel said it was "without question the most important movie you are likely to see this year" (2007: 2). A. O. Scott called it "a sober, revelatory and absolutely vital film" (2007: 3). And there are many, many more reviews in this vein.

The reviews are also important for showing why the film was so successful, at least at a critical level: its sobriety allows it to be "political" yet to avoid the "agitprop" label. Many reviewers comment on what I am calling the sobriety of the film: "This movie . . . never raises its voice" (Ansen 2007b: 12); "It seems to have been made with the kind of calm focus that is bred by deep anger, but it always stays on mission" (Harris 2007: 1). A. O. Scott calls it "temperate" (2007: 2) and, in the quote we have heard already, "sober" (2007: 3). Another describes it as "exchanging liberal complacency with wonkishly objective rigor" (Stevens 2007: 2). The sobriety of the film especially stands out against a backdrop of more flamboyant documentary filmmaking of recent years: "'No End in Sight' . . . demonstrates for all the kook-fringe documentarians how far you can get on scrupulous reporting, non-conspiratorial analysis, penetrating interviews and a fair overview" (Hunter 2007: 1). "In an era of shout-first-ask-questions-later filmmaking, Ferguson's frosty intensity is exciting" (2007: 1). Other reviews make clear who those "kook-fringe documentarians" or "shout-first filmmakers" might be, or rather, there is really only one in question: Michael Moore. "This is a documentary of persuasion to make

Michael Moore look like a dancing bear" (Burr 2007: 2). "Charles Ferguson makes the case against the Bushies in Iraq—not from the vantage of a lefty tub-thumper like Michael Moore but from that of a policy wonk" (Edelstein 2007: 2). "This is not a documentary filled with anti-war activists or sitting ducks for Michael Moore" (Ebert 2007: 1).

Moore is obviously a very controversial figure, but he is central to the emergence of the "new documentary," to which we now turn.

The New Documentary

Documentary filmmakers constitute a relatively small but passionate group, who make their films with love and devotion, and often put many years of their lives into a single film. Dan Klores, director of *Crazy Love* (2007), expressed some of this passion and love when he came up to the stage to take Q&A at Sundance in 2007: "He said first that he wants to thank everyone who makes documentary films, that he tries to see all of them, that it's not a question of good and bad, but people put their hearts and souls and years of their lives into these films and he cares for them all" (field notes, January 24, 2007). Loved too by aficionados like myself, documentaries are nonetheless considered dry and boring by most movie viewers, and in the past they have made very little money.[7]

The film that changed that story was Michael Moore's *Fahrenheit 9/11*, which came out in 2004 and grossed $119 million, putting it in a league with Hollywood blockbusters. Suddenly, as film scholar and filmmaker Eric Faden said, documentaries had become "hot" (*Media Stylo #4*, 2005). But changes were already in the air. In 1998, Linda Williams wrote of the "unprecedented popularity [of documentary films] among general audiences, who now line up for documentaries as eagerly as for fiction films," and went on to talk of "a new hunger for reality on the part of a public seemingly saturated with Hollywood fiction" (1998b: 382). The year 2002 in particular seems to have been a breakout year, as Moore's *Bowling for Columbine* won the Best Documentary Academy Award and, more importantly, made an impressive $21 million at the box office. An article in the *Hollywood Reporter* in 2003 bore the subhead "Documentary filmmaking finally begins to break into the mainstream." The article begins breathlessly, "The Oscar-winning 2002 docu [*sic*; a *Variety* magazine abbreviation] 'Bowling for Columbine' might have been the watershed, but it seems the movie industry and audiences are discovering what film lovers have known for decades: Documentary films can be every bit as compelling, if not more so, than fictional narratives" (Linden 2003: 35).

Things appeared even better over the next few years, with Michael Moore's *Fahrenheit 9/11* winning the Palme d'Or in Cannes and *An Inconvenient Truth* starring Al Gore winning an Academy Award in 2004 and 2006, respectively. Robert Redford noted with satisfaction in 2007 that it had been "Sundance's original goal [to put] docus on the same level as features" (Zeitchik and McClintock 2007). And in February 2008, film scholar Douglas Kellner gave a lecture at UCLA in which he referred several times to the present moment as "the Golden Age of documentaries" (see also his *Cinema Wars*, 2010).

What had happened to effect this dramatic transformation? In a short but very illuminating film called *Media Stylo #4: The Documentary's New Politics* (2005), film scholar and filmmaker Eric Faden explores the changes in documentary filmmaking that had been going on since the late 1980s that paved the way for this extraordinary state of affairs.[8] He looks at a variety of industrial changes but then focuses on five films that, from his point of view, "changed the genre" of the documentary, either through becoming more like narrative features, or by accustoming viewers to certain kinds of documentary conventions, or both. I'll present his list and give a brief summary of his points as to why each contributed to the breakout success of documentaries in the 1990s.

- *The Thin Blue Line* (Errol Morris, 1988) broke with cinema verité documentary conventions that eschewed narrative voice-over and thus limited the kinds of stories documentaries could tell. Morris used reenactments to tell a story about an event in the past; the film also "had a film noir lighting scheme and the plot of a thriller."
- *Roger and Me* (Michael Moore, 1989) was "part of a narcissistic genre" and "fit neatly into the persona-dominated mediascape, the journalist-as-star that emerged in the 1990s."
- *Hoop Dreams* (Steve James, 1994) "had a story so compelling and suspenseful that filmmaker Spike Lee wanted to remake the film as a fictional feature." It also acclimated audiences to some of the look and feel of documentaries.
- *The Blair Witch Project* (Daniel Myrick and Eduardo Sánchez, 1999) was of course not a documentary. However, it borrowed the docu-

mentary's conventions in order to enhance its reality effect and "acclimated huge audiences to the documentary's aesthetics of handheld camera, loose framing, and available location lighting."

- *Bowling for Columbine* (Michael Moore, 2002) represents "a new type of mainstream documentary" in which "Moore uses a patchwork of appropriated materials" to create "film essays" (like, one might note, the short theoretical film Faden himself has made).

In sum, Faden points to a general trend toward making documentaries more exciting, and at the same time toward making some exciting feature films look more like documentaries, thus in a sense naturalizing for audiences some of the documentary's aesthetics. This all seems fundamentally correct; in addition, I want to pursue several further lines of thinking about the new documentary.

I want to argue first that filmmakers of the "new documentary" persuasion try to occupy a complicated position in which they hold on to the classic truth function of documentary film but at the same time import a kind of postmodern and/or Gen X sensibility that renders the truth claim more complex and contingent, or clothes that truth in irony and humor, either way tuning into more contemporary sensibilities. This position is delicate, and it is possible to go too far in the direction of moral ambiguity or political incoherence. But when it works, it makes for a more powerful documentary, either in the sense of enhanced drama, or in the sense of being funny and ironic, either way delivering something an audience schooled in Hollywood movies may be willing, and maybe even eager, to sit down and watch.

Let me start with the first part of this equation—complicating, but not losing, the truth function of documentary film. Here I draw on Linda Williams's excellent meditation on truth in contemporary documentaries, via a discussion of Errol Morris's *The Thin Blue Line* (1988). Morris's use of fictional reenactments of the crime at the core of the film was very controversial at the time. Williams goes straight to the heart of the matter:

> Truth is not "guaranteed" and cannot be transparently reflected by a mirror with a memory [the phrase was explained earlier as referring to photographs], yet some kind of partial and contingent truths are nevertheless the always-receding goal of the documentary tradition. Instead of careening between idealistic faith in documentary truth and

cynical recourse to [charges of] fiction, we do better to define documentary not as an essence of truth but as a set of strategies designed to choose from among a horizon of relative and contingent truths. (L. Williams 1998b: 386)

Williams particularly opposes this more subtle sense of truth construction and history construction to the lament of Fredric Jameson, and other early left-(anti)postmodernists, for the loss of historical consciousness under the regime of postmodernity (L. Williams 1998b: 387). Moreover, while seeing this kind of filmmaking as "postmodern," Williams is careful to stop short of a kind of hall-of-mirrors approach to the truth: "As *The Thin Blue Line* shows, the recognition that documentary access to [the] real is strategic and contingent does not require a retreat to a *Rashomon*-like universe of undecidabilities" (L. Williams 1998b: 387). Indeed, after showing the viewer throughout the film just how complicated the truth can be, Morris does in the end arrive at a genuine (if still partial) truth, something to be compared with the ending of *Capturing the Friedmans*, discussed in chapter 6. Harking back to an earlier language, we might say that Morris explores, but does not get lost in, the "gray areas."

Once again I am interested in the complicated position held by "the new documentary" in holding on to the truth function of the genre while at the same time operating within a "postmodern" mode that would normally be taken to be highly relativistic and hostile to the idea of truth. Errol Morris represents one approach as just discussed. The other picks up on the playful and ironic side of postmodern/Gen X culture and uses humor, jokes, irony, and stunts to break up the sobriety of the classic documentary and yet make a serious point. This of course is the space of Michael Moore's films.[9] All of Moore's films are about the very serious subject of the literally inhuman nature of capitalism. But instead of the sober documentary that marches us through a "history lesson," Moore's films are organized around stunts and laced with humor. The very premise of *Roger and Me* is a stunt—to get through to Roger Smith, the president of General Motors, and confront him with the human devastation wrought by the closing of the General Motors plant in Flint, Michigan. Moore knows, and we know, that this will never happen, but it sets up the narrative line of the film, and it shows how inaccessible (read: insensitive, uncaring, etc.) Smith is to (the suffering of) ordinary people. Moore does at least one version of this stunt in every one of his films, and it has become a kind of trademark of his. In addition, in later films, Moore makes use of lively graphics, a strong sound track, and other elements to heighten the pleasure of the film even as it delivers a serious message.

This use of jokes and stunts within a plot line of a quixotic quest for truth (and for action) can be seen in a number of other contemporary political documentaries. One example is a short film by Emily and Sarah Kunstler called *Getting Through to the President* (2004). The Kunstler sisters are self-declared activist filmmakers. The film is a very charming little seven-minute documentary in which Emily and Sarah encourage people on the street to make a free call to President Bush's comment line (or they give the person a cup of quarters to make the call). The filmmakers make an effort at "balance" in that two of the fifteen or so callers tell Bush he is doing a good job. Most of them, however, say very critical things, but one is sure those comments will never get to the president. One man asks the operator to read him back his comments, but she hangs up.

Another example is Haskell Wexler's *Who Needs Sleep?* (2006). This is a documentary about the excessively long hours people making films have to work during production. Wexler wants to expose the corporate greed behind this and start a movement for shorter work hours during production. (One of the interesting narrative threads of the film is how the unions seem to be in bed with the corporations, and they try to shut down his nascent movement, telling him he is "getting ahead of the local.") At one point he goes to see the head of the Occupational Safety and Health Administration (OSHA) in Washington, DC. He tries unsuccessfully to make an appointment, so he turns to the camera and says he is going to "pull a Michael Moore" and see if he can just barge in and get access. Of course the effort fails, but the point is made.

For a final example, we may consider Kirby Dick's *This Film Is Not Yet Rated*, also from 2006. The film was about the MPAA (Motion Picture Association of America) ratings board, the people who can ruin the chances of a film by giving it an NC17 (formerly X) rating, and the fact that the membership of the board is secret. There are many interviews with filmmakers and film critics about how problematic this is, as well as about the general conservatism of the board, particularly about sex. But Dick also "pulls a Michael Moore" (though he doesn't use the phrase) and hires detectives to try to find out the identities of the board members and out them, which he does at the end. The detectives are very funny and clever, and in fact, unlike attempts in the other films, they do get the information Dick is seeking. He also succeeds in talking to some of the board members on the phone. Further, in addition to the funny-quest structure, Dick, like Michael Moore, makes clever use of animation and music to give the film a kind of antic look and sound.

In addition to the kind of tricksterism of these films, both narratively and stylistically, I want to call attention to the central role of the filmmaker in the story we see on screen. This of course was another of Michael Moore's innovations, and there is no question in my mind that it works to capture the attention of audiences who are used to "stars." Eric Faden placed *Roger and Me* within the somewhat negative context of the "cinema of narcissism" and of the promotion of even minor journalists and anchor-persons as "stars," and I take his point. At the same time, I would argue that this is one of the ways in which the film succeeds in merging the personal and the political. All the filmmakers show that they have a personal stake in the issue being examined by the film. Moore makes the strongest links between his personal life history and the films he makes, including reciting his personal history of growing up in Flint, showing his baby pictures, and bringing his father on screen (for a critical take on this, see Bernstein 1998). But even in cases where the filmmaker does not bring in so much personal material, the point is made. We know that Kirby Dick is a citizen of the community held hostage by the MPAA ratings board, and we know that Emily and Sarah Kunstler are citizens, like so many of their viewers, frustrated with the conservative and hawkish presidency of George W. Bush.

Returning to the broader point, we may think of all these films, including both those in the mode of drama (*The Thin Blue Line* and others) and those in the mode of comedy or irony (Moore and others), as using post-modern conventions in the service of truth. I would argue that this represents a very important cultural and historical synthesis, working against the darkness and moral ambiguity of many independent films discussed in the previous chapters, embracing the cultural questions (such as relativism) and styles (such as irony) of the present moment, but making them do positive political work.

The Personal and the Political in the New (Political) Documentary

I want to return here to the charge that the classic documentary was dry and boring, giving audiences a history lesson in the pejorative sense, and telling them to eat their spinach. We may translate this point in part into a question already touched on briefly several times: the split between the personal and the political, with documentaries in the classic mold being precisely too impersonal, pursuing the political (and "history") in too objectivist a way.

One of the solutions to this in the new documentary is, to extend a point begun already, the creation of "stars." The classic documentary does not have stars—attractive leading personages who constitute a focus of both eye appeal and emotional identification. The narrator is generally off-screen; sometimes there is no narrator at all. There is often a parade of individuals ("talking heads"), no single one of whom becomes a point of personal connection for the viewer.

The new documentary creates stars in at least two ways. One, as I have already indicated, involves making the filmmaker the star of the film. Michael Moore is the example best known to the wider public; Haskell Wexler (who "pulled a Michael Moore") is very well known within the film community. And although Al Gore did not direct *An Inconvenient Truth*, he did write the book, and he successfully used his own star power in the film to attract and keep the audience's attention.

The other major strategy for creating stars in the new documentary (and even in some of the more "classic documentaries" of recent years) involves making stars of one or more of the film's "talking heads." All the documentaries discussed here involved the use of very attractive and articulate individuals who engage the viewer with their intelligence and perceptiveness, but also with their looks and personalities. Examples from the discussions in this chapter would be the young journalist who first broke the Enron story, Bethany McLean, in *Enron: The Smartest Guys in the Room*; Karen Kwiatkowski, the disillusioned young (now retired) U.S. Air Force lieutenant colonel in *Why We Fight*; or Marine lieutenant Seth Moulton in *No End in Sight*. Of course, biographical documentaries by definition always had stars in this sense—persons with some kind of appeal and charisma; one could go all the way back to *Nanook of the North* (Robert J. Flaherty, 1922) for this tradition. But the stars of the new documentary are not the objects of the documentary; the object of the documentary is the political issue—Enron, or the military-industrial complex, or the Iraq War. Finding people who precisely will not seem like "talking heads," who will be not only intelligent about the issues but attractive and appealing to viewers, seems to be a further mode of drawing the viewer into a personal connection with the issues of the film.

Pushing this point up a notch, I was fascinated to see that documentary filmmakers often bring the "stars" of their films with them to screenings and film festivals, and especially to the most important festivals like Sundance. At Sundance 2007, when the lights came up at the end of *No End in Sight*, there on the stage next to filmmaker Charles Ferguson was the intelligent, articulate, and (I think not irrelevantly) handsome Seth Moulton; when the lights came up at the end of a lovely film called *Miss Navajo* (Billy Luther, 2007), there on the stage was the intelligent, articulate, and (again not irrelevantly) attractive Crystal Frazer, the young Navajo woman at the center of the film. More recently I saw a screening of *The Most Dangerous Man in America: Daniel Ellsberg and the Pentagon Papers* (Judith Ehrlich and Rick Goldsmith, 2009), and when the lights came up there on the stage with the filmmakers were Daniel Ellsberg and his wife. They received a five-minute standing ovation.

But there is another way of connecting the personal and the political in the new documentary, and that has to do with the content of the films. It is not difficult to construct story lines in which intimate personal relationships play out within, and affect the workings of, large-scale political structures, while at the same time large-scale political structures inform and deform personal relations. European and other non-American screenwriters and filmmakers have done this successfully for decades. Recent films like the Austrian/French *Caché* (Michael Haneke, 2005), the South African *Catch a Fire* (Phillip Noyce, 2006), and the German *The Lives of Others* (Florian Henckel von Donnersmarck, 2006) all involve plot lines critically linking the violence of large-scale structures of power with intimate stories of love and betrayal. Of course, those are feature films. It might seem almost impossible that this kind of plot could be constructed within the framework of a documentary, but one recent film succeeds brilliantly: Errol Morris's *Standard Operating Procedure* (2008). The film is about the abuse and humiliation of prisoners in Abu Ghraib prison in Iraq, theoretically for purposes of breaking down their resistance so that they would provide important intelligence. Naked men were forced to pose with one another in human pyramids, to wear women's underwear on their heads, to be led around on leashes like dogs, and so forth. The film is also about the fact that the soldiers and officers involved in the abuse took hundreds if not thousands of photographs of these scenes—not just the abuse of power but the pornography of power. And finally, the film is about the personal relationships among these soldiers and officers—sexual affairs, pregnancies, jealousies, betrayals. Moreover, as in *The Thin Blue Line*, Morris uses these personal relationships to give the movie—which otherwise consists of almost unbearably disturbing footage—plot, mystery, and drama. He personalizes the film not only in the sense of representing, via the story, the linkage between the personal and the political, but also in the sense of keeping the viewer fascinated by the personalities and relationships. At every level, then, *Standard Operating Procedure* shows the viewer or, in the best case, makes the viewer feel at a gut level that the political is profoundly personal.

Political Films across the Generations

The "Golden Age of documentaries" turned out to have been something of a bubble. Depending on which film one counts from, it lasted anywhere from four years to a decade. By 2008 *Newsweek* critic David Ansen declared it over, as many of the outstanding and prizewinning documentaries of that year made shockingly little money (Ansen 2008), and no documentaries have since hit the blockbuster levels of *Fahrenheit 9/11* or *An Inconvenient Truth*. But of course indie people would be the first to say that box office is not everything, and two rather more hopeful points need to be made here.

The first is that many of these films will have a significant afterlife through television broadcast and/or DVD rentals. Documentaries are known to do much better on television (McDonald 2001; Ansen 2008: 68), and television in turn has been supportive of the genre. (A special cheer here for Sheila Nevins, longtime president of HBO Documentary Films.) Since many more people watch television, and now rental DVDs, than go to the movies, many of these films may have what author Chris Anderson (2006) has memorably called "a long tail," an impact far beyond their brief (if any) theatrical distributions, and far beyond what their (usually weak) box office takes would suggest.

The second point concerns production rather than consumption. There is a saying in the world of independent film that any film that gets made is a success. If we look at the actual practices of independent filmmakers today, we see that they are turning out documentaries—many of them political documentaries—at an extraordinary rate. My list of political documentaries made since the late 1980s runs to almost fifty films, most of them made within the last five years. This suggests—to return to a point with which I began this chapter—that the younger generation is at least as concerned as the older generation to take up political issues on film, and that those who pronounced the younger generation apathetic and apolitical were perhaps not looking in the right places.

In closing this chapter, then, I want to bring out the degree to which political filmmaking spans the generations, up into the present generation of young documentarians. To do this, and also to link back to one of the central themes of this book, I here narrow the focus of "political films" to films specifically about the destructive workings of neoliberal capitalism.

To begin with, I want to pay homage to the older documentarians, starting with Haskell Wexler, born in 1926 and still fighting the good fight with *Who Needs Sleep?* (2006). And then there is the extraordinary group of boomer-generation documentarians who have further developed and sustained a brilliant and hard-hitting critique of contemporary capitalism: Michael Moore (most recently with *Sicko* [2007] and *Capitalism: A Love Story* [2009]), Robert Greenwald (*Wal-Mart: The High Cost of Low Prices* [2005] and *Iraq for Sale: The War Profiteers* [2006]), Alex Gibney (*Enron: The Smartest Guys in the Room* [2005]), and Charles Ferguson (*Inside Job* [2010]).

A brief aside here about Charles Ferguson and *Inside Job*. *Inside Job* is a brilliant account of the bad (corporation-favoring) politics and the bad (greedy, immoral, and often illegal) financial practices that led up to the near crash of the stock market in 2008; the film won the Best Documentary Oscar for 2010. I noted earlier in this chapter that political documentaries go beyond cultural critique and seek to move people to act in the real world. When Ferguson received the Oscar, he went up to the podium and made a very strong comment to the effect that many of the people and corporations discussed in the film had been involved in "massive fraud" and yet "none of these guys are in jail yet" (field notes, February 27, 2011). Ferguson clearly hopes for real-world action as a result of his films, both in the sense of moving the legal system to act and in the sense of getting the rest of us angry and politically active.

And now let us look at the Gen Xers. Several of them have taken on capitalism directly in the style of the boomers noted above. Mark Achbar and Jennifer Abbott made *The Corporation* (2003), an incisive critical history of how the American corporation has grown ever more powerful over time. Eugene Jarecki's *Why We Fight* (2005) shows the degree to which the massive defense-industry corporations have infiltrated the inner policy-making circles of the government, virtually guaranteeing that the United States will be in a perpetual state of warfare. James D. Scurlock's *Maxed Out: Hard Times, Easy Credit and the Era of Predatory Lenders* (2006) is a hair-raising account of the newly expanded predatory lending industry and the ways in which massive levels of debt are destroying both the national economy and individual lives. And although boomer Alex Gibney directed *Enron*, the investigative reporting for the book on which it was based, as well as the coauthorship of the book and the authorship of the script, were all done by *Fortune* magazine reporter Bethany McLean, another certified Gen Xer.

Gen X filmmakers have also been in the lead with critical documentaries about the relationship between corporate greed and the destruction of the environment. Only one of the films in this set (within my filmography) was made by a boomer-generation filmmaker: Louis Psihoyos made *The Cove* (2009), which looks at the annual massive roundup (for sale) and slaughter (for food) of dolphins in a certain coastal village in Japan. All the rest of the films in this group have been made by Gen Xers, filmmakers born starting in the early 1960s. Jennifer Baichwal's *Manufactured Landscapes* (2007) shows, among other things, how a certain area of China has come to specialize in removing precious metals, including mercury, from discarded American computers, and how the ground water in that area has become so polluted with mercury that drinking water must be trucked in. *Mann v. Ford* (2010), directed by Maro Chermayeff and Micah Fink, tells the story of decades of dumping toxic auto paint waste on Ramapough Indian land by a Ford Motor Company plant in northern New Jersey. Also about polluting the ground water, but on an even bigger scale, Josh Fox's *Gasland* (2010) shows how the process of extracting natural gas involves injecting toxic chemicals into the ground, and tells us as well that the natural gas industry was exempted from all regulations under the Clean Water and Clean Air acts under the George W. Bush administration.

And then there is global warming. Davis Guggenheim's *An Inconvenient Truth* (2006), based on Al Gore's book by the same name, kicked off this whole genre, graphically depicting the ways in which global warming is increasing and slowly destroying the earth. *An Inconvenient Truth* was a very powerful film, but it was in many ways the least political of the group, as Guggenheim and Gore played down the political finger pointing. Daniel Gold and Judith Helfand's *Everything's Cool* (2007), on the other hand, makes the more political argument that the Environmental Protection Agency under George W. Bush's presidency was subjected to heavy pressure, mainly by the oil industry, to undermine scientific information on global warming in all their reports. Chris Paine's *Who Killed the Electric Car?* (2006) also addresses the politics of the global warming issue; Paine shows first how the auto industry in America systematically destroyed public transportation in many cities after World War II, and then, when an electric car was developed in the early 1990s, how that too was destroyed by a combination of oil and auto interests, all in the name of profit. The preponderance of Gen Xers in the group making films about the environment intuitively makes sense. It is common knowledge that, if there is one political issue that animates the younger generation, it is the issue of the environment. What is striking in these films, however, is the degree to which environmental degradation is specifically looked at as an effect of the workings of contemporary neoliberal capitalism.

Finally, Gen X documentarians have been leading the way with a somewhat more global perspective on capitalism than the older generation. I have already noted Jennifer Baichwal's *Manufactured Landscapes*, concerned in part with what might be called the globalization of toxic waste (mercury from discarded American computers) in China. David Redmon documented the inhuman working conditions of the Chinese workers who make the distinctive beads for the American Mardi Gras (*Mardi Gras: Made in China*, 2005). Yung Chang made *Up the Yangtze* (2007), about the tribulations of a family whose land is being flooded by the Three Gorges dam project in China. Jason Kohn made *Manda Bala* (2007), about corruption in the Brazilian government, the polarization of wealth in Brazil, and the epidemic of kidnapping that is related to all this.

In sum, there has been a growing stream of good political documentary work coming out of the trenches of Generation X. In some ways it has gone in new directions—more concerned with the environment, more global—and that is all to the good. At the same time, there is a strong underlying continuity with the work of the older generation, a growing awareness of the ways in which neoliberal capitalism is destroying lives and the very planet itself.

This body of work, along with many other powerful political films (about race, for example) that I have not had time to discuss, also allows us to see that the Occupy Wall Street movement did not come from nowhere. Despite the charges, and perhaps until recently the reality, of widespread political apathy among Gen Xers, it is clear that many members of this generation were already working out their own ways of thinking about and—more importantly for present purposes—representing some of the terrible realities of today's world.

And so we move to the brief conclusions for this book, where I will consider, among other things, the future of independent film itself.

CHAPTER 9

Conclusions

I have argued throughout this book that (independent) films are part of what Appadurai and Breckenridge have called the "public culture." Public culture comprises all forms of representation—the arts, media, scholarly work, and more—that can be read as attempts to grasp and/or critique (and/or manage) some existing social reality. At any given time, some of those representations will have achieved relatively greater power than others, having greater social authority and greater scope of impact: think Hollywood movies. Others will be located in more marginal, but sometimes also oppositional, positions: think independent film.

Oppositional cultural forms like independent films work by "talking back" to dominant cultural representations. At the most general level, independent films "talk back" to Hollywood by doing everything that Hollywood generally will not do—by treating "difficult" subjects; by insisting on the importance of realism; by refusing happy endings and other things that make audiences feel good—all in the service of getting audiences to think about the harsh realities of the world. At a more specific level, any given film or group of films can be looked at in terms of its specific representations of social reality, the ways in which it seeks to subvert dominant views of everything from love and sex to capitalism and globalization. The results are often not pretty, but they can be—when they work—very powerful.

This approach to film is fundamentally anthropological. It looks at films as it looks at any cultural phenomenon, as related in the first instance to its own time and place. Of course, the first instance may not be the last instance. Some films (or any other cultural works) may achieve popularity beyond their time and place of production; some may fade at one point and be revived at another; and in all these cases one would ask new questions about their meanings. But those questions would always be—from this point of view—related to the real social world in which the films are being (re-)appropriated and (re-)appreciated.

Films are of course complex textual assemblages, involving story, visuality, and sound. If I had time, and if this were a different book, I would have discussed the films in terms of the interaction of all of these elements, for it is only through that interaction that films gain their unique power. I provided one such multidimensional interpretation in chapter 8, with respect to the documentary *No End in Sight*, precisely to try to reveal what made the film so powerful. But for the broader purpose of this book, which was to ask what the emerging independent film movement as a whole was trying to say and do in these new and difficult times, I have mostly stayed at the level of story—setting, character, dialogue, plot—as well as mood, as these are most directly relatable to the social issues at stake.

Yet to say that films both are shaped by and talk back to their social and historical context is never to say that films are mere "reflections" of that context. Every act of representation is at the same time an act of interpretation, an attempt to cast what is going on in the world around us in a particular way. Within the world of edgy/quirky/difficult independent film, furthermore, every act of representation/interpretation is at the same time meant to be a challenge to viewers—to think differently, to feel differently, and even, in the case of political documentaries, to get off our bottoms and act back on the real world.

I have argued throughout the book that the independent film movement that began in the 1980s is most productively read as addressing and critiquing a cluster of interrelated changes of massive proportions in the economy, in family life, and in patterns of political engagement that began in the late 1970s. At this point, then, rather than bore the reader with a plodding summary of what has come before, I would like to pull the discussion together around a particular theme that has been woven, in different ways, through virtually every chapter of the book: social class. Changes in the American class structure, as a result of neoliberal policies and practices, have been implicated materially and/or imaginatively in virtually every aspect of the indie movement, and I would like to take stock of that as I bring the book to a close.

Following the class discussion, I will bring the account of the indie movement up to date, at least as much as I can, since things tend to change very quickly. I will look at the crisis that hit the indie world in 2007, as many studios closed their specialty divisions and money for independent filmmaking became much scarcer. And I will look at the indie community's responses to the crisis, including, among other things, an expanded interest in exploiting the Internet. Finally, I will return to the wider world and consider what we might take away from this story in terms of political inspiration for the present and the future.

Class Transformation and Independent Film

I began the book with the observation, central to much of Marxist theory, that major cultural transformations in capitalist societies tend to be linked to major transformations in the class structure. Raymond Williams argued the point in general terms, while Jürgen Habermas and E. P. Thompson argued the point through case studies, in relation to the eighteenth-century European bourgeoisie and the nineteenth-century English working class, respectively. One could argue that Fredric Jameson, in his classic 1984 article "Postmodernism, or the Cultural Logic of Late Capitalism," was trying to make a similar argument, linking what he argued was a massive cultural shift—from modernity to postmodernity—to a shift in the order of what he called "late capitalism." Like most observers at that time, however, Jameson did not yet have a good grasp of the way in which "late capitalism," an early take on what most observers now call "neo-liberalism," was reshaping the class structures of advanced capitalist societies. The present book in a sense represents another shot at what Jameson was trying to do, but eschewing the red flag of "postmodernism," and providing greater specificity about both the cultural and social (class) changes in question.

Both Habermas and Thompson focused on emerging classes, that is, on the ways in which the French bourgeoisie or the English working class both was made and made itself under particular conditions of historical struggle. Implicit in these accounts is an awareness that changes at one level of the class structure reverberate through the other levels, but the primary focus is on the particular class in question. My class frame for the discussion in the present book has been slightly different. By starting with "neoliberalism" rather than a focus on the fate of any particular class, the whole American class structure is seen to be in motion, one might even say in convulsions, with different effects at different points in the structure and at different points in time.

This is to say, then, that class has entered the independent film story in different ways as well. Sometimes we saw it as providing the material conditions for the emergence of the indie scene. Sometimes we saw it as defining the social positioning of various players within the indie scene. And sometimes we saw it as the object of the filmmakers' critical imaginations, that is, as the subject of the films in the form of mood, metaphor, or story. I will run through the chapters here by way of following the class threads that weave through them.

Chapter 1, "Making Independence," was about the conceptual opposition between "Hollywood" and "independent film." On the surface, the chapter had little to do with neoliberalism and class. Let me suggest, however, that there is a way in which the opposition between Hollywood and independent film can be read as a Lévi-Straussian binary, lining up with an unspoken binary of class. Hollywood has a lot of money, while independent film has very little. Hollywood owns most of the means of production and distribution, while indies have to scrounge for material resources and beg for distribution deals. Hollywood is an "industry" represented by executives or "suits," while independent filmmakers are a kind of artistically defined proletariat, people who have "day jobs" and hope to make films when they can. Without pushing this interpretation too far, one might suggest that some of the anger some independent filmmakers feel about "Hollywood" can be read as a kind of displaced class resentment.

Chapter 2, "Dark Indies," was the first of the film chapters. Class issues are front and center in the chapter, both outside and inside the films. Outside the films, we meet Generation X specifically as class subjects, feeling the impact of the neoliberal economy on their prospects for decent jobs and secure futures. Inside the films this impact registers in a variety of ways: in Gen Xers' stories of soul-destroying jobs, in immigrants' stories of the brutality of work at the bottom of the economy, and most of all in the darkness of mood and look that permeates most of these films.

Chapter 3, "Making the Scene," was about the coming together of the indie scene in New York and Los Angeles in the 1980s and 1990s. Here we meet a different set of class subjects, the Professional Managerial Class or PMC. Although some of the children of the PMC began to slide downhill in this period, some of them held their own, and a few did extremely well within the economic booms of the 1990s. In addition, a significant fraction of this class has been observed to shift into more progressive politics and more adventurous relationships to the arts. It is from this more specific class sector, then, that we get many of the producers, all of the investors, and much of the audience of independent film.

Chapter 4, "Moral Ambiguity," began from the fact that so many independent films have pedophiles as central characters. I looked at these films along several dimensions, including the dimension of moral ambiguity that permeates many of the films, as well as the broader neoliberal economy. But the specific class aspects of the chapter concerned the turmoil in the contemporary middle-class family. In this context the pedophile appears as the monster let loose by negligent parents and also sometimes as the substitute for the negligent or absent parent. The full significance of the class factor in this chapter only becomes apparent later in the book, when we realize that virtually all the pedophile films were set in middle- to upper-middle-class families. Where poor mothers will be seen (in chap. 6) to be struggling to protect their children, middle-class parents in the pedophile chapters appear as self-involved and careless of their children's welfare.

Chapter 5, "Making Value," is about independent producers. It was one of the findings of the research that independent producers almost uniformly come from relatively high capital backgrounds, and thus this chapter returns us to the realm of the PMC. In this context, however, I explore the education, as well as the money, factor in PMC class positioning, and consider the ways in which the combination of the two kinds of capital allows producers to create both symbolic and substantive value for the films they produce.

In chapter 6, "Film Feminism," class entered the story through a set of films in which poor single mothers struggle to protect their children. The films can be read as straightforward stories of the harshness of life in the lower levels of the class structure, made worse for poor people in general and women in particular under neoliberalism. But they can also be read, as I argued in the chapter, as allegories of downward mobility for middle-class women, in an era in which this has become a much more real possibility. I also explored the ways in which the setting of the films in the white lower- and underclasses "changes the picture" of many aspects of gender and parent-child relations.

Chapter 7, "Making Films," was a kind of mini-ethnography of the film production process. Here class entered the story in terms of the class structure of a movie set, where, as one cinematographer said to me, "all the producers and directors are from fancy educations, while everyone else is lower class." While this is not strictly accurate—filmmakers come from much more variable class backgrounds than the largely PMC producers—it does capture the general class structure of movie production. My point in this chapter was that, amidst the general post-Fordism of the neoliberal economy, in which the working class is taking a terrible hit, film production is a kind of island of Fordist capitalism, in which unionized workers still do relatively well, and in which everyone involved will often feel a sense of satisfaction and achievement at a job well done.

Chapter 8, "Politics," does not address any specific class or classes but pulls the focus back to the workings of neoliberal capitalism that underlie the class transformations running through all of the preceding chapters. In the last section of the chapter I draw attention to a growing number of powerful documentaries that are exposing the terrible effects of this system, not only on people's lives as classed subjects, but on the earth and air and water of the planet we inhabit.

All people—male and female, white or black or brown, immigrant or native—live in capitalist societies as classed subjects. Class is often invisible, but it is always there, and when the class structure starts moving in any major way, as it has been doing since the late 1970s, the impact is enormous for everyone. Independent film is one of the sites in which these seismic shifts have registered, often as forms of violence, which they are. And independent film is one of the sites in which these shifts have been—again often violently—exposed for critique and challenge.

The Crisis and the Remaking of the Scene: Indiewood and Internet

The independent film scene continued to grow and flourish throughout the 1990s and well into the 2000s. Great films were made, more investors emerged, more screens were devoted to independent films, and audiences for the independent aesthetic continued to grow. But starting in 2007, things started to go bad. Box office takes went down, and the indie industry, if one may use that term, went into a slump. There were various theories about what was going on—that indie films were too dark given the dark state of the world today (Abramowitz 2007), or that too many indie films were being made and released and were glutting their own market (Miramax CEO Daniel Battsek, quoted in Abramowitz 2007). Here is a quick summary of the progression of the crisis:

- In May 2008 Warner Bros. announced that it was closing two of its specialty divisions, Picturehouse and Warner Independent Pictures.
- In June 2008 Mark Gill, CEO of the independent production company The Film Department, proclaimed at the L.A. Film Festival, "As relates to independent film, the sky really is falling," and the quote went viral (this version quoted in Bilsborrow-Koo 2008).
- In August 2008 Scott Macaulay, editor of *Filmmaker* magazine, convened a panel in the offices of the Independent Feature Project in New York on the "Crisis in the Funding and Distribution of Independent Film."
- In July 2009 Paramount closed its Paramount Vantage specialty division.
- In September 2009 the Museum of Modern Art in New York City hosted an "Indie Summit" to hash out the continuing crisis.
- In November 2009 Disney announced the severe retrenchment of its Miramax specialty division, closing it down completely in 2010.

An article in November 2009 titled "Indie-Film Shakeout: There Will Be Blood" summed up the dire situation:

Of the 38 indie-film financing firms—the so-called front end—that existed in 2007, only 11 remain. . . . While Wall Street investment in independent movies totaled more than $2 billion from 2005 to 2007, it has plummeted to practically nothing since then. . . . How important were those [now-closed] specialty arms? In 2007, they accounted for more than 30% of indie box-office revenues. . . . [The old funding model—preselling the foreign rights] is now dead . . . the foreign presell market has dried up." (Davies 2009)

But as we know, independent film has been pronounced dead many times before, yet it still manages to rise from its own ashes. Here we need to follow two distinct lines of development since 2007. The first has to do with developments within the specialty divisions and mini-majors, that is, within the zone of production at the more Hollywood end of the indie spectrum, the zone that has been called "Indiewood" (G. King 2009). The second has to do with developments in the more radically independent zone of indie filmmaking, where filmmakers still try to "stay out of the studios" so that they can make films as they wish, without regard to whether those films will have any commercial appeal or not. My assumption throughout this book is that both kinds of work are important. Indiewood is important in that it tries to make films that have an independent spirit and yet have a shot at some kind of commercial success; without this, there is no chance of impacting the wider American public and in some sense "changing the culture." On the other hand, truly independent film is also crucially important, as it represents the only possibility of actually saying something outside of the Hollywood hegemony, or as much outside as one can get and still have people understand what is being said. One could argue that the whole independent movement has only been possible because those two sites and forms of production coexisted, in tense modes of mutual interest and interchange.

I begin with some of the developments in "Indiewood." Reading beyond the crisis literature, one learns that the specialty divisions and mini-major independent production companies that survived what now appears as a market shakeout are actually doing very well. In an article about the "near-death of Miramax" in 2009 (when it was gutted, prior to being closed completely in 2010), Magnolia Pictures president Eamonn Bowles is quoted as saying, "The market has gotten back to a more sustainable level." The writer continues, "[Bowles] suggests that surviving companies like Magnolia, Sony Pictures Classics, IFC and Zeitgeist, who focus on marketing quality films to niche audiences, are now in a stronger position. . . . 'We've done very well since last summer. It's inherently a more reasonable situation'" (O'Hehir 2009: 2). Similarly, an article surveying the fiscal health of the independent scene at the end of 2009 is relatively optimistic: "The tumult in the independent film world continued in 2009, but there were bright spots for the sector's survivors. . . . New stand-alone companies as well as the remaining few studio specialty units continued to chug along. . . . Summit, Lionsgate, Weinstein Co., Focus Features, Overture and Fox Searchlight all scored nine-figure box office [totals]" (Swart 2009: 1).

A closer look shows one kind of business strategy being used by companies like these in order to be financially successful and yet continue to produce quality films with independent spirit. This involves returning to an older definition of "independent." The category of independent once included everything the studios wouldn't make, including horror, porn, exploitation movies, and so on, as well as serious artistic and/or experimental films. Peter Biskind remarked that the remaking of the independent "brand" in the 1990s was created in part by Robert Redford and the Sundance people, who drew the line between art and schlock and appropriated art for the independent label (Biskind 2004: 77). Today's successful mini-majors and specialty divisions have expanded the category again, with a model in which, in effect, the more popular or less reputable work supports the more artistic work. Thus, for example, the most successful mini-major of 2009 was Summit Entertainment, which had a blockbuster-level success with the release of the second installment of the *Twilight* vampire series, *New Moon* (Chris Weitz, 2009). At the same time, they also picked up and released the much more artistically serious *The Hurt Locker* (2008), which did very well at the box office and also garnered Best Picture and Best Director Oscars. A similar pattern can be seen with mini-major Lionsgate, which on the one hand continued to release crowd pleasers like Tyler Perry comedies and horror films but also released *Precious* (Lee Daniels, 2009), a very independent and "difficult" film about an abused black teenager that also won major awards (Swart 2009).

Now let's look at the more hard-core independent side. There is no question that things have become much tougher for filmmakers on this side, on both ends of the production process. It is harder to raise money to make the films, and it is harder to get distributors, which is to say the (shrunken number of) specialty divisions and mini-majors, to buy and release the film. Thus, there is a great deal of rethinking and re-strategizing going on.

I have already forecast some of these discussions in chapter 1. In September 2008, in the midst of the crisis, producer Ted Hope presented the keynote address at the "Filmmaker Forum" in Los Angeles. Whereas some people were saying that indies were dead, Hope took a strong stand against this point of view: "The proclamations of indie film's demise are grossly exaggerated. How can there be a 'Death of Indie' when Indie—real Indie, True Indie—has yet to even live? . . . When someone says 'Indie is dead,' they are talking about the state of the Indie Film *Business*, as opposed to what are actually the films themselves" (2008; emphasis in original). He also took a strong stand against the "the sky is falling" point of view: "They can say 'the sky is falling' because for the last fifteen years the existing power base in the film industry has focused on *films fit for the existing business model*, as opposed to ever truly concentrating on creating *a business model for the films that filmmakers want to make*" (2008; emphasis in original).

In a nutshell Hope called for independent filmmakers to stop waiting for a "golden deal" from a major distributor and start distributing their films themselves. Self-distribution is a daunting business, involving the development and execution of marketing strategies, booking screens wherever possible on one's own, collecting revenues, and all the other work a distributor would normally do. But the pattern seems now to be taking hold in the indie world (Cieply 2009; Levy in Macaulay 2009),[1] with new kinds of indie producers, sales reps, and releasing companies emerging to facilitate the process (e.g., Jon Reiss's Producer of Marketing and Distribution or PMD; guest post on Hope for Film, August 16, 2011).

The main alternative to DIY distribution is to give up on theatrical screenings altogether and switch to finding ways to draw revenue from releasing films on the Internet. There is a lively debate over whether Web release could or should ever become the dominant model of independent film distribution. One question has to do with giving up the "event" quality created by theatrical release. Producer Ira Deutchman, responding to the Indie Summit in 2009, wrote,

> I think there's very little chance the major studio theatrical model will die. What they produce in Hollywood is the very definition of "event," and that is exactly what drives people out of their homes and into theaters. For more subtle work it's much more complicated. Can we create the desire in younger audiences to see non-mainstream cinema on the big screen with an audience? Or will these types of films be relegated to museums? (Deutchman 2009: 5)

As Deutchman suggests, events both are social (they draw people together) and have wider cultural address (they speak to a larger public rather than to an elite niche like museum audiences). Thus, people promoting a predominantly Web-based release model now talk about how to "event-ize" Web releases. Alex Johnson, described as a filmmaker and "interactive strategist," "suggests that 'event-izing' a film can work for both big movies—

like *Twilight*-watching parties—and small movies, if a group of like-minded young folks can embrace seeing a film as a social happening" (in Kaufman 2010: 1–2). Agent Scott Beiben is quoted as saying that "filmmakers need to start touring like bands" (in Kaufman 2010: 1–2).

Many independent filmmakers are by now pursuing some hybrid strategy, continuing to seek theatrical distribution while developing strategies for exploiting the Web to maximum advantage. Filmmaker Eyad Zahra wrote a guest post on Hope for Film about the release strategy for his film *The Taqwacores*:

> What I love about our release strategy is that we are using a hybrid method towards launching this film. We are doing a standard limited theatrical launch in NYC and LA, while [also] stressing an intense grassroots campaign effort. It's a bit of the old and new wrapped in one, which allows me to be involved as much as I want to be. I have been involved in every major decision for the film. I also manage our online media (website, facebook fan page, twitter) personally. (Guest blog post, October 22, 2010)

And then, in conjunction with all of the above, there is always the tried-and-true indie method of lowering the budget. In a guest post on Hope for Film titled "Stop the Whining," producer and festival programmer Kristina Michelle exhorted the indie community to tighten their belts, lower the budget, and get out there and make those films:

> [Independent filmmaking] is NOT a dying industry. It isn't endangered or failing. . . . Our economy as a whole is in an awful state, but that should not depress filmmakers searching for a budget. Instead, they should adapt to making their films on lesser budgets—all without diminishing the quality of their work. If they are good at what they do, they don't need a million dollars to make a great film. They just need the dedication and the heart that it takes to make an independent film. (Guest blog post, February 1, 2011)

In sum, independent film is feeling the squeeze of the bad economy like every other sector outside the investment banks, the big corporations, and the security sector. Yet the news from both Indiewood and the truly independent world, in terms of both rhetoric and films, remains hopeful, as both sides reinvent themselves for the new economic reality.

Independent Film and the Future

A few final notes for this book.

First, I have argued throughout this book that Generation X did not end with the cohort born in the early 1980s, as was put forth in the original Gen X literature. Rather, insofar as Generation X is defined not only by their demographics but also by their relationship to the larger economy, everyone born since the early 1960s counts as Generation X, that is, the generation that is bearing the brunt of the new neoliberalized order. I still think this is true. But I recently gave a talk in which I presented some of the themes from this book, including the point about the continuation of Generation X. Afterward, in a Q&A session with some graduate students, one of the students, born after the end of the original Gen X time frame, offered an interesting amendment to the point. He agreed with my point about continuity, but he also said that he thought the younger generation had by now adapted somewhat to the situation and was, for better or worse, collectively in less of a state of shock, rage, and depression about the whole thing. Others in the room immediately disagreed with him, and we don't have the ethnography to say whose views were more representative than whose. But the point makes sense: younger people today are probably coming into adulthood (and going to graduate school, among other things) with much lower expectations, compared to the situation of the immediate post-boomer generation, which, I think, was truly shocked by the turn the world was starting to take.

The point about adaptation then connects to my final issue: politics. Does "adapted to the situation" mean resignation and passivity? Until 2011, the answer probably would have been "yes." As discussed in chapters 7 (feminism) and 8 (politics), the boomers who had experienced the political activism of the 1960s and 1970s viewed Generation X as politically apathetic, and many Gen Xers agreed. Yet I have tried to show that the independent film movement contained the seeds of political awakening even before the 2011 demonstrations in Wisconsin and the dramatic emergence of the Occupy Wall Street movement in that same year. Thus, I want to conclude this book with some thoughts about the ways in which the independent film movement functioned as one site in which a new critical politics was taking shape on the American scene.

I would point first to the kind of energy and agency, as well as idealism, that people put into making independent films, as we have heard through-out this book. Independent film people are people who believe, in the best spirit of American individualism, that you can get out there and make something happen. Individualism, of course, has its disastrous downsides; it is as much a part of neoliberalism as it is potentially a force against it. But people do need to believe that they can both create and change things, both individually and collectively; this is the sine qua non of any kind of political consciousness. Although the indie film world sees itself as being about art more than politics, in constantly fostering this sense of agency and idealism, the idea of both making things and making impact, it has arguably served, in some extended sense, as both a model of and a basis for political engagement.

Second, a noteworthy feature of the indie scene has been the new breed of wealthy investor, interested in putting money into socially and politi-cally progressive films. As discussed in chapter 2, these investors are part of a larger, and very encouraging, development in the American class struc-ture, a reconfiguration of the PMC. In earlier times the wealthy and power-ful wing of the PMC also tended to be politically and culturally conserva-tive, while the more progressive wing of the PMC tended to have less money and clout. In recent decades, however, an increasing number of wealthy individuals with progressive politics, or progressive individuals who have made a lot of money, have become visible on the broader politi-cal landscape. Some of these, in turn, have taken an interest in indepen-dent film, as an art form that has the potential for significant social or cultural impact.

And then there are the films. Independent film people seek to make films "that matter." Eschewing mere "entertainment," or using "entertain-ment" to make a serious point, independent films are explicitly meant to show the world "as it really is." I have argued throughout the book that this commitment to (a certain kind of) realism has a fundamentally critical edge. Sometimes, as in political documentaries, the critical function is clear and straightforward. But I have argued that even seemingly apolitical, highly "personal" independent films can work as "cultural critique," chal-lenging viewers to examine their fixed assumptions about what is normal, good, or "real." This is not to endorse a kind of hyper-relativism, and I have discussed the relativism issue (often associated with "postmodernism") at various points in this book. But pushing people intellectually and emotionally off-center and off-balance, and de-normalizing the status quo, seems to me again to create some of the conditions of possibility for political action.

Finally, and most straightforwardly, I want to reemphasize the developments in the documentary genre, which has been noteworthy in both its filmic political activism and the creative development of the genre itself. Documentarians of the past few decades have critically taken on all the important moral and political issues of our times—torture, capital punishment, war; racism, sexism, the persecution of sexual minorities; and more —and they have done this in strikingly innovative ways. In keeping with the themes of this book, I have focused particularly on the growing number of excellent films that in one way or another addressed neoliberal capitalism. I find it extraordinary that these fundamentally leftist critiques of neoliberal capitalism have been getting made in significant numbers and have been garnering both audiences and awards. The work began with the great boomer documentarians but is now continuing strongly into Generation X, as I showed at the end of the last chapter. The sheer fact of these films being shown in mainstream theaters or on HBO, and/or having a good rental life in people's homes, has seemed to me—again, even before Wisconsin and Occupy Wall Street—to be one of the best indications that many people are waking up, intellectually, emotionally, and politically, to the urgent need for action in these times.

Filmography

Films

9/11/2001 segment. 2002. Dir. Mira Nair. Prod. Lydia Dean Pilcher. In *September 11.* Creative Prod. Alain Brigand.

12 and Holding. 2006. Dir. Michael Cuesta. Prod. Brian Bell, Michael Cuesta, Jenny Schweitzer, Leslie Urdang.

28 Days Later. 2002. Dir. Danny Boyle. Prod. Andrew Macdonald.

The 400 Blows. 1959. Dir. François Truffaut. Prod. François Truffaut.

Aeon Flux. 2005. Dir. Karyn Kusama. Prod. David Gale, Greg Goodman, Martha Griffin, Gale Anne Hurd, Gary Lucchesi.

After Hours. 1985. Dir. Martin Scorsese. Prod. Griffin Dunne, Amy Robinson, Deborah Schindler.

After Innocence. 2005. Dir. Jessica Sanders. Prod. Jessica Sanders, Marc Simon.

After the Wedding. 2006. Dir. Susanne Bier. Prod. Peter Garde, Peter Aalbaek Jensen.

Aileen: The Life and Death of a Serial Killer. 2003. Dir. Nick Broomfield, Joan Churchill. Prod. Jo Human.

All the Vermeers in New York. 1990. Dir. Jon Jost. Prod. Henry S. Rosenthal, Lindsay Law.

American Beauty. 2000. Dir. Sam Mendes. Prod. Bruce Cohen, Dan Jinks.

An American Crime. 2007. Dir. Tim O'Haver. Prod. Jocelyn Hayes Simpson, Hans Ritter.

American Movie. 1999. Dir. Chris Smith. Prod. Sarah Price, Chris Smith.

American Psycho. 2000. Dir. Mary Harron. Prod. Christian Haley Solomon, Chris Hanley, Edward R. Pressman.

American Splendor. 2003. Dir. Shari Springer Berman, Robert Pulcini. Prod. Ted Hope.

Amreeka. 2009. Dir. Cherien Dabis. Prod. Paul Barkin, Christina Piovesan.

Apocalypse Now. 1979. Dir. Francis Ford Coppola. Prod. Francis Ford Coppola, Gray Frederickson.

Awake. 2007. Dir. Joby Harold. Prod. Jason Kliot, Fisher Stevens, Joana Vicente.

Babel. 2006. Dir. Alejandro González Iñárritu. Prod. Steve Golin, Alejandro González Iñárritu, Jon Kilik.

Ballast. 2008. Dir. Lance Hammer. Prod. Andrew Adamson, John J. Hammer.

Barton Fink. 1991. Dir. Joel Coen. Prod. Ethan Coen.

Before the Devil Knows You're Dead. 2007. Dir. Sidney Lumet. Prod. Michael Cerenzie, Austin Chick, William S. Gilmore, Brian Linse, Paul Parmer, Jeff G. Waxman.

Before the Rains. 2007. Dir. Santosh Sivan. Prod. Mark Burton, Paul Hardart, Tom Hardart, Andrew Spaulding.

The Bicycle Thief. 1948. Dir. Vittorio De Sica. Prod. Giuseppe Amato.

The Big Picture. 1989. Dir. Christopher Guest. Prod. Michael Varhol.

Black Male. 2000. Dir. George Baluzy, Mike Baluzy. Prod. Michael Delfay.

Black Swan. 2010. Dir. Darren Aronofsky. Prod. Scott Franklin, Jerry Fruchtman, Mike Medavoy, Arnold Messer, Brian Oliver, Joseph P. Reidy.

The Blair Witch Project. 1999. Dir. Daniel Myrick, Eduardo Sánchez. Prod. Robin Cowie, Gregg Hale.

Blood Simple. 1984. Dir. Joel Coen. Prod. Ethan Coen.

Blue Steel. 1989. Dir. Kathryn Bigelow. Prod. Edward R. Pressman, Oliver Stone.

Blue Velvet. 1986. Dir. David Lynch. Prod. Fred C. Caruso.

Bonfire of the Vanities. 1990. Dir. Brian De Palma. Prod. Fred C. Caruso, Brian De Palma.

Boogie Nights. 1997. Dir. Paul Thomas Anderson. Prod. Paul Thomas Anderson, Lloyd Levin, John S. Lyons, JoAnne Sellar.

The Bourne Identity. 2002. Dir. Doug Liman. Prod. Patrick Crowley, Richard N. Gladstein, Doug Liman.

Bowling for Columbine. 2002. Dir. Michael Moore. Prod. Jim Czarnecki, Kathleen Glynn, Michael Moore.

Boys Don't Cry. 1999. Dir. Kimberly Pierce, Andy Bienen. Prod. John Hart, Eva Kolodner, Jeffrey Sharp, Chistine Vachon.

Boyz n the Hood. 1991. Dir. John Singleton. Prod. Steve Nicolaides.

Brokeback Mountain. 2005. Dir. Ang Lee. Prod. Diana Ossana, James Schamus.

Caché. 2005. Dir. Michael Haneke. Prod. Veit Heiduschka.

Cannibal! The Musical. 1993. Dir. Trey Parker. Prod. Ian Hardin, Alexandra Kelly, Jason McHugh, Trey Parker, Matt Stone.

Capitalism: A Love Story. 2009. Dir. Michael Moore. Prod. Anne Moore, Michael Moore.

Capturing the Friedmans. 2003. Dir. Andrew Jarecki. Prod. Andrew Jarecki, Mark Smerling.

Catch a Fire. 2006. Dir. Phillip Noyce. Prod. Tim Bevan, Eric Fellner, Anthony Minghella, Robyn Slovo.

Chicago 10. 2007. Dir. Bret Morgen. Prod. Graydon Carter, Brett Morgen.

Children of Beslan. 2005. Dir. Ewa Ewart, Leslie Woodhead. Prod. Ewa Ewart, Leslie Woodhead.

Chop Shop. 2007. Dir. Ramin Bahrani. Prod. Bedford T. Bentley, Jeb Brody, Pradip Ghosh, Lisa Muskat, Marc Turtletaub.

Citizen Ruth. 1996. Dir. Alexander Payne. Prod. Cathy Konrad, Andrew Stone, Cary Woods.

Clerks. 1994. Dir. Kevin Smith. Prod. Scot Mosier, Kevin Smith.

The Company Men. 2010. Dir. John Wells. Prod. Clair Rudnick Polstein, Paula Weinstein, John Wells.

Control Room. 2004. Dir. Jehane Noujaim. Prod. Hani Salama, Rosadel Varela.

The Corporation. 2003. Dir. Mark Achbar, Jennifer Abbot. Prod. Mark Achbar, Joel Baken, Dawn Brett, Cari Green, Nathan Neumer, Thomas Shadel, Bart Simpson.

Coven. 2000. Dir. Mark Borchardt. Prod. Bill Borchardt, Mark Borchardt.

Crash. 2004. Dir. Paul Haggis. Prod. Don Cheadle, Paul Haggis, Mark R. Harris, Robert Moresco, Cathy Schulman, Bob Yari.

Crazy Love. 2007. Dir. Dan Klores. Prod. Dan Klores, Fisher Stevens.

Crimes and Misdemeanors. 1989. Dir. Woody Allen. Prod. Robert Greenhut.

Crips and Bloods: Made in America. 2008. Dir. Stacy Peralta. Prod. Baron Davis, Jesse Dylan, Dan Halsted, Shaun Murphy, Stacy Peralta, Gus Roxburgh, Cash Warren.

The Crying Game. 1992. Dir. Neil Jordan. Prod. Stephen Woolley.

Daughters of the Dust. 1991. Dir. Julie Dash. Prod. Julie Dash, Arthur Jafa, Steven Jones.

The Dead Girl. 2006. Dir. Karen Moncrieff. Prod. Eric Karten, Gary Lucchesi, Tom Rosenburg, Kevin Turren, Henry Winsterstern, Richard Wright.

Deliver Us from Evil. 2006. Dir. Amy Berg. Prod. Amy Berg, Matthew Cooke, Frank Donner, Hermas Lassalle.

Derrida. 2002. Dir. Kirby Dick, Amy Ziering Kofman. Prod. Amy Ziering Kofman.

The Diving Bell and the Butterfly. 2007. Dir. Julian Schnabel. Prod. Pierre Grunstein, Kathleen Kennedy, Jon Kilik, Jim Lemley.

Doubt. 2008. Dir. John Patrick Shanley. Prod. Mark Roybal, Scott Rudin.

Down by Law. 1986. Dir. Jim Jarmusch. Prod. Alan Kleinberg.

Edge of Outside. 2006. Dir. Shannon Davis. Prod. Shannon Davis, Dena Krupinsky, Jon Messner.

An Education. 2009. Dir. Lone Scherfig. Prod. Finola Dwyer, Amanda Posey.

Election. 1999. Dir. Alexander Payne. Prod. Albert Berger, David Gale, Keith Samples, Ron Yerxa.

Enron: The Smartest Guys in the Room. 2005. Dir. Alex Gibney. Prod. Alison Ellwood, Alex Gibney, Jason Kliot, Susan Motamed.

Eraserhead. 1976. Dir. David Lynch. Prod. David Lynch.

Everything's Cool. 2007. Dir. Daniel Gold and Judith Helfand. Prod. Daniel B. Gold, Judith Helfand, Chris Pilaro, Adam Wolfensohn.

Eve's Bayou. 1997. Dir. Kasi Lemmons. Prod. Mark Amin, Michael Bennett, M. Cevin Cathell, Caldecot Chubb, Samuel L. Jackson, Margaret Matheson.

The Examined Life. 2008. Dir. Astra Taylor. Prod. Bill Imperial, Lea Marin.

Faces. 1968. Dir. John Cassavetes. Prod. Maurice McEndree, John Cassavetes.

Fahrenheit 9/11. 2004. Dir. Michael Moore. Prod. Jim Czarnecki, Kathleen Glynn, Michael Moore.

Far from Heaven. 2002. Dir. Todd Haynes. Prod. Jody Patton, Christine Vachon.

Ferris Bueller's Day Off. 1986. Dir. John Hughes. Prod. John Hughes, Tom Jacobson.

Fight Club. 1999. Dir. David Fincher. Prod. Ross Grayson Bell, Ceán Chaffin, Art Linson.

Finding Nemo. 2003. Dir. Andrew Stanton. Prod. Graham Walters.

Firehouse Dog. 2007. Dir. Todd Holland. Prod. Michael Colleary, Michael J. Maschio, Mike Werb.

Forty Shades of Blue. 2005. Dir. Ira Sachs. Prod. Mary Bing, Margot Bridger, Jawal Nga, Donald Rosenfeld, Ira Sachs.

Frozen River. 2008. Dir. Courtney Hunt. Prod. Chip Hourihan, Heather Rae.

Fur: An Imaginary Portrait of Diane Arbus. 2006. Dir. Steven Shainberg. Prod. Laura Bickford, Andrew Fierberg, William Pohlad, Bonnie Timmermann.

GasLand. 2010. Dir. Josh Fox. Prod. Trish Adlesic, Josh Fox, Molly Gandour.

Getting Through to the President. 2004. Dir. Emily Kunstler, Sarah Kunstler. Prod. Haskell King.

Girlfight. 2000. Dir. Karyn Kusama. Prod. Sarah Green, Martha Griffin, Maggie Renzi.

The Golden Boat. 1990. Dir. Raoul Ruiz. Prod. James Schamus, Jordi Torrent.

Good Night and Good Luck. 2005. Dir. George Clooney. Prod. Grant Heslov.

Gummo. 1997. Dir. Harmony Korine. Prod. Stephen Chin, Scott Macauley, Robin O'Hara, Ruth Vitale, Cary Woods.

Half Nelson. 2006. Dir. Ryan Fleck. Prod. Anna Boden, Lynette Howell, Rosanne Korenberg, Alex Orlovsky, Jamie Patricof.

Happiness. 1998. Dir. Todd Solondz. Prod. Ted Hope, Christine Vachon.

Heart of Stone. 2009. Dir. Beth Toni Kruvant. Prod. Beth Toni Kruvant.

Hearts of Darkness: A Filmmaker's Apocalypse. 1991. Dir. Eleanor Coppola, Fax Bahr, George Hickenlooper. Prod. Les Mayfield, George Zaloom.

Hello, Dolly! 1969. Dir. Gene Kelly. Prod. Roger Edens, Ernest Lehman.

Home Alone. 1990. Dir. Chris Columbus. Prod. John Hughes.

Home of the Brave. 2006. Dir. Irwin Winkler. Prod. Boaz Davidson, Danny Dimbort, Michael P. Flannigan, Trevor Short, John Thompson.

Hoop Dreams. 1994. Dir. Steve James. Prod. Peter Gilbert, Steve James, Frederick Marx.

Hotel Rwanda. 2004. Dir. Terry George. Prod. Terry George, A. Kitman Ho.

Hounddog. 2007. Dir. Deborah Kampmeier. Prod. Ray Dowell, Jen Gatien, Deborah Kampmeier, Terry Leonard, Lawrence Robins.

How the Beatles Rocked the Kremlin. 2009. Dir. Leslie Woodhead. No Listed Producer.

The Hurt Locker. 2009. Dir. Kathryn Bigelow. Prod. Kathyrn Bigelow, Mark Boal, Nicolas Chartier, Greg Shapiro.

The Ice Storm. 1997. Dir. Ang Lee. Prod. Ted Hope, Ang Lee, James Schamus.

An Inconvenient Truth. 2006. Dir. Davis Guggenheim. Prod. Lawrence Bender, Scott Z. Burns, Laurie David.

Independence. 2007. Dir. David Brocca. Prod. Albert Brocca.

Independent's Day. 1998. Dir. Marina Zenovich. Prod. Marina Zenovich.

The Informant! 2009. Dir. Steven Soderbergh. Prod. Howard Braustein, Kurt Eichenwald, Jennifer Fox, Gregory Jacobs, Michael Jaffe.

Inside Job. 2010 Dir. Charles Ferguson. Prod. Jeffrey Lurie, Christina Weiss Lurie.

In the Bedroom. 2001. Dir. Todd Field. Prod. Todd Field, Ross Katz, Graham Leader.

In the Soup. 1992. Dir. Alexandre Rockwell. Prod. Hank Blumenthal, Pascal Caucheteux, Jim Stark.

Iraq for Sale: The War Profiteers. 2006. Dir. Robert Greenwald. Prod. Matthew Brown, Sarah Feeley, Jim Gilliam, Robert Greenwald, Richard Jacobs, Dal LaMagna, Devin Smith.

I Shot Andy Warhol. 1996. Dir. Mary Harron. Prod. Tom Kalin, Christine Vachon.

Jaws. 1975. Dir. Steven Spielberg. Prod. David Brown, Richard D. Zanuck.

Jennifer's Body. 2009. Dir. Karyn Kusama. Prod. Daniel Dubiecki, Mason Novick, Jason Reitman.

Jersey Girl. 2004. Dir. Kevin Smith. Prod. Scott Mosier.

The Joy Luck Club. 1993. Dir. Wayne Wang. Prod. Ronald Bass, Patrick Markey, Amy Tan.

Jump Tomorrow. 2001. Dir. Joel Hopkins. Prod. Nicola Usborne.

Juno. 2007. Dir. Jason Reitman. Prod. Lianne Halfon, John Malkovich, Mason Novick, Russel Smith.

Kabul Transit. 2006. Dir. David Edwards, Gregory Whitmore, Maliha Zulfacar. Prod. David Edwards, Gregory Whitmore, Maliha Zulfacar.

Kids. 1995. Dir. Larry Clark. Prod. Cary Woods.

Killer of Sheep. 1978. Dir. Charles Burnett. Prod. Charles Burnett.

King of the Hill. 1993. Dir. Steven Soderbergh. Prod. Albert Berger, Ron Yerxa.

The Kite Runner. 2007. Dir. Marc Forster. Prod. Sidney Kimmel, Laurie MacDonald, Sam Mendes, Jeff Skoll.

Lady in the Water. 2006. Dir. M. Night Shyamalan. Prod. Sam Mercer, M. Night Shyamalan.

La Sierra. 2005. Dir. Scott Dalton, Margarita Martinez. Prod. Scott Dalton.

Léon: The Professional. 1994. Dir. Luc Besson. Prod. Claude Besson, Luc Besson, Patrice Ledoux.

L.I.E. 2001. Dir. Michael Cuesta. Prod. Rene Bastian, Michael Cuesta, Linda Moran.

Like Crazy. 2011. Dir. Drake Doremus. Prod. Jonathan Schwartz, Andrea Sperling.

Little Children. 2006. Dir. Todd Fields. Prod. Albert Berger, Todd Field, Ron Yerxa.

Little Fockers. 2010. Dir. Paul Weitz. Prod. Robert De Niro, John Hamburg, Jay Roach, Jane Rosenthal.

Little Man Tate. 1991. Dir. Jodie Foster. Prod. Peggy Rajski, Scott Rudin.

Little Miss Sunshine. 2006. Dir. Jonathan Dayton, Valerie Faris. Prod. Albert Berger, David T. Friendly, Peter Saraf, Marc Turtletaub, Ron Yerxa.

The Lives of Others. 2006. Dir. Florian Henckel von Donnersmarck. Prod. Quirin Berg, Max Wiedermann.

Living in Oblivion. 1995. Dir. Tom DiCillo. Prod. Michael Griffiths, Marcus Viscidi.

Loop Dreams: The Making of a Low Budget Film. 2001. Dir. Harvey Hubbel V. Prod. Harvey Hubbel V.

Lost in La Mancha. 2002. Dir. Keith Fulton, Louis Pepe. Prod. Lucy Darwin.

Lost in Translation. 2003. Dir. Sofia Coppola. Prod. Sofia Coppola, Ross Katz.

Mad Hot Ballroom. 2005. Dir. Marilyn Agrelo. Prod. Marilyn Agrelo, Amy Sewell.

Manda Bala. 2007. Dir. Jason Kohn. Prod. Joey Frank, Jared Ian Goldman, Jason Kohn.

Mann v. Ford. 2010. Dir. Maro Chermayeff, Micah Fink. Prod. Nancy Abraham, Donald Everett Axinn, Sheila Nevins.

Man Push Cart. 2005. Dir. Ramin Bahrani. Prod. Ramin Bahrani, Bedford T. Bentley III, Pradip Ghosh.

Manufactured Landscapes. 2007. Dir. Jennifer Baichwal. Prod. Jennifer Baichwal, Daniel Iron, Nick de Pencier.

Mardi Gras: Made in China. 2005. Dir. David Redmon. Assoc. Prod. Dale Smith, Deborah Smith.

Margot at the Wedding. 2010. Dir. Noah Baumbach. Prod. Scott Rudin.

Marie Antoinette. 2006. Dir. Sofia Coppola. Prod. Sofia Coppola, Rozz Katz.

Match Point. 2005. Dir. Woody Allen. Prod. Letty Aronson, Lucy Darwin, Gareth Wiley.

Maxed Out: Hard Times, Easy Credit and the Era of Predatory Lenders. 2006. Dir. James D. Scurlock. Prod. James D. Scurlock.

Media Stylo #4: The Documentary's New Politics. 2005. Dir. Eric Faden. Prod. Eric Faden. http://www.tft.ucla.edu/mediascape/Spring08_DocumentarysNewPolitics .html.

Memento. 2000. Dir. Christopher Nolan. Prod. Jennifer Todd, Suzanne Todd.

Mimic. 1997. Dir. Guillermo del Toro. Prod. Ole Bornedal, B. J. Rack, Bob Weinstein.

The Ministers. 2009. Dir. Franc. Reyes. Prod. Jill Footlick, Aaron Ray, Franc. Reyes.

Mission Impossible III. 2006. Dir. J. J. Abrams. Prod. Tom Cruise, Paula Wagner.

Mississippi Masala. 1992. Dir. Mira Nair. Prod. Mira Nair, Michael Nozik.

Miss Navajo. 2007. Dir. Billy Luther. Prod. Billy Luther, Duana C. Butler.

Mistress. 1992. Dir. Barry Primus. Prod. Robert De Niro, Meir Teper.

Monsoon Wedding. 2002. Dir. Mira Nair. Prod. Caroline Baron, Mira Nair.

Monster. 2003. Dir. Patty Jenkins. Prod. Mark Damon, Donald Kushner, Clark Peterson, Brad Wyman, Charlize Theron.

The Most Dangerous Man in America: Daniel Ellsberg and the Pentagon Papers. 2009. Dir. Judith Ehrlich, Rick Goldsmith. Prod. Judith Ehrlich, Rick Goldsmith.

The Motel. 2006. Dir. Michael Kang. Prod. Miguel Arteta, Karin Chien, Matthew Greenfield, Gina Kwon.

Mother and Child. 2009. Dir. Rodrigo García. Prod. Lisa Maria Falcone, Julie Lynn.

Mr. and Mrs. Smith. 2005. Dir. Doug Liman. Prod. Lucas Foster, Akiva Goldsman, Eric McLeod, Arnon Milchan, Patrick Wachsberger.

Mr. Brooks. 2007. Dir. Bruce A. Evans. Prod. Kevin Costner, Raynold Gideon, Jim Wilson.

My Left Foot. 1989. Dir. Jim Sheridan. Prod. Noel Pearson.

Mysterious Skin. 2005. Dir. Gregg Araki. Prod. Gregg Araki, Jeffrey Levy-Hinte, Mary Jane Skalski.

Mystic River. 2003. Dir. Clint Eastwood. Prod. Clint Eastwood, Judie G. Hoyt, Robert Lorenz.

The Namesake. 2007. Dir. Mira Nair. Prod. Lydia Dean Pilcher, Mira Nair.

Nanook of the North. 1922. Dir. Robert J. Flaherty. Prod. Robert J. Flaherty.

Narc. 2002. Dir. Joe Carnahan. Prod. Michelle Grace, Ray Liotta, Diane Nabatoff, Julius R. Nasso.

Neighbors. 1981. Dir. John Avildsen. Prod. David Brown, Richard Zanuck.

Neo Ned. 2006. Dir. Van Fischer. Prod. David E. Allen, Mark Borman, Valerie McCaffrey.

Nine Lives. 2005. Dir. Rodrigo García. Prod. Julie Lynn.

No End in Sight. 2007. Dir. Charles Ferguson. Prod. Jennie Amias, Charles Ferguson, Audrey Marrs, Jessi Vogelson.

North Country. 2005. Dir. Niki Caro. Prod. Nick Weschsler.

Northern Lights. 1979. Dir. John Hanson, Rob Nilsson. Prod. John Hanson, Rob Nilsson.

The Notorious Bettie Page. 2006. Dir. Mary Harron. Prod. Pamela Koffler, Katie Roumel, Christine Vachon.

Ocean's Eleven. 2001. Dir. Steven Soderbergh. Prod. Jerry Weintraub.

Office Space. 1999. Dir. Mike Judge. Prod. Mike Judge, Daniel Rappaport, Michael Rotenberg.

Operation Homecoming: Writing the Wartime Experience. 2007. Dir. Richard E. Robbins. Prod. Richard Robbins.

The Order of Myths. 2008. Dir. Margaret Brown. Prod. Margaret Brown, Sara Alize Cross.

Orgazmo. 1997. Dir. Trey Parker. Prod. Fran Rubel Kuzui, Jason McHugh, John Frank Rosenblum, Matt Stone, Trey Parker.

Out of Faith. 2006. Dir. Lisa Leeman. Prod. L. Mark DeAngelis.

Outrage. 2009. Dir. Kirby Dick. Prod. Amy Ziering.

Padre Nuestro (Sangre de mi Sangre). 2007. Dir. Christopher Zalla. Prod. Per Melita, Ben Odell.

Pan's Labyrinth. 2006. Dir. Guillermo del Toro. Prod. Álvaro Augustín, Alfonso Cuarón, Bertha Navarro, Guillermo del Toro, Frida Torresblanco.

Paradise Now. 2005. Dir. Hany Abu-Assad. Prod. Bero Beyer, Amir Harel, Gerhard Meixner, Hangameh Panahi, Roman Paul.

Paris Is Burning. 1990. Dir. Jennie Livingston. Prod. Jennie Livingston, Barry Swimar.

Passengers. 2008. Dir. Rodrigo García. Prod. Julie Lynn, Judd Payne, Matthew Rhodes, Keri Selig.

Pee Wee's Big Adventure. 1985. Dir. Tim Burton. Prod. Richard Gilbert Abramson, Robert Shapiro.

Persepolis. 2007. Dir. Vincent Parronaud, Marjane Satrapi. Prod. Xavier Rigault, Marc-Antoine Robert.

Personal Velocity. 2002. Dir. Rebecca Miller. Prod. Alexis Alexanian, Lemore Syvan, Gary Winick.

The Player. 1992. Dir. Robert Altman. Prod. David Brown.

Poison. 1991. Dir. Todd Haynes. Prod. Christine Vachon.

Precious. 2009. Dir. Lee Daniels. Prod. Lee Daniels, Gary Magness, Sarah Siegel-Magness.

Pretty Woman. 1990. Dir. Garry Marshall. Prod. Arnon Milchan, Steven Reuther.

Primer. 2004. Dir. Shane Carruth. Prod. Shane Carruth.

The Prisoner or: How I Planned to Kill Tony Blair. 2006. Dir. Petra Epperlein, Michael Tucker. Prod. Petra Epperlein.

The Prizewinner of Defiance, Ohio. 2005. Dir. Jane Anderson. Prod. Jack Rapke, Steven Starkey, Robert Zemeckis.

Protagonist. 2007. Dir. Jessica Yu. Prod. Elise Pearlstein, Susan West, Jessica Yu.

Public Access. 1993. Dir. Bryan Singer. Prod. Kenneth Kokin.

Pulp Fiction. 1994. Dir. Quentin Tarantino. Prod. Lawrence Bender.

Quinceañera. 2006. Dir. Richard Glatzer, Wash Westmoreland. Prod. Anne Clements.

Rachel Getting Married. 2008. Dir. Jonathan Demme. Prod. Neda Armian, Jonathan Demme, Marc Platt.

Rashomon. 1950. Dir. Akira Kurosawa. Prod. Minoru Jingo.

The Reader. 2008. Dir. Stephen Daldry. Prod. Donna Gigliotti, Anthony Minghella, Redmond Morris, Sydney Pollack.

Reality Bites. 1994. Dir. Ben Stiller. Prod. Danny DeVito, Michael Shamberg.

Red Badge of Courage. 1951. Dir. John Huston. Prod. Gottfried Reinhardt.

Relative Evil. 2004. Dir. Tayna Wexler. Prod. John Cosgrove, Ira Deutchman, Stephen Dyer, Terry Dunn Meurer.

Restrepro. 2010. Dir. Tim Hetherington, Sebastian Junger. Prod. Tim Hetherington, Sebastian Junger.

Return of the Secaucus Seven. 1980. Dir. John Sayles. Prod. William Aydelott, Jeffrey Nelson.

The Right Stuff. 1983. Dir. Philip Kaufman. Prod. Robert Chartoff, Irwin Winkler.

Roger and Me. 1989. Dir. Michael Moore. Prod. Michael Moore.

Roman Polanski: Wanted and Desired. 2008. Dir. Marina Zenovich. Prod. Jeffrey Levy-Hinte, Lila Yacoub, Marina Zenovich.

The Royal Tenenbaums. 2001. Dir. Wes Anderson. Prod. Wes Anderson, Barry Mendel, Scott Rudin.

Se7en. 1995. Dir. David Fincher. Prod. Phyllis Carlyle, Arnold Kopelson.

Secretary. 2002. Dir. Steven Shainberg. Prod. Andrew Fierberg, Amy Hobby, Steven Shainberg.

September 11. 2002. Multiple directors. Creative Prod. Alain Brigand.

A Serious Man. 2009. Dir. Ethan Coen, Joel Coen. Prod. Ethan Coen, Joel Coen.

sex, lies, and videotape. 1989. Dir. Steven Soderbergh. Prod. John Hardy, Robert Newmyer.

She's Gotta Have It. 1986. Dir. Spike Lee. Prod. Spike Lee.

Short Cuts: The Film. 1993. Dir. Robert Altman. Prod. Cary Brokaw.

Sick: The Life and Times of Bob Flanagan, Super Masochist. 1997. Dir. Kirby Dick. Prod. Kirby Dick.

Sicko. 2007. Dir. Michael Moore. Prod. Michael Moore, Megan O'Hara, Susannah Price.

Sideways. 2004. Dir. Alexander Payne. Prod. Michael London.

Slacker. 1991. Dir. Richard Linklater. Prod. Richard Linklater.

Slumdog Millionaire. 2008. Dir. Danny Boyle, Loveleen Tandan. Prod. Christian Colson.

Slums of Beverly Hills. 1998. Dir. Tamara Jenkins. Prod. Michael Nozik, Stan Wlodkowski.

Sociology Is a Martial Art. 2001. Dir. Pierre Carles. Prod. Véronique Frégosi and Annie Madeleine Gonzalez.

The Soloist. 2009. Dir. Joe Wright. Prod. Gary Foster, Russ Krasnoff.

Sorry, Haters. 2005. Dir. Jeff Stanzler. Prod. Jake Abraham, Karen Jaroneski, Jeff Stanzler, Gary Winick.

Spellbound. 2002. Dir. Jeffrey Blitz. Prod. Jeffrey Blitz, Sean Welch.

Standard Operating Procedure. 2008. Dir. Errol Morris. Prod. Julie Ahlberg, Errol Morris.

Stephanie Daley. 2007. Dir. Hilary Brougher. Prod. Sean Costello, Lynette Howell, Samara Koffler, Jen Roskin.

Stolen Summer. 2002. Dir. Pete Jones. Prod. Ben Affleck, Matt Damon, Chris Moore.

Straight Out of Brooklyn. 1991. Dir. Matty Rich. Prod. Matty Rich.

Stranger Than Paradise. 1984. Dir. Jim Jarmusch. Prod. Sara Driver.

Sugar. 2008. Dir. Anna Boden, Ryan Fleck. Prod. Paul S. Mezey, Jamie Patricof, Jeremy Kipp Walker.

Sunshine Cleaning. 2008. Dir. Christine Jeffs. Prod. Jeb Brody, Peter Saraf, Marc Turtletaub, Glenn Williamson.

Superman Returns. 2006. Dir. Bryan Singer. Prod. Gilbert Adler, Jon Peters, Bryan Singer.

Swingers. 1996. Dir. Doug Liman. Prod. Victor Simpkins.

Swoon. 1992. Dir. Tom Kalin. Prod. Christine Vachon.

Synecdoche, New York. 2008. Dir. Charlie Kaufman. Prod. Anthony Bregman, Spike Jonze, Charlie Kaufman, Sidney Kimmel.

Syriana. 2005. Dir. Stephen Gaghan. Prod. Jennifer Fox, Georgia Kancandes, Michael Nozik.

Take Out. 2004. Dir. Sean Baker, Shih-Ching Tsou. Prod. Sean Baker, Shih-Ching Tsou.

The Taqwacores. 2010. Dir. Eyad Zahra. Prod. Eyad Zahra.

Thelma and Louise. 1991. Dir. Ridley Scott. Prod. Mimi Polk Gitlin, Ridley Scott.

The Thin Blue Line. 1988. Dir. Errol Morris. Prod. Mark Lipson.

Things You Could Tell Just by Looking at Her. 1999. Dir. Rodrigo García. Prod. Jon Avnet, Lisa Lindstrom, Marsha Oglesby.

Thirteen. 2003. Dir. Catherine Hardwicke. Prod. Jeffrey Levy-Hinte, Michael London.

This Boy's Life. 1993. Dir. Michael Caton-Jones. Prod. Art Linson.

This Film Is Not Yet Rated. 2006. Dir. Kirby Dick. Prod. Eddie Schmidt.

Three Kings. 1999. Dir. David Russell. Prod. Paul Junger Witt, Charles Roven.

The Tourist. 2010. Dir. Florian Henckel von Donnersmarck. Prod. Gary Barber, Roger Birnbaum, Jonathan Glickman, Tim Headington, Graham King.

Towelhead. 2007. Dir. Alan Ball. Prod. Alan Ball, Ted Hope.

Traffic. 2000. Dir. Steven Soderbergh. Prod. Laura Bickford, Marshall Herskovitz, Edward Zwick.

Trouble the Water. 2008. Dir. Carl Deal and Tia Lessin. Prod. Carl Deal and Tia Lessin.

Trust. 1990. Dir. Hal Hartley. Prod. Hal Hartley, Bruce Weiss.

Tulia, Texas: Scenes from the Drug War. 2003. Dir. Emily Kunstler, Sarah Kunstler. Prod. Randy Credico.

The Twilight Saga: New Moon. 2009. Dir. Chris Weitz. Prod. Wyck Godfrey, Karen Rosenfelt.

Twist of Faith. 2004. Dir. Kirby Dick. Prod. Eddie Schmidt.

Unbelievable Truth. 1990. Dir. Hal Hartley. Prod. Hal Hartley, Bruce Weiss.

Up in the Air. 2009. Dir. Jason Reitman. Prod. Jeffrey Clifford, Daniel Dubiecki, Ivan Reitman, Jason Reitman.

Up the Yangtze. 2007. Dir. Yung Chang. Prod. Mila Aung-Thwin, John Christou, Germaine Wong.

Velvet Goldmine. 1998. Dir. Todd Haynes. Prod. Christine Vachon.

The Virgin Suicides. 1999. Dir. Sofia Coppola. Prod. Francis Ford Coppola, Julie Costanzo, Dan Halsted, Chris Hanley.

The Visitor. 2007. Dir. Thomas McCarthy. Prod. Michael London, Mary Jane Skalski.

Wall Street. 1987. Dir. Oliver Stone. Prod. Edward R. Pressman.

Walmart: The High Cost of Low Prices. 2005. Dir. Robert Greenwald. Prod. Jim Gilliam, Robert Greenwald, Devin Smith.

The War Within. 2005. Dir. Joseph Castelo. Prod. Tom Glynn, Jason Kliot, Joana Vicente.

The Wedding Banquet. 1993. Dir. Ang Lee. Prod. Ted Hope, Ang Lee, James Schamus.

Wendy and Lucy. 2008. Dir. Kelly Reichardt. Prod. Larry Fessenden, Neil Kopp, Anish Savjani.

Wet Hot American Summer. 2001. Dir. David Wain. Prod. Howard Bernstein.

Whale Rider. 2002. Dir. Niki Caro. Prod. John Barnett, Frank Hübner, Tim Sanders.

What Happened Was... 1994. Dir. Tom Noonan. Prod. Scott Macaulay, Robin O'Hara.

Who Killed the Electric Car? 2006. Dir. Chris Paine. Prod. Jessie Deeter.

Who Needs Sleep? 2006. Dir. Haskell Wexler. Prod. Tamara Maloney.

Why We Fight. 2005. Dir. Eugene Jarecki. Prod. Eugene Jarecki, Susannah Shipman.

William Kunstler: Disturbing the Universe. 2009. Dir. Emily Kunstler, Sarah Kunstler. Prod. Susan Korda, Emily Kunstler, Sarah Kunstler, Jesse Moss.

Winter's Bone. 2010. Dir. Debra Granik. Prod. Alix Madigan, Anne Rosellini.

A Woman under the Influence. 1974. Dir. John Cassavetes. Prod. Sam Shaw.

The Wrestler. 2008. Dir. Darren Aronofsky. Prod. Darren Aronofsky, Scott Franklin.

X-Men: The Last Stand. 2006. Dir. Brett Ratner. Prod. Avi Arad, Lauren Shuler Donner, Ralph Winter.

Young@Heart. 2007. Dir. Steven Walker. Prod. Sally George.

Žižek! 2005. Dir. Astra Taylor. Prod. Lawrence Konner.

Television Programs

Dexter. 2006–. Showtime. Exec. Prod. Daniel Cerone, Clyde Phillips, Melissa Rosenberg.

"Failure to Protect." 2003. *Frontline,* PBS. Prod. Rachel Dretzin, Barak Goodman, Muriel Soenens.

Law & Order: SVU. 1999–. USA. Creator Dick Wolf.

The L Word. 2004–9. Showtime. Creators Michele Abbott, Ilene Chaiken, Kathy Greenberg.

Project Greenlight. 2001–5. HBO. Season 1, Episode 2. December 2, 2001. Prod. Tina Gazzero, Eli Holzman, Tony Yates.

Sex and the City. 1998–2004. HBO. Creator Darren Star.

Sherpas of Nepal. 1977. Dir. Leslie Woodhead. Anthropologist: Sherry B. Ortner. In the series "Disappearing World." Manchester, England: Granada Television. Distributed by the Royal Anthropological Institute.

The Sopranos. 1999–2007. HBO. Creator David Chase.

South Park. 1997–. Comedy Central. Creators Matt Stone, Trey Parker.

Notes

Introduction

1. Kate Hohman, then a PhD student in anthropology at Columbia University, connected me to her partner, Chad Beck, who was one of the editors of the film.
2. A "Hollywood studio film" may also originate within a separate production company that then sells the package to the studio. These companies might be called "independent production companies," but they do not make independent films in the sense defined here. They make "Hollywood" or "studio-oriented" films.
3. See also Levy (1999) and G. King (2005) for attempts to define the genre.
4. A big nod here to Netflix and DVD technology, without which this project in this form would have been virtually impossible.
5. Later represented as "the Center for Transnational Cultural Studies" rather than the "Project."
6. See Desai (2003) for a similar argument about the emergence of a new cinema in India that sees itself in terms very similar to American independent film. One could call it "not Bollywood," though Desai does not use the phrase.
7. I was living in Ann Arbor, Michigan, at the time, collecting material for my then-new project on social class in America.
8. On the ways in which the middle class and the working class in America serve as mirrors for each other's fears, see Ortner ([1991] 2006b).
9. This section represents a condensation of Ortner ([1998] 2006c).
10. The reasons for expanding the time frame have been variously given, but 1961–81 is now the generally accepted period. The whole question of defining and dating "generations" has been questioned (see Ortner [1991] 2006b).
11. There is also a book on what Gen Xers were watching on television when they were growing up, as Gen X is viewed as the first generation to have been very strongly shaped by TV (Owen 1997). Thanks to Eric Vanstrom, who assembled an excellent bibliography for me on the relationship between (independent) film and Generation X.
12. Rosten had a PhD from the University of Chicago, but he earned his living as a

popular writer and a screenwriter. As an interesting footnote to history, he was married to Margaret Mead's sister.

13. Abu-Lughod's study also includes extensive information on audience reception; the combination of production and reception ethnography is rare. Another excellent reception study is Purnima Mankekar's *Screening Culture, Viewing Politics* (1999).

14. I rarely asked questions from the audience myself. I was as much interested in the audience's questions as in the filmmakers' answers.

15. Geertz was my advisor in graduate school, and my own early work was largely in this mode of cultural-textual interpretation. My first book consisted of close interpretations of four Sherpa rituals (Ortner 1978).

Chapter 1: Making Independence

1. Brochure kept in author's files; copy available on request.

2. Of course, from the point of view of people who make Hollywood movies, things look very different. Independent films appear impractical (because noncommercial) at best, and inaccessible and elitist at worst. I had to cut a long section here on Hollywood's view of indies. For various pieces of the Hollywood perspective, thanks to Murray Chotiner, David Gale, Sheila Hanahan Taylor, Franc. Reyes, and Harold Ramis, all of whose quotes unfortunately hit the cutting-room floor.

3. The series ran for three years, but this discussion pertains to the first year, 2001–2.

4. *The Big Picture* was one of four films independent producer Ron Yerxa was taking to show at a filmmaking seminar in Berlin as illustrating, but also caricaturing, the Hollywood/indie contrast. The other three films were *American Movie* (Chris Smith, 1999), *Pee Wee's Big Adventure* (Tim Burton, 1985), and *Mistress* (Barry Primus, 1992).

5. The debate over whether independent film can maintain its independence goes back at least to the 1990s; see Hope (1995) and Schamus (1995). More recently see Hope (2008 and 2010b).

6. I am grateful to Elizabeth Traube for pressing me on the issues discussed in this section. Similar and related issues about the ways in which the dominant culture has appropriated oppositionality have also been taken up in depth in Thomas Frank's *The Conquest of Cool* (1997) and Timothy Taylor's *The Sounds of Capitalism* (2012).

7. There is also what might be called a lower boundary, by virtue of which independent films in the artistic sense are cut off from films that are made independently of the studios but are in some way or other viewed as disreputable: porn, "exploitation movies," "transgressive cinema," etc. (see Biskind 2004: 77; Hawkins 2005). Bob Rosen also discussed these in his interview. Unfortunately, space prohibits pursuing this line of discussion.

8. Echoing Schamus's metaphor to the effect that independent film has successfully "stormed the castle," several observers of the Hollywood scene have viewed the

entry of independent filmmakers into the studios as a kind of indie "conquest" (Waxman 2006) or "taking back" (Mottram 2006) of Hollywood. While this may be going too far, to the extent that the specialty divisions have been sites of intense negotiation between Hollywood and indie perspectives, it must be true that the impact has gone in both directions. This is a very interesting question but beyond the scope of this discussion.

9. Schamus transitions from this to a larger point about the conglomerization of media, the reduction of number of media outlets, and thus at the largest level a kind of censorship that operates by making it impossible for certain views to be heard. This is an enormously important point but somewhat tangential to the present discussion, so I will not pursue it here.

10. The relationship between the independent film movement and the (more or less simultaneous) explosion of the Internet is a very interesting one but is mostly beyond the scope of this book. Particular connections will appear from time to time, and I will return to the subject briefly in the conclusions.

11. David had been a graduate student in anthropology with whom I worked at the University of Michigan. He invited me to the screening and talked to me at length afterward, for which I thank him very much.

Chapter 2: Dark Indies

1. Emanuel Levy (1999) has made diversity central to his definition of independent film, calling it a "cinema of outsiders." Despite my comments above, there is a way in which the world of independent film does *seem* more diverse than the world of Hollywood movies. I'm guessing this is because of the greater audibility of diversity rhetoric and practices (like Project Involve) in the indie world, and also because films from minority and Third World filmmakers tend to have proportionally greater visibility and to win proportionally more awards in indie festivals and competitions. At this point we simply do not have the data to say anything more definitive on the subject.

2. The end of security as a broad new affective formation is the subject of Lauren Berlant's compelling work *Cruel Optimism* (2011). Unfortunately, the book came to my attention too late to be included in the discussions of this book.

3. These interviews were at the time part of a research project on my high school graduating class, the Class of '58 of Weequahic High School in Newark, New Jersey (Ortner 2003). The original project was conceived as a multigenerational study, but that proved unwieldy and the work on the Children of the Class of '58 was not included in the book.

4. Sixteen thousand people died of AIDS in New York City alone between 1986 and 1989 (Vachon 2006: 24).

5. In the film *Bowling for Columbine* (2002), about the widespread but inaccurate fear of violent crime in the United States, Michael Moore pursues a different explanation. Citing Glassner's study, Moore makes a case for the idea that powerful

forces in the United States are into fearmongering for economic and political purposes. He includes a clip of rock star Marilyn Manson saying, "It's a [media] campaign of fear and consumption. . . . Keep everyone afraid and they'll consume" (chap. 14). Moore says, "The media, the corporations, the politicians have all done such a good job of scaring the American public, it's come to the point where they no longer need to give any reason at all." He then shows a clip of George W. Bush saying, "Today the justice department has issued a blanket alert—it was in recognition of a general threat we received. . . . Given the attitude of the evil-doers this may not be [the last]" (chap. 18).

6. By invoking the idea of "master narratives of modernity," I gesture toward the work of Jean-François Lyotard (1984) on the postmodern condition as centrally involving the loss of faith in the grand narratives of modernity. I do think an argument can be made that Generation X can be seen as embodying many elements of what has been called postmodern culture, for both better and worse (see also Radwan 2000). But the idea of postmodernity/postmodernism has become a kind of red flag that attracts rather excessive contestation, and might thus distract readers from the main arguments of the book. In an earlier version of this discussion I described Generation X as "postmodernism on the ground," but it seemed unproductive for the reasons just noted, and I have dropped it. It remains a kind of ghost in the text.

7. Recent independent film has been dubbed "neo-noir" by some (Levy 1999, chap. 7). Some independent films (especially some of the Coen brothers' films) do self-consciously work with variations of the classic film noir genre, but I will not pursue this parallel here.

8. Sobchack works primarily within a subfield of film studies called "genre studies," in which scholars tend to be more interested in questions of social, cultural, and historical context. See, e.g., Braudy (1976), Schatz (1981), Browne (1998), Grant (2003), and Braudy and Cohen (2004).

9. Filmmakers themselves do not generally see these patterns, and when I tried to ask questions about patterns in the larger corpus of independent film, filmmakers seemed to find the questions unintelligible or, at the very least, uninteresting.

10. Other films take on the neoliberal economy at the top, as it were, with the lead character being, for instance, a corporate executive or a stockbroker. The earliest figure in this lineage is probably Gordon Gekko, in *Wall Street* (Oliver Stone, 1987), a corporate raider and stock manipulator who famously pronounced that "greed is good." Gekko in turn foreshadows the much more evil character of Patrick Bateman, protagonist of the independently financed *American Psycho* (Mary Harron, 2000). Bateman is a Wall Street investment banker and yuppie consumer by day and a serial killer by night.

There is also an interesting line of films in which the amoral/immoral neoliberal figure is placed in direct opposition to the Gen X (slacker/loser) character.

These include *sex, lies, and videotape* (Steven Soderbergh, 1989) and *Before the Devil Knows You're Dead* (Sidney Lumet, 2007), as well as *Reality Bites*.

11. The movie *Up in the Air* (Jason Reitman, 2009) satirizes this new state of affairs. Thanks to Rebecca Feinberg for the reminder. See also the more serious *The Company Men* (John Wells, 2010).

12. The original reference came from an online article that is no longer available.

13. There is an intertextual reference here; there are scenes in the novel *Generation X* involving human fat in the dumpsters outside of a liposuction clinic.

14. I had considered including the film *Clerks* in this discussion, as it is also centrally concerned with young people who hate their jobs. But *Clerks* is set in the working class, and its resemblance to the other films is only superficial. The guys in *Clerks* do not hate their jobs because they expected more; they hate their jobs because they are dead-ended in the working class and always have been. There are desultory conversations about going back to school and somehow moving up in the world, but it is clear that this is not going to happen.

15. There is one place in independent film where the American Dream lives on for immigrants and minorities, which is a certain kind of inspirational film (usually a documentary) about a contest involving minority or immigrant kids—e.g., *Spellbound* (Jeffrey Blitz, 2002) or *Mad Hot Ballroom* (Marilyn Agrelo, 2005). In these films the kids work really hard and someone gets to be a winner, although the odds are very long. The long odds inject a note of realism in these otherwise upbeat films.

16. In the third episode, directed by Youssef Chanine, a filmmaker (character) who narrowly escaped being a victim of the 9/11 attack is visited by the ghost of an American marine. The two argue about whether the attack was justified, with the filmmaker-character at one point shouting about all the people who have been killed in American-initiated wars around the world. In the sixth episode, directed by Ken Loach, a Chilean man writes a letter to the parents and loved ones of those who died on 9/11, detailing the American-led coup against Salvador Allende that took place in Chile starting on September 11, 1973, and in the course of which Allende and thousands of others were killed. I was told by someone that the film was considered too controversial and had trouble getting U.S. distribution, although I have not been able to track down any specific information about this.

17. I have not been able to track down birth dates for all the filmmakers of these films. Of the five I could find, Mira Nair was born in 1957 and thus counts as a boomer. For the rest I have the following Gen X birth dates: Tom McCarthy, b. 1966; Ramin Bahrani, b. 1975; Michael Kang, b. 1970; and Christopher Zalla, b. 1975.

Chapter 3: Making the Scene

1. Thanks to Kate Hohman for pointing me toward the "scene" literature, part of her research on Brooklyn country music (Hohman 2012).
2. There have been several valuable histories of independent film in America. For books, see Biskind (1998, 2004), Ferncase (1996), Levy (1999), Merritt (2000), and Pierson (2003). For an excellent documentary, see *Edge of Outside*, 2006.
3. The explosion of the home video industry had broader implications than can be discussed here. Speaking in an interview during her tenure as executive director of Film Independent, Dawn Hudson emphasized the ways in which people's easier access to a wide spectrum of films "increases the sophistication of audiences . . . , their film grammar, and their appetite for film" (interview, February 3, 2006).
4. All of this is, of course, much more complicated than I have time to develop here. Among other things, the upper edge of the PMC has become much more entwined with the true capitalist classes, as a result of the growing practice of including in executive pay packages large amounts of stock options in their own corporations (see Brenner 2003; Fulcher 2004; Taylor n.d.).
5. Film scholar Diane Negra picks up David Brooks's idea of "bourgeois bohemians" in her discussion of indie film star Parker Posey (Negra 2005).
6. With characteristic irony, he also went on to say, "The other side of this self-created poverty that producers often bemoan is that no one forced us to do this kind of work. Really. We are not out in the fields saving peoples lives, we are not working for global peace or anything."
7. For more on Berger and Yerxa, whom producer Ted Kroeber described as "the gold standard" in producing, see Ortner (2007a, 2007b).
8. Hudson is now executive director of the Academy of Motion Picture Arts and Sciences.
9. Gilmore has now gone on to become head of the Tribeca Film Festival in New York City.

Chapter 4: Moral Ambiguity

1. In *12 and Holding* (Michael Cuesta, 2006) a young boy kills another young boy because his mother said she wanted the boy dead; in *Crimes and Misdemeanors* (Woody Allen, 1989) a man kills his lover, who is threatening to reveal their affair to his wife; in *In The Bedroom* (Todd Field, 2001) a couple kill the man who killed their son; in *Match Point* (Woody Allen, 2005) a man kills his lover (who has become pregnant and too demanding) and her landlady (to make the other murder look like a robbery gone wrong); in *Mystic River* (Clint Eastwood, 2003) a man kills his friend because he mistakenly thinks that the friend killed his daughter; in *Neo Ned* a man kills another man who had abused the woman he loves when she was young; and in *Short Cuts* (Robert Altman, 1993) a man kills a young woman in a park, apparently out of rage over his wife's work as a provider of phone sex.

2. Christine Vachon, who coproduced the film with Ted Hope, wrote about Solondz, "He wrote a nonjudgmental film about a pedophile. He's my kind of filmmaker" (Vachon 1998: 13).

3. This was the title of a two-part PBS *Frontline* series about an apparently mentally disturbed little girl who died from the effects of her foster mother trying to restrain and gag her, and about a social welfare system so broken it could not protect the child and countless others like her.

4. Jesse's lawyer in *Capturing the Friedmans* states on screen that Jesse confessed to him that the father Arnie had abused him for years. Jesse denies on screen having told this to the lawyer.

5. The mother is shown several times as being very hard and cold, as her grown son weeps copiously and is clearly in a deeply depressed state. Was she really that cold, or did the filmmaker draw on what is clearly a cultural script about absent mothers and choose footage to represent her in that way? We don't really know, of course, but it is interesting that in a filmed Q&A session that appears in the bonus material on the DVD, Tony goes out of his way twice to praise his mother and say how supportive she was.

6. In the documentary, the girl, now woman, in the Polanski case defends her mother against the press's representations that her mother, an aspiring actress, had in effect pimped her out to Polanski.

7. There may be budget factors at work here, in that films set in families are for the most part much cheaper to make. But that is clearly only one small part of the story.

8. It is very interesting to compare independent films and Hollywood movies on the question of the family. Children are put at risk in Hollywood movies too—it is a basic plot device—but there is always a happy ending. Not only is loving protection restored to the child in the end, but the child is often cast as a hero who saved the day (see, e.g., *Home Alone* [Chris Columbus, 1990], *Finding Nemo* [Andrew Stanton and Lee Unkrich, 2003], and *Firehouse Dog* [Todd Holland, 2007]).

9. All of these issues will be recognizable to anthropologists as they are also issues that arise in ethnographic fieldwork. Specifically on the question of working with a "repugnant subject," see Caton (1999: 4), citing also film theorists Tania Modleski and Linda Williams.

10. It is also a major issue in the literature on postmodernity (see, e.g., Bauman 1992; Eagleton 1996; A. Ross 1988). I indicated in an earlier note that I see Generation X as the embodiment of a (certain version of) postmodernism "on the ground." I hope to treat this relationship in a separate essay.

Chapter 5: Making Value

1. One of the things indie producers do is deal with the outside world, that is, the world beyond the film. Producers were thus the participants in the independent film world who were often most available to the anthropologist.

2. Although I am interested primarily in true independent producers, I also interviewed some Hollywood-oriented independent producers; I did not interview any studio-based producers, but I will draw on several published interviews with them in the course of this chapter. Partly this relates to the fact that, especially in Los Angeles, many independent producers have worked in the studios, as producers and/or executives, at some point in their careers. Schamus is the relatively rare case of an independent producer going in the other direction.

3. The award always has a corporate sponsor, which changes often, so the name of the award changes too, but it is always called the "[name of corporate sponsor] Producers Award."

4. Closely related to the question of lack of respect is the proliferation of producer credits, a major issue in the producing world. James Schamus commented, "Right now there's been an enormous proliferation of producer credits handed out on movies. Someone's manager gets a producer credit, the financier gets a producer credit, an executive at the company that finances the movie gets a producer credit, so it's really degraded the producer credit and the idea of the producer's role" (2006: 3). Vance Van Petten, executive director of the Producers Guild of America, also discussed this with me extensively in his interview (December 13, 2007).

5. The PGA is primarily Hollywood oriented, and I do not have separate figures for independent producers. But impressionistically, I would guess that there is a similar ratio.

6. A recent article about contemporary top studio executives pointed out that they too come from elite educations, compared to their predecessors, many of whom did not have college degrees (Cieply and Barnes 2009: 1). My own limited contact with studio executives bears this out. Similarly, TV writer and screenwriter John Romano remarked in an interview that many TV writers are lawyers (interview, March 8, 2005).

7. There were other items on Drubner's list (e.g., "understanding how money works"), but I will not try to cover everything here.

8. Horberg is a studio producer who has also nurtured many independent films.

9. I have not pursued the gender association here, but it was well captured by Barbra Streisand in her famous Crystal Awards speech of 1986:

> A man is commanding—a woman is demanding
> A man is forceful—a woman is pushy
> A man is uncompromising—a woman is a ball-breaker
> He's assertive—she's aggressive
> He shows leadership—she's controlling. (Quoted in Obst 1996: 190–91)

10. There is apparently no word in French that translates as (this version of) the English word *agency*.

11. He then added, "Unless you're totally brilliant, in which case you can be an asshole."

12. It will be of interest to anthropologists that Ted Kroeber is the great-grandson of A. L. Kroeber, founder of the anthropology department at UC Berkeley, and one of the pioneers of American anthropology.

13. Ted Hope turned the metaphor upside down but made the same basic point. He compared the producer's role to that of a child in a family that had lost a parent: "I think you can actually trace a lot of my producerial instincts to different aspects of my childhood, and that's very true for many producers. They are people that try to bring peace into a chaotic experience, or that are asked to solve the problems in some sort of way, and find gratification in doing that" (interview, March 15, 2006).

14. Directors also talk about not having felt protected: "[Brian] De Palma had turned down [the line producer's] request for a more significant producing credit. He didn't feel that [that person] had protected him from the executives the way a producer would have" (Salamon [1991] 2002: 294).

15. The festival was organized by two graduate students in what was then called the Critical Studies Department in the UCLA School of Theater, Film, and Television, Adam Fish and Jason Skonieczny. It was held on April 26, 2007.

Chapter 6: Film Feminism

1. This is not to say that there are no male directors who might be considered to have a feminist sensibility. Rodrigo García, for example, has made an extraordinary series of women-focused films, including *Things You Can Tell Just by Looking at Her* (2000), *Nine Lives* (2005), and most recently *Mother and Child* (2009). But the subject of men representing women has a long and thorny history in feminist film criticism, and it would simply take me too far afield to pursue it here. Key references would include Haskell ([1973] 1987), Mulvey ([1975] 2004), de Lauretis (1984), Modleski (1988), and Traube (1992a, 1992b).

2. Sophia Coppola is one of the few exceptions. See Joshua Rothkopf's scathing review of *Marie Antoinette* (2006), in which he called Coppola "the most prominent of Generation X filmmakers" (2006: 125).

3. In a later (2007) article, journalist Sharon Waxman pointed out that many of these women had left their positions, signaling a shift in the climate of Hollywood (back) to a "boys' era." Independent producer Lydia Dean Pilcher challenged Waxman's gloomy view, emphasizing that women filmmakers were still getting much good work out and finding receptive female audiences. She concludes, "There is some good news out there, so let's get it all out and give our filmmakers of today and young filmmakers of tomorrow something to hold on to" (letter to Waxman dated April 30, 2007, shared with me by Pilcher).

4. Kathleen McHugh has pointed out (personal communication) that the figures for the 1970s may not be accurate, as more women were making films in that era but were not necessarily members of the DGA.

5. Here is the math. There are 648 references in my filmography as of July 29, 2012, representing a total of 478 directors. Of these, 87 are women, or 18 percent.

6. *An Education* was a British production directed by Danish director Lone Scherfig. Although I am not systematically looking at foreign films in this book, I treat those that do come up for discussion as independent films, particularly those that play the same festival circuits as American independent films and those that display a not-Hollywood or independent spirit.

7. In fact, she emphasized that women in the broader film/movie industry were generally very supportive of one another. Others have made this point as well; see Obst (1996), Hill (2000), and Hass (2005).

8. One of my Gen X informants in the 1990s, a young woman with a PhD in physics, talked at length about how shocked she was to encounter so much ongoing sexism in the workplace, having come from a liberal background: "Until I worked for a year I did not realize the truth in all I've heard about women, especially in the math or science related careers, about the inequalities. I went to a high school that was in a relatively liberal town. I went to a college that was all women, that pushed its women to become leaders. . . . I especially got coddled because I was the one female physics major and everybody wanted me to stay with that program. Everybody knew me and everybody liked me so I never really saw these problems until I worked for a year and I experienced a sort of harassment and I experienced inequality of women. . . . I certainly would not have believed it if I hadn't been there."

9. *North Country* is, like *Fight Club* discussed earlier, a borderline case of "independence." Like *Fight Club*, it was made in a Hollywood studio (Warner Bros.) on a relatively large budget ($30 million). But the director, New Zealander Niki Caro, had previously made the award-winning independent film *Whale Rider* (2002), and as far as I can see, she went back to making indies afterward. The film is also thematically consistent with all the other films in the discussion, and I made the decision to keep it in the pool.

10. I set aside here the whole genre of strong and physically violent female action hero stories, including (in my sample) *Aeon Flux* (Karyn Kusama, 2005) and *Blue Steel* (Kathryn Bigelow, 1989). These pose interesting questions for feminist scholars and journalists (see, e.g., Tasker 1998, Hale 2011, Scott and Dargis 2011), but mostly appear in nonrealist Hollywood movies and television shows and speak to different issues.

11. I am tempted to relate the harsh representations of senior women in some of the films to the friction between the feminist and post-feminist generations discussed earlier. All the filmmakers are part of the supposedly post-feminist generation, although none of the senior women in the films appear particularly "feminist." On the contrary, they mostly tend to be aligned with the patriarchal order. No doubt a lot could be said about these negative representations of senior women (see also the mothers who love their pedophile sons in chap. 4), but I cannot pursue the subject here.

12. *Frozen River* is the only film in this group that has a significant race theme. The

two women have a very prickly relationship because, from Lila's point of view, Ray has all the race privileges of being white but doesn't know it. This is an ongoing issue throughout the film and is only overcome when Ray finally comes to understand the privilege of her whiteness.

Chapter 7: Making Films

1. The strong authority of the director on the set represents a definite change from Powdermaker's time; it is clear in Powdermaker's text that the director often got very little respect (1950: chap. 10). The strong role of the director probably dates from the end of the studio system in the 1950s and/or the rise of auteurism (the idea that the director is the most important creative force in filmmaking) in the 1960s.

2. See the documentary *Lost in La Mancha* (Keith Fulton and Louis Pepe, 2002) for a sad account of the breakdown of a film during production.

3. Below-the-line workers were not directly part of this project. See Caldwell (2008), as well as several essays in Mayer, Banks, and Caldwell (2009).

4. Filmmakers vary in their willingness to leave a relatively porous boundary between the set and the outside world. Low-budget indie films may have no choice, but there is also some ideology to the effect that it's healthy for a filmmaker to not seal a movie production off too tightly from the real world: "There's a great piece of film advice that, in the story I heard, was told to a young Bertolucci by Renoir: 'Always leave the door to the studio open'" (Macaulay 2008: 1). Most American movie productions, however, are closed in a way that not only keeps the public out but keeps the participants in a kind of cocoon-like, low-stimulus environment. Observing the shooting of *Lady in the Water*, Michael Bamberger noted that "the real world receded quickly. It was like being in a Las Vegas gaming room, where you can't tell day from night" (2006: 197).

5. According to the documentary *Who Needs Sleep?*, the lengthening of shooting days is relatively recent and thus might be related to the neoliberalization of the economy in the past few decades. But I could not find any specific information on when and how this pattern evolved and have to leave the question open here.

6. The relationship between gift giving and social cohesion is the subject of one of the great classics of anthropology, *The Gift* (Mauss [1923] 1967).

7. Child actors have specific legal protections as well as these more general protections on set.

8. When the production is finished, especially for an independent film, there is still a great deal of work to be done—trying to get into festivals; trying to get a distributor; trying to get cheap publicity out of interviews, Q&As, and Web campaigns; and so on. Playwright Neil La Bute talks about this in a funny/frustrated way in the film *Independent's Day* (Marina Zenovich, 1998). See also Rosen (1990) and Stubbs and Rodriguez (2000).

Chapter 8: Politics

1. See Roussel (2010) for the view of a French sociologist on this subject. Roussel is codirector, with American sociologist William Roy, of a large-scale joint French-American research project called "How Art Does Politics."

2. A third version of this objection has to do with the idea that "politics" are petty, and that in certain contexts people should rise above them. Filmmaker Tim Hetherington said the following in an interview about his (nonpolitical) Afghanistan war film *Restrepo* (2010): "This is a visceral, experiential war film. And we just think there's a massive need, at this critical juncture, for people to put their politics aside in the lobby of the theater, and go into a dark room for 93 minutes to experience and share what these guys go through, and in some ways digest it and honor it" (quoted in Lang 2011: 1). I heard a similarly nonpolitical film about Iraq veterans, called *Operation Homecoming* (Richard E. Robbins, 2007), defended on similar grounds in a screening Q&A; field notes, February 12, 2008.

3. In the interests of space I had to cut here a section called "Confessions of a Documentary Junkie." I discovered documentaries in the late 1960s, starting with the work of Frederic Wiseman, and documentaries remain to this day my favorite genre of film.

4. The documentary form would obviously include all ethnographic film, and I have actually had some direct involvement in the making of one. In 1977 I participated in the making of *Sherpas*, in the Granada Television series "Disappearing Worlds." My official title was "Anthropologist," and I was involved in all stages of the production of the film—I conceptualized the framework and story; I served as cultural mediator and translator during the shooting of the film in the field (Nepal); and I consulted during the editing of the film in Manchester, England. The producer (whom we would call the director) was the prizewinning British documentarian Leslie Woodhead (see, for example, his *Children of Beslan* [2005] and *How the Beatles Rocked the Kremlin* [2009]). I hope to treat ethnographic film in a separate work.

5. Nichols's language here could easily be translated into Bourdieu's discussion of the social and cultural dynamics within a "field of cultural production." As discussed earlier, Bourdieu argues that boundaries in artistic fields, and particularly the boundary between "art" and "commerce," are always under contestation.

6. Here I assume he is talking about *Sick: The Life and Times of Bob Flanagan, Super Masochist* (1997).

7. It is interesting to note that the situation is reversed in the world of book publishing, where nonfiction does better than fiction (Donadio 2005).

8. Faden makes a certain kind of film that is at once scholarly and comic/energetic/compelling. He calls them "Media Stylos," a term he takes from Jean-Luc Godard, who defined them as "research in the form of a spectacle."

9. There are also truth issues surrounding Michael Moore's films, especially includ-

ing charges that Moore plays fast and loose with chronology. See Kellner (2010, chap. 3) for a very useful discussion.

Chapter 9: Conclusions

1. Zachary Levy is a documentary filmmaker. He points out that many filmmakers, including himself, have been doing distribution DIY for some time now. He doesn't say, but could have said, that distribution deals for documentary film-makers are relatively rare and even harder to get than for feature films, and that DIY distribution has probably been the norm for most documentary filmmakers throughout the history of documentary film.

References

Abramowitz, Rachel. 2000. *Is That a Gun in Your Pocket? The Truth about Female Power in Hollywood.* New York: Random House.

——. 2007. "Indie Films Could Use a Little More 'Sunshine.'" *Los Angeles Times,* October 25, E1.

Abu-Lughod, Lila. 2005. *Dramas of Nationhood: The Politics of Television in Egypt.* Chicago: University of Chicago Press.

Allain, Stephanie. 2007. Interview by Lisa Y. Garibay. *Film Independent Calendar,* February, pp. 5, 15.

Anderson, Chris. 2006. *The Long Tail: Why the Future of Business Is Selling Less of More.* New York: Hyperion.

Ansen, David. 2006. "The Maverick of Movieland: Robert Altman, 1925–2006." *Newsweek,* December 4, 69.

——. 2007a. "The Rage of Aquarius." *Newsweek,* March 5, 65.

——. 2007b. "The Road to Ruin" (review of *No End in Sight*). *Newsweek,* July 30. http://www.msnbc.msn.com/id/19886680/site/newsweek. Accessed on September 3, 2010.

——. 2008. "How Much Did 'Taxi to the Dark Side' Earn at the American Box Office?" *Newsweek,* July 7/July 14, 66, 68.

Appadurai, Arjun. 1990. "Disjuncture and Difference in the Global Cultural Economy." *Public Culture* 2 (2): 1–24.

Appadurai, Arjun, and Carol Breckenridge. 1988. "Why Public Culture?" *Public Culture* 1 (1, Fall): 5–9.

Askew, Kelly, and Richard R. Wilk, eds. 2002. *The Anthropology of Media: A Reader.* Malden, Mass.: Blackwell Publishing.

Bach, Steven. 1985. *Final Cut: Art, Money and Ego in the Making of Heaven's Gate, the Film That Sank United Artists.* New York: Newmarket Press.

Balio, Tino. 1976. *United Artists: The Company Built by the Stars.* Madison: University of Wisconsin Press.

Bamberger, Michael. 2006. *The Man Who Heard Voices: Or, How M. Night Shyamalan Risked His Career on a Fairy Tale*. New York: Gotham.

Baron, Caroline. 2006. Interview by Lisa Y. Garibay. http://www.filmindependent .org/news/filmmaker+interviews/carolin_baron. Accessed on September 14, 2010.

Bauman, Zygmunt. 1992. *Intimations of Postmodernity*. London and New York: Routledge.

Bennett, Stephen Earl, and Eric W. Rademacher. 1997. "The 'Age of Indifference' Revisited: Patterns of Political Interest, Media Exposure, and Knowledge among Generation X." In *After the Boom: The Politics of Generation X*, ed. S. C. Craig and S. E. Bennett, 21–42. Lanham, Md.: Rowman and Littlefield.

Berlant, Lauren. 2011. *Cruel Optimism*. Durham, N.C.: Duke University Press.

Bernstein, Matthew. 1998. "Documentaphobia and Mixed Modes: Michael Moore's Roger and Me." In *Documenting the Documentary: Close Readings of Film and Video*, ed. B. K. Grant and J. Sloniowski, 397–415. Detroit, Mich.: Wayne State University Press.

——. [1994] 2000. *Walter Wanger: Hollywood Independent*. Minneapolis: University of Minnesota Press.

Bilsborrow-Koo, Ryan. 2008. "Your Film Online." *Filmmaker* Magazine blog post, September 23. http://filmmakermagazine.com/news/2008/09/your-film-online-by-ryan-bilsborrow-koo. Accessed on September 25, 2008.

Biskind, Peter. 1983. *Seeing Is Believing: How Hollywood Taught Us to Stop Worrying and Love the Fifties*. New York: Henry Holt.

——. 1998. *Easy Riders, Raging Bulls: How the Sex-Drugs-and-Rock 'n Roll Generation Saved Hollywood*. New York: Touchstone (Simon and Schuster).

——. 2004. *Down and Dirty Pictures: Miramax, Sundance, and the Rise of Independent Film*. New York: Simon and Schuster.

——. 2007. "An American Family." *Vanity Fair*, April. http://www.vanityfair.com/culture/features/2007/04/sopranos200704. Accessed on June 23, 2008.

Born, Georgina. 1995. *Rationalizing Culture: IRCAM, Boulez, and the Institutionalization of the Musical Avant-Garde*. Berkeley: University of California Press.

——. 2005. *Uncertain Vision: Birt, Dyke, and the Reinvention of the BBC*. London: Vintage.

Bourdieu, Pierre. 1984. *Distinction: A Social Critique of the Judgement of Taste*. Trans. Richard Nice. Cambridge, Mass.: Harvard University Press.

——. 1993. *The Field of Cultural Production: Essays on Art and Literature*. Edited and introduced by Randal Johnson. Various translators. New York: Columbia University Press.

Braudy, Leo. 1976. *The World in a Frame: What We See in Films*. Chicago: University of Chicago Press.

Braudy, Leo, and Marshall Cohen, eds. 2004. *Film Theory and Criticism*. 6th ed. New York: Oxford University Press.

Brenner, Robert. 2002. *The Boom and the Bubble: The US in the World Economy*. London and New York: Verso.

———. 2003. "Towards the Precipice: Robert Brenner on the Crisis in the US Economy." *London Review of Books*, February 6.

Brooks, David. 2000. *Bobos in Paradise: The New Upper Class and How They Got There*. New York: Simon and Schuster.

———. 2005. "Karl's New Manifesto." *New York Times*, May 29. http://www.nytimes.com/2005/05/29/opinion/29brooks.html?_r=1&pagewanted=print. Accessed on August 25, 2010.

Brooks, Peter. 1995. *The Melodramatic Imagination: Balzac, Henry James, Melodrama, and the Mode of Excess*. New Haven, Conn.: Yale University Press.

Browne, Nick, ed. 1998. *Refiguring American Film Genres: Theory and History*. Berkeley: University of California Press.

Burr, Ty. 2007. "Ty Burr's Top Ten." *Boston Globe*, December 30, 2007. http://www.boston.com/ae/movies/articles/2007/12/29/ty_burrs_top_10. Accessed on August 3, 2008.

Caldwell, John Thornton. 2008. *Production Culture: Industrial Reflexivity and Critical Practice in Film and Television*. Durham, N.C.: Duke University Press.

Callahan, David. 2010. *Fortunes of Change: The Rise of the Liberal Rich and the Remaking of America*. Hoboken, N.J.: Wiley.

Caton, Steven C. 1999. *Lawrence of Arabia: A Film's Anthropology*. Berkeley: University of California Press.

Caves, Richard E. 2000. *Creative Industries: Contracts between Art and Commerce*. Cambridge, Mass.: Harvard University Press.

Chocano, Carina. 2011. "Skipping through the Popular Culture, Snarling at Everyone." (On-line title: "Thelma, Louise and All the Pretty Women.") *New York Times Magazine*, April 24, p. MM48.

Cieply, Michael. 2009. "Now, Independent Filmmakers Are Distributing on Their Own." *New York Times*, August 13, 1, 15.

Cieply, Michael, and Brooks Barnes. 2009. "In Hollywood, the Easy-Money Generation Toughens Up." *New York Times*, March 22. http://www.nytimes.com/2009/03/23/business/media/23moguls.html. Accessed on September 14, 2010.

Comaroff, Jean. 1997. "Consuming Passions: Child Abuse, Fetishism, and 'The New World Order.'" *Culture* 17 (1–2): 7–25.

Comaroff, Jean, and John L. Comaroff, eds. 2001. *Millennial Capitalism and the Culture of Neoliberalism*. Durham, N.C.: Duke University Press.

Coontz, Stephanie. 1992. *The Way We Never Were: American Families and the Nostalgia Trap*. New York: Basic.

Coppola, Eleanor. [1979] 1992. *Notes on the Making of "Apocalypse Now."* New York: Limelight Editions.

Coupland, Douglas. 1991. *Generation X: Tales for an Accelerated Culture*. New York: St. Martin's.

———. 2010. "A Radical Pessimist's Guide to the Next 10 Years." *Saturday's Globe and Mail*, Friday, October 8. http://www.theglobeandmail.com/news/national/a-radical-pessimists-guide-to-the-next-10-years/article1750609/. Accessed on March 21, 2011.

Crockford, Julian. 2000. "'It's All about the Bucks, Kid. The Rest Is Conversation': Framing the Economic Narrative from *Wall Street* to *Reality Bites*." *Post Script* 19 (2): 19–33.

Curtin, Michael. 1996. "On Edge: Culture Industries in the Neo-Network Era." In *Making and Selling Culture*, ed. R. Ohmann, 181–202. Hanover, N.H.: Wesleyan University Press.

Dargis, Manohla. 2010a. "Declaration of Indies: Just Sell It Yourself!" *New York Times*, January 17. http://www.nytimes.com/2010/01/17/movies/17dargis.html. Accessed on September 22, 2010.

——. 2010b. "How Oscar Found Ms. Right." *New York Times* Arts and Leisure section, Sunday, March 14, 1, 17.

Davies, Erin. 2009. "Indie-Film Shakeout: There Will Be Blood." *Time*/CNN, November 7. http://www.time.com/time/business/article/0,8599,1936350,00.html.

Davis, Mike. 1990. *City of Quartz: Excavating the Future in Los Angeles*. New York: Vintage.

de Lauretis, Teresa. 1984. *Alice Doesn't: Feminism, Semiotics, Cinema*. Bloomington: Indiana University Press.

Denby, David. 2010. "Image Problems." *New Yorker*, March 22, 82.

Desai, Jigna. 2003. "Bombay Boys and Girls: The Gender and Sexual Politics of Transnationality in the New Indian Cinema in English." *South Asian Popular Culture* 1 (1): 45–61.

Deutchman, Ira. 2009. "10 (9 actually) Responses to the Issues Brought Up at the 'Indie Summit.'" http://iradeutchman.com/wordpress/indiefilm/indie-film-summit/. Accessed on September 26, 2009.

Donadio, Rachel. 2005. "Truth Is Stronger than Fiction." *New York Times Book Review*, Sunday, August 7, 27.

Dornfeld, Barry. 1998. *Producing Public Television, Producing Public Culture*. Princeton, N.J.: Princeton University Press.

Dudley, Kathryn Marie. 1994. *The End of the Line: Lost Jobs, New Lives in Postindustrial America*. Chicago: University of Chicago Press.

Dunne, John Gregory. [1968] 1998. *The Studio*. New York: Vintage.

Durkheim, Emile. [1912] 2001. *The Elementary Forms of the Religious Life*. Trans. C. Cosman. Oxford: Oxford University Press.

Eagleton, Terry. 1996. *The Illusions of Postmodernism*. Oxford: Blackwell.

Ebert, Roger. 2007. [Review of] "No End in Sight." *Chicago Sun-Times*, August 10. http://rogerebert.suntimes.com/apps/pbcs.dll/article?AID=/20070809/REVIEWS/708090301/1023. Accessed on August 3, 2008.

Edelstein, David. 2007. "The Year in Movies." *New York Magazine*, December 9, 2007. http://nymag/com/arts/cultureawards/2007/41803/. Accessed on August 3, 2008.

Editors. 1974. "The Last Word. Inaugural Issue of Jump Cut." *Jump Cut*, No. 1, 1974, pages not given.

Ehrenreich, Barbara. 1989. *Fear of Falling: The Inner Life of the Middle Class.* New York: Pantheon.

——. 2001. *Nickel and Dimed: On (Not) Getting By in America.* New York: Henry Holt.

——. 2005. *Bait and Switch: The (Futile) Pursuit of the American Dream.* New York: Owl.

Ehrenreich, John, and Barbara Ehrenreich. 1979. "The Professional Managerial Class." In *Between Labour and Capital,* ed. P. Walker, 5–45. Boston: South End.

Elsaesser, Thomas. 1987. "Tales of Sound and Fury: Observations on the Family Melodrama." In *Home Is Where the Heart Is: Studies in Melodrama and Women's Film,* ed. C. Gledhill, 43–69. London: BFI.

Epstein, Edward Jay. 2006. *The Big Picture: Money and Power in Hollywood.* New York: Random House.

Faludi, Susan. 2010. "American Electra: Feminism's Ritual Matricide." *Harper's,* October, 29–42.

Feinstein, Howard. 1999. "A Tender Comedy about Child Abuse? What Is Todd Solondz Up To?" *Guardian Unlimited,* March 26. http://www.guardian.co.uk/film/1999/mar/26/features. Accessed on September 19, 2010.

Ferncase, Richard K. 1996. *Outsider Features: American Independent Films of the 1980s.* Westport, Conn.: Greenwood.

Filmmakermagazine.com. http://www.filmmakermagazine.com/main/Filmmaker Background.pdf. Accessed on February 5, 2012.

Fischer, Michael M. J. 1995. "Film as Ethnography and Cultural Critique in the Late Twentieth Century." In *Shared Differences: Multicultural Media and Practical Pedagogy,* ed. D. Carson and L. D. Friedman, 29–56. Urbana and Chicago: University of Illinois Press.

Fleck, Ryan, and Anna Boden. N.d. Interview by Rob Carnevale. http://www.indie london.co.uk/Film-Review/half-nelson-ryan-fleck-and-anna-boden-interview. Accessed on April 18, 2010.

Foucault, Michel. 1986. *The History of Sexuality, Volume I.* New York: Vintage.

Frank, Raphie, and Mindy Bond. 2005. "Todd Solondz, Filmmaker." http://gothamist .com/2005/04/13/todd_solondz_filmmaker.php. Accessed on September 19, 2010.

Frank, Thomas. 1997. *The Conquest of Cool: Business Culture, Counterculture, and the Rise of Hip Consumerism.* Chicago: University of Chicago Press.

Frow, John. 1995. *Cultural Studies and Cultural Value.* Oxford: Clarendon.

Fulcher, James. 2004. *Capitalism: A Very Short Introduction.* New York: Oxford University Press.

Gabler, Neal. 1988. *An Empire of Their Own: How the Jews Invented Hollywood.* New York: Anchor.

Gaines, Jane M. 1999. "Political Mimesis." In *Collecting Visible Evidence,* ed. J. M. Gaines and M. Renov, 84–103. Minneapolis: University of Minnesota Press.

Geertz, Clifford. 1973a. "Thick Description: Toward an Interpretive Theory of Culture." In his *The Interpretation of Cultures,* 3–32. New York: Basic.

———. 1973b. "Deep Play: Notes on the Balinese Cockfight." In his *The Interpretation of Cultures*, 412–54. New York: Basic.

Ginsburg, Faye D. 1999. "The Parallax Effect: The Impact of Indigenous Media on Ethnographic Film." In *Collecting Visible Evidence*, ed. J. M. Gaines and M. Renov, 156–75. Minneapolis: University of Minnesota Press.

———. 2002. "Fieldwork at the Movies: Anthropology and Media." In *Exotic No More: Anthropology on the Front Lines*, ed. J. MacClancy, 359–76. Chicago and London: University of Chicago Press.

Ginsburg, Faye D., Lila Abu-Lughod, and Brian Larkin, eds. 2002. *Media Worlds: Anthropology on New Terrain*. Berkeley: University of California Press.

Giroux, Henry A. 1998. "Stealing Innocence: The Politics of Child Beauty Pageants." In *The Children's Culture Reader*, ed. H. Jenkins, 265–82. New York: New York University Press.

Gitlin, Todd. 1983. *Inside Prime Time*. New York: Pantheon.

Glassner, Barry. 1999. *The Culture of Fear: Why Americans Are Afraid of the Wrong Things*. New York: Basic.

Gledhill, Christine. 1987. "The Melodramatic Field: An Investigation." In *Home Is Where the Heart Is: Studies in Melodrama and Women's Film*, ed. C. Gledhill, 5–42. London: BFI.

Grant, Barry Keith, ed. 2003. *Film Genre Reader III*. Austin: University of Texas Press.

Greenblatt, Stephen. 1999. "The Touch of the Real." In *The Fate of "Culture": Geertz and Beyond*, ed. S. B. Ortner, 14–29. Berkeley: University of California Press.

Grindstaff, Laura. 2002. *The Money Shot: Trash, Class, and the Making of TV Talk Shows*. Chicago: University of Chicago Press.

Gusterson, Hugh, and Catherine Besteman, eds. 2010. *The Insecure American: How We Got Here and What We Should Do about It*. Berkeley: University of California Press.

Habermas, Jürgen. [1962] 1994. *The Structural Transformation of the Public Sphere: An Inquiry into a Category of Bourgeois Society*. Trans. T. Burger with F. Lawrence. Cambridge, Mass.: MIT Press.

Hale, Mike. 2011. "Sugar and Spice and Vicious Beatings." *New York Times*, Sunday, March 13, Television section, 6, 26.

Hannerz, Ulf. 1996. *Transnational Connections: Culture, People, Places*. London and New York: Routledge.

———. 2010. "Field Worries: Studying Down, Up, Sideways, Through, Backward, Forward, Early or Later, Away and at Home." In his *Anthropology's World: Life in a Twenty-First-Century Discipline*, 59–86. London: Pluto.

Hanson, Peter. 2002. *The Cinema of Generation X: A Critical Study of Films and Directors*. Jefferson, N.C.: McFarland.

Harris, Mark. 2007. "Rage at the Machine" (review of *No End in Sight*). ew.com, posted August 23, 2007. http://www.ew.com/ew/article/0,,20053061,00.html. Accessed on August 3, 2008.

Hartley, John, ed. 2005. *Creative Industries*. Oxford, U.K.: Blackwell.

Harvey, David. 2005. *A Brief History of Neoliberalism*. Oxford: Oxford University Press.

Haskell, Molly. [1973] 1987. *From Reverence to Rape: The Treatment of Women in the Movies*. 2nd ed. Chicago: University of Chicago Press.

Hass, Nancy. 2005. "Hollywood's New Old Girls' Network: How Running the Studios Became Women's Work." *New York Times*, Arts & Leisure, Sunday, April 24, 1, 13.

Hawkesworth, Mary. 2004. "The Semiotics of Premature Burial: Feminism in a Postfeminist Age." *Signs* 29 (4): 961–85.

Hawkins, Joan. 2005. "Dark, Disturbing, Intelligent, Provocative, and Quirky: Avant-Garde Cinema of the 1980s and 1990s." In *Contemporary American Independent Film*, ed. C. Holmlund and J. Wyatt, 89–106. New York: Routledge.

Hays, Matthew. 1997. "Make Art, Not Politics: Gregg Araki on Going *Nowhere*." http://www.montrealmirror.com/ARCHIVES/1997/071797/film1.html. Accessed on September 11, 2007.

Hernandez, Eugene. 2004. "Dispatch from Toronto: American Auteurs Araki, Kerrigan, and Solondz Stir Festival." September 17. http://www.indiewire.com/onthescene/ontheescene_040917toro.html. Accessed on September 11, 2007.

Hesmondhalgh, David. 2007. *The Cultural Industries*. 2nd ed. London: Sage.

Hill, Debra. 2000. "Produced by Debra Hill." Interview by Ken Ross. *Produced By*, Summer, 8–15, 18.

Hohman, Anne Kathryn. 2012. Brooklyn Country: Class, Culture, and the Politics of "Alternativity." PhD dissertation, Department of Anthropology, Columbia University.

Holtz, Geoffrey T. 1995. *Welcome to the Jungle: The Why behind "Generation X."* New York: St. Martin's Griffin.

Hope, Ted. 1995. "Indie Film Is Dead." *Filmmaker Magazine*, Fall. http://www.filmmakermagazine.com/fall1995/dead_film.php. Accessed on March 29, 2006.

———. 2006. IMDb Biography. http://www.imdb.com/name/nm0394046/bio.

———. 2008. "A Thousand Phoenix Rising: How the New Truly Free Filmmaking Will Rise from Indie's Ashes." http://filmindependent.org/empower/keynote.html. Accessed on September 29, 2008.

———. 2010a. "The Good Machine No-Budget Commandments." Truly Free Film blog, July 21. http://trulyfreefilm.hopeforfilm.com/2010/07/the-good-machine-no-budget-commandments.html. Accessed on September 14, 2010.

———. 2010b. "Reflections on 'Indie Film Is Dead.'" Truly Free Film blog, August 16. http://trulyfreefilm.hopeforfilm.com/2010/08/reflections-on-indie-film-is-dead.html. Accessed on September 23, 2010.

———. 2010c. "Why Producers Are Valued." Blog post, Hope for Film, July 15. http://trulyfreefilm.hopeforfilm.com/2010/07/why-producers-are_valued.html. Accessed on September 23, 2010.

Horkheimer, Max, and Theodor W. Adorno. [1944] 2006. "The Culture Industry:

Enlightenment as Mass Deception." In *Media and Cultural Studies: Keyworks*, ed. M. G. Durham and D. M. Kellner, 41–72. Malden, Mass.: Blackwell.

Hornaday, Ann. 2006. "Women of Independent Miens: Nicole Holofcener and Mary Harron Prove a Woman's Place Is in the Director's Chair." *Washington Post*, Sunday, April 16. http://www.washingtonpost.com/wp-dyn/content/article/2006/04/14/AR2006041400300_pf.html. Accessed on May 29, 2010.

Horowitz, Josh. 2006. *The Mind of the Modern Moviemaker: 20 Conversations with the New Generation of Filmmakers.* New York: Plume (Penguin).

Howe, Neil, and Bill Strauss. 1993. *13th Gen: Abort, Retry, Ignore, Fail?* New York: Vintage.

Hunter, Stephen. 2007. "From Iraq to Alaska to Ireland, Powerful Storytelling That Hit [sic] Home." *Washington Post*, Sunday, December 30. http://www.washingtonpost.com/wp-dyn/content/article/2007/12/28/AR2007122800705.html. Accessed on August 3, 2008.

IMDb.com. 2010. "Independent Spirit Awards Overview." www.imdb.com/event/ev0000349/overview, March 5. Accessed on February 5, 2012.

Inda, Jonathan Xavier, and Renato Rosaldo, eds. 2002. *The Anthropology of Globalization: A Reader.* Malden, Mass.: Blackwell.

James, David E. 2005. *The Most Typical Avant-Garde: History and Geography of Minor Cinemas in Los Angeles.* Berkeley: University of California Press.

Jameson, Fredric. 1984a. "Foreword" to J.-F. Lyotard, *The Postmodern Condition: A Report on Knowledge*, vii–xxi. Minneapolis: University of Minnesota Press.

———. 1984b. "Postmodernism, or the Cultural Logic of Late Capitalism." *New Left Review* 146 (July–August): 53–92.

Jost, Jon. [1989] 2005. "End of the Indies: Death of the Sayles Men." In *Contemporary American Independent Film: From the Margins to the Mainstream*, ed. C. Holmlund and J. Wyatt, 53–58. London and New York: Routledge.

Kaufman, Anthony. 2010. "Youthquake: Where Is the Under 30s Audience for Indie Film?" http://www.filmmakermagazine.com/issues/spring2010/industry-beat.php. Accessed on September 22, 2010.

Kellner, Douglas. 2010. *Cinema Wars: Hollywood Film and Politics in the Bush-Cheney Era.* Malden, Mass.: Wiley-Blackwell.

King, Geoff. 2005. *American Independent Cinema.* Bloomington: Indiana University Press.

———. 2009. *Indiewood, USA: Where Hollywood Meets Independent Cinema.* London: I. B. Taurus.

King, Lynnea Chapman. 2000. "Generation X: Searching for an Identity?" *Post Script* 19 (2): 8–18.

Klawans, Stuart. 2000. "Independents' Day." *Nation*, March 16. http://www.thenation.com/article/independents-day?page=full. Accessed on July 27, 2011.

Klein, Naomi. 2007. *The Shock Doctrine: The Rise of Disaster Capitalism.* London: Penguin.

Krugman, Paul. 2002. "For Richer: How the Permissive Capitalism of the Boom Destroyed American Equality." *New York Times Magazine*, October 20, 62–67, 75–77, 141.

Kwan, Jennifer. 2009. "Cody Exorcises Demons from 'Jennifer's Body.' " *Reuters*. http://www.reuters.com/article/idUSTRE58C0ZI20090914. Accessed on September 28, 2010.

Lahr, John. 2002. "Whirlwind: How the Filmmaker Mira Nair Makes People See the World Her Way." *New Yorker*, December 9. Downloaded from Lexis/Nexus on September 7, 2007.

Lancaster, Roger N. 2011. *Sex Panic and the Punitive State*. Berkeley: University of California Press.

Lang, Brent. 2011. " 'Restrepo' Filmmaker Tim Hetherington Killed in Libya." *Wrap Movies*, April 20. http://www.thewrap.com. Accessed on April 20, 2011.

Larkin, Brian. 2008. *Signal and Noise: Media, Infrastructure, and Urban Culture in Nigeria*. Durham, N.C.: Duke University Press.

Lash, Scott, and Celia Lury. 2007. *Global Cultural Industry: The Mediation of Things*. Cambridge, U.K.: Polity.

Levy, Emanuel. 1999. *Cinema of Outsiders: The Rise of American Independent Film*. New York: New York University Press.

Linden, Sheri. 2003. "Real Genius." *Hollywood Reporter*, August, 35–37.

Linklater, Richard. 1992. *Slacker*. New York: St. Martin's.

Lyotard, Jean-François. 1984. *The Postmodern Condition: A Report on Knowledge*. Trans. G. Bennington and B. Massumi. Minneapolis: University of Minnesota Press.

Macaulay, Scott. 2006. "Playground Rules" (interview with Todd Field). *Filmmaker Magazine*, Fall. http://www.filmmakermagazine.com/issues/fall2006/features/playground_rules.php. Accessed on September 19, 2010.

———. 2008. Editor's Note. *Filmmaker Newsletter*, April 17. newsletter@filmmaker magazine.com.

———. 2009. Editor's Note. *Filmmaker Newsletter*, October 29. newsletter@filmmaker magazine.com.

Mandelberger, Sandy. 2009. "Producer Ted Hope Honored at Woodstock Film Festival." *FFT Online*. http://filmfestivaltoday.com/index.php?option=com _content &view=article&catid=38%3Afft-festival-coverage&id=237%3Aproducer-ted-hope-honored-at-woodstock-film-festival&Itemid=60. Accessed on September 14, 2010.

Mankekar, Purnima. 1999. *Screening Culture, Viewing Politics: An Ethnography of Television, Womanhood, and Nation in Postcolonial India*. Durham, N.C.: Duke University Press.

Mann, Denise. 2008. *Hollywood Independents: The Postwar Talent Takeover*. Minneapolis: University of Minnesota Press.

Marcus, George E. 1998. *Ethnography through Thick and Thin*. Princeton: Princeton University Press.

Marcus, George E., and Michael M. J. Fischer. 1986. *Anthropology as Cultural Critique: An Experimental Moment in the Human Sciences.* Chicago: University of Chicago Press.

Martin, Randy, and Ella Shohat, eds. 2003. "Corruption in Corporate Culture." Special issue of *Social Text,* Winter.

Maslin, Janet. 1996. "To Abort, Not to Abort: A Comedy." *New York Times,* December 13. http://movies.nytimes.com/movie/review?res=9F01E1DC173EF930A25751C1A96 0958260. Accessed on December 23, 2011.

Mast, Gerald, revised by Bruce F. Kawin. 1992. *A Short History of the Movies.* 5th ed. New York: Macmillan.

Mauss, Marcel. [1923] 1967. *The Gift: Forms and Functions of Exchange in Archaic Societies.* Trans. I. Cunnison. New York: W. W. Norton.

May, Lary. 1989. "Movie Star Politics: The Screen Actors' Guild, Cultural Conversion, and the Hollywood Red Scare." In *Recasting America: Culture and Politics in the Age of Cold War,* ed. L. May, 125–53. Chicago: University of Chicago Press.

Mayer, Vicki, Miranda J. Banks, and John Thornton Caldwell, eds. 2009. *Production Studies: Cultural Studies of Media Industries.* New York: Routledge.

Mayshark, Jesse Fox. 2007. *Post-Pop Cinema: The Search for Meaning in New American Film.* Westport, Conn.: Praeger.

Mazzarella, William. 2003. *Shoveling Smoke: Advertising and Globalization in Contemporary India.* Durham, N.C.: Duke University Press.

McCarthy, Todd. 2007. "It's Not Easy Being a Kid." *Daily Variety,* January 26, 1, 6.

McDonald, Kathy A. 2001. "Truth Is as Strong as Fiction on the Tube." *Daily Variety,* July 30, 36–37.

McHugh, Kathleen. 2009. "The World and the Soup: Historicizing Media Feminism in Transnational Contexts." *Camera Obscura* 24 (3 72): 111–52.

McRobbie, Angela. 2009. *The Aftermath of Feminism: Gender, Culture, and Social Change.* London: Sage.

Merritt, Greg. 2000. *Celluloid Mavericks: The History of American Independent Film.* New York: Thunder Mouth.

Miège, Bernard. 1989. *The Capitalization of Cultural Production.* New York: International General.

Miller, Toby, Nitin Govil, John McMurria, and Richard Maxwell. 2001. *Global Hollywood.* London: British Film Institute.

Modleski, Tania. 1988. *The Women Who Knew Too Much: Hitchcock and Feminist Theory.* New York and London: Routledge and Kegan Paul.

——. 1991. *Feminism without Women: Culture and Criticism in a "Postfeminist" Age.* New York and London: Routledge.

Moncrieff, Karen. n.d. [ca. December 2006]. Interview, with Mary Beth Hurt, by the NYC Movie Guru. http://www.nycmovieguru.com/karen&mary.html/. Accessed on May 9, 2010.

Mottram, James. 2006. *The Sundance Kids: How the Mavericks Took Back Hollywood.* New York: Faber and Faber.

Mulvey, Laura. [1975] 2004. "Visual Pleasure and Narrative Cinema." In *Film Theory and Criticism*, 6th ed., ed. L. Braudy and M. Cohen, 837–48. New York: Oxford University Press.

Muñoz, Lorenza. 2008. Interview with Charlie Kaufman. *Film Independent Magazine* 17 (10, October): 5.

———. 2009. "Behind-the-Scenes at the Spirit Awards." *Film Independent Magazine* 18 (2, February): 8–10.

Nader, Laura. 1969. "Up the Anthropologist: Perspectives Gained from Studying Up." In *Reinventing Anthropology*, ed. D. Hymes, 284–311. New York: Pantheon.

Negra, Diane. 2005. "'Queen of the Indies': Parker Posey's Niche Stardom and the Taste Cultures of Independent Film." In *Contemporary American Independent Film*, ed. C. Holmlund and J. Wyatt, 71–88. London and New York: Routledge.

Nelson, Rob, and Jon Cowan. 1994. *Revolution X: A Survival Guide for Our Generation*. New York: Penguin.

Nesbitt, Jim. 1991. "American Dream Fades, Changes for Middle Class." *Ann Arbor News*, September 22, A1, A11.

Newman, Katherine S. 1988. *Falling from Grace: The Experience of Downward Mobility in the American Middle Class*. New York: Vintage.

———. 1993. *Declining Fortunes: The Withering of the American Dream*. New York: Basic.

Nichols, Bill. 1978. "[Review of] *38 Families, Redevelopment, Revolution until Victory, The Beginning of Our Victory*. New from California Newsreel." *Jump Cut* 17 (April): 10–13.

———. 1991. *Representing Reality: Issues and Concepts in Documentary*. Bloomington: University of Indiana Press.

Obst, Lynda. 1996. *Hello, He Lied, & Other Truths from the Hollywood Trenches*. New York: Broadway.

O'Hehir, Andrew. 2009. "The Undignified Near-Death of Miramax." *Salon*, November 5. http://www.salon.com/ent/movies/btm/feature/2009/11/04/miramax/print.html. Accessed on September 22, 2010.

Ohmann, Richard, ed. 1996. *Making and Selling Culture*. Hanover, N.H.: Wesleyan University Press.

Ortner, Sherry B. 1978. *Sherpas through Their Rituals*. Cambridge: Cambridge University Press.

———. 2003. *New Jersey Dreaming: Capital, Culture, and the Class of '58*. Durham, N.C.: Duke University Press.

———. 2006a. "Introduction: Updating Practice Theory." In her *Anthropology and Social Theory: Culture, Power, and the Acting Subject*, 1–18. Durham, N.C.: Duke University Press.

———. [1991] 2006b. "Reading America: Preliminary Notes on Class and Culture." In her *Anthropology and Social Theory: Culture, Power and the Acting Subject*, 19–41. Durham, N.C.: Duke University Press.

———. [1998] 2006c. "Generation X: Anthropology in a Media-Saturated World." In her *Anthropology and Social Theory: Culture, Power and the Acting Subject,* 80–106. Durham, N.C.: Duke University Press.

———. 2006d. "Power and Projects: Reflections on Agency." In her *Anthropology and Social Theory: Culture, Power and the Acting Subject,* 129–54. Durham, N.C.: Duke University Press.

———. 2007a. "Notes from Hollywood: The Indie Movement." *Anthropology News,* September, 27–28.

———. 2007b. "Notes from Hollywood: *Little Miss Sunshine* Finds Its Way." *Anthropology News,* October, 22–23.

———. 2010. "Access: Reflections on Studying Up in Hollywood." *Ethnography* 11 (2): 211–33.

———. 2011. "On Neoliberalism." *Anthropology of This Century,* Issue 1, May, London. www.aotcpress.com/articles/neoliberalism.

Owen, Rob. 1997. *Gen X TV: The Brady Bunch to Melrose Place.* Syracuse, N.Y.: Syracuse University Press.

Palmer, Stephanie, and Sheila Hanahan Taylor. 2005. Interview by Chris Leeder. Done Deal Interviews. http://www.scriptsales.com/StephanieSheilaInterview .html. Accessed on November 3, 2005.

Perucci, Robert, and Earl Wysong. 2008. *The New Class Society: Goodbye American Dream?* Lanham, Md.: Rowman and Littlefield.

Pfeil, Fred. [1985] 1990. "'Makin' Flippy Floppy': Postmodernism and the Baby Boom PMC." In his *Another Tale to Tell: Politics and Narrative in Postmodern Culture,* 97–125. London: Verso.

———. 1995. "Chips Off the Old Block." In his *White Guys: Studies in Postmodern Domination and Difference,* 233–62. London: Verso.

Phillips, Kevin. 2002. *Wealth and Democracy: A Political History of the American Rich.* New York: Broadway.

Pierson, John. 2003. *Spike, Mike Reloaded: A Guided Tour across a Decade of American Independent Cinema.* New York: Hyperion/Miramax.

Porterfield, Matthew. 2011. "If We Speak with Honesty, Will People Listen and Respond?" Truly Free Film blog via e-mail, February 17.

Post Script. 2000. Special Issue on Gen X Films. Vol. 19, No. 2, Winter–Spring.

Powdermaker, Hortense. 1950. *Hollywood the Dream Factory.* New York: Little, Brown.

Radwan, Jon. 2000. "Generation X and Postmodern Cinema: *Slacker.*" *Post Script* 19 (2, Winter–Spring): 34–48.

Remnick, David. 2007. "Comment: Family Guy." *New Yorker,* June 4, 29–30.

Roberts, Johnnie L. 2004. "The Lions' Reign." *Newsweek,* July 12, 42–43.

Rosen, David, with Peter Hamilton. 1990. *Off-Hollywood: The Making and Marketing of Independent Films.* New York: Grove Weidenfeld.

Rosenfelt, Deborah, and Judith Stacey. 1987. "Second Thoughts on the Second Wave." *Feminist Studies* 13 (2): 341–61.

Ross, Andrew. 1988. "Introduction." In *Universal Abandon? The Politics of Postmodernism*, ed. Andrew Ross, vii–xviii. Minneapolis: University of Minnesota Press.

Ross, Lillian. [1952] 2002. *Picture*. Cambridge, Mass.: Da Capo.

Ross, Steven J. 1998. *Working Class Hollywood: Silent Films and the Shaping of Class in America*. Princeton, N.J.: Princeton University Press.

Rosten, Leo. [1941] 1970. *Hollywood: The Movie Colony, the Movie Makers*. New York: Harcourt, Brace.

Rothkopf, Joshua. 2006. "[Review of] *Marie Antoinette*." *Time Out New York*, October 19–25, 125.

Roussel, Violaine. 2010. "Making 'A Political Movie That Does Not Take a Political Stand': Specialization and Depoliticization in American Cinema." *International Journal of Politics, Culture, and Society* 23:137–55.

Rushkoff, Douglas, ed. 1994. *The Gen X Reader*. New York: Ballantine.

Ryan, Michael, and Douglas Kellner. 1988. *Camera Politica: The Politics and Ideology of Contemporary Hollywood Film*. Bloomington: Indiana University Press.

Salamon, Julie. [1991] 2002. *The Devil's Candy: The Anatomy of a Hollywood Fiasco*. Cambridge, Mass.: Da Capo.

Schamus, James. 1995. "Long Live Indie Film." *Filmmaker Magazine*, Fall. www.filmmakermagazine.com/fall1995/live_film.php. Accessed on March 29, 2006.

———. [1999] 2001. "A Rant." In *The End of Cinema as We Know It*, ed. J. Lewis, 253–60. New York: New York University Press.

———. 2006. Interview by Anna Martemucci. http://thecareercookbook.com/article.php?article_id=18. Accessed on November 20, 2007.

Schatz, Thomas. 1981. *Hollywood Genres: Formulas, Filmmaking, and the Studio System*. New York: Random House.

Scheper-Hughes, Nancy, and Howard F. Stein. 1998. "Child Abuse and the Unconscious in American Popular Culture." In *The Children's Culture Reader*, ed. Henry Jenkins, 178–95. New York: New York University Press.

Schickel, Richard. 2007. "*No End in Sight*: Iraq in Harsh Light." *Time*, posted Friday, July 27, 2007. http://www.time.com/time/arts/article/0,8599,1647716,00.html. Accessed on August 3, 2008.

Scott, A. O. 2007. "In the Beginning: Focusing on the Iraq War Enablers" (Review of *No End in Sight*). *New York Times*, July 27, 2007. http://movies.nytimes.com/2007/07/27movies/27sigh.htm. Accessed on August 3, 2008.

———. 2009. "Neo-Neo Realism: A Handful of Young American Directors Are Making Clear-eyed Movies for Hard Times." *New York Times Magazine*, March 22, 38–43.

Scott, A. O., and Manohla Dargis. 2011. "Gosh, Sweetie, That's a Big Gun." *New York Times*, Sunday, May 1, special section on "Summer Movies," 1, 10.

Sennett, Richard. 1998. *The Corrosion of Character: The Personal Consequences of Work in the New Capitalism*. New York: W. W. Norton.

———. 2006. *The Culture of the New Capitalism*. New Haven, Conn.: Yale University Press.

Setoodeh, Ramin. 2009. "Apocalypse Now." *Newsweek*, December 7, 70.

Shapiro, Isaac, and Robert Greenstein. 1999. "The Widening Income Gulf." April 4. Washington, D.C.: Center on Budget and Policy Priorities.

Shohat, Ella, and Robert Stam. 1994. *Unthinking Eurocentrism: Multiculturalism and the Media*. New York: Routledge.

Sklar, Robert. 1975. *Movie-Made America: A Cultural History of American Movies*. New York: Random House.

Smith, Sean. 2006. "A Flying Leap." *Newsweek*, July 3/July 10, 88–89.

Smith, Sean, and David Ansen. 2006. "Prize Fighters." *Newsweek*, February 6, 58–67.

——. 2007. "Hollywood Royalty." *Newsweek*, January 29, 56–67.

Sobchack, Vivian. 1998. "Lounge Time: Postwar Crises and the Chronotope of Film Noir." In *Refiguring American Film Genres: History and Theory*, ed. N. Browne, 129–70. Berkeley: University of California Press.

——. 2003. "'Surge and Splendor': A Phenomenology of the Hollywood Historical Epic." In *Film Genre Reader III*, ed. B. K. Grant, 296–323. Austin: University of Texas Press.

"So Little Time . . . An AIDS History." 2002. http://www.aegis.com/topics/timeline/. Accessed on August 29, 2010.

Stacey, Judith. 1990. *Brave New Families: Stories of Domestic Upheaval in Late-Twentieth-Century America*. New York: Basic.

——. 1996. *In the Name of the Family: Rethinking Family Values in a Postmodern Age*. Boston: Beacon.

Steven, Peter, ed. 1985. *Jump Cut: Hollywood, Politics, and Counter-Cinema*. Toronto, Ont.: Between the Lines.

Stevens, Dana. "The Top 10 Movies of 2007." *Slate Magazine*, December 28, 2007. http://www.slate.com/id/2180954/. Accessed on August 3, 2008.

Straw, Will. 2002. "Scenes and Sensibilities." *Public*, No. 22/23, 245–57. (My pagination refers to a manuscript version downloaded from the Web.)

Stubbs, Liz, and Richard Rodriguez. 2000. *Making Independent Films: Advice from the Filmmakers*. New York: Allworth.

Swart, Sharon. 2009. "Indies Stay Alive in 2009." *Variety*, December 29. http://www.variety.com/article/VR1118013177.html?categoryid=3768&cs=1. Accessed on September 8, 2010.

Tang, Jean. 2002. "'I Don't Think I Was Cut Out to Be a Director:' Todd Solondz Explains Why Moviemaking Is a Nightmare." http://dir.salon.com/ent/movies/int/2002/01/30/solondz/index.html. Accessed on September 14, 2010.

Tasker, Yvonne. 1998. *Working Girls: Gender and Sexuality in Popular Cinema*. New York: Routledge.

Tasker, Yvonne, and Diane Negra, eds. 2007. *Interrogating Post-Feminism: Gender and the Politics of Popular Culture*. Durham, N.C.: Duke University Press.

Taylor, Timothy D. 2012. *The Sounds of Capitalism: Music, Advertising, and the Conquest of Culture*. Chicago: University of Chicago Press.

——. n.d. *New Capitalism, Music, and Social Theory*. In preparation.

Thompson, Anne. 2005. "The Producers." www.hollywoodreporter.com. August, 36–37.

Thompson, E. P. 1966. *The Making of the English Working Class*. New York: Vintage.

Thompson, Gabriel. 2008. "Meet the Wealth Gap." *Nation*, June 30, 18–27.

Timberg, Scott. 2004. "After the Indie Revolution." theage.com.au. January 17. http://www.theage.com.au/articles/2004/01/14/1073877894564.html. Accessed on July 26, 2011.

Traube, Elizabeth. 1992a. *Dreaming Identities: Class, Gender, and Generation in 1980s Hollywood Movies*. Boulder, Colo.: Westview.

——. 1992b. "Secrets of Success in Postmodern Society." In her *Dreaming Identities: Class, Gender, and Generation in 1980s Hollywood Movies*, 67–96. Boulder, Colo.: Westview.

——. 1994. "Family Matters: Postfeminist Constructions of a Contested Site." In *Visualizing Theory: Selected Essays from Visual Anthropology Review 1990–1994*, ed. L. Taylor, 301–21. New York: Routledge.

——. 1996. "Introduction." In *Making and Selling Culture*, ed. R. Ohmann, xi–xxiii. Hanover, N.H.: Wesleyan University Press.

Turan, Kenneth. 2002. *Sundance to Sarajevo: Film Festivals and the World They Made*. Berkeley and Los Angeles: University of California Press.

Uchitelle, Louis. 2010. "American Dream Is Elusive for New Generation." *New York Times*, July 6. http://www.nytimes.com/2010/07/07/business/ economy/07generation.html. Accessed on September 28, 2010.

Ulrich, John M., and Andrea L. Harris, eds. 2003. *GenXegesis: Essays on Alternative Youth (Sub)Culture*. Madison: University of Wisconsin Press.

Vachon, Christine, with David Edelstein. 1998. *Shooting to Kill: How an Independent Producer Blasts through the Barriers to Make Movies That Matter*. New York: HarperCollins.

Vachon, Christine, with Austin Bunn. 2006. *A Killer Life: How an Independent Film Producer Survives Deals and Disasters in Hollywood and Beyond*. New York: Simon and Schuster.

Van Couvering, Alicia. 2007. "A Question of Silence" (Interview with Hilary Brougher). *Filmmaker Magazine*, Winter, 35–41.

Van Lier, Heidi. 2009. "Indie Films Q&A with Heidi Van Lier: My Indie Film Shoot Feels Lame and Small. Help." http://filmindependent.org/filmmaker-blogs/1430. Accessed on May 28, 2009.

Walley, Christine J. 2010. "Deindustrializing Chicago: A Daughter's Story." In *The Insecure American: How We Got Here and What We Should Do about It*, ed. H. Gusterson and C. Besteman, 113–39. Berkeley: University of California Press.

Watney, Simon. 1987. *Policing Desire: Pornography, AIDS, and the Media*. Minneapolis: University of Minnesota Press.

Waxman, Sharon. 2006. *Rebels on the Backlot: Six Maverick Directors and How They Conquered the Hollywood Studio System*. New York: HarperCollins.

——. 2007. "Hollywood's Shortage of Female Power." *New York Times*, April 27. http://query.nytimes.com/gst/fullpage.html?res=9507E1DF153EF935A15757C0 A9619C8B63&sec=&spon=&pagewanted=all. Accessed on April 27, 2010.

Wikipedia. www.wikipedia.org.

——. "Charles H. Ferguson." Accessed on February 5, 2012.

——. "Metro-Goldwyn-Mayer." Accessed on April 11, 2011.

——. "Leo Rosten." Accessed on February 4, 2012.

Williams, Linda. 1998a. "Melodrama Revised." In *Refiguring American Film Genres: History and Theory*, ed. N. Browne, 42–88. Berkeley: University of California Press.

——. 1998b. "Mirrors without Memories: Truth, History, and *The Thin Blue Line*." In *Documenting the Documentary: Close Readings of Documentary Film and Video*, ed. B. K. Grant and J. Sloniowski, 379–96. Detroit: Wayne State University Press.

——. 2003. "Film Bodies: Gender, Genre, and Excess." In *Film Genre Reader III*, ed. B. K. Grant, 141–59. Austin: University of Texas Press.

Williams, Raymond. 1977. *Marxism and Literature*. Oxford: Oxford University Press.

——. 1981. *Culture*. London: Fontana.

Wood, Gaby. 2006. "Hollywood's New Politics." *Observer*, Sunday, January 8. http://film.guardian.co.uk/print/0, 5369257–3181,00.html. Accessed on May 30, 2008.

Wray, John. 2007. "Minister of Fear." *New York Times Magazine*, September 23, 44–49.

Wyatt, Justin. 2001. "Marketing Marginalized Cultures: *The Wedding Banquet*, Cultural Identities, and Independent Cinema of the 1990s." In *The End of Cinema as We Know It*, ed. J. Lewis, 61–71. New York: New York University Press.

Zeitchik, Steven, and Pamela McClintock. 2007. "Redford Touts Documentaries." *Variety @ Sundance*, January 18. [Hard copy accessed on January 20, 2007, in files of author.]

Ziskin, Laura. 2002. "*Produced by* Case Study: Laura Ziskin." Interview by Chris Green. *Produced by*, Spring, 16–23.

Index

Babel (film), 225

baby boomers: films by, 256–58; generational shift and, 19–22

Bacon, Kevin, 41

Bahrani, Ramin, 30, 86, 289n17

Baichwal, Jennifer, 256–57

Bait and Switch (Ehrenreich), 18

Ball, Allen, 130

Baluzy, George and Mike, 210

Banks, Miranda J., 25

Baron, Caroline, 167

Barton Fink (film), 96

Baumbach, Noah, 132

BBC (British Broadcasting Corporation), 24

Beck, Chad, 2, 207, 285n1

Before the Rains (film), 162

Berg, Amy, 123

Berger, Albert, 98, 106–8, 116–19, 155–57, 159–60, 164

Berlant, Lauren, 287n2

Berlin Film Festival, 107

Berman, Gail, 176

Besson, Luc, 130

Besteman, Catherine, 19

Bicycle Thief, The (film), 57

Bier, Susanne, 55

Big Beach Productions, 117–18

Bigelow, Kathryn, 177, 184

Big Picture, The (film), 40–41, 286n4

biographical documentaries, 252–54

Birmingham/British cultural studies, 11–12

Biskind, Peter, 9, 95, 101, 110, 115, 267

Black Male (film), 210, 223

Blair Witch Project (film), 247–48

Blood Simple (film), 95

Blue Steel (film), 294n10

Blue Velvet (film), 95

Boden, Anna, 177

Bollywood, 72

Bona Fide Productions, 106–8

Bonfire of the Vanities (film), 54, 202–3, 211, 214, 219

Boogie Nights (film), 134

Borchardt, Mark, 39

Born, Georgina, 24

boundaries of independent film, 46–48, 502n7

Bourdieu, Pierre: on artistic value, 152, 163; on class transformation, 99–101; on cultural production, 3–4, 10, 91–92, 163–68, 296n5; documentary about, 170; on habitus of artists, 160; on taste, 157; on truth and reality, 53

"bourgeois bohemians" (bobos), 100–101, 290n5

Bourne Identity, The (film), 206

Bowles, Eamon, 266

Bowling for Columbine (documentary), 19, 65, 246, 248, 287n5

Boyle, Barbara, 111, 158, 235–37

Boyle, Danny, 206, 211, 224

Boys Don't Cry (film), 174, 186–87

Boyz n the Hood (film), 119

Brando, Marlon, 211

Breckenridge, Carol, 7–8, 259

Brenner, Robert, 99

Brigand, Alain, 83

Brody, Jeb, 200

Brokeback Mountain (film), 47

Brooks, Peter, 121

Broomfield, Nick, 187

Brougher, Hilary, 139, 222, 225

Brown, Margaret, 184

Buena Vista Motion Pictures group, 176

Burnett, Charles, 93

Burns, Michael, 61

Buscemi, Steve, 201, 212

Bush, George W., 242–46, 250–51, 256–57, 287n5

Butler, Judith, 170

Caché (film), 253

Caldwell, John Thornton, 24–25, 27, 32

Callahan, David, 151–54

Campbell, Billy, 38

capitalism: class structure and, 261–64; documentaries about, 253–58; emergence of independent film and, 99–101; in Generation X films, 75–81; moral

cultural critique: film feminism and, 173–98; in immigrant film, 89–90; independent film as, 3–4, 7–11, 29–58, 271–72; neoliberalism in film and, 70–81; political films as, 229–58

cultural production: art vs. commerce in, 34–38, 296n5; education levels and, 168–72; production of value in, 163–68. *See also* public culture

Culture of Fear, The (Glassner), 68–69

Curtin, Michael, 42–45

Dabis, Cherien, 36–37, 82

Daldry, Stephen, 142

Dalton, Scott, 184

Damon, Matt, 37–38

Daniels, Lee, 266

Dargis, Manohla, 50

darkness of independent film, 59–70, 262; in immigrant films, 83–90; patterns of, 73–81; women filmmakers and, 174, 185–89

Dash, Julie, 115

Daughters of the Dust (film), 115

Davis, Mike, 19, 65

Davis, Viola, 135

Dayton, Jonathan, 177, 224

Dead Girl, The (film), 57, 139–41, 186–87, 189–92, 196–98

Deal, Carl, 184

debt burden, generational shift in, 21–23

Declining Fortunes: The Withering of the American Dream (Newman), 15, 18

Deliver Us from Evil (documentary), 123

Del Toro, Guillermo, 39

Demme, Jonathan, 131

Denby, David, 60

De Niro, Robert, 217

De Palma, Brian, 54, 109, 211–12, 224

Depp, Johnny, 40–41

deregulation, neoliberalism and, 12–15

Dern, Laura, 122

Derrida (documentary), 170

Derrida, Jacques, 170

De Sica, Vittorio, 57

Deutchman, Ira, 268–69

Dexter (television series), 141

DiCaprio, Leonardo, 217

Dick, Kirby, 123, 169–70, 240–41, 250–51

Dinklage, Peter, 212

directors: actors and, 210–13; crew relations with, 207–10; producer relationships with, 163–68, 219–20, 293n14; production process and, 205–7; women directors, 176–79, 293nn4–5

Directors Guild of America (DGA), 176, 293n4

discourse analysis: film studies and, 29–32; for independent film, 32–34; political documentaries and, 241–42

dismissal, discourse of, 44–46

distribution strategies, for independent film, 50

Diving Bell and the Butterfly, The (film), 167

divorce rate, family breakdown and, 130–37

documentaries: classic definitions of, 238–39; ethical gray areas in, 137–41; ethnographic research and, 2–3, 296n4; future of, 272; generational shift concerning, 254–58; Hollywood ad, 32; as independent films, 5; influence of history in, 233–37, 296n3; new documentary format, 246–51; pedophilia in, 123–26, 129–31; personal vs. political in, 247–54; political documentaries, 230–32, 237, 239–46; on social and cultural theory, 170; by women filmmakers, 184–85

Documentary's New Politics, The (documentary), 238

do-it-yourself distribution, 50; Internet and, 268–69

Dornfeld, Barry, 24–25

Double Hope Films, 102

Doubt (film), 126, 135–36

Down and Dirty Pictures: Miramax, Sundance, and the Rise of Independent Film (Biskind), 9, 115

downward mobility: class transformation and, 16–19; women filmmakers' focus on, 194–98, 263–64

Film Department (independent production company), 265
Film Independent, 32–33, 111–12, 119, 178
Filmmaker Forum, 49
Filmmaker magazine, 108–9, 112–14, 138–39, 265
filmmakers: from Generation X, 74–81; political affiliations of, 233, 296n2; producers' relationships with, 163–68; production of value by, 163–68; on production process, 202–5, 264; as stars, in documentaries, 252–54; women as, 173–98. *See also* directors; producers
film schools, infrastructure for independent film and, 109–10
film-viewing practices methodology, 6, 183
financing for independent film, 116–19; current trends in, 265–69, 271–72; gender issues in, 181–82; Hollywood comparisons with, 201–2; wealth accumulation and, 151–54
Fincher, David, 74–81, 150
Fine Line Features, 101, 104
Fink, Micha, 145
Fischer, Michael, 70, 89
Fish, Adam, 38
Flaherty, Robert J., 252
Fleck, Ryan, 177
Focus Features, 47, 102, 117–18
food and catering during film production, 222–23
Fordism, neoliberalism and, 13–15
foreign film, as independent film, 72, 94–95, 294n6
Forensic Films, 101
Forster, Mark, 213
Foster, Jodie, 173
Foucault, Michel, 29–30
400 Blows, The (film), 94
Fox, Josh, 145, 256–57
franchise formulas in filmmaking, 93
Frankfurt school, 11
Frazer, Crystal, 253
Freeman, Morgan, 211–12
Fresh Air (radio program), 126–27

Friedman, Arnie, 124–26, 128, 138
Friends (television series), 134
Frontline (television series), 291n3
Frozen River (film), 189–93, 195–97, 294n12
Fuller, Sam, 92

Gaghan, Stephen, 118
Gaines, Jane, 230
García, Alberto, 115
García, Rodrigo: on audiences for indie films, 51–52, 55–57, 178; on darkness in films, 60; *Mother and Child* made by, 119; on production process, 209, 216; women in films of, 293n1
Garofalo, Janeane, 76
Gasland (documentary), 145, 256–57
Geertz, Clifford, 27, 32, 72, 286n15
gender: in independent film production, 150–54, 181–83, 292n9; in pedophilia films, 131; poverty in films and meaning of, 191–94; producer-director relationship and, 164–68
generational shift: class transformation and, 19–23, 285n10; feminism and, 294n11; independent film and issues of, 64; in political films, 254–58; post-feminism and younger women and, 179–83
Generation X, 20–23, 285n11; American Dream and, 71; class structure and, 64–70, 99, 154, 174, 262; darkness in independent film and, 64–70, 99; documentary filmmaking and, 248, 256–58; end of security and, 64–70; family life viewed by, 131–37, 192; filmmakers from, 74–81; future of independent film and, 270–72; moral ambiguity in, 141–46; political apathy of, 230–31; postmodernism and, 288n6, 291n11; producers from, 149–54; women filmmakers from, 173–74, 188–89
Generation X (Coupland), 75–76, 289n13
Generation X: Tales for an Accelerated Culture (Coupland), 20
Generation Y, 22
genre studies in independent film, 288n6

Hollywood (*cont.*)
ducers in, 292n2; public culture and, 8–11;
specialty divisions in, 43, 97–98, 105–8;
women producers in, 176–79, 181, 293n3
Hollywood Renaissance, 93, 109–10
Hollywood Reporter (journal), 155, 246
Holtz, Geoffrey, 131
Home of the Brave (documentary), 223
home video industry, independent film
and, 290n3
Hoop Dreams (documentary), 247
Hope, Ted: on decline of indie films, 267–
68; on early indie experiences, 30, 119,
158–59, 233; Good Machine partnership
and, 101–7, 113; as producer, 148, 161, 164,
167–68, 291n2, 293n13; on production
process, 51; on reality in indie films, 54;
Schamus partnership with, 47; on taste,
155–56; on "truly free film," 48–50
Hope, Vanessa, 164, 170
Hope for Film (blog), 156, 268–69
Horberg, Bill, 155, 292n8
Horkheimer, Max, 10, 44–45
Horowitz, Josh, 201–2
Hotel Rwanda (film), 248
Hounddog (film), 130–32, 186
House Un-American Activities Committee
(HUAC), 229
How the Beatles Rocked the Kremlin (docu-
mentary), 296n4
Hudson, Dawn, 111–12, 119, 233, 290n3
Hughes, John, 144
Hunt, Courtney, 189
Hurt Locker, The (film), 178, 184, 267
Huston, John, 211, 218, 235, 237

Ice Storm, The (film), 131
IFC, 266
immigrant films, 81–90, 232, 289n15
immigration, American Dream and, 16
improvisation, film production using, 209–10
Iñárritu, Alejandro Gonzales, 225
Inconvenient Truth, An (documentary), 5,
118, 247, 252, 254, 257
Independent Feature Project (IFP), 110, 265

Independent Features Project/West (IFP/
West), 32, 111–12
independent film: ambivalence concerning,
42–50; boundaries of, 46–48; class
transformation and, 12–15, 260–64; criteria for, 33–34; darkness of, 59–70;
decline of, 264–69; definitions of, 3–4,
32–34; discourse concerning, 29–30, 32–
34; ethnographic research on, 2–3;
examples of, 4–5; families depicted in,
131–37; feminism and, 173–98, 263–64;
festivals and promotion of, 114–16;
financing and investment for, 116–19;
future of, 270–72; Generation X and,
20–23, 64–70; historical overview, 92–
96; internet and, 264–69, 287n10; in Los
Angeles, 105–8; moral ambiguity in, 121–
46, 263; neoliberalism and, 12–15, 70–81;
in New York City, 101–5; organizational
infrastructure for, 110–12; politics in,
229–58; production of, 199–227, 263;
proliferation in 1990s of, 96–101; public
culture and, 7–11; "scene" in, 91–120;
selection criteria in research on, 6–7;
sociocultural infrastructure for, 108–16;
truth and reality in, 50–58; women filmmakers in, 173, 176–79
Independent's Day (film), 95–96
Independent Spirit Awards, 5; Best Feature
Film winners, 5–6; discourse on independence at, 32–33; edginess at, 61–62;
infrastructure for independent film and,
109; John Cassevetes Award, 39; Producers' Award, 149, 292n3
"Indie-Film Shakeout: There Will Be
Blood" (Davies), 265
Indie Summit, 268–69
"Indiewood," 266–69
industrial reflexivity in Hollywood, 32
infrastructure for independent film, 108–16
Insecure American, The (film), 19, 65, 69
Inside Job (documentary), 117, 145, 255–56
institutional infrastructure: for independent
film, 92; independent film and, 110–12
international films, independent films as, 55

Miège, Bernard, 10

Millennials, 22

Miller, Toby, 10

Mimic (film), 39

Ministers, The (film), 218–19, 225

minority cinema, emergence of, 94

Mirabai Productions, 101

Miramax Films, 9, 37–39; edgy movies by, 61; foreign film distribution by, 94; independent film from, 72; New York indie scene and, 101–2, 104; origins of, 95; retrenchment by, 265

Mirren, Helen, 217

Mississippi Masala (film), 82, 96

Miss Navajo (documentary), 253

Mitchell, John Cameron, 167

Moncrieff, Karen, 57, 139–41, 189

Monsoon Wedding (film), 124, 128

Monster (film), 186–87

Moore, Chris, 37–38

Moore, Michael: capitalism in films of, 249–52, 255; critique of moral ambiguity in films of, 145; economic insecurity in films of, 65; edginess in films of, 61; influence in indie films of, 96, 240, 245–46, 247–48, 296n9; middle class in films of, 19, 287n5; new documentary era and, 246–47, 252; politics in films of, 185, 232, 234, 237, 288n5; prizes won by, 5–6; working class in films of, 17

Moore, Tyria, 187–88

moral ambiguity in independent film, 121–46, 263

moral panic, pedophilia and, 126

Morgen, Bret, 236–37

Morris, Errol, 95, 247–49, 253–54

Most Dangerous Man in America: Daniel Ellsberg and the Pentagon Papers, The (documentary), 184, 253

Motel, The (film), 86–88

Mother and Child (film), 119, 293n1

Moulton, Seth, 245, 252–53

Mr. and Mrs. Smith (film), 201

Mr. Brooks (film), 141

murder, women filmmakers use of, 186–89

Murphy, Audie, 235

Museum of Modern Art, 265

My Left Foot (film), 96

Myrick, Daniel, 247–48

Mysterious Skin (film), 60, 126, 129, 148, 192

Mystic River (film), 290n1

My Two Dads (television series), 134

Nair, Mira, 82–83, 88, 96, 124, 206, 221–22, 233, 289n17

Nameless Indie (film), 209

Namesake, The (film), 82

Nanook of the North (documentary), 252

Narc (film), 202

narrative, cultural critique through, 70–81

Nation, The (magazine), 45–46

Nazism, in *Fight Club,* 79

neoliberalism: class transformation and, 11–15, 152–54, 262–64; downward mobility of women and children under, 194–98, 263–64; emergence of independent film linked to, 98–99; family breakdown and, 133–37; generational shift and, 19–23; in immigrant films, 82–90; in independent film, 70–81; moral ambiguity and, 141–46; poverty in films and, 190–94; sociology of producers and, 149–54; women filmmakers and, 174

Neo Ned (film), 290n1

neo-neo realism, 56–57

"neo-noir" film genre, 288n7

Nesbitt, Eileen, 185–86

Nevins, Sheila, 254

"new historicism," cultural analysis and, 27

New Line Cinema, 101, 104, 113

Newman, Katherine, 15, 17–18

New Moon (film), 267

"Newsreel" collective, 94

New York City, independent film scene in, 101–5, 262–63

New York Film Festival, 104

Nichols, Bill, 238–39, 296n5

Nigeria, film production in, 24, 72

Nightline (television program), 235

Nilsson, Rob, 93

postmodernism: documentary filmmaking and, 248; Generation X and, 288n6, 291n11; political films and, 230

Post Script (journal), 20, 64

poverty: moral ambiguity in films and, 122–23, 263; women filmmakers' focus on, 189–98

Powdermaker, Hortense, 2, 6, 24, 218–19

Precious (film), 62, 266

Pretty Woman (film), 174, 179–80

Prisoner Or: How I Planned to Kill Tony Blair, The (documentary), 184

Prizewinner of Defiance, Ohio, The (film), 186

producers: agency of, 154–55, 158–60; characteristics of, 154–63; contributions of, 147–72; education levels of, 151–54, 168–72, 292n6; entrepreneurial skills of, 155; influence of film theory on, 170–72; proliferation of producer credits on, 292n4; relationship networks of, 154–55; rituals during production of, 217–27; sociology of, 149–54; taste as cultural capital for, 154–57; value production by, 163–68, 263; women as, 173

Producers Guild of America (PGA), 150, 165, 176, 292n5

production companies: in Los Angeles, 105–8; in New York City, 101–5

production process for films, 199–227, 264; director and, 205–7; material conditions in, 213–16; political documentaries and, 255–58; rituals of, 216–27; set vulnerabilities and, 207–16

production studies, research in, 25–27

Professional Managerial Class (PMC): financing and investment in independent film and, 117–19; independent film and emergence of, 99–101, 262–63, 290n4; producers from, 150–54, 263

Project Green Light (HBO series), 37–38, 42

Project Involve, 178, 287n1

public culture: class transformation and, 12; demise of American Dream and, 15–19; generational shift and, 19–23; Generation X and, 68–70; independent film and, 2–3, 7–11; independent film as, 3–4, 7–11, 108–16, 259–61; moral ambiguity in, 143–46; neoliberalism and class transformation in, 11–15; pedophilia in, 123; "yuppies" and, 100–101

Public Culture (journal), 7–8

Pulp Fiction (film), 96

queer cinema, 63

Rabin, Cathy, 162

Rachel Getting Married (film), 131

racial diversity in independent film, 63, 94, 287n1

racism: in immigrant films, 82–90; women filmmakers on, 184–85, 191–94, 294n12

rape, women filmmakers use of, 185–86

Ray, Nicholas, 92

Reader, The (film), 142

reality: fakery in independent films vs., 53–58; in independent films, 50–58, 72–73; indie producers' awareness of, 291n1; moral ambiguity and, 137–41

Reality Bites (film), 21–22, 64, 74, 76–77, 80–81, 134

Red Badge of Courage (film), 218, 235, 237

Redford, Robert, 34, 95, 114–15, 267

Redmon, David, 237, 257

Reinhardt, Gottfried, 235

Reiss, Jon, 268

Reitman, Jason, 207

relationship networks, producer's use of, 160–68

Relative Evil (film), 132

representation: in immigrant film, 89–90; in independent film, 72–81; in public culture, 259–61

Restrepo (documentary), 296n2

restricted production, Bourdieu's concept of, 52

Return of the Secaucus Seven (film), 95

Rich, Matty, 115

Rider, Winona, 76

Right Stuff, The (Wolfe), 235

Robbins, Tim, 41–42, 185, 229

Roberts, Julia, 42

Rodriguez, Robert, 167

Roger and Me (documentary), 17, 96, 247, 249–51

Roman Polanski: Wanted and Desired (documentary), 130–31, 291n5

Rosen, Bob, 32, 34, 93–94, 110–11, 114

Ross, Lillian, 218, 235

Ross, Steven J., 12

Rossi, Antonio, 2

Rosten, Leo, 24, 285n12

Rothkopf, Joshua, 292n2

Royal Tenenbaums, The (film), 132

Ruiz, Raoul, 113

Rumsfeld, Donald, 242–46

Rushkoff, Douglas, 141

Russell, David O., 166, 205–6, 209–10

Safford, Tony, 115

Salamon, Julie, 208–9, 219

Sánchez, Eduardo, 247–48

Sanders, Jessica, 184

Saraf, Peter, 221

Satrapi, Marjane, 177

Sayles, John, 95, 115

Scenes from the Drug War (documentary), 184

"scenes" of independent film, 91–120, 262–63; internet and, 264–69

Schamus, James: *Filmmaker* magazine and, 113; on financing for films, 97–98; Hope's partnership with, 102–7; on indies and studios, 148, 292n2, 292n4; influence on indie films of, 47–48, 286n8, 287n9; on taste in film, 156–57

Scherfig, Lone, 294n6

Schickel, Richard, 245

Schnabel, Julian, 167, 203

Schulberg, Sandra, 110

Scorsese, Martin, 93, 109

Scott, A. O., 56–57, 245

Scott, Ridley, 174

Scurlock, James D., 256

second wave feminism, 175, 179–83; class issues in, 191–94

security: class transformation and fears about, 18–19; Generation X and end of, 64–70, 287n2

Selig, Keri, 159

Sennett, Richard, 144

September 11 (film), 83, 88, 289n16

September 11, 2001 attacks, immigrant films in wake of, 82–83, 88–90

Serious Man, A (film), 60–61

Setoodeh, Ramin, 60–61

set vulnerability, film production and, 207–16

sex, lies, and videotape (film), 60, 95–96, 115

Sex and the City (HBO series), 175, 179–80, 183, 190, 195

sexism: class issues and, 191–94; women filmmakers' critique of, 175–76; younger women's awareness of, 180–83, 294n8

sexual abuse, women filmmakers use of, 185–86

sexual harassment, women filmmakers' experiences of, 181–83, 186–88

sexuality: in children, 130–31; Generation X and, 66–70

sexual perversity in independent film, 61

Shaye, Robert, 101

Sheridan, Jim, 96

Sherpas (documentary), 296n4

She's Gotta Have It (film), 95

shooting conditions, film production and, 213–16

Shooting Gallery, The, 101

Short Cuts (film), 290n1

Showalter, Michael, 226

Shyamalan, M. Night, 222–23

Sicko (documentary), 255

Sick: The Life and Times of Bob Flanagan, Super Masochist (documentary), 296n6

Singer, Bryan, 205

Singleton, John, 119, 167

Skalski, Mary Jane, 148

Sklar, Robert, 92–93

Skoll, Jeff, 118–19

Slacker (film), 21–22, 36, 74–76, 81, 96, 115, 231

Whitaker, Forest, 119

Whitmore, Greg, 52

Who Killed the Electric Car? (documentary), 257

Who Needs Sleep? (documentary), 216, 250, 255

Why We Fight (documentary), 241, 252, 256

William Kunstler: Disturbing the Universe (documentary), 184

Williams, Linda, 62, 121, 246, 248–49

Williams, Raymond, 10, 12, 261

Willis, Bruce, 42, 211–12, 219

Winkler, Irwin, 223

Winter's Bone (film), 189–92, 195–96

Wiseman, Frederic, 296n3

Wolfe, Tom, 235

Wolff, Tobias, 106

Woman under the Influence, A (film), 39

women filmmakers: indie film culture and, 173–98; poor women in films by, 189–96; as producers, 150–54; supportive relationships among, 294n7

Woodhead, Leslie, 296n4

work: documentary films on, 250–51; in Generation X films, 74–81, 262, 289n14; in immigrant films, 87–90; job insecurity and, 199–200

working class: in Cassevetes's films, 93; film crew members from, 208–10, 264; neoliberalism and transformation of, 12–15, 151–54; women filmmakers' focus on, 189–96

Wright, Joe, 118

Wuornos, Aileen, 186–88

Wyatt, Justin, 45

Yerxa, Ron, 98, 106–8, 116–19, 153, 155–56, 233, 237

Young@Heart (documentary), 234

Yu, Jessica, 137–38

Yung Chang, 257

"yuppies," emergence of, 100–101

Zahn-Storey, Diane, 61–62

Zahra, Eyad, 269

Zalla, Christopher, 289n17

Zeitgeist, 266

Zenovich, Marina, 95, 137–38

Ziskin, Laura, 158–59, 165

Žižek! (documentary), 170

Žižek, Slavoj, 170

Zsigmond, Vilmos, 205

Zulfacar, Meliya, 5

SHERRY B. ORTNER is Distinguished Professor of Anthropology
at the University of California, Los Angeles. She is the author of
*Anthropology and Social Theory: Culture, Power, and the Acting
Subject* and *New Jersey Dreaming: Capital, Culture, and the Class
of '58* (both also published by Duke University Press).

Library of Congress Cataloging-in-Publication Data
Ortner, Sherry B.
Not Hollywood : independent film at the twilight of the American
dream / Sherry B. Ortner.
p. cm.
Includes bibliographical references and index.
ISBN 978-0-8223-5410-9 (cloth : alk. paper)
ISBN 978-0-8223-5426-0 (pbk. : alk. paper)
1. Independent films—United States. 2. Independent filmmakers—
United States. I. Title.
PN1993.5.U6076 2013
791.43—dc23   2012044750